GW00362056

MAVERICK GUIDE TO
NEW ZEALAND

mav-er-ick (mav'er-ik), *n* 1. an unbranded steer. Hence [colloq.] 2. a person not labeled as belonging to any one faction, group, etc. who acts independently. 3. one who moves in a different direction than the rest of the herd—often a nonconformist. 4. a person using individual judgment, even when it runs against majority opinion.

The Maverick Guide Series

The Maverick Guide to Australia
The Maverick Guide to Bali and Java
The Maverick Guide to Barcelona
The Maverick Guide to Berlin
The Maverick Guide to the Great Barrier Reef
The Maverick Guide to Hawaii
The Maverick Guide to Hong Kong, Macau, and South China
The Maverick Guide to Malaysia and Singapore
The Maverick Guide to Bermuda
The Maverick Guide to Oman
The Maverick Guide to Prague
The Maverick Guide to Scotland
The Maverick Guide to Thailand
The Maverick Guide to Vietnam, Laos, and Cambodia

Information in this guidebook is based on authoritative data available at the time of printing. Prices and hours of operation of businesses listed are subject to change without notice. Readers are asked to take this into account when consulting this guide.

MAVERICK GUIDE TO
NEW ZEALAND
11TH EDITION

Edited by SUSAN BUCKLAND
and JANE WARWICK

PELICAN PUBLISHING COMPANY
Gretna 2000

Copyright © 1981, 1982, 1983, 1985, 1986, 1987, 1989
by Robert W. Bone

Copyright © 1989, 1991, 1993, 1996, 2000
by Pelican Publishing Company Inc.
All rights reserved

*The word "Pelican" and the depiction of a pelican are
trademarks of Pelican Publishing Company, Inc., and are
registered in the U.S. Patent and Trademark office.*

ISBN: 1-56554-778-0

First edition, February 1981
Second edition, January 1982
Third edition, March 1983
Third edition, second printing, May 1984
Fourth edition, January 1985
Fifth edition, February 1986
Sixth edition, January 1987
Seventh edition, January 1989
Eighth edition, January 1991
Ninth edition, January 1993
Tenth edition, January 1996
Eleventh edition, March 2000

Maps courtesy of New Zealand Tourism Office.

Printed in the United States of America
Published by Pelican Publishing Company, Inc.
1000 Burmaster Street, Gretna, Louisiana, 70053

Contents

List of Maps

MAVERICK GUIDE TO
NEW ZEALAND

1

Why New Zealand? (An Introduction)

New Zealand has always been explorers' country.

Made of mountains and valleys thrust up in the remotest part of our planet, it existed for millions of years without feeling the foot of man—or of hardly any animal, for that matter.

Ice ages and glaciers came and went. New ranges and plains were formed by massive movements under the sea. Tectonic plates ground together, and volcanoes erupted again and again in island-building processes that are still going on.

Trees, plants, and flowers drifted on winds and water to this land until they caught hold of rich New Zealand soil. Seeds were also borne by birds blown from their courses on other continents until they reached an isolated haven thousands of miles from their nests.

Some of the species of vegetation that took root in New Zealand have survived to become unique examples of evolutionary change. Many of the winged creatures that contributed to the lushness of the landscape also remained to enjoy the fruits of their new homeland. (And on the forest floor below the new immigrant birds scuttled one of the world's oldest reptiles—the tuatara.)

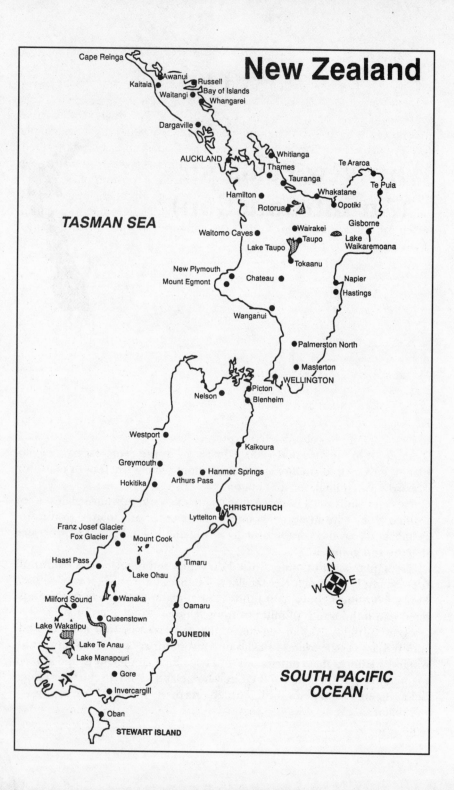

Succeeding generations of these new birds gradually began to be transformed, too. In the absence of ground predators, some found their wings
weakened; finally, having lost the need, they lost the ability to fly. A few
grew large and heavy, and one long-necked species called the moa actually
developed into a sort of feathered monster. Moa specimens reconstructed
in New Zealand museums show that some could stretch as high as 13 feet
to reach the boughs their ancestors had deserted as roosting places.

A close cousin to the moa, the small and equally flightless kiwi, survives
today in New Zealand forests, poking its long bill here and there on a
search for goodies in the ground. An endangered species, the kiwi is now
an official symbol of the nation.

The moa itself just about made it into modern times, but its demise was
accelerated by the first humans to inhabit New Zealand—Polynesians who
began exploring the Pacific around 800 A.D. The contingent that remained
in New Zealand soon developed a taste for the big bird and apparently
hunted it to extinction, perhaps as late in the game as the eighteenth century. (However, there are those who claim to have seen this elusive bird,
which in some parts of the country has gained Sasquatch-like status.)

The lesson of the moa has not been lost on conservation-minded New
Zealand. With an area totaling more than 103,000 square miles (slightly
larger than all of Great Britain), but with a population of only a little over
3.4 million, modern New Zealanders have developed a firm reverence for
nature and the soil. One of their most treasured possessions is the aforementioned tuatara, still scuttling the forest floor and still unchanged since
time in these islands began. The lizard is the last remaining example of the
prehistoric Rhynchocephalia order.

In fact, the country's ability to nurture life is its principal natural resource. Today it is considered a nation of expert farmers. You may have
heard, for example, of Sir Edmund Hillary, a well-known professional bee-
keeper.

Many New Zealanders are also amateur explorers, of course, even if not
all of them have managed to conquer Mount Everest in their spare time.
A large number seem to have flown from their country to see other parts
of the world. Until recently, at least, few stayed away for very long.

These intrepid people, who have flourished so well in a majestic and
bountiful land, have chosen to call themselves Kiwis.

A Land of Peace and Order

Despite an often violent history, New Zealand today is by and large an
English-speaking nation where you can walk in the parks and forests—even

at night—without fear. Government is strong, and there is a healthy respect for authority throughout the country.

Policemen patrol their beats on foot—and often by themselves—rather than sealed up by pairs in patrol cars. And the average cop still does not carry a gun. In the woods, there are no antisocial elements like snakes, wolves, or bears to worry about.

Camera film and cassette tapes are more competitively priced than they were six years ago. Most rooms in the plushest hotels today run about U.S. $150 for two, although excellent accommodations may also be found for less than half that price, usually in motels, all over the country. Generally a bottle of milk is thrown in, too, and most motel units contain everything you need to cook your own meals, except the food.

A good dinner in a good restaurant will run U.S. $25 to U.S. $30 per person, plus any drinks. If that's too much, the traveler can either choose a more modest place or else opt to cook with locally bought groceries in his room for a fraction of that amount.

The groceries themselves, grown in a country that has been described half-jokingly as one gigantic farm, provide some of the purest, most delicious foods in the world. Apples are sweeter and applier; potatoes are varied, unusual, and delicious; and the meat—lamb and beef—can be heavenly when prepared correctly.

Some of the best fish in the sea are caught and cooked in New Zealand. And freshwater specialties known to anglers the world over include large, tender trout and succulent salmon. The moist-textured orange roughy fish does a steady export trade to the U.S. but costs less to savour in New Zealand. Wines are good and improving yearly, and Kiwi beer just may be the smoothest, tastiest brew you've ever experienced.

New Zealand is laced with excellent, well-marked highways leading to wide-open spaces and distant, secluded glens. A recently deregulated gasoline industry has sparked a price shake-down that consumers are enjoying. Traffic is blessedly light, even during "rush hours" in this underpopulated, unpolluted country. And it seems that even the wildest and most out-of-the-way areas can be reached in jig time.

The visual delights served up in the outback are legendary. New Zealand mountains, lakes, rivers, glaciers, fiords, forests, hills, valleys, and waterfalls form eye-soothing backdrops to a nation of curiosities. There is unusual vegetation, such as the cabbage tree, whose spiked leaves were cooked and eaten by early settlers. You'll see ferns as tall as trees ought to be, and hardwood trees whose colorful timber is favored for strong, beautiful woods, such as the kauri, matai, and rimu.

Flowers, both native and introduced, flourish along city streets as well as running wild over the landscape. There are thousands of types, many of which are only now beginning to fill the frames of foreign visitors' cameras—blossoms you just won't see anywhere else. Hillsides are often paved with yellow gorse, and wild blackberries seem to grow everywhere. Both are considered scourges in New Zealand.

Somehow, birds don't seem as shy, even while they manage to stay just out of reach. Without a flashlight, considerable patience, and a lot of luck, you will have trouble spotting the nocturnal kiwi outside of the zoos. But you'll see the antics and hear the songs of many other feathered species, both the grounded type, like the curious weka, and such airborne varieties as the supermaneuverable fantail.

Man-made objects are also surprising in New Zealand. In a country where new and used cars cost twice as much as in the U.S., the citizens can hardly bring themselves to tow Annabelle away to the junk heap. You'll see excellent, well-preserved specimens of obscure prewar English and American models still tootling along the tar sealing (asphalt pavement).

If we had a flair for the antique business, we would scour New Zealand for old automobiles and other ancient mechanical bargains to bring back home. They still manufacture and use wringer washing machines, but even devices that are no longer new are kept useful by gadget-minded and resourceful Kiwis. These pragmatic people believe that if a thing is worth keeping, it's worth running. And if it's running, it's certainly worth keeping!

Most New Zealanders are descended from two distinct ethnic groups, Polynesian and European. The original discoverers came to the land called Aotearoa—the "Long White Cloud"—from islands further north. History dates some of the earliest arrivals back to more than 1,000 years ago, and it was this crowd who dined happily on the moa. Then a later migration, an often belligerent bunch of Polynesians, called themselves Maori. They had the disconcerting habit of eating their enemies.

The bulk of the population traces its roots to the British, who began to colonize the country in the wake of Captain Cook's voyages. Settlement was slow at first, largely because of fierce wars with the Maori over land. Today the two peoples participate equally under the law, and the kind of racial tension known in other parts of the world is rare in New Zealand. However, as in all countries once colonized, there are grievances and regrets, emotions that sometimes overflow. Lately, it is the 6th of February, Waitangi Day—when the nation celebrates its birth—that such complaints are bought into the open and both sides look yet again at the wrongs, real or imagined, of the past.

The Maori have kept alive a rich cultural tradition that includes songs and dances recalling an era of primitive warfare and traditional sentimental love. Distinctive styles of woodwork and other arts have also continued. Rare is the tourist who does not bring home at least some small piece of wood or greenstone carving.

The Confessional

Now here are the answers to some questions about our *modus operandi* in New Zealand. Just how much cumshaw are we taking to turn out our detailed impressions of the country? Who pays the payola? Let's bare the baksheesh!

Readers of other titles in our Maverick series have understood for more than a decade now that the word "Maverick" guarantees that we are totally honest in our opinions on the travel scene. A dirty hotel room is a dirty hotel room in anyone's language. An overpriced meal is an overpriced meal. A rip-off is first and foremost a rip-off, and that's what we call it, too.

We don't take money, friendship, or favors to say something nice. When we find a facility we especially like, we are lavish in our praise, and you can be sure that it is an honest evaluation. And we try to reflect every shade of gray between the good, the bad, the ugly, and the beautiful.

All opinions expressed, unless otherwise credited, are those of two people—the authors. We take full responsibility for them.

Our preferred standard, of course, is never to let even a hint of commercial influence waft our way, so that everyone can see we are rich and powerful enough to be pure and shiningly independent in the travel-writing world.

Unfortunately, it's too seldom stated in the business that the economics of travel reporting today hardly permit that kind of Utopian innocence. We have found to our disappointment that it is utterly impossible to do the thorough, exhaustive job necessary in a comprehensive guidebook without permitting at least some assistance during the research phase of the book, even if it is far less than some others might allow.

Given that we and the rest of the world are imperfect, then, the next best thing is to lay it on the line as to just what influences may have been directed toward us. Those who are skeptical of our judgment may then apply any correction factor they think appropriate. For this book it has been necessary for us to become more involved with the travel industry than for other volumes in the series.

We still never accept a free meal from a restaurant we are testing. Never have; never will. We usually insist on paying for our hotel rooms, too.

However, we have occasionally accepted a travel agent or journalist discount when it has been offered, especially when it was necessary to test the most expensive accommodations. On a few occasions we have been "shouted" to a hotel room, generally by the New Zealand government's Tourism Board—rarely by anyone connected with the hotel itself. Nearly all the hotels and motels we stay in never know we are doing a book at all, although we sometimes tell them after we have paid the bill and checked out.

Over the years we have traveled to New Zealand many times, usually as paying passengers on whatever airline or ship was convenient at the time. In recent years we have also accepted a few special complimentary trips on Air New Zealand, Continental Airlines, and Qantas Airways, sometimes as members of a specific press group.

In all these cases we traveled only on the firm prior understanding by those carriers that we were under no obligation of any sort and that they would not see a line of our manuscript before it was published. This is consistent with the code of ethics of the Society of American Travel Writers.

Beyond that, New Zealand's Tourism Board has occasionally provided us with a car to use while traveling around the country. We've always paid for the petrol, however. And this is no mere drop in the tank, as we have burned a lot of it while tooling around over thousands of miles of landscape in the past few years.

Last, and I hope least, we have tagged along on some sightseeing tours as guests when offered a place, on the theory that the trip was going anyway, and we would be imposing no significant financial burden on the excursion. In New Zealand this also included our guided hike over the Milford Track.

So that's all of it, right up on top of the table. And we'll wager that it is a lot more than most travel writers are willing to tell, and quite a bit less than many are willing to take.

This *Maverick Guide to New Zealand* is the eleventh edition of the sixth guide in the Maverick series, which began in 1977 with the publication of our guide to Hawaii, updated regularly since. Our second volume, *The Maverick Guide to Australia*, was first published in 1979. For any travelers winging to Australia or Hawaii on their way to or from New Zealand, we firmly recommend consulting the latest editions of those, too.

We have one more excellent source of solid information for each edition of this book—our readers. Aldous Huxley once wrote, "For every traveler who has any taste of his own, the only useful guidebook will be the one which he himself has written." Therefore, after you return from your trip, would you write us about it? Letters like that help us tremendously in preparing each edition of all the Maverick Guides.

Use either the letter/envelope form at the end of the book, or—if that's not enough room—copy down the publisher's address and write us reams on your own paper in a separate envelope. We will appreciate it no end, and we promise to read it all from start to finish.

Getting the Most out of This Book

As in our previous guides, we have arranged this one in a smooth pattern designed for superefficient use. Following our first four chapters on the basics of travel, nature, and people, we devote the subsequent "area chapters" to six important New Zealand cities and their surrounding countryside—three from the North Island and three from the South Island.

These are *Auckland,* the northern gateway and largest city; *Rotorua,* the center of Maori culture and underground thermal activity; *Wellington,* the often underrated national capital; *Christchurch,* the flowerful main city on the South Island; *Queenstown,* quaint hub of the mountain and fiord country; and *Dunedin,* Scottish enclave of the deep south.

Each of these area chapters is divided into 12 numbered sections; after you have become familiar with them in one chapter you will know where to look for information on the same subject in each of the others.

The area chapters are divided as follows:

1.The General Picture
2.Long-Distance Transportation
3.Local Transportation
4.Hotels and Motels
5.Restaurants and Dining
6.Sightseeing
7.Guided Tours and Cruises
8.Water Sports
9.Other Sports
10.Shopping
11.Night Life and Entertainment
12.The Address List

We strongly suggest that you use this book in two ways. First, go over it at home to help you plan a bang-up trip to New Zealand. In the next chapter, for example, we cover many of the choices to be made concerning airlines, tours, travel agents, and the like. The other two general chapters—one on nature and the other on people—should contribute to your knowledge of the country. The individual hotels, for which you may want to make advance reservations, are listed in the area chapters.

Second, the book is designed to be used on the scene to help solve those day-to-day puzzlers—what bus to take to MOTAT, where to find a hamburger, and generally how to budget your time and money as you travel throughout New Zealand.

SHE'LL BE RIGHT, MATE!

To explore New Zealand today still requires a certain spirit of adventure. You'll not find there the smooth, practiced hand of the European host, deftly guiding guests over timeworn cobbles on the Baedeker circuit.

Instead, things in New Zealand are a lot less formal—less polished and less in a rut—for the modern explorer. Most international travelers over the past few years have returned from New Zealand with nothing but praise for the refreshingly honest, and sometimes charmingly naive, reception they received.

You won't always snag a porter, a cab, or a waiter exactly when you want one. But when you do find him, chances are he'll be willing, able, genuinely courteous, and friendly. And he won't expect a tip, either.

When things go wrong, and they do on trips as in all of life, the self-sufficient New Zealander somehow manages to cope with the situation. A country of weekend do-it-yourselfers, New Zealand boasts businessmen who can pour concrete, gourmet chefs who can change tires, and concert violinists who fix broken plumbing.

An Aucklander who is a particularly valued friend once told us there is an optimistic phrase that sums up what is almost a national religion in New Zealand. "We like to say, 'Never mind. She'll be right!'" And you know, she really will be, too!

2

On Your Mark . . .
Get Set . . .

Pencils sharpened? Desks and tables cleared? Okay, get ready for some logical thinking about the mechanics of setting up a great vacation (or business trip, if you insist) in New Zealand.

First of all, going to New Zealand means there are several things you *won't* have to bite your nails over—language, for one, and that's a biggie. Also, personal security is of little concern, as compared to other destinations. Ditto for health (there is absolutely no such thing as Te Rauparaha's Revenge). And tipping? Hah! It hardly exists, so knock that right out of the worry column, too, along with many of those imponderables you pore over before European, Asian, or South American expeditions.

All of the details shake down to about ten categories, when arranged in manageable order. To wit: international transportation and costs (boat or plane to the country); internal transportation (planes, trains, buses, rental cars); conducted tour or no conducted tour; choice of a travel agent; baggage allowances and packing; busy travel times; weights and measures; money and prices; visas and official stuff; and how to find further information.

In short, this chapter is designed to cover the practical aspects of getting to New Zealand and of moving around efficiently once you arrive.

Experienced travelers may want to skip over some of the stuff that follows. Very experienced travelers will read every word—and come back to some of this again, after reading other chapters in the book.

To travelers covering both New Zealand and Australia in the same trip: Sorry, but in this chapter we have had to repeat several points made in *The Maverick Guide to Australia,* to help those who are not going to both countries. However, the deadlines for the editions of these two books are different, and we would humbly suggest that you consult the latest revision of the Australian Maverick as well as this one in order to get the most up-to-date picture on traveling Down Under. The tab for the two volumes together may seem a little steep, but we'll bet a pavlova to a cabbage tree that either one will save you an amount greater than the price of both.

Throughout this book, we generally quote figures in New Zealand dollars (except in this chapter when speaking of air and sea fares from the U.S. to New Zealand, etc.). To avoid confusion, we may sometimes write U.S. $10 or N.Z. $10, for example; that's the official way to do it. And all prices given in New Zealand dollars are subject to the new tax of 12 percent (Goods and Services Tax referred to and pronounced as either "GST" or "GIST"), which we'll discuss in greater detail on down the line a bit.

Sea Routes to New Zealand

If you've got the time—and the money—they've got a ship on which you can laze your way to N.Z. from the U.S. Three shipping lines in particular have fairly regularly scheduled voyages between the two countries, with the often added bonus of visiting several interesting ports en route.

Cunard has bought several of the Royal Viking Line vessels, and this has enhanced rather than detracted from the previous schedules. For information you can call toll free in the United States 1-800-5-CUNARD or write to 555 Fifth Ave., New York, NY 10017.

P & O Cruises runs several cruises over various sectors that include the Pacific. The cruise line sells exclusively through travel agents, so contact your nearest or usual agency. The company's two British cruise liners, *Canberra* and *Sea Princess,* depart on annual around-the-world cruises from Southampton in England between January and April each year. The vessels circumnavigate the global waters in opposite directions, providing opportunities for sea travel between West Coast ports of the United States and New Zealand, Australia, and Britain.

California's well-known **Princess Cruises** (Tel. 310-553-1770) brings two of its nine ships to the South Pacific during the summer months each year. Cruise durations are usually around 14 nights, and several itineraries are on offer. Some cruises operate between Hawaii and Tahiti to a variety of ports in both places. There are also cruises between Tahiti and Sydney that include several Pacific ports and visit Auckland. A popular South Pacific itinerary operates between Sydney and Auckland, visiting Melbourne and Hobart in Australia and making several stops in both the North and South islands of New Zealand. Round-trips are also available from Sydney to the Pacific islands of Vanuatu, New Caledonia, and Fiji. Cruise itineraries and schedules vary each year. Write for up-to-date information to Princess Cruises, 10100 Santa Monica Blvd., Los Angeles, CA 90067, or call 310-553-1770.

What about passenger-carrying freighters? We thought these had all disappeared in recent years, but an interesting possibility emerged when the West German-registered **Columbus Line** announced it would take a maximum of 8 to 12 first-class passengers in sailings several times a month from certain U.S. port cities bound for Australia and New Zealand. We hear the cabins are as big as the *Queen Elizabeth II*'s, and we have it on authority that the food supply is "endless," but your best bet would be to write for information from the agent, Freighter World Cruises, Inc., 180 South Lake Ave., Suite 335, Pasadena, CA 91101. The Columbus Line ships sail several times a year.

The grand lady **Queen Elizabeth II** gracefully sails her 67,000-ton way to Auckland from New York via the Bahamas and South America, thence to Los Angeles and Papeete and on to Auckland, usually at the beginning of February. Unfortunately this doesn't happen every year. Even so, in case you're one of the lucky ones, call Cunard's office for up-to-date information at 1-800-5-CUNARD or write to 555 Fifth Ave., New York, NY 10017, so as not to miss a trip on this beautiful and stately vessel.

All ashore, please. Here's where we rejoin the rest of the crowd at the airport.

The Air Ways to Aotearoa

It's a truism, of course, and we've never denied it, that First Class is the beautiful people way to fly. They feed you like an ancient Maori chief. The liquor flows like Sutherland Falls. There are chairs the length and width of Cook Strait to stretch out in. Your companions may be dripping with wealth. There are lots of professional smiles and pillow-fluffing fuss from the ever-present cabin crew. And oh, yes, some free extras like maybe a pair of slipper socks and a sleep mask.

But you'll have to decide yourself if all that—plush as it may be—is worth an outlay of about U.S. $3,000-4,000 to fly *each way* between Los Angeles and

Auckland. Maybe it is, but when you consider the fact that you will save up to $2,000 or more each way just by sitting in the middle or back of the plane, with somewhat less froufrou, well, that may color your opinion.

Repeat: *Two thousand dollars.* I don't know what you'd do with that money, but we'd use it to live better—or stay longer—in New Zealand. We have flown First Class to Auckland, to see what it was like. Admittedly it *was* grand. But you know your pocket best.

Business Class. Before we talk about true economy, though, we want to mention that most airlines in the Pacific now offer a special mid-range service called Business Class or some equivalent term. ("J" Class is the ticket code.) On Down Under flights, these tickets have been running about $550 more than full Economy Class each way, but there are inconsistent differences on what you get for the price.

Traveling on a sort of second-class First Class, business flyers usually check in at the First Class counter. They may use the airline's VIP lounge, and that means free drinks and peanuts. On the plane, liquor and movies will be free. Seats are near the First Class section, and they are wider and more comfortable than those in Economy. On Air New Zealand they are upstairs in the bubble as well as in the "nose" downstairs, depending on whether the aircraft is a Boeing series 200 or 400 aircraft. You'll be seated with other business folks, too, of course, and you may have a larger reading library and a more liberal meal menu than the backseat passengers. If your company will spring for the extra couple of hundred, or if you can cough it up yourself, then go for it! Many passengers find the more commodious ambiance well worth the relatively small difference.

There's another interesting trend, however, that may portend the future on Pacific routes. That is to give Business Class service and facilities like drinks and movies free to the regular, full-fare Economy Class traveler. This would leave only those flying on bottom-level discount fares who might need to reach for their wallets from time to time at 30,000 feet. (But even that difference seems to be disappearing now, with more and more APEX passengers also getting free movies and drinks.)

Economy Class. Now, you can cut your fares much more drastically, of course, by traveling Economy Class. While it is not very practical to speak of specific prices in a biennial guidebook, the general principles will hold true, even if the actual amounts change. And incidentally, with airlines allowed to regulate themselves more and more, competition is increasingly stiff. Fortunately, this is particularly true throughout the Pacific region. Not all the fares on different air carriers over the same routes are the same. The airline that is cheaper this week may not be so next week, and vice versa. So if you're going for bargains, you'll have to comparison shop more than ever before.

Before we start, here's a tip from David Horowitz's consumer radio program: Airlines are allowed to quote you one ticket price on the phone, but if there's been a fare hike by the time you physically pick up the ticket, they can charge you at the increased rate. However, if you go right ahead and pay for your tickets and take them home, a "fare guarantee law" assures you that you won't have to pay any additional rate—at least if you use that ticket inside of one year from the day you cracked your wallet. So it is generally worthwhile to buy your ticket just as soon as you possibly can, even if it seems far in advance of your departure date.

The full-fare Economy Class ticket, which today totes up to a little over U.S. $2,500 round trip from California to New Zealand, normally entitles you to stop off when and where you want, travel any day of the week, and stay in the country up to a year before coming back to the States. But check around carefully. Airlines sometimes offer two kinds of Economy Class tickets. The one we have quoted here applies to travel with one carrier. If you want to experience a couple of different airlines on the way, expect to pay a few hundred dollars more. Greater expense could be incurred if you opt for one that does not allow for a stopover en route.

How to get the very lowest fares. You can save a lot—maybe more than 50 percent off round-trip full-fare Economy Class tickets—if you're willing to accept some restrictions on your travel plans. Look for tickets sold under Advance Purchase Excursion (APEX) fares, for example. APEX fares vary depending on the season you travel, generally worked out in three levels for "Low," "Shoulder," and "Peak" periods. (The seasons are different for different airlines, and sometimes changed for northbound and southbound flights. You might fly out in one season and return in another, and in that case your fare will generally be prorated.) Low seasons going down on these runs may be from about March through August, but don't be frightened off. We have had some beautiful vacation weather in New Zealand for these Southern Hemisphere fall and winter months.

To qualify for the APEX fare, you will have to fork over the dough for your ticket some time in advance (from 14 to 21 days), and if you change your mind about going, some percentage of the fare won't be refunded. Among other restrictions is that there is often no stopover privilege under the APEX fare, and you may be required to remain in New Zealand for at least two weeks. As a rough guide, the lowest advance payment fares for L.A./Auckland/L.A. are, at the time of writing, U.S. $850 (during low season—from 1 April to 31 July) and U.S. $1,510 (during peak season—1

December to 28 February). There's also a shoulder fare (applicable if flying during neither low nor peak season) of U.S. $1,280.

Note that it is in APEX fares that the real price competition usually comes. At times there may be significant differences among the airlines, not only in the dollar amounts, but also in the season during which the rate applies.

If you don't live on the West Coast, ask your travel agent to compare the discount fares available from your area to New Zealand with the combination of discount fares available from California added to the best deal you can make from your home to the Coast. You may find, for example, that the bargain fares offered from New York to Los Angeles added to the best price you can get from L.A. to Auckland would be lower than the New York-Auckland fare.

What about taking off from Hawaii for New Zealand? Well, if you're already in Hawaii, or you're going there anyway, fine. Generally speaking, it will cost you between U.S. $150-250 less to fly one-way to Auckland from Honolulu than it will from Los Angeles. The trouble is that it will probably cost you more than $200 to get to Hawaii in the first place. Again, check it out with your travel agent; sometimes special fares do come along that would make this a valid technique to save a few bucks.

With the increase in traffic to the Pacific over the past year or so, some airlines, unfortunately, have been squeezing their rows in Economy Class. We try to keep up with these seat-shrinking shenanigans, but it's difficult on an annual basis. In any case, tell whomever is making your reservation that we said to ask how many seats there are in a row. We would then avoid aircraft offering 11 across, perhaps in a 3-5-3 configuration (the aisles are between the numbers). If you do draw such a plane, at least try for an aisle seat, avoiding the three middle seats in the center column of the cabin (generally seats E, F, and maybe G).

Tip: For overnight flights, request a window seat on the right side of the aircraft. Coming in to Auckland over the island-studded northeast coast of New Zealand is usually spectacular at sunrise!

Which airline to fly? From North America, you have a choice among four airlines flying direct to Auckland (AKL in the abbreviated airline jargon): **Air New Zealand, United Airlines, Qantas,** and **Air Pacific.** On the Vancouver-Los Angeles-Auckland route, Air New Zealand code-shares with Canadian Airlines. Be aware that with fare structures as they are, it is difficult to "interline"—take more than one airline—without substantial financial penalty.

After price, perhaps, you choose an airline on how well it is set up to meet your own needs—what cities it leaves from, the connections between flights, the convenience of departure times, how quickly it gets where you're going, the number and type of free or low-cost stopovers available en route, and so forth.

Making a choice between airlines should be narrowed down for practical reasons. Air New Zealand now operates five nonstop flights from Los Angeles to Auckland, cutting out the Honolulu stopover and cutting down the flight hours. The flights operate Wednesdays, Thursdays, Fridays, and Saturdays.

If you need convenient connections from one of several U.S. cities, United is a logical choice (depending on which U.S. cities are served by the airline). Its Los Angeles (LAX) terminal receives feeder flights throughout the day, and then it launches its overnight Auckland flights in the evening. (Passengers who embark in Los Angeles probably will not have to change planes in Honolulu.)

Air New Zealand has daily flights from Los Angeles—more takeoffs than any of the others—and there are different routings, too. Canadians leaving from Vancouver could choose Canadian Air Lines, which code-shares with Air New Zealand, United Airlines, and Qantas.

If you want to stop over in Hawaii, your choice will be United, Air New Zealand, or (from Canada) Canadian Airlines. If you want to see something of Samoa, your options are Hawaiian Airlines, which flies from Honolulu to Pago Pago five times a week and from Honolulu to Apia every Tuesday; and Air New Zealand, with their new Honolulu, Apia, Tonga service. If you want to experience a piece of Tahiti, you'll have to take Air New Zealand. If you want to see Rarotonga and the Cook Islands, Air New Zealand is your airline. If you are going to stop off in Fiji, choose Air New Zealand, Canadian (code-sharing with Air New Zealand), Qantas, or Air Pacific.

Here is a brief discussion on services offered by all the airlines leaving for New Zealand from the U.S.A. and Canada.

Air New Zealand. A friend of the family since 1966, Air New Zealand has carried us several times to and from the "Land of the Long White Cloud." It is especially suited for passengers who want to stop over at a selection of Pacific island ports on the way Down Under or Back Up.

Flights leave Los Angeles each evening for Auckland, and the exact departure times change about four times a year, in order to accommodate the somewhat confusing differences in daylight and standard time between California and New Zealand. Six flights a week fly via Honolulu only and five a week via Honolulu and Nadi (Fiji). Twice a week Air New Zealand flies via Papeete (Tahiti). Depending on the routing, passengers arrive in Auckland after around 15.5 hours (via Papeete *or* Honolulu) to over 17 hours (via Honolulu *and* Nadi) elapsed time. The flights from L.A. get in at Mangere Airport, Auckland, throughout the morning.

Most return flights leave Auckland in the evening, arriving at LAX in the late afternoon and early evening (on the same date). Air New Zealand operates convenient nonstop flights from Auckland to Los Angeles, reaching that city in one 12-hour hop, shaving 3.5 hours off the normal elapsed time. It flies several of these nonstoppers every week between the West Coast of the U.S. and New Zealand.

Canadians should note that Air New Zealand also operates eight flights per week from Vancouver, BC, to Auckland, and four a week from Toronto. The airline operates these flights in conjunction with Canadian Airlines, and there is a stop in Honolulu on the way to Auckland. Total elapsed flight time between the cities is about 16.5 hours.

Air New Zealand now fields a fleet consisting of Boeing 747-200s (the long-range version of the popular jumbo) and the stretched upper deck 747-400s on its international runs. In the Economy Class section, the rows of seats are split by two aisles into a usual 3-4-3 configuration. In First Class, 10 (in the 200 series) and 16 (in the 400 series) very wide sleeper seats are separated 2-2-2. The airline also flies the efficient 767 (Extended Range) Boeings on some of its international routes.

Air New Zealand also offers a Business Class service. Like First Class, Business Class travelers either ride in the upstairs dome or downstairs, depending on whether it is a Boeing 200- or 400-series aircraft. These passengers receive First-Class-type amenities like china service, slippers, sheepskin covers, over-the-ear earphones, etc. (When the plane is crowded, this area is much more comfortable than the coach seats.)

First Class passengers are given several choices in meals, and even in Economy Class Air New Zealand offers a choice of two meals on the menu. Fresh New Zealand specialties are usually featured. All drinks, including champagne, wine, and beer, are complimentary in all classes. Music, exclusive video programs, and movies are also offered to everyone, with no extra charge for headsets. Feature films are shown on flights longer than 4.5 hours in duration.

Air New Zealand offers the usual First, Business, and Economy Class fares, plus APEX fares requiring 14 days' advance purchase. These are divided into "Peak," "Shoulder," and "Low" seasons at discounts amounting to 30 percent off Economy Class in peak season to over 50 percent off in low season. Unlimited stopovers are now allowed in any fare category.

Don't hold us to it, but at this writing the lowest Air New Zealand low-season, round-trip Los Angeles-Auckland APEX fare still hovers below $990 if purchased 21 days before travel.

If all other arrangements work out (fares, seasons, convenience, etc.), we would tend to choose Air New Zealand to fly to Auckland as a way to begin experiencing something of the country right away. (Tell 'em we sent you.)

Air Pacific. Air Pacific is a familiar sight under southern skies and runs a fleet of 747 aircraft from Los Angeles on Saturdays. In the afternoon, the airline heads to Auckland via Nadi (Fiji). Economy Class seats 404 passengers in a 3-4-3 configuration, and Business Class offers 2-2 seating for 18 passengers. All Business Class passengers have access to private airport lounges at no extra cost. Contact Air Pacific at Suite 475, 841 Apollo Street, El Segundo, CA 90245, Tel. 1-800-227-4446.

United Airlines. United took over the Pacific routes of Pan American early in 1986, and has considerably expanded services to the South Pacific since.

The airline offers daily flights to Auckland and Melbourne from Los Angeles on spacious B747-400 series Boeing aircraft. Economy seating configuration is 3-4-3. APEX fares are sold on Peak, Shoulder, and Low seasons.

Qantas Airways Limited. Qantas flies from Los Angeles to Auckland every day except Tuesday and Thursday. On Monday and Saturday the service comes via Tahiti; the other days are nonstop. Business and First Class have standard in-seat videos, the only airline on the route with this facility. Qantas no longer code-shares with Air New Zealand. Qantas has also promoted a special APEX fare on flights from Los Angeles and San Francisco, allowing stopovers (three in New Zealand) at a special price. The airline now also flies between Sydney and New York.

You can choose to stop over in Honolulu. The flight continues on to Sydney with connections to *Auckland, Wellington, Christchurch,* and *Melbourne.* The details may change, but the APEX fare is a plan worth considering on an excellent airline worth flying. The carrier has also begun flights between Sydney and New York.

Flying Australia-New Zealand. Auckland is the major port of entry to New Zealand by air from North America, but the nation does have a total of three international airports. If you're flying the trans-Tasman services from Australia (Melbourne, Sydney, Brisbane, Cairns, Perth, Adelaide, or Hobart), you may choose to land in Auckland or Wellington on the North Island or at Christchurch on the South Island.

We'd pick Christchurch, if possible. It's a modern airport, a lovely city, and all in all a good place to begin a visit to the country. Auckland may be an efficient airport from which to leave, however. Wellington Airport, which is not our favorite, is sometimes closed by weather. Anyway, the runway isn't long enough to accommodate most jumbo jets.

Between Australia and New Zealand, we might select Air New Zealand to fly east, and Qantas Airways in the opposite direction, although the joint trans-Tasman services operated by Qantas and Air New Zealand to selected Australian ports could influence that. (We have no specific objection to United or British Airways, which also make these nonstop hops.) Any jet takes a little over three hours to make the trip.

There are about ten different price levels on the highly competitive trans-Tasman flights, ranging between about N.Z. $3010 Auckland/Sydney round-trip First Class to around N.Z. $700 for the lowest season EPIC (APEX) fare from Auckland to Sydney (round trip). Look at these fares carefully when you're making plans. You may find that the cheapest *one-way* Economy fare is slightly above the EPIC round-trip fare. The fares at the low end of the scale can be extremely competitive, and you may find it viable to get a cheap fare into Australia and *then* buy a fare across the Tasman. You may also find it cheaper to depart Australia for New Zealand from a different gateway. For instance, Garuda Indonesia flies over Brisbane en route to Bali and can board passengers at the Australian port. Fares therefore, between Brisbane and Auckland on Garuda can be extremely reasonable.

The airport departure tax is $20 for all passengers aged 12 years and over when leaving New Zealand for any other country.

Transportation inside New Zealand

Traveling within the nation should be scenic and fun, and if you check out all the options, it will be. Details tied to specific localities are covered in the six area chapters of this volume, but some basic aspects of getting around the country should be considered before leaving home.

Domestic air travel. Air New Zealand's "domestic services" are operated by **Air New Zealand National** and feature frequent connections between two dozen major airports. They occasionally use Boeing 767 wide-body twin jets on the nonstop Auckland-Christchurch route (1 hour and 20 minutes) and on the Auckland-Wellington run (1 hour); and Boeing 737 twin jets (3-3 seating) on those routes plus on others like Wellington-Christchurch (45 minutes) and Christchurch-Dunedin (45 minutes). **Air New Zealand Link** is an efficient amalgam of smaller airlines serving provincial routes. On all flights, check in early to get a window seat. The views are often first-class.

Depending on how much you pay for the ticket, the in-flight service will be dished up with many or few frills. Air New Zealand was faced with its first major competitor on the domestic front when a New Zealand-based offshoot of the Australian company **Ansett Airlines,** called, logically enough, **Ansett New Zealand,** began flights on major domestic routes in 1987 and has gone from strength to strength. Air travelers have benefited from the ensuing battle for market share, and New Zealanders now frequently fly around their little country for less than ever before.

For example, you can get from Christchurch to Wellington for $149 on an Air New Zealand Super Thrifty fare, which slices up to 45 percent off the normal economy ticket. This is about the cheapest in a range of cut-price fares, nearly always matched by Ansett New Zealand, and they come with a few minor conditions. However, overseas visitors should not find them too restrictive. The more dollars added to the cost of the ticket, the fewer the restrictions. Thrifty fares from Wellington to Christchurch currently cost $269 round trip. The top-cost Wellington/Christchurch fare, which carries no restrictions, costs $210. (We are talking New Zealand dollars, of course.) In-flight meals crop up at meal times with hearty A.M. and P.M. nibbles. Alcohol is now served on Ansett New Zealand. Wine is complimentary with dinner, but all other alcoholic drinks must be paid for.

Travelers who fly to and from the country on Air New Zealand are allowed to buy a special air pass called the **Explore N.Z. Pass.** It costs N.Z. $515 for three sectors or N.Z. $1,373 for eight sectors. *It must be purchased outside New Zealand.* To the Air Pass you can combine a variety of Accommodation passes, also purchased through your travel agent before you depart for New Zealand. These cover motels, hotels, and farm stay accommodations. Ansett Australia has, at time of writing, just released its "Visit Australia Pass," bought through the Australian company but valid for travel on both Ansett Australia within Australia and Ansett New Zealand within New Zealand. The Air Pass promises to be competitive. Further details can be obtained from Ansett Australia, C/O Air New Zealand, 1960 East Grand Avenue, El Segundo, CA, Tel. 1-888-4-ANSETT.

A couple of additional airlines include the Auckland-based **Helicopter Line,** which operates chartered flights to the Bay of Islands and other nearby destinations. **Southern Air Limited,** formerly Stewart Island Air Services, uses a Britten-Norman Islander to fly between Invercargill and Stewart Island (a trip we enjoyed).

Taking the train. There are two main trains between Auckland and Wellington (via Hamilton, Tongariro National Park, Palmerston North, and lots of other places). The *Northerner* is an overnight rail service, operating both ways Sunday to Friday. Northbound and southbound versions of this train leave Wellington at 7:50 P.M. and pull in at Auckland at 7 A.M. From Auckland, the *Northerner* departs at 8:40 P.M. and arrives in Wellington at 7:35 A.M. An all-night buffet, snacks, tea, and coffee are available, and pillows and reclining seats cushion the sleeping hours. Personally, we think this one is only for white-knuckle fliers, since there is nothing to see along the way in the dark. The *Northerner* fares are between $61 and $122. It operates every night except Saturday.

Far preferable to our way of thinking is the scenic daylight version, the *Overlander,* which normally makes about seven stops. Auckland-Wellington trains run from 8:53 A.M. to 7:43 P.M., and Wellington-Auckland trains from 8:45 A.M. to 7:35 P.M. There is full bar service, midday meals, complimentary morning and afternoon teas, a train attendant to attend passengers, and even a commentary en route. On the Rotorua and Tauranga runs the train is sometimes called a "rail car," which means there are probably two to four carriages—with the electric engine built right in whichever car is doing the pulling. Fares between the two cities will run N.Z. $135.

You can also take a train from Wellington north along the east coast. As far as Napier, it offers a diner on the 5.5-hour trip. The *Bay Express* from Napier to Gisborne leaves about a half-hour later and costs between $36 and $71. The service leaves at 8 A.M. from Wellington and arrives in Napier at 1:22 P.M. It returns from Napier at 2:29 P.M. and arrives in Wellington at 7:36 P.M. Some years ago we took the whole journey from Gisborne to Wellington, a tiring excursion totaling 11 hours. The scenery, however, was delightful.

A little-known rail car also runs between Taumarunui (on the main line) and Stratford and New Plymouth.

After crossing Cook Strait to Picton on the *Interislander* ferry, you can take the *The Coastal Pacific Express* from between $31-$75. It departs Picton at 1:25 P.M. and arrives in Christchurch at 6:45 P.M. after 5 hours of sea view. There's also a spur from Christchurch over the Southern Alps to Greymouth. (During the summer months keep an eye out for the Lynx high-speed ferry service—local travel agents will have details.)

The train from Christchurch through Dunedin to Invercargill is named the *Southerner.* Leaving both ends of that run at 8:15 A.M., that train takes 9 hours to make the entire trip for a fare of between N.Z. $38-$77. Both directions offer a dining car en route for teas and buffet lunch. There is a liquor service, Devonshire afternoon teas (scones with cream and jam), and lamb's-wool seats to recline on. The *Southerner* has earned the reputation of being New Zealand's friendliest train.

The scenery may be great, and it is certainly easily seen, since trains in Kiwi-land will probably never break any speed records. The Auckland-Wellington run, for example, averages less than 40 miles per hour, partly because of the limitations caused by the narrow, 3.5-foot gauge common to all tracks in the country.

One of the great train journeys of the world is New Zealand's **Transalpine Express,** which departs Christchurch at 9 A.M. each day and arrives in

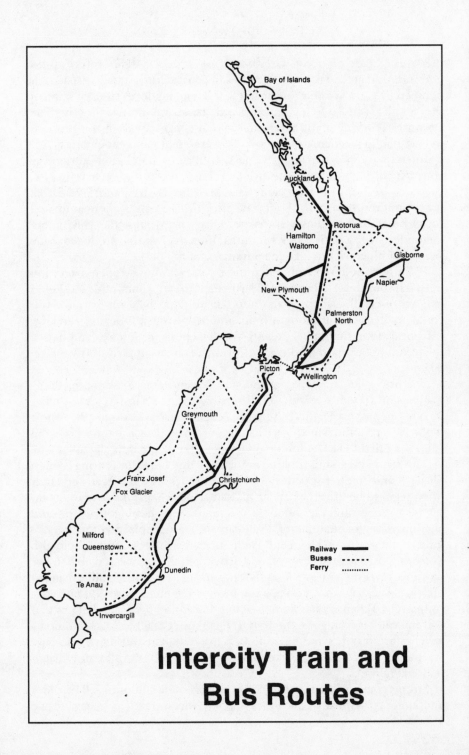

Bay of Islands

Auckland

Rotorua

Hamilton
Waitomo

Gisborne

New Plymouth

Napier

Palmerston
North

Picton

Wellington

Greymouth

Franz Josef
Fox Glacier

Christchurch

Milford
Queenstown

Dunedin

Te Anau

Invercargill

Railway
Buses
Ferry

Intercity Train and
Bus Routes

the West Coast town of Greymouth at 1:25 P.M. The return from Greymouth is at 2:30 P.M. and it arrives in Christchurch at 6:30 P.M. Cost is between $41 and $68 (day excursion $109), and it affords views of some of the South Island's best scenery from expansive train windows. The Devonshire morning and afternoon teas are also served on this train, as well as a liquor service, the sheepskin-covered seats, and commentary.

Intercity offers a special **Travelpass.** It must be purchased outside the country (through travel agents usually). The latest prices we have in N.Z. currency are from $434 for eight days, $662 for 15 days, and $774 for 22 days. Children travel for about half price. These passes allow unlimited travel on trains, the buses of Intercity (see map), and the Wellington-Picton ferry for a period of six months. Intercity has also produced some suggested itineraries to take full advantage of the deal.

It's important to remember that these passes cannot be open-dated; you must tell your travel agent what day you want to start yours, and you should make a reservation for that day also. (It wouldn't be a lot of fun if you could not get a seat on a bus or train, and had to watch your first travel day disappear down the line.) Intercity Travel Centres in New Zealand have a toll-free number should you want to contact them on arrival. It's (0800) 802 802.

The prices quoted above for the New Zealand Travelpass are for the 2-in-1 version (coach + ferry). Other versions are the 3-in-1 (coach + rail + ferry), 4-in-1 Short Flight Travelpass (coach + ferry [1] + rail [2] + short flight [1]) and the 5-in-1 Long Flight Travelpass (coach + ferry [1] + rail [2] + long flight [1]). Additional sectors are available with all passes.

The line between buses for transportation and buses for touring is often blurred, and Intercity operates conducted tours also. But even the latter often seem to be driven by cheerful, loquacious chaps who love to get on the microphone and yarn about the region they are passing through—and anything else, for that matter. Prices are, as an example, $64 for the 425-mile trip between Auckland and Wellington or vice versa during the night, departing Auckland at 7:50 P.M. and arriving in the capital at 6:50 A.M. For daytime travel the cost is $96 each way, leaving at 9:15 A.M. and arriving at 8:15 P.M. Auckland to Rotorua, a distance of 158 miles, costs $44 one way.

Intercity obligingly has a toll-free number inside the United States that you can call regarding the Intercity Travel Pass. It's 800-458-1130. Intercity coaches are privately owned, although Intercity Rail and the *Interislander* are owned by NZ Rail. The combination of the two provides an efficient national network.

Strong competition is provided by two privately run outfits. The older and larger is **Newmans Coachlines Limited,** which traces its lineage to the two Newman brothers who started a horse-drawn service from Nelson to Murchison in 1879. The firm is still in the family, offering trips and tours over most of the North Island and part of the South Island. (Their "Glacierland" tour got a big thumbs-up from the Fleischmanns of Tonawanda, New York.)

One other reputable bus company that specializes in guided tours is **Guthreys New Zealand Tours, Ltd.,** founded in 1945. This dependable firm is headquartered in Christchurch. Previously we have also mentioned the Grayline, but this company has now been bought out by Mount Cook Landlines.

A tale of three rental cars. Once upon a time, the big three in car-rental firms in New Zealand were known as Tasman, Mutual, and Dominion, three good names full of Kiwi character. Now, with international franchising having impinged on the New Zealand rental-car market, Tasman has become **Hertz,** Mutual has been transformed into **Avis,** and Dominion has acquired the familiar **Budget** label.

It may cost you more to rent a car in New Zealand than in North America. But as far as we are concerned there is no better way to see the country, and you can probably save at least some money by staying at motels, if you want. You might find a car for about N.Z. $60 daily, which would be better for small trips around town—or, for that matter, anything averaging under 150 kilometers or so per day.

We'll pass on this advice from one conscientious Hertz woman in Christchurch: When turning in the car, always ask the company to calculate the bill both on the kilometer and the unlimited-distance basis, and then pay the lesser amount. (Usually, the company will do that for you without your asking.)

For trips running from one area of the country to another, you may have to stay with one of the big three. But there are other local-area car-rental companies that may offer lower rates, and a few of them may be represented in more than one city. To get the lowest rates on a rental car, the best technique is to sit down with a telephone and the Yellow Pages (it's usually under "R" for Rental Cars in N.Z.) and call some of the lesser-known firms. When you get a good rate, ask what other cities they are represented in.

Other car-rental companies worth looking into include **Maui, Thrifty, Letz, Percy,** and **Green's.**

Driving in New Zealand. For North Americans, the big worry may be in keeping left, and I must admit we are usually concerned about that for all of a day or so. After proceeding particularly cautiously for the first couple of days, though, New Zealand driving came as easily as—probably easier

North Island Driving Times

The times, in hours and minutes, represent: driving time for a driver who travels at 50 to 55 mph on open stretches of road plus a safety factor of 5 to 10 minutes per hour for traffic delays (and short stops for petrol, refreshments, etc).

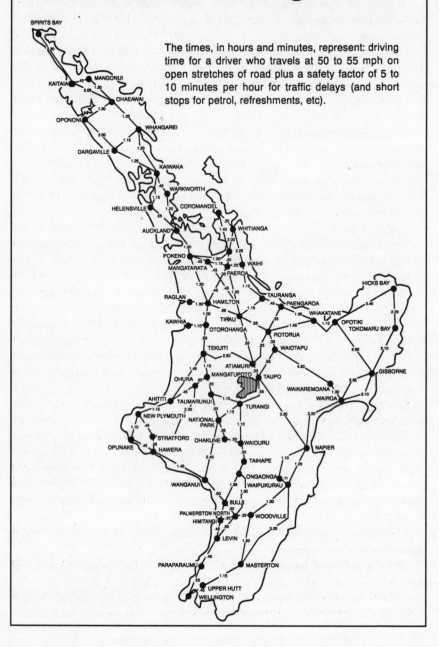

than—driving anywhere in the U.S., Canada, or elsewhere in the right-hand traffic world.

Until you get used to it, we would suggest driving with a companion wherever possible. Simply "keeping left" is not the only thing; you must remember some other aspects of that phenomenon. Since the steering wheel is on the right, remember that the vehicle extends quite a way out to your left. Your driving partner will no doubt scream when the curb comes too close. Associated with that, too, is passing ("overtaking"). Be sure to pull far enough to the right so that you don't give everyone heart failure.

You must become accustomed to the idea that right turns are made *across* traffic, and stop looking somewhere in outer space for the rear-view mirror. Be particularly careful when coming off one-way streets, and when you're looking for drivers in other cars around you, try not to be unduly surprised when you see that many seem to be either self-propelled or else driven by dogs and babies!

Here are some other driving checkpoints:

• You don't need an International Driving License if you have with you a valid license from the U.S., Canada, Australia, or certain other countries.

• In the absence of other signs or signals, remember that the car to your right has the right-of-way. And that rule is extended to mean that if you're coming up to a side street to make a left-hand turn into it, and a car coming toward you on the same route also wants to turn into that same side street, that car—*the car turning across the traffic*—has the right-of-way. (Of course you have the right-of-way over that car if you are continuing straight through the intersection—or if you both want to turn into a side street on your right.)

• Most New Zealand roads are excellent, but look out if you see a sign warning of a "metal surface." That means loose gravel, so slow down. By the way, there's something about the shape of New Zealand gravel that causes it to be tossed harder, higher, and farther by speeding cars. If two vehicles are passing at high speed, gravel tossed by one car can slam against the windshield of the second car. Broken windshields ("puckered screens") are therefore not an uncommon occurrence throughout the country.

• By and large, we do not think New Zealand drivers are as skillful and as safety-conscious as many North American drivers. They're probably spoiled by the light traffic. Most are polite, however—except perhaps in Auckland.

• Road signs, which are constructed and installed by the Automobile Association, are nearly always excellent. But look out for temporary signs

South Island Driving Times

The times, in hours and minutes, represent: driving time for a driver who travels at 50 to 55 mph on open stretches of road plus a safety factor of 5 to 10 minutes per hour for traffic delays (and short stops for petrol, refreshments, etc).

like "Detour." These are set up by the Ministry of Works ("misery works," say the Kiwis). They sometimes start you on the detour but don't get around to bringing you back to the main route again!

• Make an effort to learn what various signs mean. "P 40," for example, is not reserved for an airplane. It means parking is allowed there for 40 minutes. And New Zealand traffic officers find nothing ambiguous in the phrase "FINE FOR PARKING." It does *not* mean "okay to park here!"

• Related to the "keep left" rule, of course, are traffic circles ("roundabouts"). Take them *clockwise*, please!

• Speed limits (marked in kilometers per hour by a number inside a red circle) are strictly enforced in New Zealand. "LSZ" means Limited Speed Zone. Use your good judgment in those areas. At this writing, the maximum speed throughout the country is 100 kph.

• If a car approaches you and flashes his lights, he may be warning you that there are traffic cops ahead. It's a friendly Kiwi custom, but definitely illegal!

• A vehicle in New Zealand is not roadworthy unless fitted with seat belts in the front *and* back. All passengers must wear the belts. It is preferable that those 5 years old and under are restrained in an approved child booster seat or capsule. The driver of a vehicle is responsible for his passengers' adherence to this law and will be fined otherwise.

• Watch out for one-way bridges. Either you or the cars approaching from the other end will be politely warned to "please give way." And some long, narrow bridges have a "passing bay"—a wide place in the middle where one car can wait while the other passes.

• "Slips" are landslides, and roads through gorges or mountain passes can be temporarily closed or restricted to one-way traffic by this relatively common occurrence.

• Herds of sheep or cattle have the right-of-way on any highway. If the animals are coming toward you, it's best to stop and let them pass. If you are both going the same way, proceed very slowly and you'll probably get through. (Be sure to give a friendly wave to the shepherd or drover!)

• You'll be alerted to the possibility of the above if you see a sign warning of "wandering stock." Also be on the lookout for sheep around the bend if you notice that the road is dotted with "chocolate peanuts"!

• Rest areas are well marked along many highways. Usually these include a toilet, picnic tables, garbage cans, etc. We make liberal use of them.

• Road maps are plentiful and well designed. A rental-car company will give you some, but we advise picking up either the *Shell Road Maps of New Zealand*, a book for around $9.95, or the much more detailed *AA Road Atlas of New Zealand* (don't miss the city maps inside). The Shell Road Map can be picked up from Shell stations around the country. BP and Mobil Oil also produce reliable road and city maps.

   • Motor campers. Instead of renting just a car, some folks prefer to rent a camper in an attempt to carry their motel room right along with them. Kiwis generally call them camper vans, incidentally. If you've satisfactorily traveled that way elsewhere, you'll love it in New Zealand, where the roads are less crowded and the campgrounds are plentiful and safe. If you've never gone that route, approach with caution. Even the best and largest campers seem crowded to vacationers used to spreading out at the end of the day. And driving techniques, of course, are more those of a truck than of a car.

   Outfits dealing in this sort of thing include Newmans (the well-known bus and tour company), Horizon, Maui Campas, Budget, and Suntrek. Information on all of these is available from the New Zealand Tourism Board in the U.S., Canada, Australia, and other countries (see the last page of this chapter). Rates start at about N.Z. $169.50 per day for the smallest camper, which sleeps two adults and one child. The camper that sleeps four adults and two children ranges in price from $170 to $225—depending on the season (the lower price coincides with the lower season). (For additional information, see Pelican's comprehensive *New Zealand by Motorhome*.)

   Bicycling. Andrew Fabula, a two-wheel enthusiast from La Jolla, California, says that New Zealand is one of the best biking countries in the world. Andrew will send information on pedaling through New Zealand or Australia and answer questions on the subject for those who send a stamped, self-addressed envelope to him at 5497 Coral Reef Ave., La Jolla, CA 92037, or he can be phoned at (619) 270-1333.

   In addition, you might want to contact a commercial firm, Backroads Bicycle Touring, which has been offering special bike tours of New Zealand and Hawaii. Write them at 1516 Fifth Street, Suite Q410, Berkeley, California 94710-1713, or telephone at 415-527-1555. Outside California, their toll-free number is 800-245-3874. With the exception of a couple of phone calls that would seem to indicate that they are courteous and efficient, we have had no personal experience with Backroads, and we would be very happy to have a reader report on the company.

   Hitchhiking. Our friends who are active, mobile members of the Society of the Upturned Thumb tell us that New Zealand is the best country in the world for getting a ride—particularly for young foreigners.

   Try displaying a national or state flag. Also, signs like "please" and "have a nice day" are popular. Our good friend John Anderson, who has thumbed the length and breadth of the land, said that one of the nicest things about traveling this way is that hitchhikers often find they are invited home by their "rides" for a meal or a rest. (No guarantees, of course!)

Tours—Guided and Misguided

Travel agents and travel wholesalers (tour operators) offer a few good guided tours to New Zealand, but we have always found it difficult to keep up with exactly who is doing what in any given year.

If you're an independent sort, more power to you. You'll have a great time exploring New Zealand on your own, changing plans at will depending on whom you meet up with, the weather, phases of the moon, or just personal whim.

But if you want to make your way through the country with logical progression, meet up with others of a like mind, and leave all the logistical mental exercise to someone else, then the conducted tour could be just the ticket—especially during heavy travel periods. In fact, guided tours in New Zealand can be great if they include some fun-loving Kiwis on the bus, too.

Remember that since air fares stay basically the same regardless of how long you're in the country, you will get more per dollar spent in a long tour than in a short one. That may seem obvious, but many of our friends seem to miss the point.

A tour that will keep you independent of the madding bus crowd would be the fly/drive plan. Of course you can make your own car-rental arrangements, but there are a couple of groups offering fly/drive arrangements that wrap up several hotels and discounted domestic flying and sightseeing deals along with the car. (You can also find some camper/van tours, but we think these are not so necessary in New Zealand, where kitchen-equipped motels are plentiful and relatively cheap.) Check with your travel agent on this.

Incidentally, all fly/drive plans inevitably involve some extra financial outlay, and more than just the price of petrol. Be sure you understand just which hotels, air connections, etc., are provided, and which are not. Also, be sure to see our remarks on driving in New Zealand in this chapter.

Tour operators. Here are a few North American travel wholesalers offering New Zealand itineraries, although there are probably some other good ones, too. You'll probably book these through your travel agent, but here are the addresses to which to write for brochures and further information. Tell them we said to write, and if you take any guided tour to New Zealand, from these companies or anybody else, we'd very much like to know how it went, for inclusion in future editions.

Adventure Center
1311 63rd Street, #200
Emeryville, CA 94608
(800) 227-8747

Australian Pacific, Inc.
512 S. Verdugo Drive, #200
Burbank, CA 91502

Australian Pacific (N.Z.) Pty.
#630 West Tower, Shipp Centre
3300 Bloor Street, W.
Toronto, Ont. M8X 2X2
(416) 234-8306

Austravel, Inc.
51 East 42nd St., #616
New York, NY 10017

Brendan Tours
15137 Califa St.
Van Nuys, CA 91411-3021

Canadian Holidays
191 The West Mall, 6th Floor
Etobicoke, Ont. M9C 5K8
(416) 620-8121

Contiki Holidays
#321-40 Dundas St. West
Toronto, Ont. M5G 2C2
(416) 593-4873

Esplanade Tours
581 Boylston St.
Boston, MA 02116

Goway Travel
2300 Yonge St., #2001
Toronto, Ont. M4P 1E4
(416) 322-1034

Goway Travel
Suite 456-409 Granville St.
Vancouver, B.C. V6C 1T2
(604) 687-4004

Holiday House
110 Richmond St. East, #304
Toronto, Ont. M5C 1P1

Holiday House
900 West Georgia St., Suite 108
Vancouver, B.C. V6C 2W6

Horizon Holidays
160 John St.
Toronto, Ont. M5V 2X8
(416) 585-9922

Islands in the Sun
2381 Rosecrans Ave.
Suite 325

El Segundo, CA 90245
Jetabout/Qantas Vacations
#505-5353 Dundas St.
Toronto, Ont. M9B 6KS
(416) 234-8220

Mount Cook Line
1960 E. Grand Ave., #910
El Segundo, CA 90245
(800) 468-2665

Newmans South Pacific Vacations
6033 West Century Blvd.
Suite 1270
Los Angeles, CA 90045

New Zealand Central Reservations
6033 W. Century Blvd., #1270
Los Angeles, CA 90045
(800) 351-2317 CA
(800) 351-2323 US

Northwest Passage Outing Club
1130 Greenleaf Ave.
Wilmette, IL 60091
(800) 732-7328

Pacific Destinations Center
18685 Main St., #A622
Huntington Beach, CA 92648
(800) 227-5317

Pacific Exploration Co.
P.O. Box 3042
Santa Barbara, CA 93130

Silver Fern Holidays
#490-1090 Homer St.
Vancouver, B.C. V6B 2W9
(604) 684-9722

Silver Wing Holidays
3331 No. 3 Road
Richmond, B.C. V6X 2B6
(604) 273-9465

SOPAC
9000 Sunset Blvd.
Suite 1410
West Hollywood, CA 90069
(800) 551-2012

South Pacific Tours, Ltd.
1727 West Broadway, 2nd Floor
Vancouver, B.C. V6J 4W6
(604) 738-6976

Trek Holidays
109th Street, #8412
Edmonton, AB T6G 1E2
(403) 439-9118

Vermont Bicycle Touring Company
P.O. Box 711
Bristol, VT 05443

For further information write to the **New Zealand Tourism Board,** 501 Santa Monica Blvd., Suite 300, Santa Monica, CA 90401, or call them at 213-395-7480

Accommodations. In section 4 of the six area chapters of this book, we go into considerable detail discussing most major and many minor hotels in New Zealand's important tourist areas centered at Auckland, Rotorua, and Wellington on the North Island and Christchurch, Queenstown, and Dunedin on the South Island. (Even if you're not staying in Auckland, be sure to see our general remarks on Kiwi hotels at the beginning of section 4 in that chapter anyway.) Each of these chapters also mentions a few places to stay in nearby sightseeing areas (section 6).

Beyond that, there are literally thousands of small hotels and motels throughout New Zealand's villages and towns and even scattered in the countryside. Sometimes even a country pub, classified in most New Zealanders' minds as nothing more than a "drinking hotel," will have two or three inexpensive rooms to rent on the top floor, although often without such modern conveniences as your own private loo. You might also like to keep an eye out for signs indicating overnight rooms for rent in private homes.

If you're a member of AAA in North America, or of some other automobile clubs in other countries, and carry your card to prove it, you'll have reciprocal privileges with the AA in New Zealand. This makes you eligible for their advice and services, and you can purchase special publications and supplies at their offices all over the country. If you're not a member, consider joining the AA in New Zealand. It would be worth the thirty bucks or so for no other reason than to be able to pick up their *Accommodation Guides*, annual booklets listing virtually every hotel and motel in the country. You can use AA facilities to book ahead on your trip, too.

Farm vacations. An unusual trip idea is to spend a number of days (or weeks) living on a New Zealand farm, eating and spending time with the family, helping with the chores as much (or as little) as you like, etc. There are about three hundred farm families throughout the country acting as hosts on these unusual programs, many of them popular with city-bred New Zealanders, too.

Of course, many of the farms are located in scenic areas, and several have interesting historic and archeological sites that may be explored on the property. Some farms take children only, and this might be a way for kids and parents to effect separate vacations in New Zealand.

The "farm holiday" scene changes somewhat from season to season, and there are several different ways to make the arrangements. Some packages include car rentals, some include rooms with private baths, and there are many other variations. Rates run from around N.Z. $65 daily per person (double) and about N.Z. $85 if you are traveling solo.

If your travel agent is not up on it all, you can get the latest on farm holidays by writing the New Zealand Tourism Board at one of the North American addresses at the end of this chapter. Or write the NZTB in Santa Monica for a list of farm and home host localities. New Zealand Farm Holidays, P.O. Box 256, Silverdale, Auckland, has a comprehensive list. You can call them at 09-412-9649, fax 09-412-9651, or e-mail farm@N.Z.accom.co.NZ.

If you just want to visit a typical Kiwi home for an evening, get in touch with Mrs. Lesley Fallon at Hospitality Plus, Ltd., P.O. Box 56175, Auckland 1003; Tel. (09) 810-9175; Fax: 810-9448. Lesley can also organize dinners, farmstays, and homestays beyond Auckland. It is a good idea to take advantage of the booking system before you leave for New Zealand. The popularity of farmhouse and country home holidays means you should reserve your chosen spot well in advance if you will be traveling during the peak holiday time of January through February. One more useful home-host address is P.O. Box 51-252, Wellington. It belongs to the New Zealand Association of Farm and Home Hosts. You could write to the secretary for quality assurance.

Veterans Clubs (called RSAs) in New Zealand offer a warm welcome to Americans, along with meals and drinks. You can write to the New Zealand Returned Services Association, "Waterside House," 220 Willis Street, Wellington, for information.

Sporting Lodges is the slightly misleading name the New Zealand Tourism Board's comprehensive *New Zealand Book* gives to about fifty smaller-scale hotels dotted around the country. What they have in common is a penchant for choosing superb sites, and they combine magnificent scenery with a menu of refreshing outdoor pursuits that can get as energetic or as laid-back as you fancy. The dinner menus usually feature local specialties, cooked with flair. These character-full accommodations are often managed by the owners, and guests enjoy the personable intimacy of a small hotel. Tariffs range from about N.Z. $200 to $750 per couple and are, in most cases, inclusive of meals. We refer to various sporting lodges as we go along.

How to Use a Travel Agent

Choose a travel agent as you would a doctor or a dentist, not just blindly from the Yellow Pages or from newspaper ads. Ask some friends who travel frequently, especially if they have recently been to New Zealand or the Pacific. They'll know who has taken good care of them and not left them in the lurch.

If you don't feel like going in to sit down right away, call a few recommended agencies on the phone. If they're willing to chat about your proposed trip, drop in for some more conversation and pick up a few brochures. It would be a mistake to sign yourself up for a major trip the first time you set foot in a travel agency. No one would be more surprised than the travel agent if you walked out carrying tickets and hotel reservations on your first—or even second—visit.

Ask them several questions about New Zealand. If they give only vague replies or try to turn your attention to only one particular tour, look out. The agent might be trying to direct you to an arrangement that provides the best deal—the best commission deal for him, that is. If the agent begins to ask *you* questions, that's good. It usually signifies an honest attempt to find out something about you and your likes and dislikes, and there's a better chance you'll end up with a trip more suited to your individual personality that way. Avoid like the plague any "assembly-line" operation where they are only interested in shipping you out in one of their most expensive prewrapped packages.

Your travel agent should be a member of the ASTA (American Society of Travel Agents) or the ARTA (Association of Retail Travel Agents) and perhaps also of the PATA (Pacific Area Travel Association). Some of the most respected agents these days also have the initials "CTC" after their names, indicating they have taken special courses to become Certified Travel Counselors. (In Australia, agents should be members of AFTA—the Australian Federation of Travel Agents.)

Don't make it an absolute requirement that your travel agent must have visited New Zealand. Some agents may have received only a "familiarization" trip, sponsored by certain members of the travel industry, and some of these agents might be a little too inclined to book their clients only with those firms who provided the freebies. A good travel agent will try to give you what you want, so we suggest that you rely on this book for the important basics and then let your travel agent try to shape your preferences into a practical itinerary—or come up with a tour at a good price that closely covers what you want to see and do.

Remember that your travel agent's services should be free to you. Agents generally make their money from commissions from airlines, hotels, car rentals, etc. Of course it costs them a certain amount in postage, phone calls, etc., to set things up, so if you decide to cancel a complicated itinerary at the last minute, they get nothing after a lot of work. Understandably enough, they may decide to bill you then. (Incidentally, many will not, in the hope that you'll be back again. And that's good business, too!)

If you prefer to make all your arrangements yourself, it can be a very satisfying experience. Just be sure to write letters that are specific about your needs, and then don't forget to bring with you all your confirmation letters and deposit receipts.

Travel Facts and Figures

BAGS AND BAGGAGE

Unless you're traveling to New Zealand by ship, you're automatically limited on the total amount of luggage you can carry with you. From and to U.S. airports, now, baggage allowances are based on the "piece" system—much preferable to the old weight maximums, which seemed to require that every traveler keep a scale in his home, and one shaped to accommodate everything from a two-suiter on down.

Under the newer system, each international traveler (including children) is allowed two checked pieces of luggage plus a small amount of hand luggage. Neither of the two checked bags may exceed 62 inches in overall dimension—adding together length, width, and height. And unless you're traveling First Class, the two together may not exceed 106 inches, all told. Virtually no commercial suitcase made in the U.S. exceeds the 62 inches, so the chances are you'll be okay even if one of them is your very largest bag. (*Caution:* Some monster suitcases we saw for sale in New Zealand did indeed go over that number.) If you're in doubt, check it out with a tape measure.

You're allowed one or more pieces of carry-on luggage small enough to fit under one seat (camera bag, airline bag, etc.). The maximum outside dimensions of all those pieces combined may not exceed 45 inches per person.

If you have an extra suitcase, be aware that it will cost you from at least $80 (West Coast) to at least $100 (East Coast) to take it to New Zealand as excess baggage. Personally, we think it's a good idea to trim down your belongings to even less. Domestic flights between New Zealand destinations normally allow only *one* checked bag, incidentally, plus the same hand luggage, although this may only be a problem if you buy another domestic ticket while inside New Zealand. Our experience has been that check-in personnel for flights inside New Zealand overlook the second bag carried by international visitors to the country.

Another potential trip-up: If you break your journey and stop over at some non-American port like Tahiti or Fiji on the way to New Zealand, the airline may choose to drop back to the old weight rule of 66 pounds per person First Class and 44 pounds Economy Class for the next leg of the trip. (Overweight may then be charged at the rate of 1 percent of the First Class fare for each kilogram—2.2 pounds—of the amount over the mark.) If you have any doubts check with the relevant airline.

If this is a genuine concern, we might suggest that you limit any stopovers to those in Hawaii, where you won't get into the situation, since the piece rule applies from or to any U.S. destination, including, of course, Honolulu. It is also less likely to happen on U.S.-owned airlines. (While traveling with our kids, we've seldom been concerned with baggage problems, since children and adults have the same requirements, and all the family belongings can be pooled for calculating total baggage allowances.)

By the way, don't take cheap bags that might break on the trip. That's false economy. If you're counting pennies, see if some non-traveling Samaritan will lend you good, sturdy luggage. Always, always put some distinctive mark on your bags so you'll recognize them among all the others they have to travel with. Stickers may do the job. Otherwise use colored tape, stripped on in a distinctive pattern up near the handle.

Incidentally, if you do want to buy a suitcase in New Zealand, you might look into one of the expandable types popular there and in England but seldom seen in the U.S. The brand we bought is called Flight, and we like the double-strength model. There may be others equally good. It seems we can always pack something more in our expanding Kiwi luggage. After closing, you push down hard on the thing and four ratchets compress the contents tightly.

Airline regulations require that every suitcase carry a name and address attached. Personally, we always put on *two* addresses—the one we're coming from *and* one we're going to. It won't do much good if they return any lost bags Up Top while we're Down Under—especially if nobody's home!

Packing. Now, what to put in those bags? Of course you say it, we say it, and every traveler from Lemuel Gulliver to Edmund Hillary says it: "Travel light!" Then we throw in everything but an extra bathtub.

Nevertheless, do your best. A big advantage to New Zealand is that it is a supremely civilized country where most of the essentials of life are affordable and readily available. If you forget something, or don't have enough of something, you can usually buy a reasonable facsimile after you get there.

The male traveler. I don't care if you're going down there with a backpack, take at least one tie with you. Personally, I would add to that either a sport jacket or a blazer. Business travelers, of course, will have at least one suit. The point is that, even in an egalitarian society like New Zealand, they do a lot of judging of men by the cut of their jib. There will be times when you need to present as neat a jib as possible.

A couple of pairs of easy-care slacks will do for most everyday needs. Substitute for one of those or add to the list a pair of jeans if you're going on any bush walks. (And it would be a shame not to cover at least a country mile here and there on foot.)

Take one or two long-sleeved shirts, one or two knit pullover shirts, and perhaps one or two two-way shirts, with short sleeves, that can be worn with a tie or open-necked. I would pack a sweater any time of year, either a pullover or a button-up cardigan (although, of course, you may want to buy a good, inexpensive wool sweater in New Zealand). Some men would be thankful for a zipper jacket in cold weather.

A topcoat? Maybe or maybe not. My personal choice is a knee-length, all-weather coat (with or without lining), unless the trip is entirely during warm-weather months. Then I would tuck in a folding raincoat instead. I always have a collapsible man's umbrella and I have never regretted taking it at any time of year.

For your feet, try to find something comfortable that still looks good with your suit and jacket. Some kind of suede might do it, but remember that suede soaks up water during wet weather. Other than that, I've felt equally at home in good restaurants, on boating excursions, and stepping nimbly around the geysers in a pair of Hush Puppies.

It's a good idea to take an old, well-broken-in pair of sneakers, too, or maybe some comfortable running shoes for excursions over some of the rougher bush country. Take hiking boots (a) if you're going to do some serious tramping for a few days, and (b) only if you've already broken them in.

You could get by without a hat, but I like a crushable, roll-up model that I can keep in my pocket until such time as the sun or rain begins to make headway on the scalp. It takes up very little weight or space.

Toss in underwear, pajamas, lightweight robe, and socks to suit your fancy. You'll find coin-operated automatic laundries in hotels and motels in New Zealand (although sometimes they are not paired up with tumble dryers).

By the way, you'll notice that New Zealand men wear shorts a lot, especially in the summertime—even with short-sleeved shirt, tie, and no coat. The key to looking good in shorts, however, is the long socks that go with them. If you don't have a pair, buy them there.

Naturally, if you're going to be athletically inclined—swimming, skiing, running, etc.—then your Kiwi wardrobe requirements will be pretty much as they would be at home for those activities.

The woman visitor. No one is going to talk a dedicated woman traveler out of her pants suit. It's a comfortable, practical uniform, so we won't try. But just be aware that you'll probably only see them on other tourists.

We'd certainly suggest taking shorts, trousers, and skirts with mix-and-match tops, but remember that you might not wear shorts as often as you do at home. You'll want a couple of dresses for evening wear, of course, and take a pullover or cardigan, as evenings can be cool at any time of year.

In the winter, a medium-weight, warm, and waterproof coat would be cozy, and you should certainly take some kind of casual jacket. In the summer, a folding raincoat is essential. Most native Kiwi women would not travel in New Zealand anytime without a folding umbrella. If you're flying around the country, keep it with your hand luggage for potentially wet walks between the plane and the terminal.

You must have comfortable walking shoes for everyday sightseeing, and a pair of shoes for the evening. And, like the men, you will need jeans and a pair of sneakers or running shoes for New Zealand bushland experiences. Again, don't buy brand-new hiking boots to take. You'll pay for that mistake in blisters.

Men and women. Take your favorite toiletries, of course, secure in the knowledge that you can replace nearly anything you run out of. However, they will often be unfamiliar brands. If you forget your mosquito repellent, you can buy some there. However, throw in a facecloth if you want to be sure to have one in your hotel room.

Of course you'll take your camera. Add to that plenty of film, which is more expensive in New Zealand (although processing is often included in the original film price). If you have a telephoto lens, you'll regret it if you leave it home. There are things in the trees and hills you just won't believe without proof! We also enjoy using our battery-powered cassette tape recorder to capture tour-guide lectures, along with the clear, ringing sound of the bellbird. (Cassette tape is also expensive in New Zealand, so bring what you think you'll need.)

If you have a pair of binoculars, toss them in, too. A portable transistor AM/FM radio helps to keep you in tune with New Zealanders. And we always carry our pocket calculator now, to check our running finances and do small jobs like converting centigrade to Fahrenheit (more on that later).

A last-minute warning: Don't forget to get enough of any prescription you may need before you leave, but also write down just what that medicine is. If you do lose the bottle, New Zealand pharmacists may then be able to match it.

Don't pack that medication in your suitcase, either, just in case the bag goes astray. It's much better in your hand luggage. You know what else not to pack in your suitcase? Right. Your passport! (You'd be surprised how many people do.)

AVOIDING THE CRUSH

Watch out for busy times of the year when you make your travel plans. During those periods you should have everything booked up solid, long in advance. The heaviest periods on New Zealand roads, railroads, and planes—and in hotels and restaurants—are "school holidays," when every kid in the country seems to be traveling between boarding school on one island and home on the other island. Trains, buses, planes, and inter-island ferries are particularly packed at the beginning and end of these periods.

Christmas Holidays (the big summer vacation) begin in mid-December and continue until early February. There will be considerable traffic of old-sters and youngsters alike throughout the month of January. You won't find the crowds unpleasant, but this is not the time to tour New Zealand without reservations everywhere you go. The rest of February into March can also be difficult, due to the large number of your fellow foreign visitors.

There are two other difficult school-holiday periods—the May Holidays (about two weeks in mid-May at the end of the first school term) and the

August Holidays (two or three weeks at the end of August and beginning of September, between the second and third terms).

Public holidays. There are nine national holidays observed throughout the country. They are as follows:

January—New Year's Day. February—Waitangi Day, February 6. April—Good Friday; Easter Monday [*sic*]; and ANZAC Day, April 25. June—Queen's Birthday, first Monday. October—Labour Day, fourth Monday. December—Christmas Day, December 25, and Boxing Day, December 26.

In addition to these, you may run across the occasional provincial holiday, when stores and offices in the immediate area will be closed.

International postal and telephone services. If you're making your own arrangements by mail, send everything by air (recheck weight and postage rates with the post office). Then allow approximately a week each way for a letter to move between an American or Canadian address and three to four days in New Zealand.

With the advent of direct international dialing, telephone rates from the U.S. to New Zealand have now gone down to the point where we sometimes pick up the phone to call the country, at least during the least-expensive hours. The cheapest way to call is generally to dial 011 (the international access code), then 64 (the country code for New Zealand), then the city code (example, "9" for Auckland), then the local number. Please don't get confused, but when calling long distance *within* New Zealand, the city code is known as the "STD" code, and all these are preceded by zero (example "09" for Auckland).

THE NEW ZEALAND TIME ZONE

Since the country is long north and south and narrow east and west, it is not complicated by different settings of the clock. It is relatively easy to keep track of New Zealand standard time vis-à-vis Greenwich mean time (GMT or UTC) in London. New Zealand is just about halfway around the earth—12 of the 24 time zones into which the world is divided—so it means only substituting A.M. for P.M. That is, when it is 1 A.M. Sunday in London, it is 1 P.M. Sunday in New Zealand. (And when it is 1 P.M. Sunday in London, it is 1 A.M. *Monday* in New Zealand.)

New Zealand is just barely across the International Date Line, and a mountaintop not far from Gisborne is said to be the world's first geographic feature to be struck by the sun of each new day.

Using the time examples above, when it is 1 P.M. Sunday in New Zealand, that time is two hours later than in eastern Australia (it is 11 A.M. Sunday in Sydney); two hours earlier than Hawaii, but on the following day

(3 P.M. Saturday in Honolulu); and four hours earlier than California, but on the following day (5 P.M. Saturday in San Francisco or L.A.).

Unfortunately for businessmen, airline people, and others concerned with international timekeeping, all of New Zealand and much of America observe daylight savings time, but on approximately—not exactly—opposite schedules for their opposite summers. Thus when it is 5 P.M. Saturday in California, it might be 2 P.M., 1 P.M., or high noon in New Zealand, depending on which—if either—locale is on daylight savings time.

(Usually DST Down Under is from the last Sunday in October to the first Sunday in March. Northern Hemisphere DST means advancing the clock an hour between the first Sunday in April to the last Sunday in October. This means that New Zealand and North America are on standard time together only for most of March and perhaps early April.)

Jet lag. Daylight savings, Greenwich mean, and all the king's horses can't put you together again if you suffer, as we do, from jet lag—that disorientation of the body clock for those who fly long distances in short amounts of time.

You can't be expected to fly from California to New Zealand, across four different time zones, and not be at least somewhat bothered by jet lag. It takes us a couple of days before we stop propping our eyes open and quit yawning in everyone's face. Luckily, flying overnight tends to minimize jet lag. And although you lose a day crossing the date line, your body may notice more that you've gained a couple of extra hours to sleep. That's the advantage of flying west instead of east. Still, when your stomach tells you it's 8 A.M. and time to eat breakfast, it will only be 4 A.M. New Zealand time. And at lunchtime you may notice a distinct craving for bacon and eggs.

You'll be even more affected if you begin your trip further east, and New Yorkers, for example, would be well advised to spend one night in L.A. on the way.

We suggest seven steps to alleviate the effects of jet lag: (1) Set your watch to New Zealand time as soon as you take off. (2) Sleep as much as you can on the airplane. (3) Unless you are sleeping, stand up and walk around the plane now and then—perhaps five minutes every hour. (4) Take no sleeping pill and little alcohol during the flight, but eat when food is offered. (5) After you arrive at your hotel, pull the shades and try for a good nap. (6) Schedule no business appointments, car rentals, or demanding sightseeing your first day. (7) Eat lightly, choosing familiar foods, on your first day.

METRICS AND ELECTRICS

Metric mysteries. Officially New Zealand is on the decimal system, but psychologically the average New Zealander is still suffering from metric lag. Everything is written down now as hectares, meters, kilograms, and the like, but the average Kiwi still seems to prefer talking in terms of acres, feet, and pounds—at least all those of middle age and above.

This gives rise to some unique problems. If a New Zealander tells you something is about 10 miles down the road, and you try to find it on the map, you'll have to look for something 16 kilometers away.

Temperature. One measurement the New Zealanders have quickly accepted is the centigrade system, more commonly called the Celsius scale. Temperatures are often given on the radio, and are worth considering to plan the day's sightseeing. In order to get the Fahrenheit equivalent accurately, take the Celsius figure, multiply by 9, divide by 5, and add 32 (it's fairly fast with a pocket calculator). Two other systems are less accurate but give you an approximation you can work in your head: Either (a) "add 15 and double it," or (b) "double it and add 30." (Pick one and forget the other.)

It might be easiest of all to remember simply that the most comfortable temperatures outdoors are generally in the 20s. (20° Celsius equals 68°Fahrenheit; 29° C = 84° F) Of course, the freezing point of water is zero degrees Celsius, and the boiling point is 100 degrees, which, after all, is the principle behind the whole scale.

Distance. Making this conversion is also easier than it might seem at first. A kilometer is .621 of a mile, but for quick mental conversion along the highway we merely move the decimal point one figure to the left or sometimes just slice off the last digit entirely, multiply by six, and then round off the product. For example, 32 kilometers (or kilometers per hour) becomes either 3 x 6 or 3.2 x 6, depending on how energetic we are. The first equation gives us 18 and the second 19.2. Either one we would round off to 20 miles (or miles per hour). Try it yourself. When the speed limit sign says 80 kph, just do a quick "8 times 6" and come out with 48. Mentally round that off to 50, of course. (Naturally if you have a rented car, you won't have to worry much because your "speedo" will be marked off in "Ks," anyway!)

For shorter linear measures, a meter is just over 39 inches—or a yard, for most purposes. A centimeter (one one-hundredth of a meter) is about four-tenths of an inch—about the width of the fingernail on your pinkie.

Volume. Gasoline and milk are sold in liters in New Zealand, and a liter is darned close to an American quart. Therefore, you can figure four liters is about an American gallon. (This is not the 40-ounce quart and 160-ounce imperial gallon that New Zealanders, Australians, and Canadians remember, of course.)

Twelve-ounce bottles or cans of beer have been changed to 340 milli-liters (ml) in New Zealand (that actually totals about 11.5 ounces). For most uses, you can figure that a fluid ounce contains about 29 milliliters (or cubic centimeters).

Weight. The kilogram, which you'll meet face-to-face at the butcher shop, is 2.2 pounds. Therefore, a half-kilo of beef would be around a pound. On the news you'll also hear the word "tonnes" in stories about an-nual wool exports, etc. That's simply another way of saying a metric ton, and it's 1.1 of the kind of ton we know about. Strangely, many New Zealanders still talk about their own weight in stone (singular and plural). That's not metric, but an old English system of measuring weight. A stone weighs 14 pounds.

Area. New Zealanders still speak of a house lot as a "quarter-acre sec-tion." Officially, however, acres have been supplanted by hectares—100,000 square meters each—and that works out to be 2.47 acres in a hectare. We call it 2.5 as a close estimate. By the way, a square meter is 10.8 square feet. Multiply by 11, an easy stop toward an approximate amount—500 square meters equals around 5,500 square feet. (So actually it's 5,382-plus, but who's counting?)

Electricity. Power is at least *measured* the way it is at home, but there are important points to remember about New Zealand volts—there are 240 of them in every socket (not 110 or so, as in the U.S. and Canada). Don't take along any North American plug-in electrical appliances, then, with the pos-sible exception of low-current devices like electric razors. Most hotels and motels now have a low-watt, 110-volt electrical outlet in the bathroom. It will work satisfactorily for razors (although the motor will run a little slow), but not for heat-producing devices such as hair dryers or irons. Rechargeable razors will work fine, and they may be recharged in the spe-cial low-watt 110-volt outlets.

If you do have 220- or 240-volt appliances, they'll still need an adapter for the three-prong New Zealand/Australian electrical socket. You *might* pick one up in the five-and-dime, but we doubt it. If not, one American firm we know of—Traveler's Checklist, Cornwall Bridge Road, Sharon, CT 06069—sells them by mail for a couple of bucks or so. (We haven't dealt with them ourselves.) We've also seen them for sale at some Radio Shack outlets in the U.S.

By the way, don't think you can adapt every American electrical appli-ance to New Zealand current with a transformer. The frequency of the cur-rent is 50 cycles per second, versus the American 60 cps. This means things with 60-cycle motors like phonographs and electric clocks will move slower in New Zealand, even if a transformer is used to lower the voltage. Check with an electrical expert before taking any such devices from one country to another.

Changing a light bulb? Here's a warning we often repeat: British-style light bulbs used Down Under don't unscrew. They push in and turn left, and catch immediately. With luck you won't end up with shattered nerves and glass in your fingers.

MONEY, CURRENCY, AND PRICES

New Zealand has often changed the official value of its currency, but during the late 1970s the N.Z. dollar remained about equal to the American buck. In the past 15 years, however, it has dropped quite a bit, a monetary plus for American, Canadian, and Australian visitors.

At this writing—and, of course, subject to sudden change—the Kiwi dollar is worth about 65¢ U.S. or 81¢ Canadian. Even if the rate goes up again you'll be surprised and pleased by how much further your dollar goes in New Zealand than in many high-rolling countries in the Northern and Southern hemispheres.

Here's something new and important: the New Zealand government introduced something called the GST—goods and services tax. Similar to the VAT (value added tax) seen in several other countries, it's an across-the-board tariff of 12.5 percent added to everything bought or sold in the country. It is designed to replace many of the previous hidden taxes in New Zealand.

New Zealanders, who are accustomed to paying for everything exactly as marked, with no pernicious add-ons, have to adjust more to the new situation than visitors to the country, who are usually used to paying sales taxes of some sort back home. Ask if the advertised prices include the GST. Many do. Supermarkets always do. But it's best to check.

Buy some N.Z. dollars before you leave on the trip. Although not essential, it's a good idea to become somewhat familiar with the "notes" (bills) and coins before leaving home. Note that there are notes in five different amounts: $5, $10, $20, $50, and $100. Until a few years ago, there was a $1 and a $2 New Zealand note. No more. Coins in the $1 and $2 denominations have taken their place. Sensibly, the different denominations in notes are printed in different colors.

The one- and two-cent copper coins also went the way of the $1 and $2 notes. But the metricized currency still has 5¢, 10¢, 20¢, and 50¢ coins.

Credit cards. We use our Diners Club card often in New Zealand, and sometimes our VISA card. American Express is also accepted, as well as MasterCard. You may encounter problems using credit cards for gasoline. Later, when the bills come in the U.S., we have found the exchange rates charged by both credit card companies to be very fair. However, we have been disappointed to see that Diners, at least, charges its club members an extra fee for converting from foreign currency, after having gotten along well without that extra revenue boost for so many years.

Traveler's checks. These are also no problem, except that you have to cash them at banks in order to get the best exchange rate. You will have to pay a five-cent "clearance fee" for each check. (Hours at the "trading banks" are generally from 10 A.M. to 4:30 P.M., Monday through Friday.) If you want to be able to cash traveler's checks more frequently at shops, restaurants, etc., you might consider buying some in New Zealand dollars after you arrive there. Sometimes these can even be charged on a credit card at banks in New Zealand. It's a policy reflecting New Zealand's hunger for "overseas funds," but one that also works as a happy convenience—especially in an emergency—for foreign travelers.

Postage. It's cheap enough to send a letter to other parts of N.Z., but look out for airmail postcards to foreign addresses. At this writing the tab for an airmail postcard is the same as it is to send an airmail letter to the U.S. or Canada!

OFFICIAL FOLDEROL

Thank goodness, there's not a lot of red tape to unwind for a trip to New Zealand. Any travel agent should guide you through the governmental guff, but here it is in brief form:

Passport. Unless you're a New Zealand citizen, you'll need a passport to enter New Zealand. Americans can apply at a passport office in major American cities or at any U.S. post office. It can take a few weeks to receive your passport once you deliver or send in the filled-out form with the required photographs and fee.

A potential trip-up, however, is that the New Zealanders require that your passport remain valid for six months beyond the date you expect to leave the country. If it won't, you'll just have to apply for a new one a little earlier than you may have planned. Probably that's the most officialism you'll run across in the country.

Visas. New Zealand has lifted the visa requirement for Americans, Canadians, and a few other nationalities, providing they are staying for no more than 30 days. Visas for three-month stays are usually arranged easily in advance by applying to New Zealand consular officers in Washington, New York, San Francisco, or Los Angeles. There is no charge.

Immigration officials. Those passport-stampers in the snappy uniforms will want to see a few things before they allow you any further than the airport. The passport, of course, and the visa, if needed, and perhaps your round-trip or ongoing ticket. That's just to make sure you're not coming into New Zealand to work or to become a burden on the economy. If these chaps think there's anything out of the ordinary, of course, they're allowed to ask for some kind of proof of your financial responsibility. They're polite and efficient. No genuine visitor needs to worry about them.

Customs. You're allowed to enter New Zealand carrying items for your own personal use. You won't have any trouble unless you're loaded down with stuff like drugs, alcohol, precious stones, a dozen tape recorders, and anything anyone in his right mind knows would be prohibited. You are safe to bring in a quart of wine and a quart of hard liquor ("spirits" in Kiwish), and a carton of cigarettes. Recently introduced customs allowances have provided for a more generous liquor quota, as long as you are not already bringing more than $700 worth of dutiable items into the country. If you're concerned at all, pick up information at the consulate or New Zealand Tourism Board (addresses in the next section). New Zealand allows a separate concession for alcohol and cigarettes. *A tip:* the inbound duty-free shops at Auckland International Airport are offering some very good prices at present.

Coming home to the U.S., of course, you have to deal with *U.S.* Customs—an easier job now that some new computer-based procedures have finally been established. We can't go into all their rules and regs here, but remember that your duty-free allowance (which can be pooled with other members of your family) is currently $400 per person. If you keep it below that, you can make an oral declaration to that effect instead of writing it all out.

If you're thinking of bringing back some New Zealand wine or beer, the limit is now one liter (just over a quart) of alcoholic beverage *per person over 21.* You'll pay duty plus internal revenue tax after that amount. If you buy valuable items like sheepskins, you get the best customs deal if you carry them back with you rather than mailing them home. (You must pay duty on mailed items whether or not you have used up your exemption.) You'll clear U.S. Customs at your first U.S. port. On the way to L.A., that will mean Honolulu, if your plane pauses there.

If you're worried about any of this, the best thing to do is to pick up a free booklet entitled *Know Before You Go* from any customs office or to write the U.S. Customs Service, P.O. Box 7118, Washington, DC 20044 for Customs Publication No. 512.

FURTHER INFORMATION

In her popular syndicated newspaper column "Trip Tips," Marie Mattson once wrote that the best vacation trip begins at the public library.

Don't step on a plane for New Zealand, or any other country, until you've had a chance to read up on your destination. Several books printed in New Zealand are excellent. Although not well known in the U.S., they may be available at a public library.

New Zealand author Maurice Shadbolt's *New Zealand North and South* was published by Penguin in late 1991 and is an excellent read. You might want to pick up a copy after arriving. Another outstanding handbook, edited by Shadbolt, is the *Shell Guide to New Zealand.*

Of the books available in the U.S., we especially recommend *How to Get Lost and Found in Upgraded New Zealand* by John W. McDermott, assisted by his "Lady Navigator," Bobbye Hughes McDermott. It is less a "how-to" book, really, than an enjoyable account of the McDermotts' year-long love affair with New Zealand in 1975. The McDermotts returned to New Zealand in 1986 to update their original *How to Get Lost and Found in New Zealand.* So impressed were the well-traveled pair with New Zealand's leap forward in accommodations and restaurants and service that they slipped "Upgraded" into the title.

The even better news is that New Zealand continues to offer more quality every year. It is also acutely aware of its natural assets and the need to conserve them for the enjoyment of travelers now and in the future.

When the time comes to leave N.Z. shores, think about visiting a book store for a permanent memory of the country. New Zealand's rich endowment of physical beauty has been captured by world-class photographers in a selection of books that you would be proud to have on the coffee table back home.

As dedicated map freaks, we wouldn't think of making a trip to a new country without collecting a few maps to pore over in advance. In North America, you can order several good country and city maps at appropriate prices from the Forsyth Travel Library, P.O. Box 2975, Shawnee Mission, KS 66201.

Don't think of leaving for New Zealand, either, before seeking the latest official information, brochures, and the like from the **New Zealand Tourism Board.** Write or visit one of the NZTB branches in several countries. In North America, you'll find them at the following addresses (these are also the addresses of the New Zealand consulate offices in the same cities). Ask for copies of the *New Zealand Book.* This is a conveniently slim brochure that lists most of the facts first-time travelers to New Zealand are looking for.

NZTB, Suite 300
501 Santa Monica Blvd.
Santa Monica, CA 90401
Tel. (213) 395-7480

The tourist office is by no means our only source of information, and we certainly don't expect that its personnel will agree with all of our interpretations of the New Zealand scene today. Nevertheless, these friendly, capable folks have always been very helpful to us while we try to assemble these details, and we pray they will continue to be so as this book is revised for future editions. As always, please tell 'em we sent you.

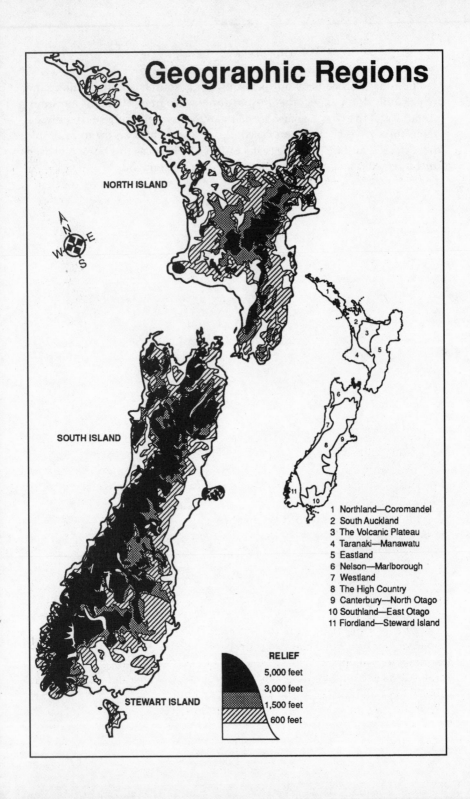

Geographic Regions

NORTH ISLAND

SOUTH ISLAND

STEWART ISLAND

1 Northland—Coromandel
2 South Auckland
3 The Volcanic Plateau
4 Taranaki—Manawatu
5 Eastland
6 Nelson—Marlborough
7 Westland
8 The High Country
9 Canterbury—North Otago
10 Southland—East Otago
11 Fiordland—Steward Island

RELIEF

5,000 feet
3,000 feet
1,500 feet
600 feet

3

The Living Land

Two very large islands make up New Zealand. They are named, rather prosaically, "the North Island" and "the South Island." Don't forget to say the "the." You can tell who doesn't really know much about the country when they mistakenly entitle these landmasses simply "North Island" and "South Island."

Some say Stewart Island is the "third island" in the country, but at 670 square miles it's only a dab in the ocean compared with the North Island's 44,000 and the South Island's 58,000 square miles.

And if you insist on getting technical, there's a group called the Chatham Islands—totaling 370 squares—scattered in the sea some 400 miles or so out in the direction of Chile, plus a few sprinkles of various uninhabited rock dots.

Nothing brings fire to the eyes of New Zealanders faster than hearing someone confuse their country with Australia. It is also true that no matter how clear the day, you can't "see Sydney from Auckland." Australia, the other "Down Under" country, is far to the west, across the Tasman Sea, about 1,000 miles measured at the closest points. There are more than 1,200 very wet miles between Sydney and Auckland.

On the globe, the two countries seem cheek by jowl, but distances in the Pacific are so vast that the close physical relationship is only an illusion. Also, Americans often have seen atlases that have decided to reduce this distance by neatly placing New Zealand as a little inset in the corner of a map of Australia, perhaps even changing the scale of the two in the process.

New Zealanders often suffer the indignity of seeing stylized world maps produced in other countries that leave their nation off the grid entirely— simply forgotten or somehow slid over the horizon at the bottom right-hand corner.

It has been suggested by more than one New Zealander that it is time a map of the world was produced with south—instead of north—at the top, pointing out that it would look much more attractive "with the top-heavy mass of the world's great continents relegated to the baseline and New Zealand floating happily in an airy bubble of ocean at the top of the world."

New Zealand certainly does seem far away from everywhere else. As the albatross flies, it is about 6,500 miles southwest of California and 4,000 miles south of Hawaii. Airplanes leaving Los Angeles daily for Auckland make the trip in about 15 hours elapsed time via Hawaii or Tahiti. From Honolulu, the flight takes about 9 hours nonstop. It's even a 3-hour hop from Sydney.

Australia and New Zealand have often been known as the Antipodes ("an-*tip*-oh-dees"), since the general area was supposed to be straight through the earth from London. In reality, New Zealand's antipode is in Spain. Nevertheless, the country is 13,000 miles from Britain, still regarded by some sentimental New Zealanders as their spiritual home. From London to Auckland is at least an all-day, all-night journey, even in the jet age.

New Zealand is a rugged, sparsely populated, very rural land, colored in intense blues, whites, greens, and yellows. Nearly three-quarters of the country is composed of snowcapped mountains or steep, verdant hills, with the most irregular territory on the South Island. The North and South Islands together add up to a length of about 1,000 miles—more, if you allow for the curvature of the nation's spine above Auckland. The country "feels" rather like the size of California, although technically its land area is about a third less.

Its elongated shape is hard to describe, except that when seen upside down, or rightside up from a New Zealand perspective, the two islands together appear somewhat like a bony mirror image of Italy's high-heeled boot. It seems to be aiming a good, swift kick in the general direction of Australia.

Weather and Climate

New Zealand tends to blame Australia for her weather. The meteorological map traditionally shows an alternating succession of highs and lows marching east across the Tasman Sea, borne by the prevailing westerlies. The high-altitude winds are so strong that smoke from massive Australian bush fires and residue from outback dust storms more than 1,200 miles away can actually cause a fine haze in New Zealand. Some of this debris even works its way through South Island glaciers after a few years, a technical fallout that tells scientists much about the life cycle of these "living" rivers of ice.

Officially, New Zealand enjoys a temperate-zone climate, but that may not mean much to North Americans used to some heavy weather extremes in their own temperate zones. Down Under winters are mild by international standards. It seldom snows at elevations below 1,000 feet, even as far south as Stewart Island.

The Northland peninsula, up above Auckland, has local boosters who like to label it "the winterless north." That's an exaggeration, for it's no Florida by any means. Nevertheless, they grow a few bananas up there, and there is a better chance of drawing a nice day in Kaitaia in August than in—well, better than in Wellington, anyway!

The west coast of the South Island is mostly dense rain forest, an effect helped by the high Southern Alps. When damp air comes across the Tasman, it is forced up by these peaks to the cooler altitude, where the laws of nature compel it to condense, dumping rain and snow on the landscape. Thus, white glaciers and viridescent tree ferns grow almost side by side, perhaps the only place in the world where this effect is seen.

Things were different during the last ice age, and for centuries the steep channels cut into the southwestern shore by dozens of ancient glaciers went unchallenged by any green, growing things. Today these gouges have been filled in by the rising sea to form Milford Sound and other deep, dramatic fiords along the coast. Glacial action also explains the unusually long and meandering lakes like Wakatipu and Te Anau on the landward side of the Southern Alps. Genuine glaciers have dwindled down to a precious few, and they have receded to an almost respectful distance at somewhat higher elevations.

The same wind that is deflected by natural barriers elsewhere finds sudden freedom in the 15-mile-wide Cook Strait between the two islands, and the funnel effect adds considerably to the turbulence of the seas at this 40-degree latitude. The nation's capital also lies directly in the path of the "roaring forties," thereby earning it the nickname of "Windy Wellington."

Although we found no Wellingtonian who would confirm it, we keep hearing of ropes occasionally being installed downtown to keep citizens from being blown away at street corners. Statistically, gusts are recorded at about 84 mph every couple of years in the capital.

Personally, we've had good experiences with Wellington weather, even in late fall, and official tables say the coldest it ever gets there is about 34° F—indeed about 2 degrees chillier than Auckland. (The respective maximums in the two cities, by the way, are 79 and 81.)

Probably the most distinctive characteristic of weather all over New Zealand is its sudden changeability, an effect caused by the narrow north-south landmass. Nowhere is this fickleness more apparent than in and around the pretty city of Christchurch, where the dominant southwesterlies may be quickly replaced by strong northeasterlies. Residents who leave their homes to walk along Christchurch's neat streets and grassy-banked river generally equip themselves for any eventuality, no matter what the weatherman said on TV last night.

The New Zealand climate is generally described as "Mediterranean," except that it is cooler than you might expect in summer because of all that water around (no part of the country is more than 75 miles from the sea). As a Down Under country, of course, its seasons are the reverse of those in the Northern Hemisphere. Generally speaking, they run like this: spring in September, October, and November; summer in December, January, and February; autumn in March, April, and May; and winter in June, July, and August.

Mountains and Volcanoes

The way geologists reckon things, New Zealand is only a youngster, and the mountain-building processes are still very much ongoing, especially in the South Island. There are 17 mountains measuring more than 10,000 feet in the Southern Alps, capped by Mount Cook, the massive white peak the Maori called Aorangi—the "cloud piercer"—at 12,349 feet. These mountains also spawn a number of short but very swift rivers.

Like California, Oregon, and Washington, New Zealand sits smack-dab on a geological hot seat, a major fault on the edge of the Pacific plate sometimes called the Ring of Fire. Eons ago she may indeed have been connected with Australia and other continents in the great Gondwanaland, the name now given to the ancient southern landmass in the continental drift theory.

New Zealand has had its share of violent earthquakes and other natural disasters throughout its existence. The worst quake in living memory occurred at Napier and Hastings on the North Island in 1931, when the Napier harbor was permanently raised above sea level and formed 7,500 acres of new land. A total of 156 lives were lost, and survivors spoke of teams of horses and drays being swallowed up whole in the ground.

Another earthquake with a similar effect "reclaimed" land along the Wellington shoreline in 1855, providing the base on which the superhighway and railroad leading out of the city were later built. And a disaster also related to the instability of the land took place on Christmas Eve 1953, when the wall of a mountain lake inexplicably burst open. The water rushed down the slope to sweep away a railway bridge, killing 151 passengers in a train that plunged into the abyss.

New Zealand experiences about 400 earthquakes a year, of which about 100 are likely to be felt by someone somewhere without instruments. These are generally taken with aplomb by New Zealanders. We've never seen it, but some motion picture theaters have a slide ready to be projected on the screen at the appropriate moment: "This is an earthquake. Patrons are requested not to panic, but to please keep their seats." Many of the minor shakers are not due to faulting, but to volcanic activity. In fact, the North Island has one of the liveliest volcanic areas in the world. It extends from the active volcanoes of Ruapehu and Ngauruhoe near the ancient caldera that is now Lake Taupo along a wide line running north through Rotorua, the thermal region known for its hot springs and geysers. The unsettled area continues into the Bay of Plenty as far as the active, unpredictable volcano that forms the treeless, sulfurous slopes of White Island.

The most famous volcanic blast took place near Rotorua in 1886, when quiescent Mount Tarawera exploded and destroyed the celebrated Pink and White Terraces—natural crystalline silica staircases that were among the country's most popular tourist attractions a century ago. The violent eruption also buried two small villages, taking a death toll of more than 150, and the still-steaming site of all this hell breaking loose is one of the most fascinating (yet often overlooked) sights in the area today.

Mount Ruapehu, the North Island's sulking centerpiece, had its biggest eruption since 1945 in September 1995. On the world's scale of things the eruption was a mere tantrum, but on this side of the world it caused a lot of interest. Air New Zealand put together an "eruption fare" for Australians to come and take a look as well as have a chance to ski on the slopes of an active volcano—a package that was eagerly snapped up.

The slopes were closed for several days, as was the Desert Road, a busy stretch of highway that passes Ruapehu. Nearby settlements had a fine covering of ash, and the Civil Aviation Authority closed the area from the mountain to the East Coast to commercial air traffic. Of course, thrill-seekers took to the skies in helicopters to view the lahar and bil-lowing steam clouds.

The ski season closed a week early due to the activity, which caused the snow to be muddy and ash-laden. There were no injuries and no damage, even though a scientist was in the crater at the time of the first eruption and several trampers were close to the summit when the first showers of boulders hurled forth.

Rotorua and Taupo are considered the centers of the country's thermal activity, with noisily boiling mud, shooting steam, hot-water creeks, and mineral odors, all resulting from the volcanic activity seething just under the surface.

In Rotorua, the area settled by the Arawa tribe around the hissing, steaming Whakawerawera village has long been one of New Zealand's "musts." Travelers generally want to take in the culture of the Maori, who sometimes cook their food in the convenient gurgling pits, as well as to see the living, breathing earth. A number of visitors find themselves compelled to cook their bodies, too, in the mineral-laden hot springs that they say are not only interesting but healthful. (Before taking the plunge yourself, be sure to see our caveats in the Rotorua chapter.)

Near Lake Taupo is the Wairakei geothermal power station, which has sunk its pipes 2,000 feet into the ground. The plant harnesses the natural steam to produce nearly 200 million watts of electricity.

Stepping away from well-marked paths in the thermal regions invites trouble. But even in some locations far from the volcanic sites in New Zealand, the ground is much less solid than in many other places in the world. Heavy rains or other causes can produce severe, costly landslides ("slips") throughout country gorges and mountain passes—so much so that signs have been erected along some highways that can be quickly changed to tell motorists whether or not the road is "open" or "closed" through unstable areas ahead. (If only a single lane is available for cars, the Ministry of Works can install timed traffic lights to regulate the flow of ve-hicles—a stop-and-go game far away from the din of any city street!)

Experienced hikers, too, are aware of the crumbly nature of much of New Zealand. "Rotten rock," they call it, as they attempt to avoid the most unreliable areas.

Natural Resources

It's often said that New Zealand boasts no natural resources, and it's true that there are no great founts of wealth like Australia's bauxite, Africa's diamonds, or America's oil. There was a **gold** rush once, spawning a romantic period during the 1860s near Queenstown and in other rugged areas of the South Island. Today the veins have mostly been exhausted, although some gold is still uncovered every year.

New Zealand is pinning many of its development hopes on a new field of **natural gas** that is now being tapped underwater a few miles offshore from the North Island city of New Plymouth. Named after the great Polynesian demigod Maui, who stood on the South Island and fished the North Island from the sea, the well promises to pull the entire country out of the economic doldrums over the next 10 years. Now they are beginning to convert Maui gas to Maui gasoline, and it is hoped that this will soon fill about half the country's liquid fuel needs. Some of the gas is also used to make other petroleum products.

Another natural resource is the massive amount of **electricity** generated by lakes and streams, mainly on the South Island. This current is then sent north on giant cables laid under Cook Strait. (Many South Islanders seem to resent the fact that they have to pay as much per kilowatt-hour as the North Island, and this controversy has sparked half-serious arguments for secession by southerners, who like to designate their home as "the mainland.")

But the country's true natural resource is not mineral, but its ability to grow things animal and vegetable. The joke that New Zealand supports over 20 times more **sheep** than people is no joke—70 million sheep compared to a total of about 3.3 million of us two-legged creatures. And the 8 million cattle (beef and dairy) also outnumber the human population by more than two to one. These animals are encouraged to range over vast pastures, a practice that keeps the grass of the hinterlands green and healthy.

Some foreigners report that the dominant characteristic of New Zealand sheep is that they are "cuter" than the sober-looking Merinos of Australia. They are usually the Corriedale, Southdown, and Romney Marsh varieties, which are bred for both meat and wool, whereas the Merino (also present in small numbers in New Zealand) is raised mainly for its wool.

There are many other types of sheep, too, some of them particularly well adapted to keeping their footing on steep hills at high stations. Driving through the countryside, you may notice that the grassy slopes often seem marked with subtle horizontal ridges. These are left by grazing sheep as they follow each other, making natural contour lines over the landscape.

Aside from their skittishness if you approach them, New Zealand sheep appear particularly happy and content. It's because they are looked after so well, of course. The costliest television and newspaper advertisements are for animal health products like sheep drench—anything to keep these valuable creatures free from the hint of disease or discomfort and to keep them producing more of their kind. ("Panacure Ewe Strength! Ups the lamb drop!"—loud TV commercial.)

Depending on their sex, however, sheep do go through one or two traumatic experiences. Except for a few rams, most males are castrated. And all sheep, except perhaps pets, must line up to have their tails chopped short ("docking"), a sanitary measure to keep these woolly appendages as free as possible from entanglement with feces and mud—a rear-end combination that dries and is termed "dags." (The Kiwi expression for "Get a move on" is often given as "Rattle your dags!")

Many station managers in the high country keep at least one black sheep for a given number of white. Reason? It makes the flock easier to spot when it's mustering (roundup) time in snowy weather! Incidentally, the number of black—and various shades of brown—sheep is on the rise in New Zealand, along with the popularity of home spinning and weaving of patterned wool scarves and sweaters from natural, undyed colors. You'll find these for sale in small shops in several parts of the country.

Cattle also lead charmed lives in New Zealand, at least up until the day they, like sheep, meet their ultimate fate at the "freezing works." Jersey cows, followed by Ayrshire and Friesian types, lead the dairy herds in New Zealand. Good beef comes from the Hereford, the all-black Aberdeen Angus, and some Friesians unlucky enough to have been born boys.

Dairy products, meat, and wool each average about one quarter of New Zealand's exports. Other important products are several **agricultural crops** grown commercially, including wheat, grain, corn, grapes, and a large variety of other vegetables and fruits. Many of these we'll discuss from the culinary viewpoint a little further on. New Zealand's largest single exporter, however, is a company that grows a native American product, the **radiata pine** tree.

A century and a half ago, the great forests of New Zealand were so dense that they severely impeded the opening up of the country by the pioneers. Gradually, however, the pioneers began to denude the land of indigenous timber—trees that produced fine, beautiful woods. (In addition to wasting a natural resource, the effect was to increase the landslides and general soil erosion to which the countryside was already all too prone.) Today many of these original trees (like the kauri) are protected by law and are seldom harvested. It is also not practical to raise them commercially, since they can take hundreds of years to mature.

In a search for a new foundation for forestry, scientists discovered that imported radiata pine trees sprang up so fast in New Zealand soil that they could be harvested about 30 years or so after planting. That's compared to the nearly 80 years it takes the same tree to mature in its native California.

Much of this *Pinus radiata* is grown today in an attractive, 375,000-acre government forest reserve south of Rotorua. Again, the natural resources of New Zealand have yielded an important environmental byproduct—the ability to keep the country clean and green.

Some Other Flora, and a Little Fauna

The most characteristic plant of the country is most certainly the fern. By this, we don't mean a few of those fuzzy things they use to dress up a bowl of flowers in America. Down in Aotearoa they come in whole forests, with ferns of all sizes and shapes, the most dramatic of which is no doubt the ponga, or **tree fern,** which can reach a height of 30 feet or more.

The national emblem of New Zealand is less the kiwi bird than it is the **silver fern.** These are difficult to find, because they usually grow below eye level, and the bright silver color is only detectable on the underside of the branch. On one recent trip, however, we kept turning over fern leaf after fern leaf off and on for days until we found just the right one. They're beautiful—a free souvenir and certainly suitable for framing against a dark background.

On the North Island, you'll still see forests of the majestic **kauri** and other giant trees once used by Maori for their seagoing canoes. Using fire and an adze, craftsmen could chip out an entire war canoe, 80 feet long, 6 feet wide, and 5 feet deep, from a single kauri trunk. Some living kauri trees are now calculated to be well over 2,000 years old. They shed their branches naturally, and the trunk can end up as an immense, even cylinder, perhaps more than 90 feet from the ground to its very first branch.

Other types of indigenous wood are produced by trees like the **rimu,** a red pine that makes attractive furniture; the **miro,** with its red berries attracting native birds; the **totara,** an easy-to-carve native pine often worked by the Maori; the **matai,** also known as the black pine tree; and the **kahikatea,** a white pine that can reach as high as 200 feet over the swamps.

You may see forests of scruffy-looking **beech** trees in the national parks. They are often brightened in the summer months by the red mistletoe or the pink rata, which use beech branches as temporary supports in their early life.

A personal favorite, which you'll see everywhere in the country, are the clumps of edible spikes that make up the **cabbage tree,** one of many endemic palms. Another is the **nikau palm,** which looks like a badly battered, totally reversed umbrella.

A few kinds of flowering trees are also native, of which the most dramatic is the **pohutukawa,** often called the New Zealand Christmas tree. No

ornaments are hung on this species, though. It breaks out in masses of
blazing crimson, but only at Christmastime. For 10 to 11 months of the
year, the pohutukawa is merely one more twisted and gnarled specimen,
clinging tenaciously to cliffs near the sea or along inland lakes on the
North Island. It has no petals, incidentally. The deep red color comes from
the stamen.

A close relative, however, is the aforementioned **rata,** a tree on its own
after it leaves its host tree and begins putting down its own roots. (Visitors
often mistake rata for pohutukawa, and both, incidentally, are related and
somewhat similar to the ohia-lehua flower of Hawaii.) A shrub-like tree
with attractive flowers is called the **manuka;** it's also known as the tea tree,
since its leaves were boiled by early settlers to make a similar beverage. Its
five-petaled blossom is usually white, but is occasionally pink or red.

During the early spring, look for the yellow **kowhai,** a tree that seems to
blossom in solid gold all over the country. At the same time, it usually loses
its leaves. The national flower of New Zealand, the kowhai is also one of
the few deciduous trees in the country.

The **New Zealand flax,** also called phormium, still grows wild in some
areas, its fibre still sought after for use in rope and twine made in New
Zealand. In coastal flats or swamps you may see waving groups of golden
(but sometimes purplish) pampas grass. Actually, these graceful plumes
are a slightly different species called **toetoe** ("toy-toy"). The stems were
used as wall coverings by the Maori. Grasslands in New Zealand are often
carpeted in **tussock,** whose brownish-yellowish blades seem to grow in
thick clumps.

Some other native New Zealand flowers include the **bush clematis,**
which crawls over trees and produces star-shaped, waxy white blossoms;
kaka beak, clusters of scarlet flowers that droop from a small shrub; **poro-poro,** purple or white flowers, also springing from shrubbery; **lacebark,** a
white, five-petaled flower that blooms in the fall; and the **celery pine,**
whose pinkish flowers are surrounded by branches that have flattened
themselves to work as leaves.

You may also find several types of **fuchsia,** which are different from the
better-known South American varieties; the **karo,** a deep purple flower
with a strong, sweet smell, appearing in the northeast in September and
October; the **North Island edelweiss,** which produces flowers in white clusters, surrounded by woolly leaves, above 4,000 feet from November to
March; the **Maori ice plant,** a seaside species producing pink or creamy
white blossoms; the **blue swamp orchid**—not really an orchid—which appears in swamps in December and January; and the **Maori onion,** a tiny
pink flower found during all seasons in mountain districts.

There are several kinds of daisies and buttercups native to the country, including the **Mount Cook lily,** which is not a lily, but a buttercup.

New Zealanders have not been satisfied with these and a few hundred other species of flowers, and have imported thousands of foreign varieties of blossoms, which many say grow better in their new home anyway. The best place to see them in rich profusion may be Christchurch, which could almost be described as the flower capital of New Zealand.

Trees that are not native include the eucalyptus, brought over from Australia, and whole glens of such old favorites as oak, walnut, etc., planted dutifully by sentimental English settlers more than a century ago in their desire to re-create something of the familiar landscape of the homes they left behind.

Some other foreign-born plants that are innocuous species elsewhere were turned into aggressive, noxious weeds once they hit New Zealand. Among these are the **blackberry bush,** which grows along so many roads, and the **gorse,** whose bright yellow blossoms seem attractive enough when they cover so many cliffs and steep hillsides in New Zealand.

Efforts to combat these thorny, hardy plants with herbicides developed during the Vietnam War have been met with considerable controversy, and most of this spraying has been stopped, since opponents claim the chemicals have harmful side effects in humans. In any case, if you see wild blackberries in New Zealand, don't eat them unless you have local assurance that they have not been treated. Even if the more virulent chemicals were not used, they may still have been recently sprayed with other solutions that could produce more than a bad stomach ache.

Animals of New Zealand. Due, apparently, to the country's long period of separation from any other land mass, the list of conventional animals native to New Zealand is short. In fact, there are only three general types of mammals we can point to. There are two species of bat; the **long-tailed bat,** which has short ears, and the **short-tailed bat,** which has long ears. You're not likely to see or hear either anywhere short of Stewart Island.

Then there are members of the seal family. You may see the **fur seal** basking on rock outcroppings at Milford Sound and elsewhere in Fiordland. There's a handsome yet frightening **sea leopard** that reluctantly performs a few tricks in Marineland at Mount Maunganui. Officially, **sea lions** are said to hang around somewhere (the Maori called them *whakaha*), as are **sea elephants,** for whom the Maori apparently had no name.

Then there are the **whales**—mammals not so numerous as they were before being hunted nearly to extinction. The whale family, of course, also includes **dolphins** and **porpoises,** and any of them may be sighted in Cook Strait and various harbors around the country.

When you consider that seals and whales are generally aquatic, and that bats do their swimming through the air, only to land on obscure islands, it's understandable that New Zealand has been called the "land without mammals." The coming of man, the ultimate mammal, however, wrought a wrenching change to all that. First of all, the first Polynesians landed with the **dog** (*kuri*) and the **rat** (*kiore*), both of which immediately set out to run several ground-nesting birds to extinction. (The *kuri* is itself extinct today, and the *kiore*, a very furry beast, is extremely rare.) The British, beginning with Captain Cook, who introduced the European **pig** (the "Captain Cooker"), also followed suit quickly enough by sentimentally tossing in destructive **opossums,** picked up in Australia (watch out for them if you're driving at night), as well as **cats** and **rabbits** from everywhere. Rabbits soon became the major scourge of New Zealand. (Government groups called Rabbit Boards until recently were dedicated to wiping out all the bunnies in the country.) The early colonists also made New Zealand a place where the **deer** and the **antelope** play. Until recently, there was an open season— even a bounty—on these foraging animals, but now a strange new market has been discovered for them. More on that later.

We've already talked about farm animals as a natural resource, and we'll meet some of them again in our food section later in this chapter. Fish and shellfish will fit in a little better there, too.

Insects? Ouch! You bet. New Zealand has no less than 10,000 species, including the most annoying **sand fly,** a tiny biter who lives along some shorelines. Even an itchy Captain Cook, who explored the coast without benefit of citronella, complained about them in his ship's log. Among the hundreds of other bugs, one of the most interesting is the **giant weta,** who looks rather like a four-inch-long cockroach. (Thankfully, you are unlikely to see them outside zoos and museums.) The **cicadas** kick up a clamor on some warm days, especially in the countryside. New Zealanders are so accustomed to their presence that the sound has to be pointed out to them before you can ask what in heck is making that constant racket. The **glow worm,** the larval stage of a type of two-winged fly, has now become a sparkling tourist attraction in the dark caves at Waitomo and Te Anau. And there are dozens of **butterflies,** nearly all introduced to the country for decorative purposes.

Reptiles. Save one or two, the scaly creatures are not distinctive. There are no land snakes in the country, a fact that New Zealanders are quite proud of. There are, however, 178 species of native earthworms, one of which stretches to about 15 inches. A couple of **sea snakes** do swim over from Australia now and then.

The **leathery turtle,** an endangered species, features a back that looks like an upturned rowboat. Then there's the **brown skink,** a friendly garden lizard, and the tiny **green gecko,** a similar creature, usually effectively hidden in the grass.

But the most interesting reptile by far is the **tuatara,** measuring up to two feet long, and considered a living survivor from the age of dinosaurs. Each individual tuatara may live to be a hundred years old or more. Outside of the zoos, you'll have to head for some uninhabited offshore islands to see the tuatara in his natural state. He has a symbiotic relationship with a petrel bird, sharing and guarding the petrel's burrow, then going out in the dark when the bird has her boyfriend in for the night. He also occupies the burrow alone in the winter, keeping it clean while the petrel is out carousing at sea for several months. Eventually outliving his roommate, the tuatara inherits the burrow entirely for himself.

Lullaby of Birdland. As much as Australia is a land of unique animals, New Zealand is a land of distinctive and fascinating birds. Even a short-term visitor to the country is likely to see and hear some feathered creatures he's never run across before.

The most famous birds, of course, are flightless, beginning with the nocturnal **kiwi** that has become a symbol of the nation. There are five types, incidentally—three of them exclusive to the South Island, one to the North Island, and one to Stewart Island. The name "kiwi" comes from the Maori interpretation of the bird's cry. Weighing three or four pounds, the 18-inch-tall kiwi is known for laying enormous eggs, far out of proportion to the size of the bird itself.

Outside of the zoos, you're more likely to run across the inquisitive **weka** in areas of thick underbrush. Also called the wood hen, the weka's wings are utterly useless, although he can take off at great speeds on two legs when required to do so. He likes to steal shiny objects, incidentally, so if you're camping, he just might get away with your spoon—or your watch!

Almost flightless, too, is the **pukeko,** or swamp hen. A long-legged blue-black bird with a red beak and red legs, its face looks almost human. A close relative is the **takahe,** once thought extinct, but rediscovered alive and well in Otago in 1948. The takahe has some green and blue markings on its body.

The fabled **moa** has not been seen for at least 150 years—perhaps for several hundred years—and is considered extinct. An intriguing story is that some early British seal hunters in southwest New Zealand—still wild, uninhabited country today—may have been among the last to see, hear, and eat a moa. They used to talk about a South Island flightless bird they called "the fireman," since it had a gobble resembling the rattling warning device then carried by fire fighters. Similar sounds are made by such grounded species as the Australian emu and cassowary. Other parts of their description also seem to point to the "bush moa," a small relative of the 10-foot monster, which could have survived into the early nineteenth century.

Other bush birds include the **native pigeon,** easily approached while busy devouring berries (the Maori once used its green and bronze feathers for their cloaks); the **tui,** a distinct species of honey-eater—dressed in gunmetal black with a white tuft of feathers at his throat—with a loud, clear call (you'll more often hear than see him); the **bellbird,** with a duller appearance but an even more bell-like voice (you'll hear him for sure in Fiordland); the **South Island robin,** who will eat out of your hand on the Milford Track but is busy catching flies everywhere else; the tiny **rifleman,** a three-inch-long greenish wren who also likes bugs and flies only short distances from branch to branch; and the **yellow-breasted tit,** sometimes called the tomtit, but unrelated to the European tomtit. The champion insect-catcher, however, is the **fantail,** who uses his extremely flexible and expandable tail to conduct what seem like impossibly complex midair direction changes in order to catch and devour his prey on the wing. (Once you see this one, you'll know it for sure!) The **morepork,** a quiet flyer, is a night owl to be sure, and eats insects, rats, lizards, mice, crabs, and even small birds. If you surprise him in the daytime, he'll look at you with sleepy, yellow-ringed eyes. The morepork's call is distinctive; it sounds remarkably like his name!

Among the high-altitude birds is the **kea,** a native parrot thought by ranchers to attack high-country sheep. It's usually vegetarian and may be easily tamed, and many hang around forest trails on the South Island, playing the clown and looking for a handout. If the aforementioned weka is a thief, then the kea is a kleptomaniac. It has a reputation for taking anything not tied down, even the laces from boots left outside a tent by an unsuspecting camper. The **kaka,** a brown parrot found on both islands, is a relative of the kea. There are two hawks in the country—the **New Zealand falcon,** which catches small birds in flight, and the **harrier,** which seeks disabled prey or carrion. The harrier is often seen on the highway in the morning picking on the opossums killed by passing cars the night before.

Wetland birds include several ducks. Two are the **paradise duck,** actually from a family between a duck and a goose, and the **blue duck,** which almost never flies, is very trusting, and is paying dearly for those traits with gradual extinction. Coastal birds include the **red-billed gull** on the North Island and the **black-billed gull** on the South Island; the **white-fronted tern,** which appears to wear a black beret as it wheels and turns looking for fish near the surface; the **oyster catcher,** of which there are several types, all sometimes using their long bills to probe under the sand for shellfish; the **pied stilt,** with long, slender legs good for wading; and the **wrybill,** one of New Zealand's most unusual birds, with a beak that is bent sideways like a sailmaker's needle.

Several seabirds make New Zealand their home, during at least part of the year. These include the **wandering albatross,** which can be found in a nesting colony at the end of the Otago Peninsula, not far from Dunedin; the **muttonbird,** a type of shearwater that was important in the Maori diet; and the **spotted shag,** an attractive species in its breeding plumage.

There are scores more native birds, plus a large variety from other lands who have come to find a happy home in Aotearoa. Bird watchers who tour New Zealand can pick up several well-produced books illustrating and describing native and introduced birds of nearly every type.

Two common introduced birds that should be recognized by all include the **Indian myna,** a dark bird whose wing tips flash with white during sudden flight; and the Australian **magpie,** a large black-and-white bird whose melodious voice belies an often vicious nature. You'll see these magpies from the car, usually in pairs or in larger gangs. When out in the open, however, stay clear of these toughies. They sometimes defend their nesting territory by diving suddenly and attacking violently those humans they perceive as intruders.

A LAND OF MILK AND HONEY—AND MORE

In his 1951 book *Return to Paradise,* James A. Michener was not entirely complimentary in his observations on New Zealand. It almost seems that he felt duty-bound to criticize such aspects as governmental interference in private life, the white immigration policy, the way the footpaths are rolled up on the weekends, and so forth in an attempt to balance his almost embarrassing adoration of the country and its people.

"New Zealand is probably the most beautiful country on earth," Michener wrote at the outset, and gradually he worked his way around toward the food.

"Life in New Zealand is wonderfully pleasant. Each home has a garden of glorious flowers. Evergreen trees abound and make the landscape lovely. The sea is always available, and no home can be far from mountains and clear lakes.

"New Zealand food is superb, even if the cooking is apt to be pretty dreadful. There are, however, five unique delicacies: soup made from sauteed toheroa clams, pronounced by the Prince of Wales to be 'the finest soup ever made,' an understatement; grilled muttonbird, a baby sea fowl whose parents cram its rubber belly with so many fresh fish that it cannot move, so that when it is cooked it tastes like chicken with a streak of trout;

Colonial Goose, which is strong mutton sliced wafer thin and served with onion stuffing and an almost black gravy; the best little tea cakes in the world; and whitebait . . ."

Eating your way through New Zealand can be a problem or a blessing, depending on how you approach it. If you spend all your time toying with the tucker they dish out in the "international" restaurants, there will be some delicious surprises and some disappointments. But if you keep your eyes peeled for local specialties, you'll have some unique culinary experiences. You'll find them either in a good, standard New Zealand hotel dining room or local restaurant. Otherwise, eating well involves your own personal finds at the fishmonger's, butcher's, and greengrocer's—products and produce you prepare yourself rather than choose off a menu.

If you're inclined to do at least some of your own food preparation, staying at New Zealand's motels is ideal. Virtually every *motel* (not hotel) room has cooking facilities, including all the dishes, cutlery, pots, and pans that are needed. We do a healthy amount of cooking while motoring around the country, and those experiences—combined with picnicking at the ubiquitous roadside rest areas—have given us some of our most delicious memories.

Until recently New Zealand food suffered from the view of many restaurateurs who either didn't believe that foreigners were interested or didn't give a fig whether they were or not, since most of their customers were fellow Kiwis. They used logically to ask who in their right mind would order roast lamb at a restaurant, when everybody makes it so well at home. Then there are all those weird fruits and vegetables—feijoas, Chinese gooseberries, tree tomatoes, black boy peaches, purple potatoes, kumaras, and more. Who would want all that stuff?

We would, that's who. And so, these days, do the locals. In the last few years, New Zealand has been exploring its culinary potential and making some appetizing discoveries. If you see a copy of *A Taste of Kiwi* in the New Zealand book shops, grab it. Edited by a New Zealand food connoisseur, Jan Bilton, *A Taste of Kiwi* presents New Zealand on an haute cuisine platter. Bilton's book is edible proof that New Zealand has finally realized its eat-out (as well as eat-in) potential. It explores regional dishes throughout the country and supplies recipes. You'll want to eat the illustrations as well.

The Marlborough region at the top of the South Island decided to put their high-quality food and wine on display a few years ago and staged its first Marlborough Food and Wine Festival. It was a roaring success. Successive annual festivals have been held in the sunny outskirts of Blenheim every year on the first Saturday in February and, as the word spreads about the fun and fine food, Marlborough hosts a growing number of visitors from around New Zealand and from overseas at each festival.

The government has also woken up to New Zealand's fine foods. Early in 1988, it launched a giant "Taste New Zealand" campaign to tempt palates, not only at home, but also abroad. New Zealand's culinary awakening is great news to those of us who believe quality foods deserve quality cooking.

We'll discuss these incredible edibles in five categories: meats and poultry, fish and seafoods, fruits and vegetables, dairy products, and cakes and desserts.

Meats and Poultry. Mutton, of course, is meat from an adult sheep, and most Americans, if they haven't grown up on it, would probably never choose mutton at a restaurant. They might, however, go for **lamb.** But even if you never eat lamb in the U.S., you still might like it a lot in New Zealand. For some reason, the Down Under lamb just doesn't develop that gamey taste so prevalent in North America, probably due to the different kinds of grasses they eat.

But here's a hot tip on lamb. Don't order "lamb." Try **hogget** instead. That Scottish word means lamb that is a year old, and it is much tastier than the younger meat—although still without the very strong flavor of mature mutton. Any time a good restaurant offers "Colonial Goose," the stuffed mutton dish that Michener remembered, or "Roast Hogget," which would be called lamb many places in the world, the house will be catering to a discriminating New Zealand palate. It almost has to be excellent (although other mutton dishes or lamb would be good, too).

Lamb, a traditional New Zealand dish, is also getting red carpet treatment in the kitchen. Adventurous chefs are serving leaner cuts in a variety of imaginative ways. But the old-fashioned lamb roast is still an old favorite.

By the way, lamb, hogget, or mutton is often served with a piquant (not sweet) mint sauce. Some diners love it, and some hate it. Try a little on the side of your plate first.

Now what about **beef?** New Zealand beef has suffered from bad press in years past. Now, anyway, it's delicious, although with a more robust, beefier flavor than you might be used to. Roast beef is dependable in a good dining room. You'll have to speak up if you like it rare, however, as Down Under preferences do not run toward the bloody. Sometimes you can find it served with horseradish, but don't count on it. More likely they'll offer it with Coleman's or some other hot-hot-HOT mustard. (Again, put a little on the side, and dip in just a wee corner of the meat.)

Incidentally, if you like American mustard on anything, you might want to consider bringing it along with you from home. It *can* be bought in New Zealand—sometimes; it's usually labeled, strangely enough, "American Mustard." But you're not likely to pick it up just any day of the week in any corner dairy (deli).

Ordering **steaks** is also safe in a good restaurant. T-bone or maybe filet mignon are the best bets; perhaps not sirloin, which can be tough. If you're buying your own raw meat, tell the butcher you are a foreigner; it might help. Otherwise, the best cuts may be roast sirloin or wing rib. Other restaurant beef dishes—Beef Wellington, for example—are also generally dependable. Harold McKee from Kansas City maintains that no one in New Zealand has the "slightest clue" of how to prepare steak, and he soon "gave it up as a total loss." It seems he couldn't get a steak that wasn't "covered with deep-fried onion rings" or "covered with gravy." This is very unfortunate and a mystery to the editor—deep-fried onion rings are not a normal New Zealand dish (except at Burger King), and I have never had a steak presented covered in gravy. However, some roast beef dishes will have gravy as well as a side order of onions (not deep-fried). We wonder if there has been a misunderstanding between American English and Kiwi English. New Zealand was definitely not a culinary delight to Mr. McKee, and we hope it didn't ruin his holiday. However, there was one saving grace—Lion Brown beer. Mr. McKee agrees that it is one of the "greatest beers brewed." Thank you.

Often overlooked by visitors to New Zealand is the excellent **corned beef.** The best is called "silverside," and if it is to be served with that wonderful, tangy mustard sauce they make there, please do yourself a favor. Don't pass it up.

Still on the meat file, don't forget **pies!** In New Zealand, when you say "pie" it means meat—usually minced (ground) beef in a fine flaky crust, traditionally bought from a street-corner pie cart, although now it's more readily available from a bakery or a corner dairy. Some pie carts may offer other specialties, too, like beef-and-kidney pie, bacon-and-egg pie, etc. Outside of the deep-dish pies, mentioned later, pies are not thought of as sweet things or desserts in New Zealand.

As part of the fallout from the deer market revolution, described elsewhere, some of the most delicious **venison** is sometimes available (although an awful lot is exported to Germany). You may see it most often offered as a stew. Some diners think it's a little sweet, but that's a characteristic of venison, and we like it.

Ham, chicken, and **turkey** are much the same in New Zealand today as in the U.S. (There are even Kentucky Fried Chicken stores in many cities.) If you're going to buy chicken or turkey in the supermarkets, look for the Tegel brand in the refrigerated area. They're practically ready to pop in a pan.

We think **sausages** in New Zealand are perhaps the best outside of England or Ireland, although some of my fellow Yanks don't share the opinion, since they are very different from most American varieties. My personal favorite is a kind called saveloy, which, for some reason, the Kiwis won't call a sausage ("there are sausages and there are saveloys"). Be warned that there are many who can't stand them by any name. You'll often find sausages offered with those gargantuan N.Z. breakfasts, but they can be good any time of day. (Incidentally, what Kiwis call hot dogs are cooked sausages, either plain or "battered," with a crunchy crust around them, and sometimes served on a stick, and can be found at fish-and-chips shops.) New Zealand **bacon,** milder and leaner than American-style, also has its fans. (It's not crispy enough for me.)

By the way, Michener's **muttonbird** is not loved by our family, although perhaps we weren't lucky enough to have his cook. They're virtually never on a menu, and they might be best when smoked. Gordon McBride, a savor-savvy scribe from Christchurch, tells us that if you like what amounts to a greasy, salted seagull, you can buy cooked muttonbirds in fish shops.

Fish and Seafoods. Some gourmets believe that New Zealand's finny fare is the country's finest offering to the culinary world. That may be exaggerated, but there is no doubt that some of these ocean and freshwater delicacies are unsurpassed.

One dish you absolutely will not find on any restaurant menu is **trout,** whether brown or rainbow. It is simply against the law for trout to be offered commercially in any form. The only way to enjoy New Zealand trout is for you or someone in your family or traveling group to catch it. Then you may take it to the dining room of a good hotel, and they'll prepare it for you. (See our Rotorua chapter for more details.) **Salmon** is another delicious freshwater fish in New Zealand. There are also two species of **eels** that are especially popular when smoked.

Whitebait, mentioned by Michener, is sometimes served as "whitebait fritters." If you can take the idea of a batch of five-inch minnows, cemented in batter from head to tail, it is supposed to be one of the country's choicest delicacies.

Some of the best-tasting *ocean* fish to be found in New Zealand, offered on the menus of good restaurants, include the following: **trevally**—fried, steamed, poached, baked, or soused; **sole**—try Sole Duglere or Sole Veronique, for example; **tuna**—baked, barbecued, or poached; **snapper**—poached, as in Snapper Mornay, or baked, steamed, fried, in a casserole, or smoked; **mullet**—somewhat oily, but good baked or barbecued; **John Dory**—the same as St. Peter's fish in Europe, and prepared in several ways; **grouper**—a versatile fish also called by the Maori word *hapuku;* **flounder**—usually cooked whole, but sometimes filleted; **blue cod**—a white-fleshed, south coast specialty; and **tarakihi**—a firm, juicy, and delicately flavored fish. Try the moist and popular **orange roughy,** exported in large quantities overseas. It's cheaper on the home front.

The same tarakihi (pronounced "*tear*-a-key") is often used in fish and chips. Not always, however. Tarakihi is becoming more expensive, and many fish-and-chips shops now serve **shark,** which is remarkably tasty in New Zealand. Shark, incidentally, is also called "lemon fish" or "flake." (Chips, of course, are French fries. Eat the fish after sprinkling a little vinegar on it.)

Crayfish is almost legendary in New Zealand, and by this we mean the size of crayfish that would be called lobster most places in the world. (Some New Zealanders are now calling it lobster, too, but there are no big pincers, the sign of a true lobster.) Unfortunately, crayfish has become expensive in New Zealand due to the export market. They are sent to the U.S. and Britain, where they are sometimes passed off as local lobster. The "cray" have a sweeter flavor than American lobster. They're a treat—when you can find them.

New Zealand's most famous shellfish is the unfortunately rare **toheroa.** This succulent clam may now be dug from the sands of certain beaches only during very restrictive seasons, although sometimes you will see it on a hotel menu in the form of toheroa soup. When toheroa is unobtainable, another shellfish, the sweeter-tasting **tuatua,** is sometimes substituted. Some people prefer tuatua anyway. Another type of clam, the **pipi,** is also favored, but it is not used in soup. **Paua** is virtually the same as abalone. **Mussels** are also extremely popular.

New Zealand **scallops** are also good and popular ("queen" scallops are the largest), and are often available either as appetizers or main courses in good dining rooms.

But the country is particularly proud of its three types of **oysters.** The Pacific oyster is not native, but it is now farmed on the North Island. The New Zealand rock oyster is much smaller and has a stronger flavor, not unlike the Sydney rock oyster. But the third type, the dredge oyster, is the most famous and the strongest-tasting, too. Usually known as Bluff oysters, or sometimes Stewart Island oysters, they are actually dredged in the Foveaux Strait between Bluff and Stewart Islands, only from April through August or September.

Fruits and Vegetables. Fruit is grown in several parts of the country, but if you're touring by car and keeping your eye out for the bushels of bargains at roadside stands, remember that there are several specific areas specializing in certain varieties.

Tropical and citrus fruit like **oranges** and the New Zealand grapefruit called **poor man's orange** will be found August through November, mostly in the Kerikeri area, near the Bay of Islands 150 miles north of Auckland. Other subtropical varieties, like **Chinese gooseberries** (or kiwi fruit) are grown principally along the crescent coast of the Bay of Plenty from Waihi to Te Kaha (April to December).

Orchards and gardens in the outskirts of Auckland (both north and south) seem to make sure that urban motorists on weekend drives can return with delicious finds in apples and pears in the winter and peaches and strawberries in the summer. Similar suburban growing areas are along Route 1, about 50 miles north of Wellington, centered around the town of Levin.

There are wonderful orchard areas on the North Island in the Hawke's Bay area, especially around Hastings and Taradale, but the heaviest concentration, particularly for "stone fruit," is in Central Otago on the South Island, generally between Queenstown and Dunedin along the Clutha and Roxburgh Rivers. Central Otago, in fact, produces 90 percent of the country's **apricots** and at least half its **cherries, peaches,** and **plums.** Anyone driving to, say, Cromwell or Roxburgh can count himself lucky to be able to load up on these goodies, as well as others like **nectarines** and sometimes **boysenberries.** The small town of Ettrick, eight miles south of Roxburgh (still on Route 8), is particularly identified with **loganberries** in December and January and **strawberries** October through March. Look for **elderberries** in December and January at Geraldine, between Dunedin and Christchurch.

Apples may be found in several fruit-growing areas, but some of the most famous and delicious varieties are grown around Hawke's Bay on the east coast of the North Island and near the city of Nelson on the north coast of the South Island. They may be less expensive in those areas, but you'll find them available in most of the country between about March and November, depending on the types. We've always thought New Zealand apples to be about the crunchiest, sweetest, and freshest available. Two personal favorite varieties are Cox's Orange and Gala. Also popular are Delicious (either red or golden), Granny Smith, and Sturmer. (Incidentally, we usually carry a few cans of New Zealand apple juice in the car. Fresh-Up is one brand you see everywhere, but there are others that are just as good.)

Some other interesting New Zealand fruits (familiar and unfamiliar) include **cherries,** usually only available in December and January; **feijoas,** a fruit rather like a pineapple guava, and usually only available in April and May; **rock melon,** a good breakfast fruit from about December to May; **tree tomatoes,** or "tamarillos," available generally in the fall and winter; **black boys,** a type of peach with a dark indigo pulp, available perhaps January through April, at least in Central Otago; **passion fruit,** grown on the North

Island between about February and July; beautiful varieties of **nectarines,** available January through March or April; and New Zealand **watermelons,** February through April or May.

Vegetables. New Zealand offers at least four dozen different types of vegetables, many of them with long growing seasons. Connoisseurs may go absolutely dewy-eyed over the idea of Hawke Bay **asparagus** in October and November, and I must admit we always think of Poverty Bay for **sweet corn,** January through April. But we're not going to go into any more of that kind of detail here.

It's worth noting, incidentally, that New Zealand seems to have eleventy-seven varieties of the **pumpkin/squash** family like buttercup, butternut, courgettes (called zucchini elsewhere, and sometimes in New Zealand), marrow, choko, and more. (The orange pumpkin, by the way, looks very different from anything you would make a jack-o'-lantern out of in North America!)

Some other vegetables you might not recognize by their New Zealand name include **aubergine** (eggplant), **beetroot** (red beets), **capsicum** (green bell peppers), **swedes** (rutabaga), and **silver beet** (Swiss chard).

In addition to the garden varieties of potatoes, New Zealand has two more interesting types of tuber. My personal favorite is the **kumara,** the New Zealand version of the Polynesian sweet potato found throughout the Pacific. But somehow the kumara—especially when roasted—has a superior flavor to those found in the soil of Hawaii, Samoa, Tahiti, etc.

Much rarer is a somewhat conventional-tasting but startling-looking potato called the **purple potato** or "Maori potato." Its flesh really is a bright purple. (We had some in Gisborne, although many New Zealanders from other parts of the country claim there is no such thing.)

Dairy Products. New Zealand milk, butter, and cheese are world famous, and the latter two products are now even available sometimes in the U.S. As you might expect, all three are relatively inexpensive in New Zealand—perhaps half the price you pay in the U.S., sometimes even less.

Milk seems to be almost a national right. You'll usually find a bottle of it compliments of the house in your hotel or motel room. In theory, it's to put in your morning tea. (Milk comes in glass bottles, often with the cream at the top, just as it did in the U.S. before World War II. It also comes in cartons, and the varieties are similar to those available in the U.S. You can, of course, arrange to have it delivered to your door daily.) In the morning you might want to try it on a popular brand of breakfast food called Weet-Bix—Canadians may know it, too; it looks rather like Shredded Wheat but tastes more like Corn Flakes. (By the way, New Zealanders virtually never go out for breakfast unless they're too far from home to prepare their own.)

New Zealand **butter** seems designed especially to be spread on fresh bread, scones, and other delicious baked products. We can't bring our-selves to ask for margarine in New Zealand, although it is generally available.

You can buy a New Zealand version of any kind of cheese available any-place in the world. Many varieties are based on cheddar—mild, medium, or sharp—and colored from white to strong yellow. Look for two types made from port wine, as well as New Zealand Camembert and Brie.

Egmont is a New Zealand cheese rather like a combination of cheddar and gouda. Also, three other cheeses—blue vein, Gruyère, and Nuzano—have been combined to produce Erbo, which has its own tangy flavor. There are also processed cheeses flavored with curry, caraway, celery, and onion. One brand we look for is Waikato, from a North Island cheese fac-tory. Another label is Ararua. New Zealand cheeses are of a high standard and the varieties have increased in the last few years.

All other dairy products, like cottage cheese, cream cheese, yogurt, etc., are available in profusion, and all for amazingly low (to Americans, any-way) prices.

Cakes and Desserts. New Zealanders love cakes, but usually not for dessert. Instead they accompany the seemingly endless cups of tea served throughout the day. The first items in the following group may be served either at morning tea (about 10 A.M.) or afternoon tea (about 3 P.M.). You may find any of these at a coffee shop and sometimes a milk bar in New Zealand, or you can buy an assortment at any of the many bakeries estab-lished in the main streets of even the smallest villages. Ideally, of course, they would be served to you in a private home. Tea and cakes together at any time of day are also known collectively as "Devonshire Tea," and you'll see this advertised at tea shops and restaurants from one end of the country to the other.

Fruitcake is a dark, heavy cake, sometimes yellow, filled with dried fruits and nuts; **scones** are either plain, cheese, date, or raisin, and are similar to baking-powder biscuits but are served with butter and jam or whipped cream and jam; **Madeira cake** is similar to the American pound cake; and **Sultana cake** is rather like a Madeira cake with sultanas (white raisins).

Dundee cake is a type of round fruitcake with almonds decorating the top; **filled or layered sponge cake** is a sponge cake sandwiched with either passion fruit, jam, or mock cream filling; and **Pikelets** are similar to small pancakes but are eaten cold, spread with butter and jam or with whipped cream.

Cream puffs are similar to the American variety, but are filled with whipped cream instead of custard; **meringues** are two small dollops of meringue pasted together with whipped cream; and **vanilla squares** are squares of custard between puff pastry, with a thin icing on the top (similar to what are known as Napoleons in some parts of the U.S.).

Fruit squares are a mixture of dried fruits between puff-pastry squares; **Lamingtons** are oblong pieces of pink sponge cake dipped in liquid red Jell-O or chocolate and rolled in shredded coconut; and **tarts** are little pastry cups filled with jam or lemon honey.

Hokey-pokey biscuits are cookies with a sweet, hard-to-describe flavor; **rock cakes** are small buns with raisins or currants inside; **shortbread** is similar to others, but particularly tasty when made with New Zealand butter; **nut loaf** is a sweet loaf made with walnuts, sliced thin, and served with butter; **date loaf** is similar to the above, but is made with dates; **apple shortcake** is a thin layer of sliced apples between two layers of buttery shortcake, sprinkled with confectioners' sugar. It is sometimes made with apricots instead of apples; and **cream buns** are somewhat similar to doughnuts, but are shaped differently and filled with mock cream. (One expatriate Kiwi dietician we know says that the entire population appears to be fueled by cream buns!)

Some goodies that are served as desserts, and not for tea, include the following:

Claimed by both New Zealand and Australia as a national dish, **pavlova** is a large meringue cake, topped with whipped cream and seasonal fruit—traditionally strawberries or Chinese gooseberries. (It was named in honor of Anna Pavlova, whose Russian ballet company toured the two countries in 1926.) **Trifle,** a heritage from Mother England, is a sponge cake soaked with sherry and containing, variously, custard, jam, flavored gelatin, and/or canned fruit, and topped with whipped cream. **Chocolate blancmange** (pronounced "blah-*mahnge*") is a type of chocolate pudding. **Plum pudding,** a steamed, cake-like dessert, contains dried fruits (no plums, by the way!) and is served hot with thin custard and cream.

Steamed pudding is made from a sponge-cake batter, steamed in a bowl with jam or golden syrup, and sometimes served with thin custard and cream. **Christmas pudding** is similar to plum pudding, but is also served with a brandy hard sauce. **Pancakes** are always the French-style crêpes, on which you sprinkle sugar and lemon juice. **Fruit sponge** is made of apple or another hot fruit baked with a sponge-cake topping. **Deep-dish fruit pie** is a hot fruit pie with the pie crust on the top only. Any of several flavors are possible. **Fruit salad,** a popular cold dessert, is made with a mixture of canned and seasonal fresh fruits.

Miscellaneous. Most often, you'll get your **toast** delivered hard in New Zealand, with the crusts snipped off around the edge. If there is still a little warmth left in it, you might try quickly slapping on the butter. But give up trying to ask for it to be brought hot. It's useless, unless you're making it yourself in a motel.

New Zealanders make a delicious assortment of **jams and jellies,** but don't be surprised if the dining room *you* have chosen only offers **marmalade**—much less sweet and more tart than the kind we Yanks are used to. Try asking for **honey;** New Zealand has several wonderful types, often named after the flower in which the bee has been doing his pollen-gathering—kowhai honey, manuka honey, etc. You may develop your own favorite.

Be warned that Kiwis often spread on their toast or bread a concoction difficult for most Americans to appreciate called **Marmite**—a type of yeast extract, containing salt, with the consistency and complexion of used axle grease. In fact, New Zealanders usually consider themselves deprived when they can't find the stuff in otherwise civilized countries. A version of it with a vegetable derivative is called **Vegemite,** and that is actually preferred to Marmite by most Australians. The formulae for both are closely guarded commercial secrets. I'm the only one in our family who can't stand either goo, and who knows? You may love it, too!

Population of Principal Cities

4

Who Are the New Zealanders?

Travelers who have visited Britain or Australia often think they already know the New Zealander, but in either case they would be wrong.

New Zealanders, who like to call themselves Kiwis, are generally friendlier than the British, although certainly not as immediately ebullient as the Australians. Strike up a casual conversation, and you'll likely be met by an initial shyness and lack of response. Keep talking, however, and after he or she sees that your interest is genuine, the average New Zealander will warm up very quickly. If you can't talk about sheep or rugby, try the relative quality of beer or wine, or the scenic wonders of the North and South Islands— always diplomatically giving the best review to the island you happen to be on at the moment.

To the American ear, the speech of the New Zealander sounds similar to that of the Australian (but don't tell him so). You'll hear many of the same expressions, to be sure, plus several more that are distinctly Kiwi slang. A favorite expression of approval goes, simply, "Good as gold!"

The tone of voice, at least among men, seems to have more of a sandy twang. The letter "R" can disappear entirely. "Farm" may be uttered as "fam" (rhyming with "ham"). The word "Maori," which should be pronounced

something like "*mow*-rie," is sometimes interpreted as "mary" or "mayerie."
More on that later.

Just between us, the Kiwis and the Aussies do have many things in common, although both hate to admit it. A New Zealander may view an
Australian with considerable suspicion, seemingly believing that every
Aussie is some kind of sharpy who will con the well-meaning, overly trusting Kiwi. In American terms, it's the way a man from Peoria might look at
a Chicagoan. The Australian, for his part, often tends to look down on New
Zealanders, perhaps the way a New Yorker looks at a man from
Philadelphia: "I went to New Zealand last week, but it was closed," goes a
typical (and unoriginal) Australian quip.

The Australian attitude can be patronizing, like that of a "big brother"
carrying little New Zealand over the stream. But there is also resentment
among some Australians toward the thousands of New Zealanders who, in
times of economic troubles, have left their country to seek work in Sydney
and other Australian cities: "Help stamp out New Zealand!" is a bumper
sticker we've seen in New South Wales.

New Zealanders and Australians move freely between their two nations.
No visas or work permits are necessary. If citizens of one country stay long
enough in the neighboring country across the Tasman they can vote there.
They also share in each other's social services.

A decade or so ago, New Zealand was indeed "good as gold," and she
can still look forward to a prosperous future. But today the lack of good
job opportunities and a much tougher economic climate have combined
to send many New Zealanders out of the country.

The traffic between New Zealand and her neighbor is still moving more
to Australia, which New Zealanders seem to see as some kind of El Dorado.
Wages are higher in Australia and there is a perception that jobs are more
freely available. But Australia is undergoing its own painful readjustment,
having lived beyond its means in recent years, and some Kiwis are returning to greener pastures back home, where a head start on chiselling a
more efficient economy out of a social-welfare-based system has started to
pay dividends.

The Kiwis certainly seem to live well enough. Nearly every New
Zealander has a telephone, television, plenty of appliances, good plumbing, a car, excellent and inexpensive food and shelter, and easy access to a
countryside of unparalleled loveliness. On an international standard,
wages seem much lower than those for comparable work in the U.S. and
Canada. As the *Wall Street Journal* pointed out, "It's hard to find a neighborhood that is either blatantly rich or brutally poor."

We like Californian Shelley Pogorelsky's description of New Zealand, which she included in a recent letter. We feel that she sums up New Zealand's real riches succinctly in the following: "My general impression of the country is that it's very refreshing. The environment is clean, there is plenty of water (unlike California), the traffic is not congested, and the air is pure. Likewise the people; they, too, are refreshing. They were open and honest and I felt safe there. If New Zealand were 1000 miles away instead of 6000 miles away, we'd truly consider moving there."

To support its extensive social welfare program, successive governments have imposed a heavy tax burden on the population. The effect of this, critics have suggested, has been to keep everyone within narrowly defined limits of rich and poor, acting also to maintain a strict egalitarian attitude. More recently, while maintaining its commitment to social welfare, the Labour Government has ventured to loosen the once tightly controlled economy. New Zealanders now pay a lower rate of direct taxation in exchange for a sales tax. A more competitive market has also grown up as import duties and restrictions have disappeared.

Some international critics of New Zealand have suggested that this egalitarian system also acts to maintain a strict egalitarian attitude among its citizens—a disposition that is not at all inclined to approve eccentricity or to reward any sort of brilliance. In fact, they say, the average New Zealander is apt to be very suspicious of the oddball, particularly one who demonstrates any sort of successfully innovative approach to anything.

Words like "clever" and "original" often have derogatory connotations in New Zealand, and for reasons related to that some of the country's most talented young people seem to have flown the coop. One Australian magazine said not long ago that statistics suggest that "just about every New Zealander with some get-up-and-go has got up and gone." On the other hand, New Zealanders seem to do pretty well in Australia and just about wherever they go. And some are returning home to try their international experience out on the local population.

It is for this reason that the government has tended to shrug its shoulders at the practically zero population growth in recent years, partly due to the emigration of its people to other countries. If nothing else, the outgoing numbers have relieved the pressure on unemployment and housing. However, the government attitude may be turning more in favor of the steady queues (lines) of foreigners who still want to live in "Godzone."

While he was the Australian premier, Gough Whitlam once said that New Zealand's troubles stemmed from her position as an "offshore farm" for Great Britain. Without being blessed with the minerals of Australia,

New Zealand has had to make do with her talent—and her life-giving soil. But now that Great Britain has joined the European Common Market, she can no longer give preferred status to the wool, meat, and dairy products of New Zealand.

With a population of only 3.3 million, New Zealand must "export or expire." There are just not enough people within the country to buy all the agricultural products 6.6 million green thumbs can turn out, and there are not enough other products she can make for her citizens.

The Kiwis have gamely set about finding new customers for their agricultural products in recent years. Britain is still an important customer, but Japan and the United States are also being successfully courted. Frozen New Zealand lamb, Fern Leaf brand butter, New Zealand "lobster tails" (from the ocean crayfish caught near Stewart Island), and other products are seen more and more in American supermarkets, particularly in Hawaii and California. New Zealanders have also begun to export several unusual horticultural products like "Kiwi fruit." Renamed for foreign markets, they were once called "Chinese gooseberries."

New Zealanders have managed to find new Middle Eastern markets for their lamb and are even getting used to strange requirements like facing toward Mecca at the moment they slaughter the beasties. In a similar vein, enterprising Kiwis have discovered that a former plague, the deer that once foraged uncontrolled over the countryside, could be turned into a useful commodity based on ignorance and superstition in other parts of the world. The horns of those animals are now scraped of their "velvet," which is sold as the principal ingredient in aphrodisiac potions in Korea and elsewhere.

Deer are now being raised in New Zealand, and those that do not develop the profitable horns are finding their way to Germany and western countries as delicious venison.

The country has recently proved very fortunate in the appearance of two more natural resources. First, with her many hydroelectric systems, she is now enjoying a surplus of electricity. Also giving great promise is the ambitious "Maui gas," from a natural methane field being tapped offshore, 34 miles west of Cape Egmont. The well leads to the site of the world's first production-scale plant to convert the gas to gasoline. The Maui gas field is divided into "A" and "B" platforms. Field A is the largest and accounts for 76 percent of the total production, offering 16,900 barrels per day. Maui B is still being completed and when operational will be an unmanned facility.

But perhaps New Zealand's most dramatic natural resource—tourism—is still in relative infancy. Her natural wonders are a combination of those offered by several other countries, plus several of her own. Add to those scenic benefits a hospitable, English-speaking atmosphere; the availability of exciting sports like skiing, rafting, and jet-boating; an interesting, indigenous Polynesian culture; a stable society without significant crime or political disorder; good food and wine; and certainly reasonable prices. The sum total is one of the best bargains for the world's travelers and potentially one of the most profitable enterprises for New Zealand.

In the past few years, New Zealand inflation exceeded 18 percent and unemployment rose to 6 percent. When the foreign debt increased to more than $11 billion in 1984, New Zealanders voted the conservative National party out of the country's leadership, forcing the resignation of the pugnacious prime minister, Sir Robert ("Piggy") Muldoon. Muldoon, who ran the country with an autocratic hand, was replaced by David Lange, head of the New Zealand Labour party. That party introduced a new style of administration and economic policy that brought inflation down to below 5 percent.

Not entirely unrelated to economic difficulties are the attitudes New Zealand has been displaying toward the Maori population during the past decade. Although the country's record on race is hardly unblemished, it is decidedly not a racist society today. In fact, it is difficult to imagine the stalwart, optimistic, fair-minded New Zealander of today as hating anything outside of poverty, war, and injustice.

But in difficult times the Maori, along with the Pacific islanders resident in New Zealand, find themselves socially and economically discriminated against, even if the discrimination is far more subtle than that suffered by blacks in the U.S. or the aborigines in Australia. Stereotypical reactions still exist, and members of what is otherwise an almost classless society still manage to look down on—or perhaps away from—the Maori.

Nearly 70 percent of all Maori are under 20, and the pressures of city life in Auckland, Wellington, and Christchurch have led some young Maori to form gangs with frightening names like the Head Hunters, Black Power, Stormtroopers, and the Mongrel Mob, a reflection on the high unemployment rate amongst the Maori. The government has made attempts to channel their energies into useful projects, and some of these have proven effective.

While Maori are having trouble competing for jobs, they also are seeking to reassert their ethnic identity and to recapture their culture before it slips away from them. Kara Puketapu, New Zealand's former secretary for Maori affairs and a Maori himself, told us that part of the answer has been discovered in a successful attempt by several tribes to conduct summer programs in the country for young Maori whose roots have gotten lost under the sidewalks of the city.

"Imagine the effect when they meet an old man there who says, 'Look, son. I knew your grandfather, and he was a good fisherman. I'll show you what he used to do,'" Puketapu said.

He also indicated that Maori are no longer happy simply to melt into the dominant white culture: "In New Zealand, we're really more like a mosaic," he said. Until recently New Zealanders, brown and white, liked to speak of themselves as "one people." With renewed Maori identity, however, they have been describing themselves as a multicultural society.

There are others who say Puketapu is an apologist for the establishment, and they warn that racial tension is being ever more deeply felt and even more clearly shown in New Zealand. Official attempts are being made to integrate Maori philosophy, culture, and language into New Zealand institutions. However, it will take more than these gestures to quiet the new tensions that are being felt by both Maori and Pakeha (whites). Maoris now number about 400,000—about 9 percent of the population.

A Canadian writer suggested in the *New Republic* magazine that the main difficulty with New Zealand was that it had no history. He's dead wrong. New Zealand's history is one of the great sagas of recent discovery and development—comparable to that of Australia, the United States, or Canada.

The First New Zealanders—A.D. 900 or So to 1642

New Zealand was first settled by Polynesians who are thought to have arrived around the tenth or eleventh century A.D. The generally accepted theory is that the islands were settled by successive small groups arriving from East Polynesia. The parallels between the original settlement of Hawaii and New Zealand are fascinating.

In Hawaii, it is generally accepted that the first people who arrived there were from the Marquesas, and the second group from Tahiti and that vicinity. Today, scholars seem to throw up their hands at narrowing down the home of the first tribes in New Zealand, other than to say they were from "East Polynesia." This could mean Tahiti, the Marquesas, or the Cook Islands. One oral legend, anyway, describes the immigration as having come from a place called Hawaiki.

Although there is some evidence that this Hawaiki was indeed Hawaii (or "Hawai'i," to use the classical spelling), there are also a considerable number of indications that it was not. Nevertheless, the word Hawaiki is merely Hawai'i, with a "k" substituted for the glottal stop of the Hawaiians. (The word for "canoe" in Hawaiian is *wa'a;* in Maori it's *waka,* for example.)

But then the ancient name for the island of Raiatea, near Tahiti in the Society Islands, was Hawaiki, too. Also, the largest island in Samoa is named Savai'i, and the *s* is considered to be interchangeable with the *h* in Polynesian languages. And to confuse the picture still further, some anthropologists believe that despite all this Hawai'i/Savai'i business, there is strong evidence pointing to the island of Tonga as an ancestral homeland for the second wave to populate New Zealand. (It seems that the only fact agreed upon is that the population did not come from the direction of Easter Island, the mysterious dot of land considered the western point of the Polynesian Triangle.)

The first group of New Zealanders are generally referred to as the "moa hunters." Archeologists poking through thousand-year-old campfires have discovered that some of them dined regularly on the now-extinct flightless bird. Not much is known of their culture, except that they may have been a relatively peaceful people compared to the warlike character that evolved in later centuries.

It appears the moa hunters gradually knuckled under to the dominant Maori, militarily and culturally, even if the two groups did live side by side at least for some years. Today's Maori is thought to be descended from both of these peoples.

The Maori oral tradition that survives today claims that a great early explorer from Tahiti named Kupe ("*koo*-pay") discovered New Zealand, named it Aotearoa—the "Long White Cloud"—and eventually returned home with the news. Later another group of explorers, led by a warrior named Toi, is said to have checked out the two large islands. Eventually others launched a great fleet of 7 to 12 seagoing canoes to bring whole families with their fruits, vegetables, and dogs to the land of Kupe and Toi.

The recitation of genealogies and other chants memorized by the Maori has placed this "great migration" at around the year 1350. The canoes, all of which received romantic names, are reported to have landed at certain places in New Zealand. Today, the 45 or so chief tribes of Maori still trace their ancestry back to one of a dozen specific ancient vessels.

For centuries the Maori had no written language, and there are several variations of these stories told in the different tribes. Also, much of the history of the people is tied up with supernatural explanations for the world around them. One of the most significant involves the very creation of New Zealand, a story woven around the Polynesian demigod Maui. According to the legend, the South Island was Maui's canoe, and Stewart Island was its anchor. Standing in his giant *waka*, Maui is supposed to have caught a huge fish. When he finally brought it up from the sea, it became the North Island, and it is known in the Maori language as "Te Ika-a-Maui," the "Fish of Maui." The South Island, of course, was called "Te Waka-a-Maui," the "Canoe of Maui."

It is intriguing that the Maori had a pretty good idea that a map of the North Island does somewhat resemble the profile of a fish, its head to the south, with Taranaki and the East Cape its fins, and Northland forming its long tail.

Americans who have visited the state of Hawaii may recognize Maui as the namesake of the Island of Maui. During his exploits there, he is supposed to have lassoed the sun as it arose from an ancient volcano crater. Tahitians and other Polynesians also tell of adventures by the same Maui.

There is scholarly opinion that the fellow actually did exist—perhaps as a captain in the ancient Asian navy that first carried his people to the islands of the Pacific thousands of years ago—although whatever his human accomplishments may have been they were certainly exaggerated in the fish stories of his descendants.

Without either the benefit or threat of European contact, the Maori culture developed very well over the centuries. Art and dance were raised to a high degree of sophistication. If the Maori had had a written language, literature surely would have been strong, too, as there was a great tradition of storytelling and complicated historical recitation. That they were good farmers is especially evident in the cultivation of the *kumara*, a delicious sweet potato still enjoyed in New Zealand. They wove clever clothing out of New Zealand flax, at times decorating their cloaks with colorful bird feathers.

Also, the science of war was highly advanced, and, according to Maori legends, an honorable avocation. Tribal and family units were close and affectionate, but the Maori cooked and ate members of other tribes defeated in battle. In a land without mammals, perhaps cannibalism did help satisfy the desire for meat. But it was also the ultimate degradation to members of rival tribes, and an old Maori insult goes: "The flesh of your grandfather still sticks in my teeth!"

By the seventeenth century A.D., the great navigators of Spain and Portugal had crossed the Pacific several times over a period of more than a hundred years, although none is known to have happened across Aotearoa. It is difficult to be positive about these facts, however, for those governments kept many of their discoveries secret in their rivalry with the Dutch and the English for supremacy of the seas.

These Iberians did come in contact with Polynesia at least once, in the Marquesas. There is one theory that they made a landfall in Hawaii, too, and another that they caught sight of New Zealand in 1576.

If the Maori had any idea of any of this nautical European activity, there is nothing remaining today to show it. They apparently would not have cared very much, for there is not even a Maori version of the appearance of the very first European known to have visited New Zealand.

Voyages of Discovery—1642 to 1813

In 1642 the Dutch East India Company, headquartered at Batavia (now Djakarta) on the island of Java, charged Captain Abel Janszoon Tasman with a mission to discover the "great southern continent" thought to exist in unknown seas to the southeast. Tasman set out with a pair of somewhat overcrowded ships. He managed to miss the continent of Australia entirely, except for a brief landing at the island now known as Tasmania, from which he retreated after hearing frightening voices and receiving some indication that the place might be inhabited by giants.

He sailed on across the sea that now bears his name until, on December 13, he virtually ran straight into the Southern Alps near the site of present-day Hokitika. Deciding there was no safe place to land, he continued up around the northeast tip of the South Island to the protected anchorage now known as Golden Bay.

On December 18, 1642, Tasman found himself in the company of no less than 22 canoes of fierce-looking natives. Following some unintelligible shouts to each other, the two societies exchanged trumpet sounds, and for some reason one of Tasman's ships fired a cannon. The sound may have been resented by the local residents, for the following day a message boat shuttling between the two Dutch ships was suddenly attacked, and four of the six sailors were killed.

After picking up the survivors, Tasman weighed anchor and his two ships left the bay, firing stern volleys at the few canoes that seemed inclined to follow. The Dutch explorer described the event as a "monstrous deed and detestable thing," and his real parting shot was to name the place where it occurred Mordenaers Baij—"Murderers' Bay." (Much later it was renamed Massacre Bay, then Coal Bay, and finally—when gold was discovered nearby in the nineteenth century—Golden Bay.)

Tasman sailed on up the coast of the North Island—not too closely, however, for he did not even sight the 8,000-foot prominence of Mount Egmont en route. He contemplated landing at Three Kings Islands, saw some spear-carrying Maoris there, and then thought better of the idea. He left the land for good on January 5, 1643, without ever having set foot on the discovery he named Staten Landt, honoring the States General of the United Netherlands. A few years later the Dutch government renamed it Nieuw Zeeland after a part of Holland and placed it on world maps in Latin as Nova Zeelandia. It seemed logical at the time to designate the country as New Zealand, since by that time the Dutch had already given the name New Holland to the known portion of Australia.

Tasman was criticized by Dutch authorities for being overcautious, and they said he should have made more detailed investigations of his discoveries. In any case, his report of savage *mordenaers* was enough to repel the interest of the world from this hostile place for more than 125 years.

A more definitive discovery of New Zealand occurred October 7, 1769. Lieutenant James Cook of the British Royal Navy was leading his first of three voyages to the Pacific. He had just completed some astronomical observations from Tahiti and was then on his way specifically to make contact with the land discovered by Tasman.

The actual first sighting of New Zealand was made by Cook's cabin boy, who spied a headland near the present city of Gisborne. Cook promptly rewarded the lad, Nicholas Young, by charting the point as Young Nick's Head, a name it still holds.

When Cook stepped ashore two days later, accompanied by two scientists, they also took with them an assistant who might have served Tasman well—a young Polynesian chief brought from Tahiti. He could speak immediately with the Maori, the first indication that his people and those of Aotearoa had descended from the same ancestors. More important to Cook, there was now hope that there would be no misunderstanding of his peaceful motives. Unfortunately, the first Maori he met were not particularly friendly. He named the place Poverty Bay, a name that belies the rich farmland in the area today.

Cook had several skirmishes as he sailed around the country, many of the Maori taking him and his men to be some kind of goblins who came in a giant goblin canoe. War was a way of life to the Maori, and they seldom showed any intimidation before the goblin chief's superior weapons. Amazingly, Cook recorded their fierce facial expressions and the taunts hurled from the canoes: *Haere mai* ("Come here!") and *Haere ki uta he patu ake* ("Come to the shore and be clubbed!").

Gradually, some of the Maori came to accept the English explorer as a *rangitira*, a chief of sorts, and eventually Cook made firm friends among them. He found no Maori with any knowledge of Tasman's unfortunate contact a century and a quarter earlier, even though he interviewed some living in the same neighborhood. Cook's visit was more memorable, apparently, and one Maori chief who lived to be 108 remembered to his death in 1872 that at the age of 5 he had been befriended by Cook and fed some delicious roast pork.

On Cook's first voyage he carefully charted the perimeter of the entire country. His maps look very much like those of today, with only two significant errors: He judged Banks Peninsula to be an island and Stewart Island to be a peninsula. He and his men made considerable forays into the countryside, marveled at kauri and kahikatea trees, fortified *pas*, and kumara gardens. He finally left New Zealand on April 1, 1770, after a six-month tour, going on to similar dramatic successes in Australia.

Cook made three scientific voyages to the Pacific altogether. He stopped for periods in New Zealand on the other two, as well, using Ships Cove of Queen Charlotte Sound as his home away from home. (Ironically, it is almost impossible to visit this spot in New Zealand today, except by boat.)

While Cook was in the midst of his first New Zealand explorations, a French captain, Jean de Surville, also arrived in the country and began to look around. Both recorded some of the same phenomena—even the same weather on the same dates—but despite the fact that their ships were as close as 60 miles apart, neither ever knew of the other's presence.

De Surville, who treated the Maori badly, died before reaching France again. His ship was impounded by the Spanish in Peru, and it was years before anyone compared the logs of the two captains.

After 1770, many ships began to call in the wake of Cook's discoveries. Cook, now promoted to the official rank of captain, revisited New Zealand with two ships in 1773, 1774, and 1777, and no doubt would have been back again had he not been killed in Hawaii in 1778.

Two more French vessels were under command of the easygoing Captain Marion du Fresne in New Zealand in 1772. He camped at the Bay of Islands, made a few mistakes, and may have violated a *tapu*. He was attacked by the same Maori that de Surville had mistreated nearly three years earlier. For whatever reason, du Fresne and two dozen members of his crew were killed and eaten.

After the founding of the British penal colony in Australia in 1788 (an event hastened by the American Revolution, since Britain could no longer dump her criminals across the Atlantic), there were more visitors to New Zealand, many of them from Sydney. Captain George Vancouver, who had been with Cook on his final voyage, sailed into Dusky Sound in 1791, as did Alejandro Malaspina, commander of a Spanish expedition, in 1793. Then there were Admiral Joseph-Antoine Raymond de Bruni d'Entrecasteaux, who represented France in 1793, and some casual stopovers by American whaling vessels at around the same time.

A famous boondoggle was the 1793 capture of two Maori chiefs by one Lieutenant Hanson, commanding the British ship *Daedalus*, so that they could be brought to Sydney to teach convicts how to make flax into fibre. The chiefs, of course, knew nothing about such "women's work," and when they refused to cooperate they were eventually brought home again.

Several sealers also operated along the New Zealand coast, but these ships jealously guarded their hunting grounds, so many of their discoveries have gone unreported and unrecorded. However, an American sealer, Captain

Owen F. Smith, is credited with an important discovery—he established once and for all that Stewart Island is separate from the South Island. His 1804 map of Foveaux Strait survives in Wellington's Alexander Turnbull Library.

Some trade took place between Australia and New Zealand in the early nineteenth century, but relations were often strained in what was then a lawless, godless region. One of the more brutal incidents took place in 1809 and became known as the Boyd Massacre. After carrying convicts from England to Sydney, the brig *Boyd* called in to New Zealand for lumber. Among some Maori in the crew was a young chief who had been whipped for a minor offense on the voyage.

After reaching the bay at Whangaroa, the chief secretly called on local Maori to help him exact *utu,* the sacred principle of revenge. Subsequently the entire crew and nearly all of the passengers were killed and eaten, and the ship was burned and sunk. Later, a group of white whalers attacked Maori at Whangaroa in retribution, killing more than 60 of them. (The attractive but lonely bay is still sparsely settled today, apparently a legacy of the horror that occurred there.)

Missionaries and Muskets—1814 to 1838

Maori who occasionally showed up on the streets of Sydney in the early 1800s attracted the sympathetic attention of the Reverend Samuel Marsden, who had come to Australia from England to be chaplain to the convict colony. In 1814 he sponsored an Anglican mission at the Bay of Islands in New Zealand, and the missionaries were welcomed by the chiefs, who quickly grasped that there was much that was important to be learned about the ways of the Pakeha, even if it was not necessarily religion.

The missionaries made several mistakes, like trying to teach bootmaking to people who wore nothing on their feet, and they were also slow to pick up the Maori language. Eventually the Maori threatened to throw the men of God out of the country entirely unless the tribes were provided with muskets. Although there was considerable debate over it, the missionaries did come up with some guns, as well as hatchets and axes, not all of which were used for saintly purposes.

Meanwhile, many Maori were suffering and dying from diseases unwittingly introduced by Pakehas—illnesses to which the indigenous people had developed no natural immunity. The religious teachings of the missionaries were hampered when many Maori began to blame the white man's *Atua* ("God," but the word also means "unknown") for the onslaught of so much mysterious suffering.

After about a decade the missionaries caught on to the fact that many of their troubles were caused by language problems. The Reverend Henry

Williams took over the mission in 1823 and began to push transliteration and translation of the Maori tongue.

Gradually—and then avidly—the Maori began to read, and the missionaries began to understand something of the syntax and grammar of the Maori. (The three mission stations established in the area—at Rangihoua in 1814, Kerikeri in 1819, and Paihia in 1823—are today among the most charming areas in the North Island, although Rangihoua is difficult to reach by road. In Kerikeri, the mission house is open to the public.)

Several Maori chiefs in the area were headed for greatness, in one way or another. Outstanding among them was Hongi Hika, protector of Marsden's missionary stations and one of its less-talented pupils. He visited Sydney several times and was presented in London to King George IV.

"How do *you* do, Mister King George?" the carefully rehearsed Hongi asked.

"How do *you* do, Mister King Hongi?" the British monarch responded.

On his return from London, Hongi passed through Sydney and there exchanged nearly all the gifts he had received for muskets. These he used in wars with rival tribes in New Zealand; as solicitous as he was of the missionaries, his name was written in the blood of his own race in other parts of the country. Many Maori escaped the musket wars of Hongi and other chiefs by taking refuge at the mission settlements.

The tribes, bearing genuine firepower for the first time, were able to create slaughter on a scale undreamed of before their contact with Europeans. Another disruptive effect was that the Maori neglected food cultivation so that they could process the tons of flax needed to trade for muskets. The warriors, of course, took prisoners, and these slaves became a mobile food supply, especially during the winter months.

Among the strange characters who showed up in New Zealand during this period was the Baron Charles de Thierry, a half-French adventurer who claimed he had bought enough land from the Maori to make him "sovereign chief" of New Zealand. This threat was only taken seriously enough to help the British decide to appoint James Busby as official British resident in New Zealand. When the baron showed up, however, the Maori only turned over a few acres of land to him. De Thierry faded away, eventually winding up as a music teacher in Auckland. For his part, Busby talked a group of Maori chiefs into drawing up a national flag and declaring their sovereign rights over all New Zealand.

Colonial Days—1838 to 1854

The British government was reluctant to establish authority in New Zealand, but it was gradually talked into doing so by missionaries pleading for the influence of law. Without waiting for the wheels of government to grind to the inevitable, a somewhat brash fellow named Edward Gibbon Wakefield took things in his own hands, formed the New Zealand Association in 1837, and began to recruit settlers. The following year the British extended the boundary of Australia's New South Wales colony to include New Zealand, or as much of it as could be negotiated from the Maori.

The year 1840 marked the official beginning of New Zealand as it exists today. In January the first of Wakefield's immigrant ships arrived, and the following month saw the signing of the Treaty of Waitangi. The chiefs debated the treaty for three days first, many of them speaking loudly against it. But the tide was apparently swayed when one well-respected chief and lifelong friend of the British, Waka Nene, ended his argument saying, "I am walking beside the Pakeha." When the shouts subsided, 46 chiefs signed or made their *moko* (an abbreviated version of their facial tattoo) on the document that gave Britain sovereignty over New Zealand, gave the Maori protection of the crown, and guaranteed them "the full exclusive and undisputed possession of their lands and estates, forests, fisheries and other properties. . . ." (February 6 is now celebrated as Waitangi Day in New Zealand, and the house of James Busby, where it was signed, is a historic reserve.)

Today it is generally agreed that the Treaty of Waitangi only helped delay the decisive struggle for land until 20 years later, when there were considerably fewer Maori and many more Pakeha in the area.

The first governor of New Zealand, William Hobson, is regarded as the architect of the ambiguously worded treaty. In May, after it had been signed by 400 chiefs from all over New Zealand, Hobson declared British sovereignty over the land. From the British point of view it was none too soon, and when a colony of French immigrants arrived in August to settle at Akaroa, on Banks Peninsula, they found the Union Jack already flying there. (They remained, anyway, and today Akaroa stands as a subtle French influence among the settlements in the South Island.)

The first capital of the new colony was Kororareka, later renamed Russell, across the bay from Paihia at the Bay of Islands. However, Hobson had the capital moved south the same year to the narrow neck of land between the Waitemata and Manukau harbors. The governor named the new site Auckland, after the governor-general of India.

More immigrants soon arrived, both directly from England and from the colony of New South Wales. Several towns were formally founded, and all went well with the Maori for more than two years. But on one occasion the British sought to arrest a feisty old chief named Te Rauparaha, who had ruled in the South Island almost as fiercely as Hongi Hika did in the North Island. The chief responded then in the time-honored way—by shooting the posse down.

A yearlong war began in 1845 at Kororareka, where, as every New Zealand schoolchild knows, a chief named Hone (John) Heke (not to be confused with Hongi Hika) regularly chopped down the flagpole as a demonstration of defiance. On other occasions, Heke's troops and the British fought each other, both in the white settlement and at Heke's well-fortified *pa* conveniently located not far away.

Under the leadership of the new governor, Sir George Grey, who was equipped with a strong military background, both Heke's troops and those of Te Rauparaha in the south were surprised and then fairly quickly disarmed. Eventually Grey came to be well loved by the Maori, who usually admired men of decisive action, in any case.

By this period, a Presbyterian Scottish colony had been established in Otago, headquartered at Dunedin, and Anglicans soon set up an agricultural settlement on the fringe of the rich Canterbury Plains at Christchurch in 1850. Descendants of pioneers in Christchurch still like to talk of their forefathers who arrived there on the "first four ships."

Other important new settlements included Nelson, which attracted a number of German newcomers, among others; New Plymouth, where the population was first welcomed by friendly Maori; and Wellington, once the immigrants learned to love the wind and live with the frequent earthquakes. There, too, the settlers printed New Zealand's first newspaper on April 18, 1840. That same year workers banded together in Wellington to successfully achieve the eight-hour workday.

In 1841 the new colony was ready for an Anglican bishop, and George Selwyn was appointed and sent out from London. Making his headquarters at Waimate, near the Bay of Islands, he became a good friend of the Maori and was known for traveling to all parts of his diocese—the entire country—on foot.

The first Roman Catholic bishop, Jean Baptiste François Pompallier, also moved around the country regularly, but in his special missionary schooner, the *Sancta Maria*. The French cleric, too, made friends among the Maori, baptizing many of them, and promising that there would be priests to follow him. The priests did not follow, however, and most of his "conversions" did not stick.

Governor Grey began to lead the colony toward self-government, which was finally achieved after the British Parliament passed the Constitution Act in 1852. It provided for a two-chamber government. The upper house would be appointed, and property owners in New Zealand could vote for members of the lower house. "Property owners" ostensibly included the Maori, but since there were few natives who owned individual property, there were few who could cast a ballot. The act also divided New Zealand into six provinces: Auckland, New Plymouth (later called Taranaki), Wellington, Nelson, Canterbury, and Otago. (Later additions included Hawke's Bay, Marlborough, Westland, and Southland.)

During that period of difficult travel and communication, provincial government was more important than the faraway national government. In fact, very little travel was done overland at all. Not the least of the problems were the many dangerous rivers, and drowning became known throughout the British Empire as "the New Zealand death."

Grey stepped down as governor and left New Zealand in 1854, but he was destined to return in a later emergency.

The Provincial Government and War—1854 to 1876

While the new Parliament argued about such things as provincial powers, there was, as the Maori say, "fire in the fern"—flames of native discontent only temporarily hidden under the cool, green surface of the North Island.

There was considerable buying of land, much of it used to amass the great estates needed to run large flocks of sheep. At the same time, the discovery of gold in California and Australia sparked similar interest in New Zealand. Major finds began to be turned over in the South Island beginning in the late 1850s, nearly always in difficult and dangerous territory. (Today the gold era is recalled in relics preserved in the wild, mountainous country around Queenstown in Northern Otago.)

In March 1859 a group of musicians in New Plymouth picked up their instruments and formed the Band of the Taranaki Volunteer Rifles, probably the first band in New Zealand. Exactly a year later, music was forgotten in New Plymouth. It was 1860; 14 years of peace had passed since "Heke's War" in the North when the fire broke out of the fern right there in Taranaki—where settlers had been welcomed so warmly a few years before. It was the beginning of a 10-year period of death and destruction, generally called the Maori Wars, although some historians say they should more correctly be called the Land Wars.

The Maori tribes had begun to see their land taken away from them through indiscriminate purchases by large numbers of Pakeha and unwise selling by naive Maori. Without the influence of Governor Grey, relationships between the two groups had deteriorated. The development of the "King Movement" in the center of the North Island was designed to unite all the tribes under a single chief, and it helped to focus the discontent. It now appeared that the Maori would have to fight for their very right to survive as a race.

The first shots were fired by the government at Waitara in March 1860, against a *pa* erected by a chief on Taranaki land who opposed the sale of the land to whites. The Maori soon evacuated the *pa,* but began to kill settlers elsewhere in reprisal. Both groups suffered grievously in the confrontations throughout the province.

Following this "Taranaki War," which lasted a year, there was the "Waikato War," and then the Second Taranaki War. A desperation move was to bring Sir George Grey back to New Zealand to talk to the Maori. This did forestall a planned major attack on Auckland, but the wars were largely being waged by a younger generation—most of the chiefs Grey had known were now dead. Also, under the new system of government, Parliament was too slow to give Grey the funds he needed.

Not all Maori supported the King Movement, incidentally. The Arawa tribe of Rotorua, for instance, fought together with the British. More importantly, they managed to keep the east coast Maori—known to be in sympathy with those fighting along the Waikato River and in the King Country—from joining in the battles.

Unfortunately the wars were prolonged by the establishment of two new fanatical religions among some Maori, the doctrines made up of a mishmash of traditional Maori beliefs and fragments of Christianity. The Hauhau, led by Te Ua, believed, among other things, that certain chants would ward off any enemy bullets. Before their numbers were decimated by this belief, they wrought considerable havoc. (In Opotiki, they slew the missionary Carl Volkner in his church; you can see the bloodstained pulpit today.)

Adherents of the Ringa-tu religion, led by a bitter chief named Te Kooti, raided Gisborne and other east coast settlements. The religion, incidentally, survives as a Maori cult in New Zealand today.

By the time the decade of wars ended, many Maori who had sought to defend their land were completely demoralized. Also, it seemed to Maori and Pakeha alike that the very numbers of the original New Zealanders were decreasing—that they were a dying race.

Land was confiscated indiscriminately, and the Maori felt a strong sense of injustice that in some cases has continued through several generations, up to the present. Nevertheless, except for a couple of brief incidents, Maori and Pakeha never fought each other again after 1870. For its part, the government henceforth made sure that the Maori were represented in the decision-making processes of the land.

New Zealanders now turned their attention to unifying their difficult land with the construction of roads, railroads, telegraph lines, and—most importantly—bridges. Due to the gold rushes, the balance of population was soon held by the South Island. New Zealanders were also beginning to make a go of sheep running, although the isolated stations (ranches) made for a lonely and often unhealthy life. They welcomed the accelerated public works program.

The treasurer (and soon prime minister), Sir Julius Vogel, financed many of these capital improvements by borrowing money overseas, and he also encouraged the immigration of 100,000 Britons. The improved communications made governing the country from a central city more practical. The capital was moved from Auckland to Wellington, and the provinces were abolished as governmental units in 1876. Their names still linger on as unofficial designations of areas of the country, but the only units of elected government below the national level are counties or boroughs, whose concerns (streets, water systems, etc.) are extremely local. This change was apparently the beginning of the "big government" concept that now pervades New Zealand life, taking over and centralizing many functions that are handled by private industries in other democracies.

Self-Government and the Welfare State—1876 to 1907

As New Zealand began to make more and more of her own decisions, she retained that British governmental system so difficult for other nationalities to grasp. Parliament (then consisting of an upper and lower house) is a lawmaking body of elected members, headed by a prime minister. He is voted into the top job by other M.P.s in his party—usually even before his party has won the majority in a general election. New Zealanders vote only for candidates to represent their own districts. The party with the most elected members then forms the government, headed by the man they have selected from among themselves. There is also a royally appointed governor, or governor-general, representing Britain's king or queen, who is officially the head of state.

Although the governor is not supposed to initiate any bills, he must sign the legislation passed by Parliament. As the years have passed, he has acted more and more on the advice of government ministers, and his role, in common with that of the British monarch, has become more ceremonial than representative of real political power.

The Maori had gained the right to elect four representatives to Parliament back in 1867, even while some Maori were still fighting the government. But when immigration was encouraged, the country's racial attitude was not as tolerant. A play produced in Auckland in 1980 reproduced a parliamentary debate of a century earlier that resulted in a resolution that New Zealand should be "for white men" and that only those of British nationality "and not naturalized British either" should be admitted.

There was strong hostility toward the Chinese in the gold fields, although the government issued a declaration coming to their defense—at least to those who were already in the country. Soon there was a special tax on the head of every Chinese person coming into New Zealand.

Despite this hindrance, many did try their luck with mining, and some stayed, eventually taking up such occupations as operating laundries, running fish-and-chips shops, or "market gardening" (truck farming). Today there are about 12,000 New Zealanders of Chinese descent, and until recently about the only ethnic restaurant that could be found in New Zealand was Chinese.

An era of social legislation began with the 1877 passage of an education act that said that public schools should be free, compulsory, and secular. An 1879 law gave every man over 21 the right to vote, and that right was extended to women in 1893—ahead of anywhere else in the world (except the state of Wyoming in the U.S. and Pitcairn Island).

Prosperity turned to depression in the 1880s, and many blamed former premier Vogel's "extravagant" public works policies. Farmers were also discouraged by the plague of rabbits that swept over the countryside, eating the grass supposedly reserved for sheep.

But these were only temporary setbacks, because an era of technology—particularly the invention of refrigeration—was beginning to help the country on its way to prosperity. In 1882, mutton was successfully shipped to Britain for the first time, and "freezing works" (that wonderful Kiwi euphemism for slaughterhouses) began to be built all over the country. Butter and cheese were also packed in the new refrigerated holds, and the mother country responded by purchasing large quantities of New Zealand's exports. It marked the beginning of small-scale intensive farming in New Zealand.

New Zealand's reputation as a law-and-order country has seldom been seriously challenged, although the gold rushes attracted several unsavory characters, generally recent arrivals from Australia, England, and the U.S. The most famous outlaws were members of the Sullivan Gang, who committed the last of several brutal murders in June 1866, ambushing four miners for their gold dust.

Investigations were perhaps easier in those days, for the technique was to immediately detain four suspicious foreigners. Under questioning, one of the four Londoners eventually informed on the other three, who were forthwith tried and executed. (The site of the ambush, "Murderers' Rock," is visited today by hikers on the Maunatapu Track, near Nelson.)

The only hanging of a woman in New Zealand occurred in 1895, when Minnie Dean, the "Winton Baby Farmer," was found guilty of murdering illegitimate babies she had accepted for adoption. (She turned out to be from Tasmania, incidentally; part of her sentence was to be buried in an unmarked grave in the Winton cemetery.)

New Zealand's best-known "criminal," however, is James McKenzie, the supposed sheep stealer, although much of his real story is unknown. With the aid of a remarkable dog, said to possess supernatural powers, the Gaelic-speaking Scot rounded up 1,000 stolen sheep and took them for great distances over what is now called the Mackenzie Country (misspelling his name) in Southern Canterbury, west of Timaru. There was considerable doubt as to his guilt, however, and McKenzie was eventually pardoned.

In the late 1800s, not everyone was engaged in sheep farming, gold mining, and road building. Labor was becoming important, and many people worked in the flax mills. Also, an unusual occupation surfaced in Northland, above Auckland, when hundreds of Dalmatians (Yugoslavs) began to poke in the earth with long sticks to search for the solidified resin from kauri trees. These "gumdiggers" sold their product for good prices, since the material was in demand for making varnish and linoleum. After the industry died, the Dalmatians remained; some took part in the wine industry, but more became farmers, and many mailboxes in the far north today bear Slavic names.

Labor unions were legal after 1878, and New Zealand suffered its first strike, a walkout of maritime workers, in 1890. The strike failed, however, and labor began to look more toward politics for help. Acts were soon passed prohibiting child labor, limiting working hours, enforcing safety and health standards, etc.

In 1895 New Zealand received a visit from an influential American tourist, the author and humorist Mark Twain. Among other things, Twain admired the Maori he met, noting with satisfaction that their population was again rising. In the book on his travels published two years later, Twain paid tribute to Maori boatbuilding, their artistic carving, and their general ability in several fields. He also praised their patriotism, loyalty, and devotion as equal to that of the British during the Maori Wars—and all this when it was not fashionable to recognize the talents and dedication of non-Caucasians.

"I do not call to mind any savage race that built such good houses or such strong and ingenious and scientific fortresses, or gave so much attention to agriculture, or had military arts and devices which so nearly approached the white man's," Twain wrote.

The Liberal party took office in 1891, and two years later the rough-talking Richard John Seddon, a former gold miner, took over its leadership. As prime minister, "King Dick" brought a dynamic, commonsense approach to government. Probably no New Zealand politician has enjoyed more personal popularity.

After the passing of an arbitration act, which sent labor-management disputes to court, his administration was practically strike-free. With the aid of Minister of Lands John McKenzie, the Seddon government set about breaking up the large estate holdings that were hampering development in the hinterlands.

A strong imperialist, the corpulent, bearded Seddon is credited with helping to establish New Zealand as an important and loyal British nation. When the Boer War opened in 1899, 6,500 N.Z. volunteers marched off to fight under British command in South Africa.

With the decline in power of the governor, Seddon set the mold for nearly autocratic rule by the prime ministers of New Zealand, a style that has generally continued into the present.

In 1900, the country declined with thanks the invitation to become part of the new Commonwealth of Australia.

Under Seddon, the government became more involved in business, not only running such things as the mail, telegraph services, telephones, and railroads, but also purchasing most of the shares of the Bank of New Zealand, establishing a national coal mine, and even buying an insurance company.

Seddon, incidentally, was not popular only in New Zealand. He visited several times in London, where he also cut an imposing figure. *Punch* once published a verse honoring him:

"When in the streets a Prince rode by
We looked at him with careless eye;
Even the most distinguished peer
Passed through our midst with scarce a cheer,
But nothing in the world would deaden
Our interest in Mister Seddon."

Seddon's most-remembered accomplishment, however, is the establishment of old-age pensions in 1898. It was the beginning of New Zealand's enlightened public welfare laws, for which it has become known throughout the world.

It was a law that went beyond a law, helping to shape a piece of the New Zealand character—one that absolutely refuses to worry unduly about the future. One story told was that of an elderly South Island miner, who was visited in his isolated cabin by an old friend. The friend asked if there was something he could do to make the miner's final years more comfortable.

"No thanks," the old man said. "Dick's seen to all that."

Seddon died in office in 1906, and he was mourned by many around the world.

The Dominion—1907 to 1945

The world has often seemed to ignore New Zealand. Due to the configuration of communication networks, lots of interesting things happen in the country that seem never to get noticed north of the equator.

In 1903 or 1904, an eccentric South Island farmer and mechanical genius built and flew a powered aircraft on a controlled path either a few months before or just after the Wright brothers accomplished the same feat. But the name Richard Pearse is never seen in a discussion of the development of aviation. (You may see his flying machines at MOTAT—a museum in Auckland.)

This intellectual isolation has been less true in the community of economic and social thinkers, however. As a successful laboratory for social legislation, New Zealand soon made her mark with these academic observers. The eminent American political scientist Frank Parsons was an early admirer. "New Zealand is the birthplace of the Twentieth Century," he wrote.

Britain changed New Zealand from a "colony" to a more dignified "dominion" in 1907, a formality that did nothing to lessen her loyalty to the mother country. As war approached in Europe, the most far-flung piece of the empire pledged full support to London, even building a warship and sending it to the British Navy. New Zealand also began compulsory military training.

Without Seddon, the Liberal party managed to hang on to the reins of government until 1911, when the Reform party squeaked into power. Dairy farmer William F. Massey was the premier destined to lead the country through World War I.

The labor arbitration court that had functioned so well under Seddon soon failed under the new government. When the court refused to grant some wage increases, there were widespread strikes in 1912 and 1913. One long waterfront strike almost spilled into a revolution. Meanwhile the working force had increased somewhat; the invention of the typewriter put hundreds of young women into New Zealand offices for the first time.

In 1914 New Zealand went to war for four years. About 8,000 men sailed for Egypt in October, and in January 1915 they helped repel Turks attacking the Suez Canal. But it was on the Gallipoli Peninsula that the New

Zealanders, together with the Australians, were to distinguish themselves while suffering heavy losses.

The ANZAC—Australian-New Zealand Army Corps—forces were ordered to land on the seaward side of the cliff-lined peninsula on April 25, capturing the Turkish positions there. The objectives were heavily defended, however, and despite vigorous fighting most Allied troops never got beyond the beaches. By the time the soldiers were evacuated at the end of the year, 8,587 Anzacs were dead and about 25,000 had been wounded. Today April 25, "Anzac Day," is marked as a national memorial holiday in New Zealand and Australia.

Later in the war a New Zealand division fought in France, and a cavalry brigade joined the British in Palestine. All together, 17,000 New Zealanders out of about 100,000 sent overseas lost their lives. It was a hard blow to a country that then numbered only a little over one million in population.

Almost forgotten today is another tragedy that took place at home—the 1918 influenza epidemic. It took the heaviest toll among the Maori, who apparently were less immune than the Pakeha. Sometimes several family members would die. The epidemic soon gave rise to a new Maori religion called "Ratana," based on a faith healer of that name. Former Maori servicemen back from World War I were not then eligible for the farm loans being offered to Pakeha. Many then joined the Ratana church, which supported traditional tribal values. The church today has about 30,000 members and exists alongside the smaller Maori church, the "Ringa-tu," established by Te Kooti.

Between the wars New Zealand joined the rest of the world in embracing new technological and cultural influences like radio and motion pictures, and welcomed the development of commercial aviation. In 1928 the first flights were made across the Tasman Sea between Australia and New Zealand.

The country's heavy dependence on British and other distant overseas markets for its meat, wool, and dairy products was its curse in 1929, and New Zealand suffered hard throughout the Great Depression. Joseph Coates, the Reform party prime minister, put many stringent measures into effect, but either they were not enough or they also contributed to the unrest. Bloody unemployment riots took place in several cities, notably the violence in Auckland's Queen Street on April 14, 1932.

There was no well-established relief system, and even disabled men had to show up for some kind of "light" government work like shoveling dirt for no apparent reason. When working, women paid into the wage unemployment fund, but out of work they were allowed no relief work or benefits.

Dr. William B. Sutch, an economist and social critic, once wrote of the situation in Christchurch: "Some of the men suffering from asthma, arthritis, rheumatism and epilepsy took from 8 o'clock to noon to cover two miles to report for duty; one woman pushed her husband in a wheelchair to Bottle Lake to call for him again in the evening. This was administrative incompetence, but there was no invalidity pension, and the principle laid down was 'no pay without work.'"

The new Labour party swept the election of 1935, although some feared that Michael J. Savage, the new prime minister, was out to destroy capitalism in New Zealand. But the policies instituted were inspired more by Franklin D. Roosevelt than by Karl Marx.

Savage set out to establish the Social Security Act. When passed, in 1938, it greatly expanded the former old-age pension plan into a retirement policy with special benefits for widows, orphans, and invalids; provided free hospital and maternity services and free medicine for all; subsidized all medical care; and guaranteed many other benefits that made New Zealand the undisputed leader among the welfare states of the world.

The 1920s and 1930s saw some rise in cultural activity in New Zealand, including art, drama, music, and literature—all perhaps stimulated by the taste of Depression adversity. Interest in the ballet seems to have begun with the 1926 visit of Anna Pavlova and her company. Opera and concert artists also began placing the major cities on their itineraries around the same time, although there was no homegrown version of these musical activities until well after World War II.

In art, Frances Hodgkins was already famous in the early years of the century; she eventually settled in England. New Zealand artists Rita Angus, Colin McCahon, and Toss Woollaston began to establish local reputations in the thirties, even if they received much less encouragement than they might have elsewhere.

The first well-known New Zealand writer was Katherine Mansfield, who settled in England before the first world war. She produced most of her short stories there, although many of her works were on New Zealand themes. Others, like Daniel Davin, followed her, leaving the country for wider stimulation and a larger market. John A. Lee's novels are mostly identified with New Zealand in the 1920s, and Ngaio Marsh began writing her successful detective thrillers in the 1930s.

During the Depression era, poetry came alive for a small coterie led by Arthur R. D. Fairburn. His satirical approach to New Zealand life may be seen in a few lines from a later poem:

"Don't be content to live in
a sort of second-grade heaven
with first-grade butter, fresh air
and paper in every toilet."

Another poet-novelist was Robin Hyde. Although wracked with illnesses, she finished six books by 1936, when she was just 30 years old. Her *Passport to Hell,* published that year, was set during World War I. In China, in 1939, she was arrested as a spy by the Japanese occupation forces, an experience she wrote about in her final book, *Dragon Rampart,* published the same year. She committed suicide that August, on the eve of World War II.

Then, the majority of New Zealanders regarded all high-toned cultural pursuits with suspicion, believing more rugged activities to be more genuine. That attitude has mellowed over the decades and the arts have attracted an increasingly strong following. Rugby, the all-consuming team sport, dates back to 1870, when it became an immediate favorite of the Maori as well as Pakeha. The national team, which seldom loses, has been known since 1905 as the All Blacks, and Maori have always been prominent on the team. Until recently, however, the Maori stayed home when the All Blacks played in South Africa.

"Ya got no 'horis' in the scrum, eh?" Maori entertainer Howard Morrison would say in a comic routine. The underlying principle was serious, however. And when New Zealanders finally did refuse to compete without the Maori, it is perhaps significant that the South Africans eventually backed down and issued the Polynesian players visas, too.

Horse racing is the second national passion, and, apparently because of its climate and soil, New Zealand consistently breeds successful Thoroughbreds, although many of them achieve fame only when running in Australia. In the depth of the depression, the biggest tragedy for many New Zealand race fans was hearing the fate of the New Zealand-raised, Australian-owned horse Phar Lap, winner of the 1930 Melbourne Cup. In 1932 Phar Lap won the Agua Caliente Handicap in California, but died after the race. New Zealanders still join with Australians in blaming the death, somehow, on the inept handling of a fine horse by the "Yanks."

When Britain declared war on Germany on September 2, 1939, New Zealand repeated the declaration just one and one-half hours later. Prime Minister Savage, who had previously opposed conscription and other defense measures, then left no doubt as to the country's position in the conflict.

"Where Britain goes, we go! Where she stands, we stand!" he said. Unfortunately, he was not able to see the war through; he died in office a few months later. He was succeeded by a fellow Labour minister, Peter Fraser, a former dockworker from Wellington.

New Zealand land forces were placed under the command of Major General Sir Bernard Freyberg, and were sent to Egypt. They saw action in the mountains of Crete, against Rommel in North Africa, up the boot of Italy, and later under General Douglas MacArthur in the Pacific, notably in the Solomon Islands.

New Zealand naval forces took part in several campaigns, including the Battle of the River Plate, when the German battleship *Admiral Graf Spee* was destroyed. Many RAF pilots and enlisted men also were New Zealanders. Later the RNZAF carried out operations against the Japanese.

Almost 200,000 New Zealanders went to war, and more than 10,000 were killed—a larger proportion of sons than many other countries gave to the campaign. One irony was that New Zealanders entered the war so quickly that they took part principally in the defense of Britain in European campaigns. When the war against Japan was declared in 1941, it was largely the United States forces who defended the Kiwi homeland. Many Americans were eventually based and trained in New Zealand, and in 1942 the U.S. became the first country outside the British Commonwealth to give full diplomatic status to its relations with New Zealand.

There is some doubt among historians that New Zealand was ever a Japanese objective, but in recent years we met a Japanese woman who said that during the war she was once employed in printing Japanese military scrip specifically marked to be used as occupation money in New Zealand.

The Postwar Period—1945 to the Present

Fraser's Labour party carried the country into the immediate postwar years with little trouble, although butter and meat rationing continued for a few years. Import controls were in effect, a frequently employed technique that keeps a lot of low-priced foreign manufactured goods from the New Zealand public. Restrictions on products from other countries have been a fact of life in New Zealand economics in greater or lesser degree for more than 50 years. In 1949, farmers and small businessmen thought there were too many controls of all types, and this became a factor in the election of the National party and Prime Minister Sidney Holland that year.

The National party, in existence since 1936, is the more "conservative" of the two main political organizations, although there is some doubt whether any party that favors so much government and so many social programs deserves that label. It has always stood for at least limited regulation of business and voluntary membership in labor unions.

The Labour party (unlike the party in Australia, they spell the word with the British "u") has strong ties with unions and their umbrella organization, the Federation of Labour (similar to the AFL-CIO in America or the ACTU in Australia). National and Labour remain the two official opposing parties in Parliament today.

All forms of art and literature began to flourish in the decades following the war. Popular culture bent enough to embrace such "man alone" themes as those used by Barry Crump in his book, *A Good Keen Man*. On a higher brow, some literary and poetry journals were established, and literature even began to attract government support. Other novelists who came to the fore were Janet Frame (*Owls Do Cry*), Ian Cross (*The God Boy*), and Sylvia Ashton-Warner (*Spinster*). Well-known poets were James K. Baxter and Kendrick Smithyman.

The founding of a dramatic group called the New Zealand Players brought some original productions to the stage, including Bruce Mason's *Pohutukawa Tree*, an exploration of Maori-Pakeha relations. Other playwrights were Allen Curnow and the poet James Baxter, equally talented and respected in the field of drama.

Art galleries were formed and welcomed the paintings of Peter MacIntyre, the prints of Mervyn Taylor and John Drawbridge, and the sculpture of Richard Cross and Molly Macalister. Except for the traditional wood carving, Maori influence has not been strong. Today, pottery is thought to be among the most advanced New Zealand art forms, with many of the potters influenced by work from Japan.

The late forties and early fifties also saw the formation of the New Zealand National Orchestra, the New Zealand Opera Company, and the New Zealand Ballet Company. Without considerable government support, though, it is doubtful that the lively or fine arts would continue to be prominent. Stewart Maclennan, once the director of the National Art Gallery, has said New Zealand life is "too even, too temperate and too secure economically, socially, and in politics and climate to foster a deeply emotional or violently expressive art."

In 1950, the weak Legislative Council—or upper house of Parliament—was abolished, leaving New Zealand as one of the very few democratic nations of the world with a streamlined, unicameral legislature.

In the past 40 years or so, New Zealand has come to regard itself more and more as a Pacific nation and to realize that it can no longer rely on Great Britain either for its markets or for its protection. In 1951 the country joined Australia and the United States in signing the ANZUS mutual security pact. While the Southeast Asia Treaty Organization (SEATO) existed, New Zealand was an active member, and sent troops to Malaysia to help fight the guerrillas there. The country was also led by the United States into the Vietnam conflict, at least to the extent of providing a small fighting unit beginning in 1965. The participation became every bit as controversial in New Zealand as it was in the U.S., however, and the New Zealand troops were pulled out in 1972.

In the 1957 elections the Labour party squeaked through, winning a majority of one in Parliament. Walter Nash became the new prime minister, and Keith J. Holyoake became leader of the opposition National party.

Holyoake didn't have to wait long for the top job. A drastic fall in overseas prices for New Zealand products forced Nash to take strict measures to deal with the deficit in the balance of payments. As ever, the increased controls were unpopular, and the National party was swept back into office in 1960.

Holyoake served for 12 years, throughout a difficult period in New Zealand's history, with many defense and trade problems. The country was still underpopulated, and the 1960s saw programs to help more British immigrants come to New Zealand. As in Australia, the immigrants were not popular with the average New Zealander, who felt these "Poms" or "Brits" thought they were coming out to "run New Zealand." Still, the majority of them soon melted into New Zealand society. There was a color bar written into the law, which prohibited nonwhite British from immigrating—a measure that has been modified today.

Except for the Maori—who have surprised everyone by increasing in population since 1896—New Zealand has always been overwhelmingly British and white. Some Chinese were willing to pay a "poll tax" to come in during the gold-rush days in the nineteenth century. In 1939 the government allowed some wives and families of New Zealand Chinese to settle in the country.

Handfuls of Indians began to immigrate to New Zealand following World War I, and have continued to do so. Some Yugoslavs and Dutch have been assimilated into the society at large; they came after World War II. A few Hungarian refugees were admitted after the Hungarian Revolution of 1956. A limited number of Vietnamese refugees were accepted following the fall of South Vietnam, and Indo-Chinese residents in the country now total many thousands.

Auckland is now described as "the largest Polynesian city in the world." To the urbanized Maori in Auckland have been added Cook Islanders, Tongans, Western Samoans, and others from islands for which New Zealand has accepted some measure of responsibility over the years. Today they are known collectively as Pacific Islanders, although many have New Zealand citizenship. There has been a certain amount of racial tension associated with them—not so much in their relations with white New Zealanders, who generally ignore them socially, but between young members of the different groups or between the islanders and city-dwelling Maori who compete with them for low-paying jobs or low-income housing.

In July 1967, New Zealand converted to decimal currency. The pound was abolished; 10 shillings (half a pound) became a New Zealand dollar;

shilling coins became 10¢ pieces; florins became 20¢ pieces; sixpences be-came 5¢, etc. The two systems existed side by side for a while, and occa-sionally today you still receive an old shilling in change instead of a 10¢-piece.

Conservation consciousness was awakened in New Zealand with the Lake Manapouri issue. Throughout the 1960s a campaign raged against raising that Fiordland lake in order to help produce cheap hydroelectric power for an Australian aluminum smelter at Bluff. A compromise was eventually reached: the lake was not raised, but the power was produced anyway. The entire power/smelter project is still debated today, long after it became a going concern. A similar campaign is being waged against an-other planned aluminum smelter in the bird sanctuary at Aramoana on the Otago Peninsula.

New Zealand officially began to object to French nuclear testing in the Pacific in the 1960s, and set up radiation laboratories to monitor radioac-tivity in the region. The opposition to nuclear weapons and nuclear power has not been strong enough for some, however, and there have been many radical demonstrations on these issues.

The massive bureaucracy produced by a government that extends into nearly every aspect of a New Zealander's life has at times proven unfair and unbending in the solving of individual problems. For this reason Parliament took a cue from the Scandinavian countries and in 1962 estab-lished the position of parliamentary commissioner—a special ombudsman to help cut through red tape in any department of government.

The idea was an almost immediate success, and the hundreds of stories of unfortunates who have had lost pensions restored or boundary fences moved, been released from mental institutions, or experienced other happy endings have served to bolster the average New Zealander's confi-dence in his way of life. The ombudsman has also explained to persons making complaints the reasons behind situations that seem at first to be unjust.

In 1967 a law on Maori participation in Parliament was changed to re-move a vestige of racism from the government. Although there are still four "Maori" members of Parliament (northern, southern, eastern, and western), even full-blooded Maori may compete for any of the 80 "European" seats. New Zealanders of part-Maori blood may also choose whether to vote as Maori or European, giving them the option to elect one of the four Maori members or one of the European members.

By the late 1960s it was apparent that Britain's entry into the European Common Market was going to doom much of New Zealand's traditional market for meat, wool, and dairy products. It was the end of an era that died hard, and as late as 1970 one New Zealand politician visited London and spoke bitterly of the Common Market as "a gigantic swindle of the British public."

But the decade was not entirely the "serious sixties." During the same years New Zealanders found themselves cheering for a polite automobile thief, convict George Wilder, who managed to relieve the boredom of confinement by escaping from prison several times, remaining at large for months on end. Wilder seemed to wander from kitchen to kitchen, at night or when nobody was home, and several North Islanders today like to boast that they once had a midnight visit from the man Howard Morrison wrote a song about—the "Wild New Zealand Boy." (The former escape artist began painting as his new prison hobby, becoming reasonably accomplished. He served his time and was eventually released—legally. An excellent outdoorsman after all that experience evading capture, he has now disappeared somewhere in New Zealand, where he may be painting still.)

Also livening things up in 1966, Captain Fred Ladd, an old-time daredevil pilot, startled everyone one March day by flying a biplane under the eight-year-old Auckland Harbor Bridge.

Labour won the elections of 1972 by a narrow margin and ran the government for the next three years, two of them under Norman Kirk as "the P.M."

An era came to a close when Kirk announced that New Zealand would no longer allow uncontrolled immigration of British and other Commonwealth citizens of European ancestry. The government also unveiled a free accident insurance program for all persons in New Zealand. (Even foreign tourists are covered today!)

An economic crisis led to more controls. After Kirk died in August 1974, Wallace (Bill) Rowling became the party—and government—leader. The New Zealand dollar was devalued twice in less than a year, and import curbs were again placed on many products. The Labour party attempted to rescue the economy by borrowing abroad and taking other desperate measures. Inflation rose to a high of nearly 18 percent.

An election in November 1975 routed Labour and gave the government to National, led by the authoritarian Rob Muldoon. He attempted to deal with rising unemployment and inflation by further immigration bans, tough price increases on government-controlled commodities, more devaluations of the New Zealand dollar, and strict wage and price freezes, which placed him in almost constant conflict with the nation's unions.

One of New Zealand's most traumatic events of the past decade was the 1981 visit of South Africa's Springbok rugby team, which played a series of exhibition matches throughout the country. The month-long tour sparked violent confrontations between two strong-willed groups. Those who were consumed by the rugby instinct said that politics and sports are two different worlds. Many others felt that South Africa's apartheid policy was so repugnant that their team should be prohibited from entering New Zealand. There were demonstrations wherever the Springboks played, and several persons were injured.

Muldoon, who sat on the fence on that issue, in other ways began aggressively running the country almost like—as one British statesman put it—a "one-man band." He assumed powers never before exercised by an New Zealand P.M., at times seemingly ruling by decree in a desperate attempt to whip the country's unwieldy economy into submission. New Zealand has never had a written constitution, and major changes in the law can be made by a simple majority vote among leaders of the party in power, a fact that makes the rights of its citizens dangerously vulnerable to autocratic decisions. It is not surprising, therefore, that the succeeding government has undertaken to create a written constitution in the form of a Bill of Rights.

If one industry and its unions reached an agreement on new salary levels, Muldoon might have stepped in and cancelled the pact, calling it "inflationary." He once negotiated a government loan from Saudi Arabia, for which the terms were kept secret. And he was criticized for using the official Security Intelligence Service (similar to the American FBI) to gather information on members of the Communist-inspired Socialist Unity party. His combative methods also extended to his relations with the press. When he took exception to articles written about him in one newspaper, he refused to seat that paper's representative at his news conferences.

Many New Zealanders liked the belligerent style of Sir Robert (he was knighted in early 1984 by Queen Elizabeth II), saying that tough times called for tough measures. He was also talented in financial affairs.

Eventually, however, he not only lost the unions, but business leaders also began to criticize him for cutting back on interest rates and investments. In the 1984 elections, Muldoon's National party was roundly defeated by Labour, bringing the rotund David Lange (pronounced "*long*-ee") into office. At 41, he became the youngest prime minister in New Zealand history.

Two crises that began in 1985 managed to thrust little New Zealand onto the world diplomatic stage and then place Lange himself directly in the international spotlight. Both dramas are related to the controversy over nuclear power and nuclear weapons in the South Pacific. In Act 1, Lange put himself in conflict with the United States, and in Act 2 his antagonist became the Republic of France.

Lange had campaigned partly on a promise to ban visits of nuclear-pow-ered and nuclear-armed ships to New Zealand; many New Zealanders be-lieve such visits by U.S. Navy vessels only make the country a strategic target in case of a future war. In a surprise to many, the new prime minister stuck to his guns and prohibited port calls by all ships suspected of either carry-ing nuclear weapons or using atomic power, which meant he had to stand up to strong diplomatic protests by the American government.

While the nation has remained a friend of the U.S. and Australia in every other way, this issue apparently invalidated the 1951 ANZUS mutual defense pact between the three countries, or at least New Zealand's par-ticipation in it. In 1986 the United States formally withdrew its commit-ment to come to the aid of New Zealand in case it is attacked. Many have forgotten, however, that New Zealand previously prohibited such visits—between 1964 and 1976—apparently without adversely affecting ANZUS. In any case, the no-port-call policy remains controversial within New Zealand, despite the efforts of the National party, now back in power, to re-vitalize New Zealand's longstanding relationship with the United States.

For at least two decades, New Zealand had been at odds with France over its testing of atomic bombs near Mururoa Atoll in the South Pacific. Then, on July 10, 1985, the ship *Rainbow Warrior*, owned by the interna-tional anti-nuclear and environmentalist organization Greenpeace, was mysteriously sunk in Auckland Harbor by an explosion that also killed one crew member. The ship had been preparing to sail to Mururoa to protest the nuclear testing. The French secret service was eventually found to be responsible for the ship's sinking, and two French agents captured in New Zealand were tried and found guilty of the crime. After serving part of their sentence in a New Zealand prison, they were handed over to French authorities on the condition that they served the remainder of their sen-tence on the French atoll of Hau. Perhaps predictably, the pair have pre-maturely returned to France. This despite the fact that the French government admitted responsibility for what Lange denounced as an act of "state-sponsored terrorism."

Since France has been an important ally in the European Economic Community, providing a good market for New Zealand's agricultural prod-ucts, and the U.S. has always been an important defense partner, both these events that have put New Zealand "on the map" have also acted to make the country somewhat nervous about the long-term effects of its un-bending stand on the two issues.

"It boosts New Zealand's profile in the world, although the point of that is somewhat moot," Lange told the *New York Times*. "We would also have a higher profile if we had a calf with eight legs."

In the face of a devalued New Zealand dollar, the Labour Government tackled other problems such as the nation's high foreign debt. The brave attempt to reduce the rate of inflation has been embraced by the National government, which came to power under former King Country farmer Jim Bolger in 1990. His government's efforts to continue what the Labour team set in motion has managed to stem the growing debt and make New Zealand's economy look healthier. Critics, nevertheless, point to subsequent job losses and other unfavorable byproducts of the change in economic direction.

As critical as New Zealanders may be of the individual forces leading them into the future, and as vulnerable as their still small-country economy makes them feel, they seem to remain optimistic about their country and its position in the world as a whole. In the same way that each house owner is possessive of his "quarter-acre section," the average New Zealander seems to retreat philosophically to the country itself, believing it to be a beautiful and basically serene bastion located safely far, far away from the ugly, dirty, and violence-prone areas of the world.

The election of 1993 introduced a new form of voting for New Zealanders—MMP, Mixed Member Proportional representation, based on a German model known as the additional member system. Under MMP, voters have two votes. The first is for a candidate standing in their electorate. The other vote is used to choose the party the voter wants to see represented in Parliament. This vote decides the number of seats each party gets in Parliament. Under MMP, when a party has a majority of seats it can form a government by itself. If no party wins a majority of seats in Parliament, the leader of the party with the most seats may try and form a government. Before a government can be formed, it may be necessary to enter into a coalition, or form an agreement with one or more parties represented in Parliament.

New Zealanders still tell the story of dynamic Prime Minister Seddon who, at the completion of a triumphant tour of Australia in 1906, boarded his ship and headed east again across the Tasman Sea. With the cheers and toasts of Australians ringing in his ears, the "fighting premier" was filled with quiet but joyful anticipation at the thought of getting under way. He sent a telegram saying he was leaving for "God's own country."

New Zealanders have often taken that phrase and played with it, asking themselves from time to time about the nation's qualifications to be the revered "Godzone." But underneath the satire there seems to be a genuine assumption that the term is basically true.

For his part Mr. Seddon, having sent his telegram, sat down with his wife on board the New Zealand-bound ship, laid his head on her shoulder, and quietly died. Many have since wondered aloud if the great man ever realized the difference between the shore he was headed for and the one he landed upon.

A Short Kiwi Who's Who

Active New Zealanders manage to dig, delve, and dive into every area of life, as do the residents of any other nation. The fame of some has spread north of the equator, of course. Others may only be well known from Bluff to Cape Reinga.

Here is an alphabetical lineup of influential New Zealanders designed to help a visitor pick up quickly on just who is doing what today in N.Z. (or what they did). Naturally they are only a few of the notables whose names you will read in the newspapers and hear on TV and radio. Generally speaking, we chose them to cover the widest range of different fields of interest and accomplishment, and we pared them down from an impossible list nearly twice as long.

BARRETT-BOYES, Sir Brian. Well-known open-heart surgeon.

BAX, Kylie. Model now residing in New York. Friend of the rich and famous and sometime escort of Donald Trump.

BEATTIE, David. Former judge and governor-general of New Zealand.

BIDWELL, Charles. Chief executive of Ceramco Corporation, one of New Zealand's most successful export companies.

BLAKE, Peter. Champion yachtsman and winner of both the 1991 Whitbread Round-the-World Race and the America's Cup.

BOLGER, Jim. Former prime minister of New Zealand. Now N.Z. ambassador to the U.S.

BRATHWAITE, Errol. Writer and author. Best known for his trilogy of novels on the Maori Wars.

BRIERLEY, Sir Ron. Stock market impresario and multimillionaire. Now lives and works principally in Australia.

BUNGAY, Mike. Wellington attorney who has defended more murder trials than any other lawyer.

CAMPION, Jane. Film director most famous for her film, *The Piano.*

CHARLES, Bob. Left-handed golfer. Probably New Zealand's best-known sportsman.

CLARKE, Helen. Leader of the Labour Party.

CLARKE, John. Real name of "Fred Dagg," New Zealand's best comedian, now a resident of Australia.

CONEY, Sandra. Feminist and author who has recently brought about a thorough investigation of medical ethics.

CROSS, Ian. Author of *The God Boy* and other books. Also chairman of the Broadcasting Commission.

CROSS, Tina. Well-known singer of popular music.

CROWE, Russell. Actor now based in Hollywood.

CRUMP, Barry. Semiretired writer. Author of *A Good Keen Man* and other books.

DEVOY, Susan. World champion squash player.

DIXON, Rod. Well-known runner. Winner of several prizes in the U.S.

DOBBYN, Dave. Top New Zealand vocalist and musician.

ELIAS, Dame Sian. First woman justice.

EWING, Barbara. Award-winning actress, now appearing in London productions.

FARR, Gareth. Percussionist and composer. Has conducted the New York Philharmonic. Precocious and talented.

FAY, Sir Michael. America's Cup challenger and Auckland merchant banker.

FITZPATRICK, Sean. One of the most famous All Blacks of recent times, and the most capped of all rugby players (Each cap denotes the number of times you have played for your country).

FLETCHER, Hugh. Head of the huge Fletcher group of companies.

FRAME, Janet. Poet and author. Known for *Owls Do Cry* and other themes of human tragedy.

GADSBY, John. One of New Zealand's best-known comedians.

GEERING, Lloyd. University professor who was tried for heresy by the Presbyterian church.

GIERINGER, Dr. Eric. He was the outspoken and controversial president of the New Zealand Medical Association. He has died, but his influence continues.

HADLEE, Sir Richard. The country's best-known cricket star.

HALBERG, Sir Murray. 1960 Olympic 5000m gold medalist and world-record holder.

HALL, Roger. Prolific playwright. Well known for recent works like *Middle Age Spread, Prisoners of Mother England,* and *Fifty/Fifty.*

HARROW, Lisa. Accomplished New Zealand stage and screen actress who frequently plays the leading role in U.K. and Australian, as well as New Zealand, productions.

HARDIE-BOYES, Sir Brian. Governor-general.

HERCUS, Dame Ann. Former government minister and now N.Z.'s permanent UNO representative in New York.

HILLARY, Sir Edmund. All-around explorer and the first to climb Mount Everest. Also famous for Antarctic explorations.

HOLMES, Paul. Television and radio host, currently one of the leading television presenters.

HOPKINS, John. National Orchestra conductor.

HOUSTON, Michael. Accomplished New Zealand pianist.

HULME, Keri. Author of *The Bone People*, which won the prestigious British literary award, the Booker Prize.

HUNT, Sam. Modern poet and a controversial character.

HUNTER, Rachel. Successful international model, once married to singer Rod Stewart.

HURST, Michael. Actor popular with Americans as Iolos, sidekick to Hercules in the popular *Hercules: The Legendary Journeys*, filmed in N.Z.

IHIMAERA, Witi. Novelist and former member of New Zealand's diplomatic staff in New York.

JACKSON, Peter. Film director. Now based in Hollywood, where he is in big demand.

JAMES, Dame Naomi. Sailed single-handedly around the world in 272 days in 1978, breaking Sir Francis Chichester's record.

JONES, Sir Robert. Self-made millionaire, property speculator, TV personality, and author.

JONES, Vaughan. Distinguished mathematician who won the world's highest accolade in math in 1991.

KOEBERGER, Anneliesa. Top New Zealand skier and silver medal winner at her first Winter Olympics in 1992.

LAIDLAW, Chris. Former All Black, high commissioner to Zimbabwe, and now race relations conciliator.

LANGE, David. Former Labour government prime minister of New Zealand.

LAWLESS, Lucy. Actress most famous for her part in *Xena, Warrior Princess*, a series that reached cult status worldwide.

LEWIS, Chris. New Zealand's biggest tennis star today.

LEWIS, David. Explorer and yachtsman. Sailed around the world alone and crossed the Pacific without instruments, etc.

LOMU, Jonah. Young rugby star and hero to aspiring All Blacks. Nearly as famous for his emotional life as his professional life.

LYDIARD, Arthur. Famous athletic coach and trainer.

McINTYRE, Peter. Popular landscape artist who works in oils and watercolors.

McPHAIL, David. Impressionist and comedian. Now rivaling Fred Dagg (John Clarke) for title of N.Z.'s number-one funnyman.

MAUGER, Ivan. Six-time world champion motorcycle racer.

MOLLER, Lorraine. Runner. Top women's finisher in the 1984 Boston Marathon.

MOORE, Mike. Former leader of the Labour Party and N.Z.'s representative at WHO.

MORRISON, Sir Howard. Comedian, singer, and probably the best-known all-around N.Z. entertainer. Also works with Maori youth projects.

MORRISON, Temuera. Nephew of Sir Howard. Actor who has enjoyed considerable success and appeared in two Hollywood movies.

MULDOON, Sir Robert. Former prime minister and former leader of the National party. Now deceased but still making an impact.

MURPHY, Geoff. Award-winning New Zealand film producer.

MYERS, Douglas. Well-known business executive and chief of New Zealand Breweries, brewers of Lion Red.

NEILL, Sam. Actor who has enjoyed considerable success not only in Hollywood but worldwide.

O'NEILL, Sharon. Well-known pop music singer.

PALMER, Geoffrey. Former prime minister of New Zealand.

PAQUIN, Anna. Actress now based in the U.S. One of the youngest winners ever of an Oscar, at age 11.

PORTER, Nyree Dawn. N.Z. actress, living in London. Remembered for her role as Irene in the TV production of *The Forsyte Saga*.

RATA, Matua ("Mat"). Former member of Parliament for Northern Maori region. Now leader of the Motu Manahaki party.

REEVES, Sir Paul. Former bishop and governor-general, the first Maori to hold this post.

RICHARDSON, Ruth. Former finance minister in the Bolger Government of New Zealand.

ROE, Allison. Runner. Set world's record for women in the 1982 New York Marathon.

SCHAFFER, Peter. American violinist, now concertmaster with the New Zealand Symphony Orchestra.

SHADBOLT, Maurice. Prominent New Zealand novelist.

SHIPLEY, Jenny. Prime minister.

SINCLAIR, Sir Keith. Historian.

SKELTON, Bob. N.Z.'s best-known jockey and the leader of a family of Skeltons, all jockeys.

SNELL, Peter G. Athlete who was a champion middle-distance runner during the 1960s. Won gold medals at the Olympics.

TAMAHORI, Lee. Film director now based in Hollywood.

TE ARIKINUI, Dame Te Ata I Rangi kaahu. Queen of the Maori, a title inherited from the "King Movement" of a century ago.

TE KANAWA, Dame Kiri. Maori woman who has become New Zealand's most famous operatic star. She sang at the royal wedding of Charles and Diana in 1981.

TELFORD, Max. Marathon runner. Now lives part-time in Hawaii.

TIZARD, Dame Catherine. Mayor of Auckland and governor-general of New Zealand.

TODD, Mark. Equestrian gold medal winner (on Charisma) at the 1984 and 1988 Olympics.

UNKOVICH, Nick. The country's best-known bowls star.

WALKER, John. Runner and former world's record holder and Olympic gold medalist in the mile.

WARING, Marilyn. Outspoken feminist and former M.P.

WHITEHEAD, Gillian. British-based N.Z. composer. Her opera *Tristan and Iseult* premiered in 1980.

WILDER, George. Escape artist and "lovable crook." An excellent bushman and self-taught painter.

WILLIAMS, Peter. Perhaps N.Z.'s most tenacious defense attorney. Has successfully defended many on drug charges.

WOOLLASTON, Toss. One of New Zealand's most renowned artists.

A Dash of Enzeddish and Godzone Slang

Traveling Americans will find more similarities than differences between the speech patterns of New Zealanders and Australians. In both cases, some mysterious sickness seems to adversely affect their vowels and contract their syllables.

Those very familiar with both countries will notice some subtle changes in tone as well as temperament on crossing the Tasman. To American ears, the phrase "six hours" might be rendered by Australians as "seeks Oz." Now listen to the New Zealanders, some of whom seem to utter the same words as "sex as."

It's not true that New Zealand English is influenced by the collective "baa" of 70 million sheep. But if a Kiwi tells you that the person you're looking for is "at a tan," you'll soon learn he is out of town. (Now practice this: "Haa naa, bran caa?")

Understanding accents is, to a large extent, just a matter of learning how to tune in. Once you're in New Zealand for a few days, you'll notice it's fun to apply the necessary correction factors. You'll also see that there is considerable variation in the New Zealand accent from one person to another.

If you're introduced to someone named "Tiny Woolsin" (or was it "Donny Wallsen"?), wait a minute and the penny will drop: Tony Wilson, of course! Similarly, "Freed Janes" or "Frid Jines" (or did he say "Janz"?) will eventually be distilled into Fred Jones.

There are also many expressions for which the meaning, if not the origin, is usually obvious. Some kindly Kiwis insist on liberally throwing out enthusiastic clichés like "Good as gold!" or "Go for your life!" Some more interesting phrases include "It's about as useful as a glass eye at a keyhole," "He's as happy as Larry," and "She's as silly as a two-bob watch!"

Another odd habit, perhaps most prevalent on the North Island, is to finish off what is undoubtedly a flat statement with just a hint of a question: "We're going to the pictures, eh?" (Sometimes the final syllable is pronounced more like "aye," but it is always written "eh.") Strangely, the final inflection does not rise in tone as you might expect.

A statement that puts forth the speaker's opinion about something is sometimes given a more prominent interrogatory tag, seemingly seeking approval of some kind: "It doesn't seem worth it, does it?" or "It's much better to be polite, isn't it?"

The major problem for most Yanks is simply that Kiwi English includes many terms that are virtually unknown in North America. Some may have simply been forgotten in the dust of history, like the "wee" and "chain" they're so fond of in Dunedin.

Others, of course, are locutions still in daily use in England (petrol, bonnet, chemist, etc.), and are generally understood throughout member nations of the British Commonwealth. If you've traveled in the U.K., or see a lot of Rank movies, you'll already be considerably ahead of the linguistic game in New Zealand. With apologies to British subjects who may be following our etymological tour, we have had to include at least a few essential Pom terms in our list over the next few pages.

Incidentally, a phrase often used by newspapers and on radio or television news in New Zealand—as in Britain—has apparently been adopted for legal reasons. Following a story about some sort of disturbance—a fight in a pub, perhaps, or even a more serious crime—the report will state rather dryly: "A man is assisting police with their inquiries." We doubt that the anonymous helpful citizen referred to is dispensing quite as much good will as it might appear. Translated, of course, it means they think they caught the bloke who caused all the trouble.

Don't forget that British English has set the standard for grammar and spelling in New Zealand. Words like "government" and "corporation" are collective nouns and take plural verbs—"The company are going to . . ." etc. Also, abbreviations are written without periods after them (Mr Jones, Main St, etc).

Although the less frivolous New Zealanders do not seem to have embraced the Australian's fondness for rhyming slang and the like, many words and phrases have been imported from Australia. With a tip of our bush hats toward the west, we've inserted a few of these that have been thoroughly adopted ("tucker," "dunny," and other colorful outbackisms) in our list. (Some other Aussie terms New Zealand may have picked up you'll have to fossick for from our Australia volume.)

Many Maori words and phrases have been carried over into the Pakeha language. Some have held up almost intact in the original vernacular: "Taihoa!" for "Hey, wait a minute!" Others have been bowdlerized. The Maori word *pakaru* meaning "broken" has been changed by no-nonsense New Zealand-ers into "puckerooed." Entries in the following list that retain their original Maori identity nearly intact (like *hangi* and *haka*), we have marked with an "M" in parentheses. (We have not included Maori words for things like certain birds and vegetables that would duplicate lists that appear elsewhere.) Most Maori words are accented on the first—or sometimes second—syllable.

Incidentally, before we forget it, there seems to be no final authority you can go to hear the "correct" pronunciation of all the Maori names for rivers, towns, etc. Pakeha have been fouling up Maori words for at least two hundred years now, and many of the bastardizations have become standardized.

Even the Maori don't agree on pronunciation, what with tribal differences and especially the debate between the North Island and the South Island tribes. New Zealand radio announcers (who often sound more Pom than Kiwi) do try to keep up with the latest trends on Maori pronunciation (faithfully enunciating the town of Whakatane as "*fah*-kah-*tah*-nay"), although to others their efforts often seem affected.

Until you get used to them, it may seem that Maori words all sound alike, most of them an unpronounceable bag of mixed-up *k*s and *w*s. And by the way, some New Zealanders may swear to you that there is really a place somewhere in the country with the Maori name Waikikamukau. We've hunted everywhere, however, and now think the story is strictly apocryphal. Waikikamukau, of course, would be pronounced "Why-kick-a-moo-cow?"

Lastly, there are several words in the New Zealand language whose origins are more obscure and that do not appear to be Britishisms, Australianisms, or Maori. "Grotty," meaning very dirty, is one of those, and the *New Zealand Dictionary* suggests it may have been a flippant interpretation of "grotesque." (Another theory, held by our Auckland actress friend Margaret Blay, has to do with the fact that "underground men's lavatories" in New Zealand are sometimes called "grots"—and that, in turn, may simply be a contraction of "grotto.") But then what about "jack up"? And "how's-your-mother"? And "opportunity shop"? No one seems to know for sure.

We've also included a few common abbreviations in the following list, which should at least help interpret some newspaper headlines. The entire list is far too long, but we simply couldn't bear to cut it down any more than we have done already. You'll find some of these as well as some other Kiwi terms used throughout the rest of the book, too. Hopefully that will put you ahead of the language game before you arrive.

For an exhaustive and amusing study of New Zealand terminology, we highly recommend a pocket-size volume entitled *A Personal Kiwi-Yankee Dictionary,* by Louis S. Leland Jr., an American psychology professor who has lived in New Zealand for more than a decade. (In the U.S. it's published by Pelican Publishing Company.) If we had only discovered that excellent collection before preparing this list, we could have avoided a lot of work!

A

Afters. Dessert. (See also "pudding.")
Airy-fairy. Idealistic. Impractical.
All Blacks. New Zealand national rugby team.

B

Bach. Vacation cabin. Weekend cottage (pronounced "batch").
Backblocks. Remote area.
Bail up. Trap in a corner. Put a cow in a pen.
Barrack for. Cheer for.
Barrister. Type of lawyer who goes to court.
Bat, off your own. Independent. Without help.
Beautiful. Sometimes means "delicious."
Bent. Mentally twisted. Also drunk.
Biff. Throw or toss.
Biscuit. Cookie or cracker. Sometimes "bickie."
Bloody. The all-purpose adjective. (Somewhat profane.)
Bluey. Pack. Equipment. Also a traffic ticket.
Bob. Formerly a shilling. Now sometimes a 10¢ coin.
Bonnet. Hood (over a car motor).
Boohai. Remote area. Outback.
Boot. Trunk of a car (where the spare tire is).
Boozer. Party.
Bore. Well.
Bowser. Gasoline pump.
Box of birds, a. Feeling healthy (like "fit as a fiddle").
Braces. Suspenders.
Browned off. Disgusted. Irritated. Angry.
Bush. Woods. Forest. Wild area.

C

Cabinet ministers. M.P.s appointed to cabinet posts by the P.M.

Campervan. Camper (truck).

Caravan. House trailer. Mobile home.

Casuals. Hotel diners not staying in the house.

Cattery. Boarding kennel for cats.

Cattle run. Ranch for cattle.

Cert. school. Short for school certificate (high-school diploma).

Chain. 22 yards (used in Dunedin and Southland).

Chain, pull the. Flush the toilet.

Cheesed off. Fed up. Exasperated.

Chemist. Pharmacist. Druggist.

Chilly bin. Portable cooler. (What Aussies call an Esky.)

Chips. French-fried potatoes.

Chockablock. Filled to the brim. Overstuffed.

Chooks. Chickens. (Mainly Australian. Less common than "fowls" in N.Z.)

Chunder. To vomit.

Cloakroom. Toilet (seen printed on doors).

Coach. Long-distance (not city) bus.

Cobber. Friend.

College. High school.

Come a gutser. Make a bad mistake.

Compere. Moderator. Master of ceremonies.

Concession. Discount.

Cooey. An attention-getting cry. Also, shouting distance.

Coot. Guy.

Cornies. Corn flakes.

Cot. Baby's crib (important for room reservations).

Cotton. Thread. (Tuft cotton is "cotton wool.")

Cowbail. Cow pen (usually for milking).

Cow cocky. Dairy farmer.

Cowshed. Barn.

Crib. Vacation home or cabin. (Used in the south of the South Island.)

Crikey! General exclamation.

Crook. Broken. Sick. No good. (Also criminal.)

Cuppa. Tea ("cup of").

D

Dag. Funny person. Also piece of wool encrusted with mud and feces.

Dairy. Small grocery. (Like "deli" in the U.S.; often sounds like "dearie.")

Daks. Undershorts in N.Z. (Trousers in Australia.)

DB. A brand of beer (Dominion Breweries).
Docket. Receipt or bill.
Domain. Public park.
Drapery. Shop selling cloth, thread, yarn, etc.
Dressing gown. Bathrobe.
DSIR. Abbr. for Dept. of Scientific and Industrial Research.
Dummy. Baby's pacifier.
Dunny. Toilet (especially if outdoors).
Dustbin. Garbage can.

E

Ear-bashing. Talking too much.
Enzed(er). New Zealand(er).

F

Facilities. Bath and toilet (a hotel euphemism).
Fair go. Good chance.
Fancy dress. Costume.
Flash. Fancy. Ostentatious.
Flat out. As fast as possible. (Also "flat to the boards.")
Flex. Electric extension cord.
Flog. To sell.
FOL. Abbreviation for Federation of Labour.
Footpath. Sidewalk (not a trail; "pavement" in England).
Forms. Intermediate and high-school levels. (Form 1 is usually equivalent to grade 7, for 12-year-olds.)
Fortnight. Two weeks. (14 nights.)
Fowls. Chickens.
Franking machine. Postage meter.
Freezing works. Slaughterhouse.
Fridge. Refrigerator.
Frock. Dress.
Fruiterer. Person who sells fruit (and sometimes vegetables).

G

Gaol. N.Z./British spelling of jail.
Gear. Clothing or equipment.
Get cracking! Get a move on!
Give way. Yield (a traffic sign).
Go. A chance, an opportunity, or an attempt.
Godzone. New Zealand (from "God's own country").

Good screw. High wages.
Grog. Liquor or any alcoholic drink.
Grotty. Very dirty (more so than "scungy").
Gubbins. Ingredients.
Guff. Nonsense. Something unwanted and unneeded.
Gumboots. Knee-length, waterproof boots. ("Wellingtons" in England.)
Gumdigger. One who digs for kauri gum (resin).
Gumfield. Area where kauri gum is found.

H

Haere mai (M). Hello.
Haere ra (M). Good-bye.
Haka (M). A fast Maori dance, traditionally done as a challenge.
Handle. Stein of beer (usually 12 ounces).
Hangi (M). Maori feast, usually with entertainment.
Hard case. Amusing person.
Header. A farm combine.
High country. Mountainous area.
Hoe into. Dig into (your "tucker") enthusiastically.
Hokonui (M). Illegal liquor. Moonshine.
Holiday. Vacation.
Home. Nostalgic term for Great Britain.
Homestead. Ranch house. Farmhouse.
Home unit. Condominium apartment.
Hori (M). George. Now slang for any Maori man.
Hotel. Sometimes means only bar or "pub."
Housie. Bingo.
How's-your-mother. Whatchamacallit. Miscellaneous.
Huli (M). Party.

J

Jack up. Arrange for.
Jersey or *jumper.* A pullover sweater.
Joker. Guy.
Judder bars. Speed bumps.

K

Kai (M). Food. A meal.
Ka pai (M). Okay. Good.
Kerb. Curb (British spelling).
Kia ora (M). Welcome.

Kilos. Short for kilograms, usually.

Kit. Basket made of flax. (Maori: kete.)

Kiwi (M). Originally, the flightless bird. Now slang for New Zealander or anything associated with New Zealand, such as Kiwi land, etc.

Kiwi fruit. More commercial name for Chinese gooseberry.

Ks. (Pronounced "kays.") Slang for kilometers or kph.

L

Ladder. Run in stocking.

Least, at. Often used by the speaker to correct himself, similarly to "I mean." (Perhaps originally an equivocation.)

Left luggage. Baggage room.

Letter box. Mailbox.

Lift. Elevator.

Lollies. Candy. (Lollipops.)

Loo. Toilet.

Lot, the. The whole thing. All of it.

Lounge. Living room.

Lounge suite. Set of living-room furniture.

Lucerne. Alfalfa.

M

Maimai (M). Hunter's duck blind.

Main. Main course on a menu (never an "entree").

Marae (M). Maori meeting place, cultural center.

Mate. Friend. Good buddy. (Does not mean spouse.)

Mere. (M). Hand club. (Sometimes made of greenstone.)

Metal surface. Gravel.

Mighty. An adjective of admiration. (A "mighty" woman.)

Mil. Short for milliliter. (Abbreviated ml.)

Milk bar. Soda fountain.

Milk factory. Dairy.

Mince. Chopped meat.

MMP. (Mixed Member Proportional) Current political system based on proportional representation.

Mo. Mustache.

Monkey's birthday. Rain while the sun is shining.

Mozzies. Mosquitoes.

M.P. Abbreviation for member of Parliament.

Muckin' about. Fooling around.

Mug. Idiot. Butt of the joke.

Muster. To round up.
Muttonbirding. Hunting a type of shearwater (muttonbird).

N

Nana. Brain (like head).
Nappies or *napkins.* Diapers.
Narc. Spoilsport.
Netting. Screen (when fine). Chicken wire (when coarse).
Nip. Small measurement of liquor (about half a shot).
Nippers. Young children.
Notes. Paper money (dollar bills).

O

Ocker. In Australia, this usually means an unsophisticated person. But in
    New Zealand it usually means "Australian." (Careful!)
Old boys/old girls. Alumni.
Opportunity shop. Secondhand goods store.
Outback. Rural areas.

P

Pa (M). A fortified Maori village.
Paddock. Field. Meadow.
Page boy. Bellhop.
Pakeha (M). White person (non-Maori).
Panel beating. Automobile body and fender work.
Passage. Hallway.
Paua (M). Abalone.
Penny drops, the. Delayed, but sudden, understanding.
Perm. Permanent wave.
Phone box. Phone booth.
Planted, get. Get punched, socked.
Plurry (M). Maori interpretation of "bloody."
P.M. Abbreviation for prime minister.
Pommie or *pom.* Englishman (somewhat derogatory).
Pong. Unpleasant smell. Stink.
Pongo. Englishman (definitely derogatory).
Poofter. Homosexual.
Popsie. Unmarried woman.
Post a parcel. Mail a package.
Postie. Letter carrier.
Pram. Baby carriage.

Prang. Crash. Wreck.
Primers. Primary school.
Pub. (Short for public house.) Bar. (Also sometimes means "hotel.")
Publican. Barkeeper. Bartender.
Puckerooed. Ruined. Broken.
Pudding. Dessert (of any kind).
Punter. Bettor (on a race, etc.).
Push bike. Pedal bike (not motorized).
PYO. Abbreviation for Pick Your Own fruit.

Q

Queue. Line of people waiting for something.

R

Rail car. Short passenger train (usually two or three cars long).
Railway. Railroad.
Railways Road Services. (NZRRS) Intercity bus line (believe it or not).
Ratbag. Mischievous child. Eccentric person.
Rates. Property tax.
Reel of cotton. Spool of thread.
Return ticket. Round-trip ticket.
Ring up. Call up on the phone.
Ripper. Something outstanding (or sometimes very funny).
Road works. Sign indicating highway is under construction.
Rot. Nonsense.
RSA. Abbr. for Returned Services Association (like the VFW).
Rubber. Eraser.
Rub out. Erase.
Rugger. Rugby football.

S

Sack. To fire from a job. (Also "get the sack," to be fired.)
Scatty. Unstable (person).
Scheme. Method or system. (Not necessarily with a nefarious connotation.)
Scone. Type of pastry. Also slang for "brain."
Scrub. Bushland. Underbrush.
Scrum. Scrimmage (in rugby).
Scungy. Dirty (but not as dirty as "grotty").
Sealing. Paving. Paved surface.
Section. House lot.
Serviette. Napkin.

Shed. Barn.
She's right! Everything's okay.
Shift. Move location (houses or offices).
Shop. Store.
Shop assistant. Sales clerk.
Shout. Buy a drink for or treat someone.
Singlet. Undershirt.
Sing out. Call. Cry out.
Sitting. Taking an examination.
Slip. Landslide.
Slog. Hard going.
Smoko. Short break for coffee or cigarettes.
Solicitor. Lawyer who doesn't appear in court.
Sound. Fiord.
Spa pool. Jacuzzi or natural mineral pool.
Stalls. Ground-floor theater seats.
Starters. Appetizers (on a menu); sometimes called "entree."
Station. Ranch or farm.
Sticky tape. Clear (Scotch) tape.
Stirrer. Troublemaker. Activist.
Stock. Farm animals.
Stockyard. Corral.
Stone the crows! All-purpose exclamation.
SUP. Abbreviation for Socialist Unity party.
Suspenders. Garters.
Swedes. Rutabaga.
Sweets. Candy or dessert.

T

TAB. Abbr. for Totalisator Agency Board (off-track betting shop).
Taiaha (M). Maori long club.
Taihoa! (M). Wait a minute!
Tangi (M). Mourning ceremony.
Tapu (M). Sacred. Taboo. Forbidden.
Tariffs. Hotel rates.
Tar sealing. Asphalt. Blacktop.
Teem. Rain heavily.
Telly. Television.
Test or *test match.* International championship game.
Tick. Check mark.
Tip. Rubbish dump.

Togs. Swimming suit.
Tolls. Long-distance phone calls.
Too right! Definitely! (Emphatic expression of agreement.)
Track. Trail.
Tramp. Hike.
Trendy. Avant-garde. Very stylish.
Trotters. Feet.
Trots, the. Harness races.
Try. Four-point score in rugby.
Tucker. Food.

U

UE. Abbr. for university entrance examination.
U-ey. (Pronounced "UE") U-turn in traffic.
U.K. Abbr. for United Kingdom (Great Britain).
Unit. Commuter train (principally in Wellington).
Ute. Pickup truck (utility).

V

Varsity. University.
Venue. Staging area. Site. Headquarters.

W

Wahine (M). Woman (usually Maori woman).
Warrant of fitness. Auto safety inspection certificate.
Wee. Small.
Whare (M). House out back for the hired help.
Wharfy. Longshoreman. Dock worker.
Wireless. Radio.
Wool. Also used to mean yarn.

Y

Yank. American.
Yarn. Conversation.

Z

Zed. New Zealand/British pronunciation of "Z."

What's in a Name?

The names sprinkled over the map of New Zealand form a strange mosaic consisting of traditional appellations imported from Great Britain or the titles of various patrons and public benefactors, combined with the sometimes lilting, sometimes staccato sounds of Maori.

The longest name in the country, by the way, belongs to a hill on the North Island, near Dannevirke, which tells a whole story in a single word: Taumata-whakatangihanga-koauau-o-Tamatea-turi-pukaka-pikimaunga-pokai-whenua-ki-tana-tahu ("the hill on which Tamatea with the big knees, who roamed the country, played his lament on his flute to the memory of his brother") Understandably, there are some variations in the spelling in different accounts. Locally, they usually just call the hill "Tamatea" for short.

Maori words with a background in the Pakeha culture also have shown up in some places. There's a tiny mountain town on the North Island named "Hihitahi," whose name is usually translated as "one stitchbird." But Auckland radio personality Merv Smith gave us the lowdown on that one. Smith, a steam-railroad buff, said that the name comes from a whispering interpretation of the train sound as it came puffing around a nearby bend: "*Hīhi-ta*hi, *hī*hi-*ta*hi."

In a third category of names are the simple descriptive labels given out a century or so ago by settlers, shepherds, sailors, and prospectors who took a no-nonsense approach to naming the land—even while others tried to dignify the process.

Some of our favorites include the following:

Terrible Billy, a swamp not far from Mount Hutt, was first named in Latin by an academic type as Pupus (meaning "marsh") Terribile (pronounced "Tear-*ree*-be-lay"). Understandably that was a little too much for the neighborhood. "Pupus" eventually sank into the muck and "Terribile" was turned into "Terrible Billy."

Gummie's Bush, a town near Riverton in the South Island, once belonged to an old Maori. That's right; he had no teeth.

Fright Cove is near the southernmost tip of Stewart Island. Its story is best told in a ship's log, dated May 6, 1850: "At dinner time yesterday, one of those absent on duty was solacing himself with 'a pipe among the bushes' not dreaming anything that lives or breathes intruded itself between him and his messmates. But a huge seal had previously emerged from the waters and gone ashore to take his siesta beneath the shelter of this very spot.

"Annoyed doubtless by the unwanted odor of the weed, he elevated his bull dog visage right vis-à-vis to the smoker. Their astonishment was mutual. . . ."

5

Auckland and
the North

1. The General Picture

Auckland, principal city of an island nation, is itself almost an island. If the ancient volcanic forces that built the northern peninsula of New Zealand had given an extra hiccup—or perhaps another sigh—the waters of Waitemata Harbor and the great Hauraki Gulf to the east might have rushed in to join with Manukau Harbor and the Tasman Sea to the west in a pair of swirling straits.

As it is, however, the site of Auckland is a one- to-seven-mile-wide isthmus, seemingly (but not quite) surrounded by cool, clear water. Genuine islands there are aplenty in this maritime environment. Just a short distance from the bustle of business, many of them appear almost as wild as the day they were "born." The lovely symmetrical island visible from many areas of the city is Rangitoto, a sleeping volcano that last erupted only about 252 years ago.

Auckland was founded in 1840 as the capital of New Zealand because Governor William Hobson valued its strategic—not scenic—importance. The narrow, hilly strip provided panoramic points from which to witness the activities of the Maori tribes. The white settlements to the north were to be protected by the new capital, acting as both an observation post and first line of defense against any war canoes that might be launched by the original New Zealanders against the newcomers. The settlement remained the seat of government for 25 years, until Wellington took over the job in 1865.

Perhaps Hobson's only mistake was in his choice of a name. "Auckland," a squawking, awkward sound, after all, has little meaning today. It was chosen to honor George Eden, the first Earl of Auckland and Viceroy of India, whose personality and exploits have now dimmed in international recollection.

It might have been better if Hobson had taken the Maori name, Tamaki ("*Tom*-a-key"), or Tamaki-makau-rau—"the spouse of a hundred lovers." From this far corner of the earth, an exotic city called Tamaki might have attracted more romantic attention from the world over the past century and a half.

The Tamaki Isthmus was known and loved by the Maori. It was originally marked by more than 60 distinct volcanic cones, and many of these elevations were further carved by the Polynesians into elaborate *pa*—fortified villages with sophisticated earthwork redoubts. Two of the tallest hills, Mount Eden and One Tree Hill, today form the green nuclei of city parks. In clear weather, when the sun angles low on the horizon, the intricate breastworks of the ancient Maori may be briefly seen in soft, shadowy outline. Many of the other hills of Auckland have been excavated completely out of existence.

To stand today in Queen Street, the mercantile axle of Auckland, is to conclude that here is not really a glamorous city. However, its physical setting is certainly glorious, and it is still one of the few urban areas in the world where the cries of seagulls often drown out the noise of traffic. In fact the city is as it has always been, an efficient gateway to the charms of the North Island and thence to the nation as a whole. In recent years local boosters have begun to play down such traditional sobriquets as the "Gateway City" or the "Queen City," drawing instead on the cheerful aspect of Auckland's wonderful bays and harbors, often full of pleasure craft. Now they call it the "City of Sails." The name has become even more apt since Auckland wrested the America's Cup from the Santiago Yacht Club in 1996. Team New Zealand, captained by Whitbread Round-the-World yachtsman Sir Peter Blake, was defending its hold on yachting's most coveted prize on the Hauraki Gulf as the eleventh edition of this book went to print.

The large majority of Auckland's almost 1,300,000 population consists of the white descendants of New Zealand's British settlers. Nevertheless, the Tamaki Isthmus is not far from the centers of Maori culture, and the commercial glitter of the metropolis has drawn many Maori into a crowded urban existence. Add to these the thousands of Pacific islanders who have immigrated over the past few decades, and today's Auckland rivals Honolulu for the title of the largest Polynesian city in the world.

It is by far New Zealand's healthiest city, financially speaking. In a country with a generally static population, Auckland is growing. Afflicted more than any other city in the country with urban sprawl, it has expanded for miles north and south in a colorful mosaic of single-family houses, each on the quarter-acre island of tranquility that most New Zealanders seem to believe is their God-given right.

Until the 1980s, there were almost no apartment buildings in the high-rise sense. Many have now been constructed, and apartment living is increasing, especially on the fringes of the inner city. Some of the large older homes near the inner city have been carved into "flats" (separate dwelling units). A few of them are low-quality housing occupied mostly by students and others of modest means. They are the closest things in the city to slums, although the word does not quite fit in this egalitarian, socially conscious nation where the rich are seldom *very* rich and the poor are apparently never quite destitute.

The expanding network of limited-access motorways is evidence of Auckland's municipal foresight; together with the Auckland Harbor Bridge, a landmark linking the older streets with the northern suburbs, it makes the city easy to get into—and out of—even during heavy traffic periods.

To the north, some of New Zealand's brightest and sunniest countryside coaxes city dwellers and travellers alike into a green land of rolling hills and attractive coastlines. In the northwest are the great *kauri* forests, the last sanctuaries for the magnificent giant trees that once grew in dense abundance over the entire island. East of there is the appealing mixture of sea and shore that Captain Cook named the Bay of Islands. There are also orchards and mission stations, established by the first European settlers, which still nourish the bodies and poetic souls of those who seek them out.

Further up the people-scarce peninsula is the land local boosters call the "Winterless North." It's not quite in the tropics, but you may notice a balmier feeling as you drive at 80 km/h right on top of the wide, white sands of Ninety Mile Beach up to Cape Reinga and its lonely lighthouse. This was once the jumping-off place from which the old Maori propelled themselves from the North Island into the spirit world.

To experience and appreciate the life and times in this faraway country of islands, "Tamaki" and the Northland together form the ideal launching point.

2. Long-Distance Transportation

If you're lucky enough to arrive in Auckland by ship, you'll sail through the magnificent Hauraki Gulf, glide past scores of inviting islands, and eventually turn into the Waitemata Harbor on the northeast side of the city. Ships nose in at Princes Wharf, conveniently right downtown, at the foot of Albert Street.

We docked there on a sunny day one year after having cleared customs aboard the *Royal Viking Star*, had a reserved Hertz car waiting at the pier, and then drove right off into New Zealand. It was one of the easiest, most pleasant entries we've ever made into the country.

When Auckland found itself host to the next America's Cup Challenge, plans to enhance the city harbor area and Princes Wharf were accelerated, and the place is now buzzing with restaurants and apartments. The word is that a Hilton Hotel has secured the prime site on the end of Prince's Wharf.

Air Travelers. If you're flying into Auckland, you'll touch down at **Auckland International Airport.** The airport is more often called "Mangere" (*Man*-gary) by locals and frequent travellers, named for the suburb where it's located, 13 miles south of Auckland itself.

Mangere processes about 80 percent of the air arrivals to the country and is served by 26 international airlines. It has recently been expanded, and facilities are modern and welcoming. You collect your baggage directly in the customs hall. Porters are few, so it's best to load your goods and chattels onto one of the little carts that are plentiful and provided free, and then push them to the inspection station.

The domestic and international terminal buildings are about a mile from each other—a pleasant walk, without luggage; a shuttle bus is available for about a dollar. Several airlines are represented at the airport, including **Air New Zealand** (Tel. 357-3000); **Air Pacific** (Tel. 379-2404); **British Airways** (Tel. 356-8690); **Canadian Airlines** (Tel. 309-0735); **Ansett New Zealand** (Tel. 0800-267-388); **Polynesian Airlines** (Tel. 309-5396); **Qantas** (Tel. 357-8900); and **United** (Tel. 379-3800). You will also find airline desks for **Thai Airways, Cathay Pacific Airlines, Japan Airlines, Malaysian Airlines, EVA Air, Aerolineas Argentinas, Lan Chile,** and **Garuda.**

The domestic terminal underwent extensive renovations in the late 1980s, prompted by the arrival of **Ansett New Zealand,** which built its own airline terminals in Auckland, Wellington, and Christchurch. There are smart Business Class lounges for passengers happy to pay the Business Class premium. Arrivals are in the center, near the moving baggage belt. Most arriving and departing passengers use air bridges.

Both terminals have the standard complement of bookshops, souvenir shops, etc., open from 6 A.M. until the last flights in the late evening. There are four rental-car companies at the airport—**Avis** (Tel. 275-7239), **Hertz** (Tel. 256-8680), **Budget** (Tel. 256-8451), and **Thrifty** (Tel. 256-1698) If you want to turn in a Budget car and catch a late flight, Budget's domestic terminal office closes at around 11 P.M., but office hours are around the clock over at the international terminal. More on rental cars in a moment.

Airport Coach. To taxi into town will cost from $38 to $40 (NZ), and that may be worth it for three or more traveling together. Otherwise, take the **AirBus** (Tel. 275-7685), which runs every 20 minutes from 6:20 A.M. to 10 P.M. daily. It's $12 a seat between the airport and the airport bus terminal at the corner of Quay and Albert Streets. Stops are made at the Airport motorhome hire centre and the major hotels. (To go to the airport by car, take State Highway 20, follow the special signs, and turn onto the George Bolt Memorial Drive, which leads right into the airport.)

A good service from city to airport and back is operated by an outfit called **Super Shuttle.** They will deliver you to your hotel or city address for more than the bus but less than the taxi fare. An average fare to the city from the airport is around $18 per person, or $10 per person if you are traveling with another. Super Shuttle's telephone number is 307-5210. **Airport Shuttles** is another mini-coach, door-to-door shuttle service (Tel. 256-0950).

Train and Bus Travel. You arrive or depart Auckland through the large railway terminal of **Tranz Rail** (Tel. 0800-802-802) for train information), just east of the central city on Beach Road. That's where you get the daytime *Overlander* or the overnight *Northerner* trains to Wellington (as described in chapter 2). Fares are $135 and $120 respectively. The *Geyserland* travels daily between Auckland and Rotorua for a fare of $63.

Intercity Coachlines buses (Tel. 913-6100) fan out to all parts of the country. It will cost about $43, for example, to take the bus to Rotorua, a four-hour trip. To Wellington, the fare is $94 during the day. The overnight trip goes down to $64 to compensate for the lack of daylight views. **Newmans Coachlines** (Tel. 913-6200) operates from the same Sky City Coach Terminal in Hobson Street. Their prices are marginally higher, a reflection of their slightly smarter coaches.

You might want to consider some charter buses operated between Auckland and the hinterlands. Some of them are more likely to provide commentary services during the trip. **Mount Cook Coachlines** (Tel. 375-4705) operates from their Auckland office at 445 Karangahape Road.

RENTAL CARS. We've placed them in this section because we believe driving is more practical for seeing all of New Zealand than for merely running around the Auckland area. Luckily, Auckland has several firms to choose from. Outside of the first trio below, be sure to ask each company what other cities they are represented in.

Avis Rental Cars (Tel. 275-7239), **Budget Rent-A-Car** (Tel. 256-8451), **Hertz** (256-8680), and **Thrifty** (Tel. 256-1698) all have desks at the airport.

Those are the big four, and from them you should expect full service at premium rates. If you're going for the lowest prices, however, check out some of those below to see who will give you the best rate for what you need. Don't forget that many firms offer different types of deals—some with unlimited distance rates, some charging by the kilometer, some with a number of kilometers included, as well as certain weekend specials, eight-hour specials, etc.—and all on cars of varying sizes.

Letz Rent A Car (Tel. 275-6890) is on Kirkbride Road near the airport; **Percy Rent-A-Car** (Tel. 303-1122) is on 110 Nelson Street.; **Maui Econocars Ltd.** (Tel. 275-3013) has its depot conveniently near the airport; and **New Zealand Rent a Car** (Tel. 308-9004) is on the corner of Sturdee Street. **Greens Rent-A-Car** is at 87 Great South Road (Tel. 298-4170). If you are staying on Auckland's North Shore, **North Harbour Rent-A-Car** (Tel. 09-415-1955) could be handy. **Cliftons Rentals** (Tel. 444-6699) is another North Shore-based company at 107 Wairau Road.

A reminder: When renting a car in New Zealand (or anywhere else), be sure to ask what extras are not quoted in the rates—required insurance, etc. And by the way, no auto renting company we know of allows its cars to be taken between the North and South islands on the ferry. You have to turn in the car and then rent another from the same or a different firm on the other island.

If you rent a camper, however, chances are you will be allowed to ferry it between the two islands. Two-berth campers, which can run from about $55 in the low season to over $140 a day in the high season, can be rented from **Maui Motorhomes** (Tel. 0800-651-080); **Pacific Horizon** (Tel. 275-9349); and **Adventure Vans** (Tel. 0800-844-255). In the past couple of years the camper market has been booming, however, and you may find some newer companies on the scene. We would be very interested in hearing how you liked yours. As a guide for what you might pay for a six-berth campervan, in the low season it would be around $140 a day and about $285 per day in the high season. Insurance must be added to this.

3. Local Transportation

Since we've already covered U-drives, local transportation in Auckland pretty much comes down to taxis and buses. You're allowed to hail a cab on the street, but it just isn't done often, and the cabs don't normally "cruise" the way they do in American cities. Normally, you look for a "taxi rank" near certain corners in the business district, or you can telephone taxi companies.

Deregulation of the taxi business in New Zealand has stiffened the competition, but the oldest established companies still tend to offer the most reliable deals. Reach members of the **Auckland Co-Operative Taxi Society,** which serves most of the city, by telephoning 300-3000. Another large firm is **Alert Taxis** (Tel. 309-2000). **Corporate Cabs** (Tel. 631-1111) and **CitiCabs** (Tel. 379-9199) are two newer ones. Rates at either are consistent with those of taxis in other large cities. Most places we needed to go in the city center seemed to cost between four and five dollars. Unless a cabbie does something unusual for you, do not leave a tip. Many drivers would find it embarrassing, unless you were just rounding off 10¢ worth of change. And a passenger traveling alone can sit up front beside the driver if he or she chooses.

Buses. If you want to hop on and off public buses all day while seeing Auckland, the "Busabout Day Pass" is a good deal. It's sold by bus drivers for $7 and gives unlimited travel on the Stagecoach Yellow buses and on the inner harbor ferries.

The **Bus Information Centre,** known as **RideLine** (Tel. 366-6400), is at Hobson Street, but unless you're right around the corner, you'd be better off phoning them. They're on duty most days until at least 9:30 P.M. to answer questions on how to get there from here. (The Municipal Bus Terminal itself is in the block bounded by Galway, Commerce, and Tyler Streets and Britomart Place.)

The bus service is generally divided into two main areas. There is the North Shore, which international visitors might be less likely to visit; it may help to know that bus numbers there are all in the 800 or 900 series. (If you get on an 800 or 900 bus, chances are you'll be across the Harbor Bridge before you can say "Waitemata wait a minute!") The South Shore services are all numbered below 800.

A handy downtown bus is any of the **streetcars** that run from the railway station via Beach Road and Customs Street, and generally up the length of Queen Street to Karangahape Road ("K" Road). Buses are numbered from 01 to 04. The efficient new **Link** buses operate through the central city and to inner-city "suburbs." The service costs $1 every time you board, and operates every 10 minutes. As in many countries, you pay by how far you go. Fares start at around 50 cents for an inner-city fare.

Ferryboats? Happily there are some, but it's hard to tell where to draw the line between simple water rides and cruises on the harbor.

Consequently, we cover everything that floats in section 7, Guided Tours and Cruises.

4. Hotels, Motels, and Places to Stay

North American travelers often become befuddled by the hotel situation in New Zealand. Mostly the problem is just a matter of terminology. First of all, a place of accommodation is not permitted to call itself a "hotel" at all, unless it is "licensed"—i.e., has government permission to serve alcoholic beverages on the premises. Then there are also buildings that may be labeled "hotels" in New Zealand that are nothing more than public bars (pubs). Once there was a law that any pub also had to offer at least a few rooms for rent upstairs, but that is no longer true. (However, a few country pubs still do, and they can be real bargains in the backblocks.) Places to stay overnight that do not have liquor licenses must use some other term, like "private hotel," to indicate that they are, after all, a place to bed down for the night.

Confusing the picture still further is the term "motel." In New Zealand a *motel* is not simply a hotel that caters to auto traffic. The main difference is that nearly all motels (or "motel flats," to use the technical term) offer cooking facilities—usually entire kitchens, fully equipped with almost everything you need to prepare and serve your own meals. Often, such a motel unit will have a separate sitting room as well as the bedroom(s). In many other countries these neat little units would be dubbed suites and charged for accordingly by greedy hoteliers without batting an eyelash. In New Zealand, motels are usually less expensive than hotels of comparable quality, and of course they cater to family travel. Don't think you have to have a car. Some of them are conveniently located near the center of towns, often right on the bus lines.

Motels around the country cost from about $65 to $150 a couple, and a few dollars extra for children. Some motels are "licensed," by the way, but most are not. Some are as luxurious in their individual units as any top-grade hotel. Some may call themselves "motor hotels," or something equally exalted (if they have that liquor license), but if they do they just might not have the kitchen. The few motels that do not offer cooking facilities are technically called "serviced motels." If they don't have a restaurant, they may offer B&B—"bed and breakfast"—at an all-inclusive rate.

The handiest listings for motels around New Zealand are the annual editions of two *Accommodation Guides*, one for each island, produced by the New Zealand Automobile Association. The motels (or "motel flats") in these manuals are rated by a rigid star system, but we don't pay much attention to that. (Without going into a lot of technical detail, we feel the star system is largely pedantic.) Nevertheless, the guides are handy for keeping up-to-date on the address, telephone number, and general price level of virtually every motel in every town and hamlet in the country. Just as in the U.S. and Canada, you can phone ahead to make reservations, either to a particular hotel/motel or to the tourist public relations office (see later).

The *AA Accommodation Guides* also list several *hotels,* but do not try to rate them at all. In 1995 the AA and New Zealand Tourism Office introduced Qualmark, an accommodation grading and rating system. Many motels are now sporting the Qualmark logo, and hotels are being graded for this new mark of quality.

The *New Zealand Bed and Breakfast Book* (a recent New Zealand Tourism Award winner) is another good source of accommodation information. You could buy one before departing for New Zealand or pick one up from a bookshop on arrival.

Here are some other things to consider when looking for a place to stay in New Zealand:

• Throughout this book we divide our hotel sections into price categories—sometimes into expensive, medium-price, and budget rooms, and sometimes just into two categories. These may include hotels, motels, guesthouses, cabins, or whatever we inspected on our rounds.

• Some of the best hotels in New Zealand include things that might be considered "extras" in other places—free delivered newspapers, refrigerators in the rooms, an electric jug with everything you need to make tea or instant coffee, etc. Therefore we tend to rank down hotels that do not keep up with what is expected by local standards.

• Virtually every hotel/motel will provide you with a free carton of milk. In theory, it's to be used with your morning tea. Some establishments will deliver breakfast ("cooked"—a big one—or "continental"—cold, but still relatively hearty—either included or at an extra charge) to your room in the morning (or sometimes served in a separate dining room).

• In the pages that follow we generally report on or estimate the price of a room for two people given in New Zealand dollars. Single rates would be about 10 percent less, on the average. Don't forget that the 12.5 percent goods and services tax, described in chapter 2, will be added to your total. In any case, you will note that when converted to American currency, the cost of most New Zealand hotel rooms, including the GST, is generally less than that of comparable rooms in cities and towns in the U.S.

• If you're making your own reservations, don't forget to be very specific about what you want. A "double" is a double bed in New Zealand; a "twin" means twin beds (although we tend to use the terms interchangeably in this book, since the price is nearly always the same). If you want a baby's crib, you ask for a "cot." The word "bath" generally means bath*tub* Down Under. If you want your room with tub or shower, say "bath or shower." If you prefer one or the other, say which. And by the way, the genteel euphemism for the whole plumbing thing is "private facilities."

• Frequent users of the telephone should ask the management whether they charge for outgoing phone calls, and how much. Some do, but now that New Zealand hotels have direct outward dialing from the rooms, calls may be free in the local area.

• If you're counting every penny and trying to do New Zealand as cheaply as possible, consider the youth hostels. You don't have to be a youth to be a member of the New Zealand Youth Hostel Association, just more than five years old. Auckland International YHA is in the heart of the city. There are 56 youth hostels in New Zealand, and accommodations within each generally range from dormitory style to ensuite. At the brand-new YHA property in Auckland city there are shared as well as ensuite rooms, kitchen facilities, and well-equipped rooms for disabled travellers. Rates are from $17 to $66 per night.

• The Auckland YHA reservations centre number is 303-9524, or you can write to them at P.O. Box 68 149 Auckland. The fast e-mail way is to contact them at book@yha.org.nz. If you join affiliated youth hostel organizations in the U.S., Canada, or other countries, your membership will be recognized in New Zealand. If you don't hold YHA membership, you can purchase a Hostelling International Card for NZ $24.00, which is valid in all countries for a year. Youth hosteling is not for everyone, so if you're at all doubtful do plenty of reading up on it before you go.

• Also for penny squeezers: Consider the various motor camps that have been established throughout the country, some of them run by local county councils, etc. Even if you're not carrying your own tent or camper, many of these camps will rent out somewhat rustic cabins from $20 to $25 or so per night. Normally you're supposed to have your own sheets and blankets, but sometimes these can be rented for two or three dollars. Facilities like toilets and showers are in a separate building—sometimes a cold jog across the wet, grassy tennis courts. Again, the AA is the best source for lists of camping grounds. You can book these places, incidentally, and many do in peak seasons. If you've never traveled this way before, approach cautiously. Some of these places could be just too basic for your blood.

• If you arrive in Auckland or anyplace else without hotel reservations, it may be easiest to go to the city Visitor Centre and ask them to find a room for you. Of course this may be impossible in December/January and other busy periods; in normal times it will save you a lot of phone dialing and a lot of shoe leather. In Auckland, the Visitor's Centre has desks right at the international airport (Tel. 275-6467) and domestic terminal (Tel. 256-8480), and are open for all arrivals and departures. In the city the centres are at 1 Queen and at Aotea Square (both share Tel. 366-6888). Throughout New Zealand, some 36 towns and cities have their own PR offices, and they're well worth a visit. We've always found the staff at such offices to be genuinely helpful and interested in showing you what their area has to offer. Either office will provide you with a wealth of useful visitor information. At the Auckland Visitors' Centre on Aotea Square there is a rack of little guides. It's open every day. Try the *A-Z Auckland Free Visitors Guide*.

EXPENSIVE AUCKLAND HOTELS

Not so many years ago, Auckland was almost a hotel wasteland, offering virtually nothing of so-called "international" standards. Happily, the picture has mightily improved with some recent additions to the scene.

The overall score is close among the top three, but we must give the edge to the swell-elegant **Stamford Plaza** (Tel. 309-8888). Located downtown behind the historic old Customhouse, the twin-winged establishment fronts on Albert Street, extending to the corner of Swanson Street. This was one of our Auckland headquarters a few years back when it was known as the Regent of Auckland, and here's the way we saw it:

Eleven-story, red-brown, tan, glass, and stainless-steel angular exterior; cheerful porters usually waiting to take your car and your bags; 30-foot-tall, recently refurbished lobby with polished Swedish granite underfoot; special business center to one side; lobby lounge for morning coffee and afternoon tea (choice of many types of tea); piano bar; the Brasserie, open for breakfast, lunch and dinner, occupying a glassed-in verandah for viewing Albert Street; pastry shop and Japanese sushi bar tucked in a couple of corners somewhere; other public areas including a ground-floor ballroom and a rooftop pool and health club; lots of flowers around from its own private florist operating on the premises.

Three high-speed elevators to the eight guest floors; accommodations divided into four types—the Queen, the King, the Twin, and the suites, all of the types occasionally designed in unusual shapes; some upper-floor accommodations with terrific vistas over the harbor; each room at least reasonably large and showing off excellent furnishings trimmed in naturally light N.Z. tawa wood; all units with twin-, king-, or queen-size beds, deep-pile wool carpets, sofa and chairs, business desk with accessories, good closets, lots of lighting, color TV hidden in an armoire (radio-TV controls at bedside), minibar, a fridge, and facilities to make tea and coffee; superior Spanish marble bathrooms (all with tub *and* shower) with lots of room and a second phone within reach of the loo; minimum rates from $385 for most rooms; executive rooms are on the top (10th) floor and cost from $400 and the suites from about $700 on up to infinity, depending on size and view. Add GST to these prices.

Some say the Stamford Plaza can be a little stuffy and pretentious like its regal predecessor (e.g., routinely serving French Evian drinking water, when N.Z. tap water is among the world's safest and best). Putting aside these and some other nitpicks we had, though, the convenient, luxurious Stamford Plaza continues to reign supreme in the Queen City this year. We happily pay homage with a low bow and a high recommendation.

That said, we must go on to say that despite the inconvenient site, we liked the **Sheraton-Auckland Hotel and Towers** (Tel. 379-5132), located above the hustle and bustle up where Symonds Street meets "K" Road. It's right next to its own special shopping mall and a block of newly developed shops. At 410 rooms, the 10-story, three-wing establishment is one of the city's larger hotel and conference centers, although somehow it doesn't look like it. Again, our capsule impressions:

There is a bright, cheerful, and "outdoorsy" lobby with large skylight, flowers, and a bubbly fountain; pink and peach marble on walls and floors; burnished wood and brass touches; large, comfortable, sunken-floor Rendezvous conversation and cocktail pit opposite the lifts; two dining rooms, including the popular Steam Biscuit Factory and the more distinguished Partington's for fine dining (this restaurant has an award for the best service in N.Z. awarded by noted N.Z. food critic, Michael Guy); large convention rooms; and Sheraton Health Club with heated outdoor swimming pool, sauna, and exercise rooms on the second floor. The Some Place Else bar is open late and offers live entertainment. Snack meals are on hand.

The rooms come with luxury furnishings, some with twin beds (with one bedside table) and some with king-size beds (with two flanking lamp tables); all with direct-dial phones, color television, radio, refrigerator, minibar, individual temperature controls, and operable windows; good views over the city with some top-floor units on the north picking up Rangitoto Island in the Hauraki Gulf; southern exposures with pleasant vistas of Mount Eden, etc.; and room service is rather uneven in our experience. Double rates currently are competitive, ranging from $195 to $249 in the main building and $260 to $332 in the Towers (plus GST). Like some of its American cousins (the excellent Seattle Sheraton Hotel and Towers, for example), it offers a superior service for a higher tariff: exclusive check-in complimentary cocktails for about an hour each evening, breakfast each morning, and a butler on tap. Suites in the main hotel cost from $620. All rooms have recently been refurbished.

This handsome addition to the cityscape was a revelation to Aucklanders when it opened back in 1983 and it has been the salvation of many outlanders since then. We've always enjoyed our own stays, although we must admit that we've usually had a car to get to the centers of action and then back to the hotel. The establishment is close to Auckland's velvet-green park called the Domain and the much less inviting motorway system. As long as cabs remain plentiful, anyway, the Sheraton still earns our affection for pleasant surroundings and a generally efficient staff.

The only hotel in Auckland we ever really hated was the old Inter-Continental, known for many years as "the Big I." Happily, the Big I blinked closed for the last time a while back, and in the same building has opened the wide-awake **Hyatt Regency Auckland** (Tel. 366-1234). A top-to-bottom reformation has been performed, and we checked in here, too, on our last Auckland ramble. It's looking and feeling good. And its Top of the Town top-floor restaurant with magnificent harbor views is still one of the best in town.

The Hyatt Regency features a single rectangular building with 274 rooms; eye-soothing, hilly location, just across Waterloo Quadrant from Auckland University; inconvenient though free parking (ask at the desk for a brass razoo to work the gate); thoroughly reamed out, enlarged, and soothingly elegant lobby with massive pillars, potted plants, and sink-down couches; lots of echoes, especially noticeable when the evening piano music begins; Crostini's café-style restaurant on the ground level, open for breakfast, lunch, and dinner; Top of the Town Restaurant on the highest (14th) level also open for delicious buffet lunches; and rooms a little smaller than those in the Sheraton, one of the limitations imposed by the building's late-fifties, big-city-hotel construction.

Our high room at the back on the Regency Club floor had a wonderful view of a harbor full of sails and Rangitoto Island. (Those on the front overlook Albert Park and the university.) It also had all the standard luxury amenities, including American TV via the hotel's own satellite dish. Rates for double, twin, and single rooms start at $300 plus GST. Suites start at $420 plus GST. The plush presidential suite is up at $1050 and you can add GST to that one, too! Regency Club guests pay $370 a night for a standard room, and receive additional pampering for the extra dollars—complimentary breakfast and cocktails, for example, as well as all-day coffee and tea with a hostess to serve it and look after the guests. Those smiling, willing faces made up for a lot of outdated plumbing and strange wiring.

Be aware that trudging up the steep hill home after Queen Street shopping is tough, so plan to hike out and then take a cab back. Recommended—as amended.

Before the trio above made their debut, the leader in Auckland was the venerable South Pacific Hotel, then the handsomely renovated and re-named Parkroyal Hotel; now it is called the **Novotel** (Tel. 377-8920), and it still wins for the prime location. It has its entrance on Customs Street, just around the corner from Queen Elizabeth Square at the end of Queen Street and that shopping center named Downtown.

About half the 188 units in this 15-story structure overlook the nearby harbor, and the other half face the city itself. It's within walking distance of the passenger-ship terminal, the ferry terminal, the airline bus terminal, and most shops, banks, and businesses. There is a friendly lobby, with street noise evident on the ground floor but not much at higher levels; the rooftop Vertigo Restaurant overlooking the harbor; five types of rooms, all with good New Zealand furnishings, including TVs, refrigerators, sound-proofing, air conditioning, phones, etc.; breakfast available from room service; and rates in the $175 to $265 range for singles and doubles. All in all, it's a respectable four-star choice for a comfort/convenience combina-tion, and the views make up for the clutter of rather neglected buildings east of the Customs Street entrance to the hotel. The city is about to pull them down to build an ambitious new public transport terminal and more apartment and office buildings. Let's hope they don't block the view.

Auckland is one of Australasia's fastest-growing cities, so new hotels are opening their doors to increasing numbers of visitors. Guest staying at the four-year-old **Sky City Hotel** (Tel. 912-6000) have no trouble finding it. Towering above the hotel is Auckland's Sky Tower, the tallest structure in the Southern Hemisphere and already one of the city's most popular tourist attractions. Since the 338-room-hotel above Auckland's Sky City Casino offers a theatre, ballroom, and numerous bars and restaurants, Sky City is a kind of entertainment destination. If anyone needs to cool off, the hotel pool does the honours. The hotel rooms are competitively priced, starting at $199 and ranging to $259 for the rooms with more bells and whistles. These prices include breakfast and good old GST.

Quay West (Tel. 309-6000) one block over on Albert Street, opened about the same time as Sky City and offers apartment-style accommodation (bedrooms, fully equipped kitchens, and living areas). The nightly charges start at $450 plus GST. On the heels of this "all-suites" hotel came two more regular hotels. **Rydges** (Tel. 375-5900) has nestled its four-star accommo-dation into the heart of the city with pleasant, air-conditioned rooms over-looking either the city or the harbor. The Circa Restaurant, Bar and

Delicatessen entices many passing pedestrians, and at 188 guest rooms, the hotel is small enough to feel friendly. Rooms are from $145 (plus GST), and breakfast is often included in the price at weekends. The rate quoted here is the so-called "corporate" rate, as opposed to the "rack" rate. Corporate rates are always more attractive because they are quoted on rooms, subject to availability. Factor in the stronger American dollar and all these rates, quoted in dollars here in our guide, look reasonable for four- to five-star hotel accommodations.

Newer than Rydges is the slightly larger but still personable **Heritage Auckland** (Tel. 379-8553). The Heritage has been transformed from the famous Farmers Department Store into a stylish and very comfortable suite-style hotel. It has traditional hotel rooms as well as suites with one to three bedrooms and separate, open-plan dining and living areas with cleverly planned kitchens containing all the mod cons, including a combined washing and drying machine. The Heritage Auckland Tower Wing opened in late 1999, adding 218 rooms to the main hotel's 269 rooms. All rooms in the Tower Wing come with kitchens and are impressively spacious. Many look out over Auckland's sparkling Waitemata, three minutes' walk away. Like most hotels around the world—and in Auckland—The Heritage and its newer Tower Wing offer cheaper rates over the weekends, so we are looking at prices from about $150 (including GST) for weekend rooms with those dinky little kitchens. The same room would be closer to $200 during the week. The suites with separate bedrooms cost from around $180 on weekends and $230 during the week. Be sure to take a look at the indoor pool. You'll be able to see the sky through the ceiling.

Citylife Auckland (Tel. 379-9222) is one of Auckland's new suite-style hotels with personality and an already established reputation for quality. While not luxurious in the Stamford Plaza sense of the word, Citylife Auckland is certainly well set up. Its four-star one-bedroom suites come with the "corporate" price tag of $189 plus GST, ranging up to $720 for the three-bedroom penthouse. There's also an indoor heated swimming pool.

The seven-story **Copthorne Anzac Avenue** (Tel. 379-8509) is near the railroad station at 150 Anzac Avenue, but it's a huff-puff of a climb by foot from mid-city. The Copthorne has a white-and-blue exterior with wrought-iron balconettes fronting the rooms; small lobby, ground floor dining room and houseguests' bar with live piano music; extras including a sauna and billiard room; and free parking. There are a total of 110 comfortable sleeping chambers with TV, coffee and tea makers, and the other usual frills; most doubles start at $172 plus GST. If the Copthorne Hotel were closer to downtown, we would rank it higher. As it is, it's still a very pleasant outpost.

The **Carlton Hotel Auckland** (Tel. 366-3000) on Mayoral Drive is a hop and step from the city's Aotea Centre, the prime city venue for top concerts and other artistic performances. Rates are currently kicking off at $390 for twin rooms. The butler service gets going on the 10th and 11th floors, and expect to dig a bit deeper for these rooms, which start at $440. Royalty may consider a night in the new Royal Suite for a tag of $1,600. GST gets added to all of these rates, of course.

The top restaurant is the Katsura, an excellent Japanese restaurant. Café Pacific is a brasserie that's open around the clock, as is the hotel's room service. Tennis players should bring their rackets along. The courts are on top of the car park. And the swimming pool is close by to cool off in.

Auckland's **Centra Hotel,** at 128 Albert Street (Tel. 302-1111) is a conveniently located 242-bedroom hotel that charges from $200 up for double rooms and around $950 for the penthouse suite (from which the views are terrific).

Directly across from the harbor, the **Copthorne Harbour City Hotel** (Tel. 377-0349) at 96-100 Quay Street is within easy shooting distance of many of the traditional tourist targets in Auckland. Other features include a recently completed larger lobby, popular first-floor bar, and available covered parking. The individual rooms are not outstanding, but the front ones still have harbor views, despite all the new water-side developments. All units have a fridge and minibar; double and single rooms run from about $250.

A place we look forward to sampling is the **Hotel du Vin,** in the Mangatawhiri Valley south of Auckland. (Tel. 0800-838-846). The nightly rates are from about $300 for deluxe accommodations (plus GST). This attractive hotel is aimed at a clientele who enjoy haute cuisine and rural tranquility. You can ride horses, play tennis, splash in the indoor swimming pool, and walk through the bush. There's also a golf course just 15 minutes' drive away. The meals are often accompanied by commendable De Redcliffe wines. Helicopters whirl guests from the airport to the hotel in 15 minutes. Otherwise, expect a ride of about 45 minutes. The hotel sits amidst its own vineyard, the De Redcliffe estate, and tastings are available daily on site. If you get to Hotel du Vin before we do, let us know what you think of it.

A 10-minute drive out of the city center, **Aachen House** (Tel. 520-2329) continues to win the praise of our readers. Joan and Greg McKirdy are the new owners and have considerably enhanced the Victorian mansion at 39 Market Road, Remuera. There is now a sunny conservatory added to the house, and antiques furnish most of the rooms. Rates are about $170 to $310 with GST, which includes a big cooked breakfast. You can inspect upmarket Aachen house on the Internet at www.aachenhouse.co.nz.

MEDIUM-PRICE AUCKLAND HOTELS

Out near Auckland Airport, the **Centra Auckland Airport** (Tel. 275-1059), has been packing them in two miles from the runways at Mangere, but so far we've never managed to work it into our schedule. Besides a dining room and coffee bar, you'll find a sauna, gymnasium, swimming pool, and other luxury facilities. You may see sheep and cows from this contented country establishment. Doubles (or twins) have been going from about $145 plus GST, perhaps a good bargain if you don't have to go into town more than once. Weekend specials drop down to about $120. It's on the corner of Kirkbride and Ascot Roads.

Across the street is the **Hotel Grand Chancellor** (Tel. 275-7029), a 160-bed hotel with corporate rates from around $135 for a double room. Suites go from about $250. There is a restaurant and oyster bar that serves those tasty morsels year-round. A swimming pool and gym are also part of the hotel complex.

The 112-room **Quality Hotel Rosepark** (Tel. 377-3619) is a popular choice with Auckland visitors. The Parnell Rose Gardens bloom just opposite. Rates begin at $140 plus GST. There are also attractive villas. This Quality Hotel is on the bus route into the city, a ride that takes about three minutes.

The **Barry Court Motor Inn,** at 10 Gladstone Road in Parnell (Tel. 303-3789), has rooms with kitchens or tea- and coffee-making facilities. There's also a restaurant, bar, and private spas to sink into. The establishment is on 1.5 acres of park. Rates are from around $86 to $300. **Grafton Oaks Motor Inn** (Tel. 309-0167), about a three-minute drive from the city's heart on Grafton Road, is another well-equipped motor inn with mod cons and a tariff of $145 double or twin. **Manor Inn** (Tel. 522-0160) at 13 Alpers Avenue is in the buzzy suburb of Newmarket. Rates are from $95. There's a licensed restaurant on the premises, and good old room service. This goes to prove that even in the suburbs New Zealand doesn't close down after dark.

Three newer entries to the medium-price scene include **New President** (Tel. 303-1333), **Park Towers** (Tel. 309-2800), and **Seibel of Auckland.** The New President is in the city centre, and some people like the microwave ovens that are in the guest rooms. Park Towers Hotel is close to the university and, like the New President, comes with a restaurant. The Seibel is in the same stable as the Quay West Hotel and was opening its doors down in the Viaduct Basin near the America's Cup Village as we went to print. The location right beside Auckland's harbor is likely to cement a good future for the Seibel.

City apartment-style hotels are increasing in number in the medium-price range, as well as in the luxury bracket. Our recommendations are the

Quest Auckland (Tel. 366-5190), **Cintra** (Tel. 379-6288), and **Auckland City Apartments** (Tel. 303-0306). They offer one- and two-bedroom apartments that are serviced each day. Nightly rates range from $100.

If you fancy staying in a peaceful spot, 12 minutes from the city centre and overlooking the velvet expanse of Cornwall Park, head for **Quality Hotel Logan Park** (Tel. 6324-1269). Or you could go bush at **Waitakere Park Lodge** (Tel. 09-814-9622) in the tree-clad hills 30 minutes west of the city and close to the wild, wonderful west coach beaches. Rates range from $120. The hills are threaded with bush walks and the hotel has a pool, squash court, and restaurant. In Auckland's elegant old suburb of Remuera, a 7-minute drive from the city, is **The Devereux Boutique Hotel** (Tel. 524-5044), and we hear it's a quality establishment. The hotel has been fashioned from a 110-year-old villa and has just 12 rooms. Prices range from $135.

Auckland's North Shore can be a pleasant base too, with many beaches close by. The **Browns Bay Motor Inn** (Tel. 479-5016) offers family units, smaller units, and three individual guest rooms. Cost is from $85 per person including continental breakfast. A little pricier but smack alongside Takapuna Beach, nearer to the city, is the **Emerald Inn** (Tel. 488-3500). Rates are from $120 and all the rooms come with small kitchens and living areas. The three-bedroom apartments have pride of place overlooking the beach. Takapuna also has a small lake called Pupuke, and the **Killarney Lakeside Resort** opened mid-1999 on its shores. Since the lake (and the new hotel) are close to the excellent Bruce Mason Theatre and Takapuna's lively beachside shopping and restaurants, you could be well located.

The grand old, 25-room, historic Edwardian-style **Esplanade Hotel** (Tel. 445-1291) is on Devonport's main street, just across the water from downtown Auckland. Tariffs for suites overlooking the harbour cost $195. Auckland city is 10 minutes away by harbor ferry. Devonport, on the tip of Auckland's north shore and facing the city, is one of Auckland's oldest suburbs, and several of the fine old villas have been converted to small, "boutique"-style hotels. **The Devonport Villa Inn** (Tel. 445-8397) is one of the best and the NZ Tourism Board presented the hotel with an award a couple of years ago. The rates are from $165.

Oakwood Manor (Tel. 275-0539) has a ring of "mock" in its name, but this member of the airport accommodations scene (Kirkbride Road) is recommended. Some of the units have spa pools. There's a restaurant on the premises, too. Rates are from $90 for two. And while we are at the airport, the **Airport Kiwi International Hotel** (Tel. 275-1005) has 32 pleasant motel units, some with facilities for the disabled. A courtesy coach to and from the airport is available. Rates are from $79 single/double. Just about next door, the **Airport Kiwi International Motor Inn** (Tel. 256-0046) is easily distinguished by the enormous kiwi on its roof. This bird is well loved by Aucklanders and stood for years on the roof of the Kiwi Bacon Factory. When the factory was no more there was some consternation about the fate of the bird, but it was soon rescued and is still a part of Auckland's skyline. Tariffs here are from $95 single/double. (Don't forget to add GST to these rates. In fact, it is safest to add it to all the hotel rates even where we have not included a mention of it.)

Also out at the airport (on Kirkbride Road with the majority of the other airport accommodations) is the **Auckland Airport Pacific Inn** (Tel. 275-1129), which operates a courtesy car to and from the airport and has rates of $79 single or double.

ROOMS AT A BUDGET

The **Kiwi International Hotel Queen Street** (Tel. 379-6487) offers a budget rate of $45 for an economy room with shared facilities. It also offers a standard room with private facilities for $75 and a business room with private facilities for $90. There is alcohol available, but the hotel is not fully licenced. There is also a restaurant. The Kiwi International is just above the Town Hall, at 411 Queen Street.

The Parnell Inn (Tel. 358-0642) at 320 Parnell Road, amidst Parnell's atmospheric browsing and brunching area, is a typical motel of about 18 rooms with tellies, phones, and kitchen facilities. It has rates of from $110 double.

In response to pleas from our readers, we finally inspected the **Ascot Parnell** (Tel. 309-9012), and it is indeed a charming choice. A residential address at 36 St. Stephens Avenue, quite removed from Queen Street, but within walking distance of Parnell Village, with its interesting shops and restaurants, the Ascot Parnell is a 1910-vintage house with a historic past; off-street parking; family-style breakfast room, where the loudest noise is sometimes the ticking clock; cheerful sun and TV porch adjoining; 130-year-old pin oak tree outside; just nine commodious guest rooms with high, rimu-wood ceilings—at least one a converted ballroom, all with telephones; all probably with private baths by the time of your check-in; classic prints on the walls; singles are $86, doubles from about $135 (and remember, these are New Zealand dollars and the price includes a good breakfast). We liked the place a lot for the type, and we think you will, too. Previous managers Heidi and Alfred Hassencamp have retired, and the hotel is now owned by Bart and Therese Blommaert from Belgium. They inform us that their intention is to "maintain the good reputation of this very fine hotel and even make improvements where possible." Many of their guests, they inform us, carry this guidebook to explore New Zealand. They are now on the Internet at ascotparnell.com.

You could also try the **Chalet Chevron** (Tel. 309-0290), another good possibility in Parnell, situated at 14 Brighton Road. Charges are about $100 double, including breakfast. Cindy Gulbranson of Monroe, Washington, wrote to tell us that she loved it. The **Bavaria Guest House** (Tel. 638-9641), at 83 Valley Road in the central Auckland suburb of Auckland, is a pleasant villa, and hosts Rudi and Ulrike from Germany make guests feel welcome. B&B rates are $110 double.

We like the look of **Millars Homestay,** in the leafy Auckland suburb of Epsom (Tel. 625-7336). Hosts Janet and Jim Millar charge from $75 for double rooms. The **Ponsonby Potager B&B** sounds fun (Tel. 378-7237). It's described as quality accommodations in tranquil cottage gardens. Ponsonby is one of the inner-city "suburbs," close to trendy Ponsonby Road with its cheek-to-cheek restaurants. The tariff for the Potager is $120 double. In Mt. Eden, another area close to the city centre and filled with interesting old houses, is **Pentlands Bed & Breakfast Hotel** (Tel. 638-7031) with kind hosts Julie and Brian. Rates are from $79 double. And in one of Remuera's quiet streets with views of the sea is **The Brooks** (Tel. 523-3746), a restored 120-year-old farmhouse. Rates here are from $75.

Also in the bargain file is the **Aspen Lodge** (Tel. 379-6698) at 62 Emily Place, just off Shortland Street. It's clean, but cold in the winter. Rates are still a very reasonable $75 double, with breakfast included. On Waiheke Island, a half hour's ferry ride from the central city, is **Waiheke Island Resort,** run by Helen and Chris Younger (Tel. 372-7897). They have a pool and tennis court to add to the resort feel of the island and its superb ocean beaches. This island will make you feel light-years from the freeway. That's probably why Gene O'Neill and his wife Liz built **Te Whau Lodge,** a getaway on Waiheke for a maximum of eight guests. Te Whau has just four guest rooms, but with great views and unobtrusive hospitality. Gene and Liz can be contacted at 372-2288.

Auckland Central Backpackers (Tel. 358-4877) offers dormitory-style accommodations from around $16 per person. They also have beds for $35 single and $47 double. The hostel has special rates with the Airbus shuttle company. Central Backpackers has security arrangements that have satisfied the Olympic Committee's strict requirements, and hosted athletes for the last Oceania Games. There is a 24-hour reception and rooftop café and bar offering breakfast and à la carte dinner. The New Zealand Tourism Board awarded the hostel Best Budget Accommodation in 1994.

There are two NZYHA youth hostels in Auckland. The flashy new International Hostel at 5 Turner Street (Tel. 302-2802) has rates from $17 for dorms to $66 for ensuite doubles. There's also a hostel in the city at the corner of City Road and Liverpool Street (Tel. 309-2802), offering beds for a nightly, per-person rate of $19.

5. Restaurants and Dining

Dining in New Zealand's best restaurants is easy. Things work pretty much the same as they do at home. All you need is money, but luckily not nearly as much as you would for a fine meal in the U.S., Canada, or (Bacchus forbid!) Europe.

Right off the bat, now, New Zealand restaurants take one night of the week off—usually a Monday or Tuesday. But there are plenty to go round, so if you find one door closed, you'll find another open close by. Some establishments charge a small supplement, maybe 50¢ per adult, for meals on Saturdays, Sundays, and holidays (that's to help pay the staff the extra rate they get on those days). BYO restaurants sometimes charge a "corkage fee" of about 50¢ to take care of opening your wine, setting it up, etc.

Tipping. The first time I tried tipping in a New Zealand restaurant, in 1966, a New Zealander who was with us immediately scooped up the change and deposited it back in my hand. "You're not starting that kind of thing in this country!" he said.

Since that time, the emphasis has changed a little. Still, we now tip in New Zealand (a) only in the best restaurants; (b) only for exceptional service; and (c) never more than 10 percent. Remember that no matter what restaurant you're in, some of the other patrons won't be tipping at all, and no one is going to chase them out the door hurling epithets in their wake. Not only that, they will be treated just as well or better the next time they show up in the same restaurant.

What about wine? BYO (or BYOG) stands for "bring your own grog," and many restaurants that are not in a position to get a license to sell alcohol are allowed to take care of you if you care to pick up some wine at a bottle store and then bring it along. Hand it to the host or waiter, and he'll whisk it away and do the rest, just as if you had ordered from their cellar. (Of course you don't go through the tasting ritual.) Don't forget to buy cold wine if it's white. Wine shops like the Glengarry and Wine Masters chains in Auckland have excellent varieties in stock at competitive prices. If you forgot to buy wine at all or didn't know that the restaurant was BYO, ask if they can send out a kitchen boy to buy it for you. (It's illegal, but a few restaurants won't have to send that lad any further than their own basement.)

Don't neglect to try New Zealand wine. The whites are often superb and have been winning prizes all over the world. The reds are palatable, but less dramatic on the whole. Brand names to look for include Montana, Matawhero, Collards, Vavasour, Vidals, Nobilo, Hunters, Villa Maria, and Te Mata. Esk Valley, Cooks, Morton Estate, De Redcliffe, and Ngatarawa are other names to look for. New Zealand produces good Sauvignon Blancs and Chardonnays in particular. Cloudy Bay is another name to look for when shopping for these varieties.

Of the whites, the champion types are Chardonnay, Sauvignon Blanc, Riesling, Sylvaner, Müller-Thurgau, Moselle, Chablis, Traminer, and Hock. For the reds, try Pinotage, Cabernet Sauvignon, Cabernet Merlot, and Claret. Good New Zealand wine will cost from $10 to $25 in a bottle store, and half again to twice as much in licensed restaurants. If your taste runs to sweet, try the new kiwi fruit wine. If you take it on its own merits, it's pretty good!

There are four main wine-growing areas on the North Island, and they include the Gisborne and Hawke's Bay regions on the east coast. Then south of Auckland there are vineyards at Te Kawhata and the Thames Valley. The Henderson area just west of Auckland is popular for Saturday-morning wine crawls. If you can find some local oenophile to do the driving, you can hit 8 or 10 wineries before noon—or so they say!

La cuisine. Many items on New Zealand menus are in French, but they are usually translated directly underneath. Such a listing does not necessarily mean you have found a French restaurant; using French is just the style for many EnZed restaurants. And by the way, the word *entree* on the menu means "appetizer"—not "main course" as in so many parts of North America. A much more sensible translation, *n'est-ce pas?*

Servings tend to be very large. No one knows why, but it may have something to do with New Zealand's reputation as a nation of hungry farmers who come in ready for beer after a hard day's work out in the boohai. And if you're a fellow Yank, be forewarned that you'll play "Hail Columbia" trying to get a glass of water. Many restaurants just keep forgetting it after you ask. *Here's a tip, though:* Ask for water from the wine waiter, and tell him you'll order your wine after the water comes.

It is also difficult to have coffee or tea *with* your meal, even with dessert, instead of *after* everything else is consumed. One fading New Zealand custom is to serve the coffee in an adjoining room. It is also difficult to get your salad served in advance of your main course. Sometimes it comes right on the same plate. You might try to ask for it as an appetizer, but in general Kiwis like it all together—except the coffee.

Credit cards. Happily, you will be able to use credit cards in New Zealand, although some restaurants do not take all cards. We carry Diners and VISA, and usually get by on one of those two. American Express,

MasterCard, and Australia's Bank Card are also accepted in many dining rooms. In some cases it is far easier to use a credit card because of the annoyance of having to pay twice—once to the wine waiter and then later for the food. You may still have to pull out your card twice, but that's not as gauche as fiddling around with filthy lucre all during the evening. The best arrangement of all when dining in your hotel is to put both wine and meal on the hotel bill. By the way, sometimes you pay the waiter or waitress, other times you go to the cashier, even in a fine restaurant.

Semi-self-service. Where the confusion comes for us Americans is ordering from more modest eating houses. There are several, for example, where you are your own sommelier. You order your food; then amble over to the bar to pick up your wine, beer, etc., pay for it, and then carry the booze back to the rest of the party.

There is another type that is partly cafeteria-style. In these, you line up with your tray, pick up the cold and prepared goodies you want (salads, desserts, etc.), then order the hot stuff when you get further down the line. They may or may not give you a number. Pay for the whole thing and go sit down. Sometimes they'll call out your number and you go collect your steak, sausages, or whatever. Sometimes they cart it around to your table, somehow managing to recognize you despite the large number of patrons.

Don't worry if you don't understand the system. Many genuine Kiwis don't either, and there are varying refinements. We hit one where, instead of the nonalcoholic drinks, you received little colored tokens. These had to be used to pay for drinks in another area of the restaurant!

Soft drinks. Some of these can be a little strange at first. If you want a lemonade, you'll have to ask for lemon juice. There *is* something called "lemonade," but it's carbonated and more like a Seven-Up than anything else. There's also an L & P—lemon and Paeroa water, a specialty of a little town called Paeroa that cans its mineral water after flavoring it with lemon.

Milk shakes are sometimes made *without* ice cream, by the way, and you'll find a lot of strange flavors. There will be very little chocolate in the chocolate shakes. Better ask for hokey-pokey instead, and hope for the best!

Exotic fare. With the exception of French and Chinese, ethnic-food restaurants are relatively new in New Zealand. However, there are some dependable, long-lived Greek, Lebanese, Japanese, Italian, Middle Eastern, various Asian, and Indian restaurants. Some say there was a sort of restaurant revolution in Auckland during the 1970s and 1980s. Certainly now it is possible to eat out in a different restaurant every day of the year.

As we reported in chapter 3, New Zealand food itself can be superb. The smaller BYO restaurants are sometimes the places where you find the best food. It is really only in the last five years that restaurants with identifiable character have started to emerge. The theory has probably prevailed that most of the patrons are not foreigners, but New Zealanders; why should they hoe into the same tucker that they whip up themselves at home? There's some commercial logic to that, so if you don't find a satisfyingly "New Zealand" restaurant, you may get invited to a good cook's home while traveling in the country. It's interesting that so many visitors do just that.

PRINCIPAL AUCKLAND RESTAURANTS

Visitors Centres stock guides to Auckland restaurants, and you'll discover that this city is well served by creative chefs with New Zealand's fresh produce at their disposal. The **Harbourside Seafood and Grill** (Tel. 307-0486) is one of the best "New Zealand" restaurants in Auckland in this "Taste New Zealand" tradition. It opened in 1992 and has been maintaining a steady trade ever since. The view may be part of the reason. Alfresco dining is a popular option because the Harbourside overlooks Auckland's sparkling Waitemata Harbor, and tables shaded by blue-and-white umbrellas spill onto the balcony. Main courses are around $18, entrees are about $12. There's also a bar to warm up in before dinner. You'll find the Harbourside on the second floor of Auckland's cleverly restored Ferry Building on Quay Street.

Parnell is an area that boasts a collection of restaurants to rival those of Ponsonby, Auckland's other main eating-out suburb. **Antoine's** (Tel. 379-8756) is a French dining room at 333 Parnell Road. Its setting in a charmingly restored villa has fresh white tablecloths and some alfresco seating on the verandah. Tony and Beth Astle offer a menu to compare with the best restaurants, and everything is cooked to order by Tony personally. The evolution of New Zealand's traditional lamb dish into a leaner, rarer, and more exciting dish (no doubt encouraged by the introduction of a national lamb cuisine award), is evident at Antoine's. Try the lamb loin or plump New Zealand salmon Tony has delivered from Stewart Island, at the southern tip of New Zealand. Main dishes are around $26 to $30. Tony's wine cellar includes first-rate international and New Zealand wines. Some may consider Antoine's a little expensive, but we saw only professionalism, pure and simple. The restaurant is open for lunch Monday to Friday, dinner Monday to Saturday.

In the North Shore suburb of Takapuna, the popular **Killarney Street Brasserie** (Tel. 489-9409), has a lively atmosphere and good food but plenty of competition, especially on Hurstmere Road, one block over towards Takapuna Beach. Taking advantage of Auckland's mild winters and Mediterranean summers, the parade of restaurants offer alfresco dining almost year-round. Many also feature either doors or windows that fold right back to let the outside in.

Plusone (Tel. 376-5112), offers plenty of wicker below and fans overhead at 13 St. Mary's Bay Road, right behind the Ponsonby post office. Owned and operated by an exuberant Finnish immigrant named Rosa Kullstrom, Plusone specializes in roast duck and venison and does magic things with humble foods like brains, kidneys, liver, and sweetbreads. Plusone is licensed, and main dishes go from $14 to $25 and include salads, vegetables, and bread. **Prego's** (Tel. 376-3095) is perennially popular with its Italian-oriented menu and wood-fired pizzas. Along the road is the **Bronze Goat** (Tel. 378-4193), with specialties including Tua Tua chowder and wholemeal bread in terra cotta pots, green-lipped mussels, oysters, char-grilled king salmon, and rack of lamb with herb bread. They serve homemade desserts, too. Sound good? If you think so, head over to 108 Ponsonby Road. If they're booked out you'll find plenty of good fare to choose from in the other numerous area restaurants. Around the corner on Jervois Road are several more of note. **Vinnies** is an award winner.

In trendy Parnell is the **Metropole** (Tel. 379-9300), at 223 Parnell Road, café-style, with large windows that open onto the street and siren the passers-by in to dine on dishes costing around $18. **Igacu,** further up Parnell Road, hops most nights (Tel. 358-4804). Asia and Pacific Rim dishes are served in this large brasserie-style restaurant that seems to suit the Auckland scene. Across the road is **Portobello,** a durable little Italian restaurant that is well patronised every night, because it keeps serving good food for reasonable prices.

Cin Cins, on Quay Street (Tel. 307-6966), is an innovative addition to Auckland's restaurant scene. It's on the street level in the Ferry Building, and diners enjoy interesting views of both patrons and harbor. Cin Cins is a brasserie style of bar/restaurant (in the Spago's of Los Angeles tradition) and serves either snacks or main meals right through the day and well into the night. Main dishes average $25. You add the cost of vegetables and salad to that, but one salad tends to satisfy two and costs around $3. **Sails,** on Westhaven Drive (Tel. 378-9890), is another good Auckland restaurant that takes advantage of the city's great harbor views. **Gaults on Quay** (Tel. 377-1200) also offers great harbor views seven days a week.

There has been a lot of development on Auckland's waterfront, with fresh impetus from the America's Cup event that kicked off in late 1999. Several more restaurants have popped up along the viaduct basin adjacent to the America's Cup Village. Two with good reputations are **The Loaded Hog** (Tel. 366-6491), a bar and brasserie, and **Kermedec Ocean Fresh Restaurant** (Tel. 309-0412). Both look over the water and moored yachts.

Newer still and buzzing over on Princes Wharf are at least a dozen new eateries, ranging from casual cafés to trendy restaurants. We tried **Euros** and were served culinary works of art on huge white plates that must be helping muscular development amongst the waiters.

Among the concentration of restaurants in Auckland's inner-city suburb of Ponsonby are some we'd like to go back to. **Java Jive** (Tel. 376-5870) on Pompalier Trace, just off Ponsonby Road, is a lively BYO restaurant with a jukebox churning out all the favorites and chefs who dish up appetizing main courses for around $18. Java Jive deserves its good-value reputation. Around the corner on Jervois Road is **Mosso Restaurant and Bar** (Tel. 376-5367), which we liked for atmosphere as well as food—especially the fritters made from the tiny, tasty fish called whitebait. Say hello to owner Tony from us if you dine there. Another talked-about restaurant is **Armadillos,** on Karangahape Road (called "K" Road locally). The bar seems as popular as the restaurant. A word of warning: Armadillos is one of those confident places that doesn't take bookings.

Newmarket, east of the city, is shaping up as the restaurant rival to Ponsonby. Notable is **Ramses** (Tel. 522-0619) on Khyber Pass, with its ceiling-to-floor windows, cocktail lounge, and interesting menus. If all this sounds too cosmopolitan, fall back on McDonald's on Broadway, Newmarket's main drag. There is also the ubiquitous Kentucky Fried Chicken.

The Village 8 and Rialto cinemas in Newmarket have several restaurants around the complexes. Across the road you can find American cuisine, and tucked in behind, Viva and the Safran Café and Bar seem to generate customers and laughter.

SEAFOOD RESTAURANTS

You may get excellent fish dishes at any really good Auckland restaurant, including many of the above. But of the half-dozen or so dining rooms specializing in *fruits de mer,* the **Harbourside Seafood and Grill** has been mentioned under the section of principal restaurants, but is included here as a good place to go for the best in New Zealand fish dishes. As a fun alternative, climb aboard the *Pride of Auckland,* a cruise vessel that serves fish for dinner. Bookings can be phoned through at 373-4557.

Heading east around Auckland's waterfront is **Hammerhead's Seafood Restaurant and Bar** (Tel. 521-4400) at 19 Tamaki Drive. The views out over the bay combine with cocktails and bar snacks. And a further word on Auckland's eastern suburbs: They curve around in a series of bays with names like Kohimaramara, Mission Bay, and St Heliers. Sitting across from the ocean they have the semi-permanent holiday atmosphere of beachside places. You won't be short of choice for dining. At St Heliers, **Saints** has built up a reputation for good dining. Seafood in this seaside place is naturally on the menu. One more fish place to note, **Alhambra Restaurant and Wine Bar** (Tel. 376-2430) sounds worth the trip to 283 Ponsonby Road in Ponsonby. It serves east coast prawns, Waiheke mussels, and South Island salmon.

STEAK HOUSES

Auckland beefeaters often praise a chain of restaurants all called Tony's, and all with a no-reservations policy. We hoed into **Tony's Lord Nelson** (Tel. 379-4564) at 37 Victoria Street West. My selection was a prime ox Scotch fillet with Sauce Nicholas—ten ounces of beef under a brown-onion-and-mushroom sauce, which was fine. (By the way, "fillet" or "filet" in New Zealand is usually pronounced with a hard *t*, sounding rather like "Fill it!") Other branches include the original **Tony's** (Tel. 307-4196) at 27 Wellesley Street West, and **Tony's Lorne Street** (Tel. 373-2138).

ETHNIC RESTAURANTS

Auckland's steady growth has seen the rise of a multitude of small new restaurants. A quick glance at the efficient Yellow Pages telephone directory under "Cuisine Guide" reveals the extent to which the city hosts a United Nations of food outlets. They range from Mongolian and Russian to Persian and Polynesian.

Chinese food, as in many other places of the world, abounds. The **New Orient** (Tel. 379-7793), at the top end of the Strand Arcade off Queen Street, is consistently good and sometimes offers live music and dancing. Other good Chinese addresses include the **Imperial Garden** (Tel. 303-4141) at 100 Albert Street, and **Empress Garden** on Jervois Road in Herne Bay (Tel. 376-5550). Many of the main courses cost under $13, and the Empress Garden got thumbs up from a recent review by Auckland's main newspaper, the NZ *Herald*.

Also in the go-ahead suburb of Newmarket is **The Pearl Garden** (Tel. 523-3696) at 1 Teed Street, where the tables are rarely empty. And try the **Ding How** (Tel. 358-4838). James Lincoln from Sunnyvale, California, wrote to us recommending the **Good Fortune Restaurant** (Tel. 302-0928) at 16 Emily Place in the city. Thanks, James. We'll try it next time 'round.

The **Chang Thong Thai** (Tel. 379-8704), at 195 Khyber Pass in Newmarket, is also receiving thumbs up from Auckland diners.

For *Italian* fare, **Da Vinci's** (Tel. 377-5428), at 508 Queen Street, is a popular BYO. **A Little Italy** (Tel. 379-5813) on Victoria Street West has similarly reasonable prices. More expensive but the genuine article is **Toto**

Italian Restaurant on Nelson Street (Tel. 302-2665). In the same league is **Cibo** in Parnell (Tel. 309-2255), where we found the ambience *simpatico.*

A merry and inexpensive place to dine is the **Mexican Café** (Tel. 373-2311), at 67 Victoria Street West. They turn on margaritas and Mexican musicians after 9 P.M. This BYO really does serve tacos, enchiladas, and other Mexican specialties. **Limon** on Princes Wharf is the new place to go for Tapas and good cheer.

If you like tandoori you might try the **Oh Calcutta** (Tel. 377-9090) in Parnell. The **Poppadom Restaurant** (Tel.529-1897) in Newmarket is another worth trying. Main dishes at Poppadom go for $10 to $20.

Japanese restaurants have also gained in popularity. One is **Ariake** (Tel. 379-2377), which serves up *teppanyaki* specialties at the corner of Albert Street and Customs Street West. Ariake has also a sushi bar in the Stamford Plaza Auckland hotel (Tel. 377-8881). The entrance is on Swanson Street. The increasing popularity of New Zealand with the Japanese, doubtless stimulated by the increase of Japanese tourists to the country, led to the opening also of **Daikoku Sushi** (Tel. 309-81512) on Quay Street opposite the Ferry Building, and to an even more recent addition called **Daikoku** (Tel. 302-2432), next door. The larger Daikoku is a Japanese steakhouse, and food is cooked at the table in *teppanyaki* style. It's easy to find at 48 Quay Street, facing the harbor, and it's open seven days a week.

If *American* can be considered an ethnic cuisine (a sobering thought), one restaurant lays claim to that title—**Rick's Café Américain** (Tel. 309-9074), in the Victoria Park Market (see section 10). Rick's, evocative of Bogart's gin mill in *Casablanca,* is supposed to serve American breakfasts (waffles and all that), plus genuine Yankee hamburgers, steaks, and the like. Sorry, we have no first-hand experience, but we'll be in As Time Goes By.

The Middle East Café (Tel. 379-4843) on Wellesley Street has been around for a long time, a sure sign of good food and good value for a BYO restaurant.

So impressive is the variety of ethnic restaurants in Auckland these days you could freewheel from the **Caravanserai Teahouse** in the city to the **Fez Café** in Ponsonby to practically whatever cuisine you feel like. The number of late-night café/restaurants is also healthy, especially in Parnell, Ponsonby, Herne Bay, Newmarket, and the central city. The cafe just across the square from the city's Aotea Centre, where many of the top concerts are performed, is also another late-night rendezvous. The Aotea Centre also has **Albert's Restaurant,** which we haven't had a chance to try yet, but the word is that it mostly gets thumbs-up.

LIGHT LUNCHES

Downtown shopping? Some of those little coffee bars where you pick up tidbits with tongs and order other things over the counter are hanging on to serve quick lunches. No alcohol is served, of course, but plenty of coffee, tea, milk shakes, and soft drinks are available. Some love those little sausage rolls, meat pies, and quiches—what Kiwis call "savouries." But they are gradually giving way to more European style cafés serving interesting, easy-to-eat light fare, accompanied by excellent varieties of coffee and tea. New Zealanders returning from the U.S.A. often can't wait to get back to their New Zealand knack of serving frothing cappuccinos, lattés, and long blacks.

When you are down on Princes Wharf, try **La Sierra.** Over in Parnell, **Frazer's Place** (Tel. 377-4080) is an interesting mix of deli and sit-down lunch bar on Parnell Road.

The basement floor of the **BNZ Tower** on Queen Street is an international food hall and a colorful place to watch the world go by. If you insist on a quarter pound of Yankee-ana, **McDonald's** is at 260 Queen Street, in the most interesting old un-McDonald's-like rococo structure you ever saw (the former Bank of New Zealand building). The **Sitting Duck Café** (Tel. 376-0374) is a delightful lunchtime spot at Westhaven, especially in the warmer months. The tables outside overlook Auckland's myriad yachts. Across the road from Kelly Tarlton's Underwater Museum is **Kelly's Café** (Tel. 528-5267), with a great view of the Waitemata Harbour.

On the other side of the Waitemata, at Devonport, is **Clarry's** (Tel. 445-4173), a café/restaurant at 18 Clarence Street. As you wander through this quaint, maritime Auckland backwater, you'll be impressed with the number of good eating places and specialty shops.

Auckland's Domain, on a hill above the city, is a green and wooded retreat from the city. You will find the impressive War Memorial Museum here (Tel. 373-4229). It's in the Domain near the museum. The café in the museum itself has fat ham sandwiches.

It's hard to find the right spot for **Death by Chocolate,** a strictly dessert restaurant in Mission Bay. You can be sure of one thing—calories. Drop in for one of their delicious desserts at your peril. The Mission Bay Death by Chocolate is on Tamaki Drive.

NATURAL AND HEALTH FOOD

These places open and close faster than Bugs Bunny chomping on a carrot. But probably the best-known at present is the **Simple Cottage** (Tel. 303-4599) at 50 High Street, behind Whitcoulls bookstore. They have no meat, fish, or eggs, limiting everything to salads, homemade cakes, vegetable shepherd's pie, bean sprout and pea salads, etc., along with several

kinds of fruit juices. Some nights the Simple Cottage goes all out with ethnic vegetarian dishes from Indonesia, India, China, Japan, or Mexico.

6. Sightseeing in Auckland and Up North

We find no absolute "musts" in Auckland sightseeing for anyone who is
going on to experience the rest of the country. In fact, many find it practical to tour Auckland *after* seeing the nation from top to bottom. But
Auckland should not be regarded merely as a gateway into and out of the
country. It has many scenic treats of its own.

North Americans getting used to driving on the "wrong" side of the
road will find it easier outside the city, and any traveler who wants to do
some shopping in New Zealand may also find Auckland to be a more practical alternative the second time around.

There are a half-dozen or so standouts within the city limits; these are
listed below. Many of them can be seen on standard city sightseeing tours
(section 7).

A personal favorite, and now becoming one of the outstanding museums of its type in the world, is MOTAT—the **Museum of Transport and
Technology** (Tel. 846-0199), on the Great North Road out in the Western
Springs neighborhood. MOTAT's scope is so wide it's hard to describe, but
in general it seems to include everything you remember from the past, and
a lot more, all in bright and shiny condition, and most even in working
order. There are cars, trains, and planes, of course, but you'll also find old-
fashioned printing presses, typewriters, music boxes and player pianos, pioneer cottages, schoolhouses, telephones, fire stations, motion pictures,
rockets, computers, spacecraft, mechanical organs, open-top electric trol-
leys, telegraph equipment, and so on.

War buffs have plenty to interest them there, too. In fact MOTAT's original seven-acre site is now linked by a tram and double-decker bus service
to the new Sir Keith Park Memorial Airfield, a 30-acre extension re-creating
a World War II military airport, and to the Auckland Zoo. Admission price
runs at $8 for adults, half that for youngsters. It's open 9 to 5 during the
week and 10 to 5 Saturday and Sunday. Take Bus 045 from Customs Street
or drive west on Route 19 for a couple of miles. If you're spending at least
one overnight in Auckland, you shouldn't miss MOTAT.

Auckland's most traditional cultural attraction is the **Auckland War
Memorial Museum** (Tel. 377-3932), which crowns the center of the
Auckland Domain, just east of the city center. This may be the best place
to begin an investigation of Maori history. The 82-foot carved war canoe is
magnificent. Be sure to push the button to hear the recording about it and

about Hotunui, the nearby Maori meetinghouse. Somewhere in the museum, too, is a reconstruction of the giant moa. It's open from 10 to 5 daily, and it is free. Small donations are politely requested and left to individual discretion. (Take Bus No. 645 or 655 from the Municipal Bus Terminal.) Its museum shop is one of the better places to buy genuine New Zealand artifacts.

There are two main hills in Auckland. We've been up them both and recommend you hit at least one of them. Both are the remains of ancient volcanoes, and each was fortified as a Maori *pa* in ancient times. **Mount Eden** is the tallest hill, at 643 feet, and gives a good view of all of Auckland. It might be worth visiting after you know something of the city and can recognize other sites. (Take Bus No. 274 from Customs Street East.)

Then there's **One Tree Hill,** 600 feet tall; it really is capped by a single pine tree, as it has been more or less continuously since ancient times. The monument beside it honors one of Auckland's earliest settlers, Sir John Logan Campbell, whose 1841 cottage is also further down the slopes in Cornwall Park. It's the oldest building in the city. By the way, you may see cattle grazing on Mount Eden, or sheep wandering on One Tree Hill—bucolic touches right in the center of a major metropolis. (Take Buses No. 302, 304, 305, or 312, from Victoria Street East.) Mt. Hobson, in the wealthy suburb of Remuera, is another peaceful stroll close to the city. The views from here out over the harbor are splendid.

The city is awfully proud of its **Harbor Bridge,** built in 1959 to link it with the North Shore. There were four lanes originally, but it soon needed four more. These were attached to the sides by a Japanese construction firm, and the addition was popularly dubbed the "Nippon Clip-on." There are still a few ferryboats in operation, however (see section 7).

On Wellesley Street East, just at the corner of Kitchener Street, is the **Auckland Art Gallery** (Tel. 379-2020), which houses works by New Zealand, American, British, and European masters. (Hours vary considerably by the season and day of the week and are frequently changed.) Stop for a coffee in the gallery's café. If the sun is shining you could sip it outside on the terrace.

We've seen lots of aquariums at one time or another, but nothing quite like **Kelly Tarlton's Underwater World** (Tel. 528-0603), where the fish might believe that you are the one in the aquarium. A moving belt carries you through a clear acrylic tunnel under the sea, almost allowing you to rub shoulders with sharks and other down-deep denizens. The aquarium has now opened its new Antarctic Centre, complete with live penguins and a ferocious Orca killer whale, a fake beast along the lines of the *Jaws* shark that springs at you at Universal Studios in Hollywood. The center offers an intriguing insight into life at the South Pole. Tickets are $20 for adults and

$10 for children and include admission to both the Antarctic Centre and the aquarium. It is well worth it. You can drive or taxi to the entrance along Tamaki Drive to the old Orakei Wharf. Buz-a-Bus (Tel. 366-6400) and the Explorer bus both pass by Kelly Tarlton's from the center of town. (The aquarium is open 9 A.M. to 9 P.M. daily.) And just over the road, overlooking the harbor, is Kelly's Café, a good lunch spot.

You'll find many more Auckland "sights" listed elsewhere. The zoo is nice, and two special attractions are the nocturnal Kiwi house and the tuatara reptile, which has an ancient heritage. Admission is $12 for adults and $4.50 for children. There are several lovely gardens and parks, like Cornwall Park, where sheep and cattle graze. Rainbow's End is bumper-boat dizzy and appeals more to local fun-seekers than to international travelers, but some young American United Airline crewmembers spotted there were having a good time. "Like an old-fashioned fair," one giggled. I'm not sure about that, but it could be worth a visit. Be sure to stop by the Auckland Visitor Centre (Tel. 366-6888) in Aotea Square to see what's going on and to pick up some pamphlets.

The popular **Victoria Park Market** (Tel. 309-6911) is open every day now. As previously mentioned, there has been much work done on Auckland's waterfront, and a new attraction is the **NZ National Maritime Museum** (Tel. 358-1019), very much a hands-on experience. It has been receiving good reviews. Find it at Hobson Wharf.

Near Auckland's Domain is the **Cathedral of the Holy Trinity,** which blends Gothic with Pacific style, controversially some would say, imaginatively in the opinion of others. For many the beautiful wooden Church of St. Mary, sitting beside the much newer cathedral, is the star attraction. At the other end of the spectrum, **Sky City** is worth inspecting for its indigenous works of art representing different aspects of New Zealand's heritage and drawing on Maori legend and early settlement. Murals and sculptures by leading New Zealand artists have been involved. The ride to the top of Sky Tower is rewarded with knockout views of the city and harbor.

Speaking of the harbor, the **America's Cup Village** should be added to your list of walkabouts in downtown Auckland. In this sail-oriented city it's a must-see.

Escaping from Sky City's casino and revolving restaurant to rural Auckland can take just half an hour. If farms are of interest, a visit to **Montgomerie Farm** (Tel. 09-292-8724), just a few miles south of Auckland, will prove a good day out. This 760-acre sheep, cattle, and goat farm offers an interesting day with BBQ lunches and friendly Kiwi hospitality.

The Explorer All Day Bus Pass costs $20 and stops at all the major attractions in the city area. Buy your ticket from the Downtown Airline Terminal. (Tel. 571-3119).

Finally, how about a visit to a genuine Auckland home and a chat with a friendly family? Nothing could be easier. Just ring up Polly Ring, secretary of **Auckland Tourist Hospitality** (Tel. 575-6655), and she'll take care of the rest. If Polly is not at home when you call, try Jean Mahon at 624-3398 or Valerie Blackie at 625-9373. This volunteer group has taken pleasure in meeting overseas visitors for several years. If you can write in advance, do so to 775 Riddell Road, Glendowie, Auckland 5, New Zealand. The charge? Don't be silly. It's absolutely free.

THE BAY OF ISLANDS

We'd head across that Harbor Bridge early in our trip and generally follow Route 1 to see what's up in the Northland peninsula, the site of some of the first and most important settlements of the country. En route north, stop by **Sheepworld,** four kilometers north of Warkworth. It's a kind of mini-farm under one roof. You will see wizard farm dogs rounding up the animals and other techniques of farming that city dwellers don't usually get the chance to see. Sheepworld's shop and café make this a good stop as well as fun.

The number-one destination for New Zealander and foreigner alike is the Bay of Islands, centered principally around the town of **Paihia,** 170 miles north of Auckland. This beautiful, ragged coast is the birthplace of the nation. Don't miss the Treaty House, where the Treaty of Waitangi between the British and the Maori was signed in 1840. (On the map Waitangi and Paihia seem to be different towns, but they're within a mile of each other.) You might have a look also at the Museum of Shipwrecks.

But the most fun in Paihia is to take one of several **launch cruises** that wind through the islands of the bay. The most popular excursion is **Fuller's Hole in the Rock Cruise,** (Tel. 09-402-7422), a four-hour ride. Wait till they take you right through the middle of hollow Piercy Island. It costs $55 per adult and $28 per child. If that is too long for you, take one of their shorter cruises of three hours that departs both morning and afternoon. These cruises have names like Dolphin Encounters (and you do encounter real dolphins), Cream Trip (this is one of the old favourites), and Tall Ship Tucker Thompson. Fuller's are longtime operators in Northland, and they also run coach trips from the Bay of Islands to Cape Reinga on the tip of the North Island.

King Tours & Cruises (Tel. 0508-888-282) offer a speeded-up version of the Hole in the Rock—one and a half hours of an exhilarating 60-knot ride for 30 passengers. The price is $50 for adults and $25 for children. More leisurely by a long shot is *Windborne,* a 51-ft. schooner built in 1928 like a Bristol Channel pilot cutter. Comfortable, safe *Windborne* charges $60 for her ride. (Tel 403-7538.)

The Bay of Islands is a mecca for fishing folk, and **Earl Grey Fishing Charters** takes you out in a light-tackle fishing vessel with skipper Steve Butler (Tel. 407-7165). Prices are $140 per person. Divers should get in touch with **Paihia Dive & Charters** at 402-7551 to explore the many fine dive sites in the bay, including the wreck of the *Rainbow Warrior,* the Greenpeace vessel destroyed by French agents in 1985. Prices range from $85 to $145. There are plenty of kayaking opportunities in this neck of the woods, too. **Coastal Kayakers** guide half-day tours costing from $40 and will give the uninitiated full instruction (Tel. 402-8105). And before we depart the water, **Dolphin Discoveries** (Tel. 402-8234) takes people out to see the dolphins and to swim with them, weather permitting. They provide the wetsuits. We haven't done this yet but want to. Those lucky enough to have swum with dolphins rate the experience as very special.

Be sure to take the ferry (or the more expensive Aquataxi) across the channel to the town of **Russell.** The first capital of New Zealand, Russell was originally called Kororareka, and it is the site of that flagpole that Chief Hone Heke kept chopping down in the 1840s. Difficult to get to by road, the village has an ancient charm about it, and one local pub still holds New Zealand's first liquor license. Don't miss the museum.

The Bay of Islands turns from a sleepy backwater into something more reminiscent of its wild colonial past during the New Zealand holiday season of January. The Duke of Marlborough pub on the waterfront bulges with revelers, game fishermen, and "yachties," who converge on the tiny town to enjoy its many offerings.

A couple of restaurants to call into while you are in Paihia are Only Seafood (Tel. 402-7444) on the waterfront overlooking the Bay of Islands and serving fresh local seafood. Close by is Bistro 40 (Tel. 402-7444) on the waterfront at 40 Marsden Road. Saltwater Café on Kings Road (Tel. 402-7783) is a recent award winner for its New Zealand cuisine, heaps of fresh seafood, beef and lamb, and blackboard specials. We also recommend Waikokopu Café in the Waitangi Treaty Grounds (Tel. 402-6275).

Do drive up the road 15 miles to the village of **Kerikeri** (actually, just the other side of it), and stop in the Old Stone Store and the next-door **Kemp House.** Built in 1822 as the original mission house in the area, it's now the oldest building in New Zealand. Just across the little bridge is Rewa's Maori Village, a re-creation of a pre-European settlement. The whole immediate area with its rapids and meandering estuary is a lovely, peaceful spot. A charming tearoom overlooks the surrounding countryside, too. The old mission house at **Waimate North** is said to be equally delightful, but we haven't seen it. Kerikeri oranges sell throughout New Zealand and are deliciously seedless.

If you're staying in the Paihia area, you can choose from backpacker up to top-notch accommodations. Backpackers should head for Centabay Lodge (Tel. 402-7466) or Peppertree Lodge (Tel. 402-6122). You'll be paying from $15 for dormitory beds and shared facilities. Campers can pitch the tent or park the motorhome at the Bay of Islands Holiday Park or Russell Top 10 Holiday Park at Long Beach. Our B&B recommendations are Craicor (Tel. 402-7882) and Seascape (Tel. 402-7650), in the $80 range. At the top end is Pukematu Lodge, set in native bush (Tel. 403-8500). Motels receiving good comments from guests include Edgewater Motel (Tel. 402-7875), Marline Court (Tel. 0800-800-959), Kauri Park in Kerikeri (Tel. 407-7629), and Commodores Lodge (403-7899). These four all charge room rates from about $60 to $190.

If you like the thought of staying in an apartment, try Pioneer Apartments (Tel. 402-7924) on the waterfront on Marsden Road, where you will be paying from around $175 to $260, kitchens included. On Seaview Road are the very comfortable units of the Beachcomber (Tel. 402-7434). Host Bryan Williams is proud of the many facilities Beachcomber offers guests. Rates range from $120-170 double. If it's a suite you are after, expect to pay between $260 and $330.

In the high season, Kerikeri could be the more peaceful place to stay. The pick of the motel selection includes Riverview Chalets Park Lodge (Tel. 407-8741), where the hosts are German immigrants Angelica and Helmut Letz, who scoured New Zealand before falling in love with Kerikeri. Peak season rates are $350 double with breakfast. They have completed extensive renovations, which have piled on the charm. Helmut knows all the good places for his guests to visit and where to put his finger on all the ingredients that make the most of excursions. We enjoyed our stay at Riverview Chalets. The Colonial House motel (Tel. 407-9106) also scores an excellent rating from the trusty *AA Guide*. Rates are from $140 double.

Russell, across the water from Paihia, has accommodations at the Duke of Marlborough (Tel. 403-7829) from $95 to $235 double. The Te Maiki Hill Villas (Tel. 403-7046) have kitchens and the rate is from $149 double. We can recommend the old colonial Ludbrook House, where genial hosts Sam and Christine Ludbrook will make guests feel warmly welcome. Christine is the local physiotherapist and has an equal interest in art. Paintings by some of New Zealand's well-known artists are for sale in the gallery in Ludbrook House.

Orongo Bay Homestead (Tel. 09-403-7527), an historic colonial house (originally owned by the American Consulate), has been rejuvenated by hosts Michael Hooper and Chris Swannell. You will find it in a secluded bay just around the corner from Russell. Michael is a superb chef and Chris is a natural host. What could be better?

Get all the dope on the Bay of Islands from the folks at Tourism Northland, P.O. Box 365, Paihia, Bay of Islands (Tel. 402-7683). Or check Northland out on the Internet at www.northland.org.nz. You can also call in to the Bay of Islands Information Centre (Tel. 402-7426) on Marsden Road. They will book you into anything that moves—or offers sleep or food. They are open from 8 A.M. until 5 P.M. We drove to the Bay of Islands in about 3.5 hours, but you may also get there by bus or charter a Helicopter Line flight right from downtown Auckland to downtown Paihia (Auckland Tel. 377-4405). It takes about an hour each way from Mechanics Bay. There are also scheduled flights from Auckland Domestic Airport to a small strip at Kerikeri.

CAPE REINGA AND THE FAR NORTH

Many go up to the cape as a day trip from Paihia. Fuller's and King's Tours and Cruises run daily trips that people speak of with enthusiasm. But we preferred to drive it ourselves, staying in **Kaitaia** overnight. The Orana Motor Inn (Tel. 09-408-1510) at 238 Commerce Street is comfortable and comfortably priced from $75 double. The Wayfarer Motel (Tel. 408-2600) at 231 Commerce also looks comfortable and rates are $66 single and $92 twin or double. Sierra Court Motor Lodge has 16 spacious, self-contained units and a swimming pool. Prices are from $65 double (Tel. 408-1461). Kaitaia has a strong Yugoslav community dating from the years of the last century when they slogged in the gum fields, felling the native kauri tree.

Tour companies like Harrisons Cape Runner, based in Kaitaia, run local tours from Kaitaia up to **Cape Reinga.** The "Cape Trip" takes you over the sands of **Ninety Mile Beach** (which, strangely, is 64 miles long—about 90 *kilometers*), then drives right on top of a running stream, and finally carries on up to the very tip of New Zealand, the lighthouse at Cape Reinga. We wouldn't have missed it for the world. We hear that beach buggies and *waka* rides are now part of the fun. Check it out. The telephone number is 408-1033.

There's another trip that looks like fun. Tuatua Tours (Tel. 409-4875) uses a special dune buggy to travel over the sand and rocks of Reef Point. We note these guys are licensed by the government's Department of Conservation, so that's a comforting thought.

Tall Tale Travel 'N' Tours (Tel. 408-0870) are Maori tour operators in the Far North, and offers tours that bring participants in touch with Maori culture. Peter, from the Te Aupouri tribe, is in charge.

You're allowed to drive over Ninety Mile Beach yourself, if you want. Speed limit is 100 km/h, same as the maximum in all New Zealand, and of course you're to keep to the left. (We advise you *not* to drive the entire length, because traversing the Te Paki stream at the very end is dangerous without local knowledge of the quicksand!) The Adriaan Lodge Motel (Tel. 409-4888) in Ahipara at the southern end of Ninety Mile Beach offers comfortable accommodations with sea views. Rates are from $50 double. You could also try The Park, 90 Mile Beach (Tel. 406-7298), where cabins range from $45 to $60 double and there's a restaurant and bar. Our other recommendation is Whatuwhiwhi Holiday Park (the name appeals, too). It is out on the magnificent KariKari Peninsula and rates are from $85 double. (Tel. 408-7202).There's also a good seafood restaurant called **The Albatross.** To walk the beach and soak up the magnificent scenery you'll need three days and stout boots. There are camping grounds at Tepotupotu and Spirit's Bay.

On the way back to Kaitaia on the paved road, keep an eye out for the privately owned **Wagener Museum.** You may never have seen such an intriguing pile of junk before. Adjacent to the museum is the **Wagener Tourist Park** (Tel. 409-8850), which has an 18-hole golf course and camping site among its attractions. The **Sullivan's Glow Worm Grotto** is also a worthwhile stop. An interesting glimpse into the history of the Far North is provided by the **Far North Regional Museum** (Tel. 408-1403) at Houhora Heads. There's also a camping ground at Houhora (408-1400).

WAIPOUA KAURI FOREST

If you've gone up the east side of the peninsula, the interesting and scenic way down is via the west, through the magnificent Waipoua Kauri Forest. Call into the Waipoua Visitor's Centre for directions. Be sure to recheck the operating hours if you're planning on using the daily *Kohu-Ra* vehicle ferry between Rawene and Kohukohu. Sometimes the last boat leaves at 4:45 P.M. The crossing takes about 15 minutes and costs about $12 per car. At **Opononi,** you may want to glance at the statue of the boy with the dolphin in front of the hotel. It commemorates Opo, the animal who played with children out in the bay during the summer of 1955-56, until it was tragically killed. Much has been written about it.

Both the golden beach towns of Opononi and Omapere have motor camps and motels. Try the Opononi Resort Hotel (Tel. 405-8858), which has rates from $90 double. There's a restaurant and bar in the hotel. It was once a gracious old Kauri villa, but alas has been extended beyond recognition. Still, the hospitality is genuine. As Omapere is a long gold stretch of a beach, the Omapere Tourist Hotel (Tel. 405-8737) is well placed and units here cost from $90. The Northland Tourism people recommend Riverhead Guest House (Tel. 405-8815), a fine old Kauri home where rates are $65 double.

The Hokianga Harbor is steeped in Maori and European history. Call the Hokianga Express Cruises (Tel. 405-8872) in Rawene for sandhill trips along the mountainous dunes that shawl the mouth of the harbor. This company also offers harbour cruises as well as water taxi services. Alma 80 Scow is a boat charter company for fishing and cruising along the Hokianga's waterways. Kokukohu Carvers (Tel. 405-5846) is where you will find handcarved bone, stone, and wood in traditional as well as contemporary designs. Commissions are undertaken and visitors are welcome to watch carvers at work. In this leisurely part of the world you feel time is on your side forever.

The road (Route 12) leads to the forest. The specific sights to see in the Kauri forest reserve are one or two of the big trees that are pointed out there. At one rest stop you can walk for a few yards into the woods to admire Tane Mahuta ("God of the Forest"), a kauri that is well over 1,200 years old and measures 170 feet in height and 44 feet around the middle. Time stands still in the lush, cool greenery of the Waipoua State Forest. The **Trounson Kauri Park,** about 10 miles south of the Waipoua forest, is a small but superb stand of trees. A track through the park takes about half an hour. Then, about 28 miles southeast of Dargaville, at Matakohe, there's the interesting **Matakohe Kauri Museum** (Tel. 431-7417), with an unusual collection of kauri gum. Merv Sterling is its creator; please say hello to him from us. This solidified resin used to be mined in the area, traditionally by Dalmatians equipped with long poles for poking into the ground. (The museum will explain it all.)

On your way south again, it is worth the detour into a tranquil and lovely harbor called **Whangaroa.** If you are tempted to stay over—and we could not blame you for that—a recommended dinner place is Kingfish Lodge (Tel. 406-0164). With restaurant, bar, and seemingly limitless sporting kingfish, the doubles rate of $250 (including breakfast and dinner) is palatable.

The North is not short on local visitor and information centers. You will find them in Whangarei, Kaitaia, Dargaville, Hokianga, and the Bay of Islands.

7. Guided Tours and Cruises

Before we forget it, let's just say that in general guided tours in New Zealand lean toward the superb, largely due to the skill and humor of the driver/guides. Once in a while you draw a dud, but there seems to be a tradition that bus drivers are entertaining as well as informative, and most seem to establish a friendly rapport with their passengers, especially on the longer trips. An extra bonus is that this is often the best way to meet traveling Kiwis, too.

Sightseeing tours are volatile businesses in New Zealand, with each year seeing several new companies starting up, then merging with or selling out to others. As of this writing, we know of at least five outfits in Auckland specializing in tours of the city and immediately outlying areas. By the time you arrive, there may be more. All will probably pick you up at your hotel, but it's always a good idea to make sure.

Gray Line Tours (Tel. 375-4707) has a half-day Auckland city tour that can be extended to include the seaside suburb of Devonport, returning on the ferry, or a cruise to the island of Rangitoto (now an extinct volcano). The same company has a one-day trip to Rotorua and extensive coach tours throughout New Zealand. They have plenty of travel experience to go with these tours.

Scenic Tours (Tel. 634-2266), another well-established company, also divides their main Auckland tours into morning and afternoon excursions and one- and two-day tours to Rotorua and Waitomo and one- to two-day trips to Cape Reinga and the Bay of Islands. Day trips to Rotorua cost from $139 and depart Auckland at 8 A.M., arriving home again at 8:15 P.M. Lunch is included in the pricier versions of this day trip. There's a one-day tour to Waitomo to visit the fascinating glow worm caves. The day trip to the Bay of Islands takes travelers all the way up to Cape Reinga, cruising out to Cape Brett and the famous Hole in the Rock and into Russell. It's a long day, departing Auckland at 8 A.M. and getting back to town 12 hours later. You pay around $180 for this adventure, but we recommend spending a little more to stay overnight in the Bay of Islands.

Great Sights (Tel. 375-4700). A half-day Auckland city tour costs from about $40. Great Sights includes visits to Sky Tower, a harbor cruise, and Kelly Tarlton's. This company used to call into Auckland's vineyards half an hour west of the city and heading toward the forested Waitakere Rangers. Alas, this is no more. "Not enough interest," say the tour operators. That surprises us, given the number of excellent wines on sale from the cellar door, and the good restaurants in the area, let alone the attractive scenery.

Auckland Adventures (Tel. 379-4545) could be the answer to a winery tour. The company picked up a NZ Tourism Award a couple of years ago for their specialty tours. **Exclusive Tours** (Tel. 815-1696), run by owner Sharron Hickman, could be another. Sharron and her team tailor tours to fit the bill.

Another good choice is **Bush and Beach** (Tel. 478-2882), which concentrates on gentle walks through subtropical rain forests and along surf beaches west of the city. Ask for Tim Sherring or Russell Leese, the owner/operators. One of their most rewarding excursions is to view the rare mainland gannet colony on Auckland's Muriwai Beach from August through April. **Maori Heritage Tours** (Tel. 235-1341) has been going since 1993 and offers guided half-day tours of Auckland from a Maori perspective. You'll be treated to a Maori welcome ceremony and visit to a marae (Maori meeting house). Half-day tours cost $60, full day $99, including lunch. For chartered tours outside of Auckland, two of the best-known companies are the **Mount Cook Coachline** (Tel. 375-4705) and **Guthreys** (Tel. 846-4144).

Just $20 buys an all-day bus pass on a double-decker London bus called the *Explorer*. It does a round of major city attractions and departs from the Ferry Building on the harbor every half hour from 9:30 A.M. to 4 P.M. The Satellite Bus operates over the summer, does a wider circuit, and you can swap between the two buses for no extra cost. Tickets are available from the driver.

Buz-a-Bus passes, which cost $7, enable you to ramble off to a variety of interesting destinations at your leisure. Use them on Auckland's yellow buses. Buy the passes from the driver.

PRIVATE TAXIS AND LIMOUSINES

There is a lot of competition in the private limo business, but two of the bigger companies are **Limousines & Tours** (Tel. 0800-454-6670) and **Hallmark Limousines & Tour Coaches** (Tel. 629-0940). They provide services in Auckland and around the country. From any such service the cost quoted is usually for the car and driver only. All sightseeing, meals, etc. (for you and the chauffeur) will be extra. (We would like to hear from any travelers who have tried these or similar services anywhere in New Zealand.)

WATER TRIPS AND GULF ISLANDS

There are several ways to get out on Auckland's lovely Waitemata Harbor and the channels in the Hauraki Gulf. Unless you have friends with their own boat, nothing is available for the Manukau Harbor on the Tasman Sea side.

Regular ferries run between Auckland and Devonport and out to Waiheke Island. The trip across the inner harbor to Devonport takes 15 minutes, and the round trip costs $7. From Devonport there are several public buses to popular beaches.

Boats leave from the terminal several times a day for *Waiheke Island*. Telephone 367-9102 for reservations. This number belongs to **Fullers,** who also operate ferry services to Devonport and other islands in the gulf. The largest island right in the Hauraki Gulf, Waiheke boasts a few villages, several farms, and some nice beaches. Either ferries or a high-speed *Quick Cat* operate the run to Waiheke; both cost $23 round trip, but the *Quick Cat* takes 35 minutes to the ferry's one hour.

Fullers has their booking office in the Ferry Terminal building on the harbor. Pick up a copy of their cruise guide for all the instant options. They have tours on tap of Waiheke, which include a visit to the island's reputable **Stonyridge** vineyard, producers of one of the world's classiest Cabernets. You can stay over on the island if you wish. There are several motels. One choice spot could be in "the Loft" at Stonyridge, overlooking its olive grove and vineyard. There are also several restaurants on the island. The **Fig Tree Café** (Tel. 372-6363) could also be a good bet. It has picked up awards from the Taste New Zealand panel.

Cruises for *Rangitoto Island,* whose graceful, symmetrical silhouette is seen from many parts of Auckland, are run by **Fullers Cruises** aboard boats departing from their own wharf across from the Downtown Terminal by the Ferry Building. Cruise time is about one hour, and the cost of the ticket for the ride and tour is $35. Rangitoto, a "dormant" (not extinct) volcano, was formed only about 800 years ago and may have erupted as recently as 250 years ago. Today it's a recreation reserve and a favorite picnic and bushwalking destination for Aucklanders. It's connected by a causeway to *Motutapu Island,* which has some interesting archeological sites and World War II fortifications. Motutapu, like nearby Tiritiri Matangi Island, is being turned back into the native forest it once was so it can become a sanctuary to threatened native bird species. Put on your walking shoes and head up the road as far as your constitution permits. The view from the island back toward the city is worth the pant. Ferries depart Auckland daily at 9:30 in the morning and at 12 and 2:30 in the afternoon. There are cruises to the neighboring islands. We recommend the cruise to Tiritiri Matangi, where New Zealand's native birds are not threatened by predators. The trip costs $30, and a Department of Conservation guide on the island can show you around for $5. One inexpensive way to cruise through many of the Hauraki Gulf Islands is on the mail run trip. The ticket is $20.

During summer, Fullers operates cruises ($39 return) to *Kawau Island,* home of the century-old Mansion House, built for New Zealand's first governor, Sir George Grey. More regular cruises to Kawau are run by Kawau Cruises daily from the Sandspit, about an hour's drive north of Auckland. Hop on their "Royal Mail Run," a day cruise leaving the Sandspit mid-morning. The ticket is $39, and the telephone number is 425-8006. If you are going to stay on the island, the return ticket is $22.

The commodious *Jet Raider* operated by Fullers cruises to *Great Barrier Island*, the furthermost island in the Gulf, with magnificent beaches and thick native forest. The cost for these trips is from $79 return. You may be escorted by dolphins and whales, and be drowned by native birdsong on arrival. Even penguins live on hospitable Great Barrier. Jump on the *Island Adventure Bus* with Bob's Tours. It's well worth the $45 ticket for the day. Tipi and Bob's **Waterfront Lodge** is on the waterfront at Puriri Bay. Fullers can book you in if you've a mind to stay over. Prices are from $95 and Tipi and Bob are proud of their new restaurant, bistro, and bar. You can call them direct (Tel. 09429-0550). Accommodation on Great Barrier that is clean and comfortable and will leave change in your pocket includes **Medlands Backpackers' Hostel** and **Stray Possum Backpackers.** Rates are from $20 per night.

A novel transport mode to Great Barrier is aboard **Gulf Trans** vessels (Tel. 373-4036), which take up to 85 passengers as well as vehicles and freight. Cost is $65 return including a BBQ lunch, and travel time is 6 hours.

The Fullers people also run cruises from Auckland to **Motuihe** and back. Featuring Norfolk pines and olive groves, Motuihe has an interesting history as a camp for prisoners during World War I. It was from there that the famous Count Felix Von Luckner made a dramatic escape in 1917.

The Pride of Auckland, a 60-foot catamaran launched by the **Charter Cruise Company** (Tel. 373-4557), currently offers one of the best sails in the City of Sails. If you catch their 12:30 P.M. departure, you will dine on fresh N.Z. *Schnapper.* The dinner cruises depart at 5, 6, and 8 P.M. Catch the boat or make your bookings at the Launch Steps, near the ferry building. The dinner cruise ticket costs $80, and lunch $60. Or you could step back a couple of centuries and sail a handsomely re-created squarerigger called *Tall Ship Soren Larsen* (Tel. 411-8755). She goes out on the harbor for short cruises or longer trips up to the Bay of Islands. Three-hour cruises cost $49.

Before we leave the water, **Auckland Adventure Kayaking** will take you on a guided eco-tour of estuaries and coastline. Chris Gulley and his experienced team pick you up from the hotel, provide all the gear, and show you how to kayak. Members of the NZ Outdoor Instructors Association, they do a professional job, give kayakers a good time, and charge $89 for the adventure.

AIR TOURS

An aerial sightseeing operation is the **Helicopter Line** (Tel. 377-4406). Their hangars are at Mechanics Bay, just off Quay Street. Sightseeing flights over Auckland and the inner gulf islands range from $125 to $285. They can also be chartered for an array of flightseeing adventures, excursions to

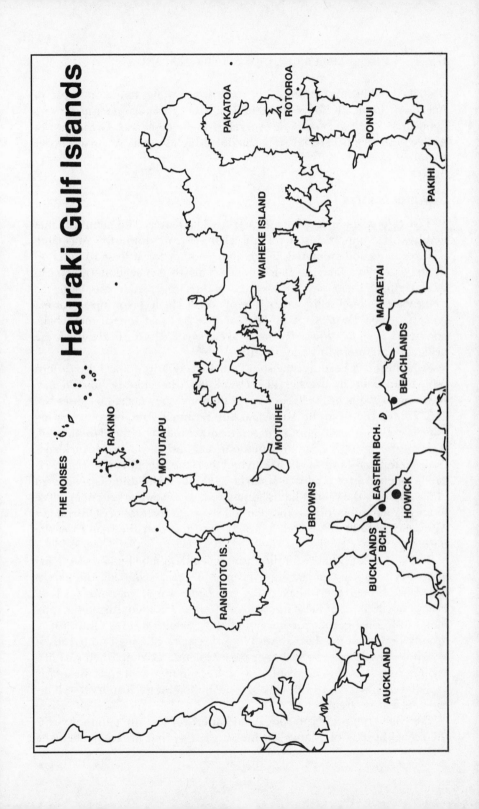

Hauraki Gulf Islands

THE NOISES

PAKATOA

ROTOROA

PONUI

PAKIHI

WAIHEKE ISLAND

RAKINO

MOTUTAPU

MOTUIHE

MARAETAI

BEACHLANDS

EASTERN BCH.

BROWNS

RANGITOTO IS.

HOWICK

BUCKLANDS BCH.

AUCKLAND

Waiheke, helifishing in the Gulf, and wine-tasting tours out west of Auckland. **Scenic Air Tours** (Tel. 09-256-8699) has a similar operation using light aircraft. Their 30-minute Auckland flight costs $88. **Great Barrier Airlines** (Tel. 0800-900-600) runs scheduled flights across to Great Barrier Island every day.

8. Water Sports

Take a look at a map of the greater Auckland area. The peninsula that ends with Devonport, just across the channel from downtown Auckland, features one good **swimming** beach after another for at least 10 miles on up the east coast. Take the 15-minute ferry across (see section 7). You can swim right at Devonport or take the connecting private bus either to *Cheltenham Beach,* just the other side of North Head, or on up to *Narrow Neck, St. Leonard's, Takapuna, Milford, Castor Bay,* and several more bays, ending at *Long Bay Regional Park.* (Take a bus back to Auckland via the bridge for an interesting round trip.)

Swimmers can head out the shoreline Tamaki Drive toward the eastern suburbs to swim at beaches like *Okahu Bay* (the closest), *Mission Bay, Kohimarama Beach,* or *St. Heliers Bay.* All these may be reached by buses No. 715, 716, or 766 from the Municipal Bus Terminal. And, of course, swimming is excellent at Rangitoto and several other islands in the Hauraki Gulf.

Swimming pools, indoor and outdoor, abound throughout Auckland. Dedicated natatorians might like to look into the "Tepid Baths" (Tel. 379-4794), open every day. Hearty breakfasts, lunches, and dinners are served in Champions, the "Tepid Baths" restaurant. The Newmarket pool is close to town. Yet another pool is the "Parnell Baths" at the foot of St. Stephen's Avenue near Judges Bay (Tel. 373-3561) and just over the road from the harbor front.

The west coast beaches on the Tasman Sea should be limited to **surfing** (but they're not). One big-wave favorite is *Piha,* about 25 miles from Auckland through the Waitakere Ranges. Another is *Muriwai Beach,* a little farther north. Both of these iron-sand strips have excellent surf in the summer, but are dangerous for the uninitiated. As one surf-wise Kiwi put it, "You have to treat the Tasman with lots of respect. She's got no friends at all!" Both beaches are patrolled by New Zealand's accomplished surf life-saving teams, and they are kept busy on hot summer weekends. Be aware, too, that that black sand will stick to you. You'll want to clean it off well before leaving the area.

Ever since the American sportsman Zane Grey took up temporary residence in the Bay of Islands during the 1920s, that area has been the headquarters for serious **deep-sea fishing,** especially from January through April. There are about two dozen charter boats berthed at *Russell,* and a few more just across the way at *Paihia.* Most go out for over $700 a day, or you may get something on a share-boat basis of about $140 per person. Anglers mainly pull in three types of marlin, several kinds of shark, king-fish, and large tuna. Records are broken there every year, often at the big international tournament in January that draws teams from Hong Kong, California, Hawaii, Australia, and elsewhere. Charter boats can be booked through the *Earl Grey Fishing Charters* (Tel. 407-7165). Your skipper Steve Butler specialises in jigging and live baiting for kingfish, schnapper, John Dory, and hapuka. On the scene, drop in to the information centers at Russell or Paihia, and they'll set you up with a boat. You can feel better about the cost when you realize it's easily split amongst a crew of several. Fishing is a prime attraction in the Bay of Islands.

If you're interested in **sailing,** the best way is to develop friends in the yachting community. This may be easier than you might imagine, and the Auckland Visitor's Centre will probably help you to get in contact with a yachting club. If you want, you can also charter your own boat, or you can hire a skipper to do most of the work. In Auckland, you could also check into **Corporate Cruising** (Tel. 021-736-820) who have a 62-ft. vessel called *Radar Blue* for daytime and evening charters and plenty of trimmings.

Day cruises in the Bay of Islands are a lot of fun. We would really like to try one of these that goes by the name of *R. Tucker Thompson,* aboard an old schooner. It must be romantic sailing this tall ship. BBQ lunches are part of the trip. It's operated daily out of Opua and Russell by Fullers, who run the historic Cream Trip. The same company operates an underwater viewing vessel called the *Nautilus.* This is the boat to catch for a tour of the ocean floor, reefs, and caves. It costs $10. Fuller's Paihia telephone is 09-402-7421. *A Place in the Sun* has skippered sailing vacations (Tel. 403-7615). Prices range from $600 per day. *Great Escape* is the bareboat yacht charter company in the Bay of Islands (Tel. 402-7143). This is where you explore the bay yourself with 2- to 6-berth yachts and all the necessary gear on board. Prices are from $75 per day.

9. Other Sports

It's often said that New Zealanders spend more time on outdoor sports than the citizens of any other nation, and it could be true. Physical educa-tion is required for the young, and sport of all kinds—organized or spon-taneous—is almost considered a national right and duty among their elders.

SPECTATOR SPORTS

Absolutely *the* national passion is a rugged type of football called **rugby,** particularly Rugby Union, the amateur form of the sport. (However, professional participation in sports is on the rise in New Zealand.) The national team is the famous All Blacks, a formidable gang dressed, naturally enough, in all-black uniforms. They are unaccustomed to defeat in the great "test" (international) matches with England, South Africa, and the few other countries who field good teams in the sport. In the winter (June to September), you can see Rugby Union matches played at *Eden Park* (Tel. 849-5555) off Sandringham Road, Route 17.

Rugby League is still the underdog but is becoming more popular and has a growing band of devoted fans who show up for matches around Auckland, especially when the home side, the Auckland Warriors, are battling it out at Ericcson Stadium with a team from the provinces or across the Tasman. **Soccer** (also known as Association Football) is also played during the winter. Its home in Auckland is North Harbor Stadium.

The summer passion in Auckland and throughout the rest of the nation is **cricket.** Eden Park (see above) plays host to that game weekends and holidays from November through April. Cricket involves bowlers (pitchers) and batsmen (batters), with attempts by the bowler to knock over the wicket and by the batsman to prevent that from happening. Cricket is thought to be the game that provides the most important character-development influence on New Zealand children.

In a contest with New Zealand a few years ago, an unfair though technically legal trick by an Australian team member won the Aussies the match but caused great animosity between the two countries. Eventually members of the Australian team, and even the Australian prime minister, apologized for the action.

Partly due to New Zealand's success in raising champion horses, but (probably) mainly because of the mania for gambling, horse racing is extremely popular. To go out to "the gallops," you head out the South Motorway (Greenlane exit) for the beautiful *Ellerslie Racecourse.* If you lose all your dough on the ponies, you can stroll through the extensive gardens on the 30 acres of property. Some prefer to go out the Great North Road to the *Avondale Racecourse.* Harness races are run at *Alexander Park,* nearly always at night.

Incidentally, Ellerslie is the only track in New Zealand that runs counterclockwise, like American tracks. The rest all send the horses around in the opposite direction (perhaps logical in a country where the water goes down the drain the other way around and where the numbers on telephone dials have been turned topsy-turvy).

PARTICIPATION SPORTS

Believe it or not, there are more than 400 **golf** courses in this small country—one for every 7,000 citizens—and this means that New Zealand has the highest number of courses per capita in the world! Two of the best are in Auckland. The *Titirangi Golf Club* (Tel. 827-5749) at New Lynn is a sleeper you don't find much published about. It hardly differs from the 50-year-old design of Dr. Alister McKenzie, the immortal Scot who helped Bobby Jones with the Masters course at Augusta, Georgia. The *Muriwai Golf Club* (Tel. 411-8454) in North Auckland features attractive seaside views next to the famous beach. There are about a dozen others in or near the city; greens fees run between $30 and $35. There are no motorized carts or caddies. Instead, you use two-wheel "trundlers" rented for $5 or so at each course. The main public course welcoming all duffers is *Chamberlain Park Municipal Golf Course* (Tel. 846-6758), across from MOTAT at Western Springs. Greens fees run around $15 during the week. It is usually hopelessly crowded on weekends and costs more. The *Takapuna Golf Course* (Tel. 418-4164) also has a $15 greens fee during the week. It's $20 Saturdays and Sundays. The *Aviation Country Club* (Tel. 275-6265), near the airport, is also open to casual players. Green fees are $20. If you can produce a membership card proving you are a fully paid-up member at a club anywhere else in the world you can do a round for $15.

Up at the Bay of Islands the champion is supposed to be *Waitangi,* but many golfers come back heralding the *Kerikeri Golf Club.* If you try them both, let us know what *you* think.

Some public **tennis** courts, grass and cement, are in the parks, but if you want to eliminate waiting time you might make bookings at the *ASB Tennis Centre* (Tel. 373-3623), open 8 A.M. to 8 P.M. You can rent racquets and balls there, but you'll have to have standard tennis attire to get on one of the 12 Laykold courts. It's about a 10-minute walk from Queen Street. The *Auckland Squash Centre* (Tel. 3794-4115) is at Karaka Street.

Skiing? There's none near Auckland. It's too warm. See our sections on *schuss*ing in the next chapter as well as in the Christchurch and Queenstown chapters.

Hiking is called "tramping" in New Zealand, and, again, we might save it for other parts of the country. If you are interested in hiking in the Auckland area, or seek detailed information in general, contact the Federated Mountain Clubs of New Zealand, P.O. Box 1604, Wellington, New Zealand, and see section 7 for a few possibilities.)

Gambling of all types is almost a national sport. If you want to bet on the horses, you don't have to go out to the track. Just step inside any of those shops labeled T.A.B. (Totalisator Agency Board). You can bet anything from a dollar up on your bobtail nag running in any race in New Zealand, and some in Australia. There are no odds at all. Whatever you win, you win, and the rest of the profit goes to charity. Or you can bet the national lottery, called the *Lotto*. Tickets cost from $2 to however much you want to splurge (usually bought from news agents), and there are many prizes of up to several million dollars. Be sure to check the results of the drawing in the newspaper. (Since we've never won, we're not quite sure where to go to collect.) It is worth buying a ticket, as the percentage of people who win the New Zealand Lotto defies logic, so much so that an expert was brought out from New York to try to find out why statistically Kiwis are luckier! It is more usual than not for the grand prize to be struck every week, often by more than one person. Some Malaysian tourists found themselves very well off after indulging in a ticket.

10. Shopping in Auckland

New Zealand's provincial towns used to shut up tight as a toheroa on Saturday afternoons and Sundays, but have now come out of their shells. But you can buy a reasonable variety of grocery-type items at the corner "dairy" in-between times. The same goes for the evenings, except in areas designated for one late-night shopping per week (Fridays, in the central city, Thursdays in most suburbs). In the major cities, particularly Auckland, an increasing number of shops and suburban shopping malls are staying open until 6 P.M. On Saturdays major supermarkets are open until 8 P.M. and/or 10 P.M. at least three nights a week. Sunday trading is now common, with most malls open from 9 A.M. until 4 or 5 P.M. Many main street shops are open on Sundays, too.

WHAT TO BUY

The best bargains in things to take home are products made of wool, and this includes, first of all, **sheepskins.** These might be short-pile sheepskins, used for things like car seatcovers (which really do keep the driver cooler in summer and warmer in winter). Short-pile sheepskins are also used on the insides of slippers and moccasins. Deep-pile sheepskins are most often made into dramatically fuzzy floor rugs (although they can be hung on walls, too).

These soft rugs may be from a single fleece or up to a combination of eight. ("Quartos," four skins sewn together, are beautiful, if you can afford them.) The natural (undyed) colors are usually white or ivory, although occasionally you will find a black sheepskin, at a much greater price.

Ask if your deep-pile sheepskin is from the South Island. Some say the sheep in those colder climes grow thicker coats to protect themselves from the weather. Quality is usually rated in "stars," usually from two stars on up to a top quality of five stars. (Some dealers have a supreme quality that they call "Gold Star.") Sheepskins are completely washable, by the way, but to keep them really beautiful be sure to follow the instructions carefully, and buy a special wire brush for combing down the skin afterwards.

Relative bargains can be find in sheepskin coats (suede on the outside, sheepskin for the lining and trim). Of course there are lots of "cuddle toys" and novelty items like powder puffs, cushions, etc., as well.

We hate to mention prices, but, as a very general guide, you can sometimes find small, natural-colored single-fleece rugs from about $100. However, the best ones are at least doubles (from two sheep) from about $200 to $300, depending on quality. Comparable rugs would usually cost you twice as much (if you could find them) in the U.S.

Car seatcovers from quality whole skins might start at $190 or so, but you can get much less expensive ones sewn from little diamond-shaped sections of several skins for around $120. Also, there are seatcover bargains that have the *backs* of the seats covered with a synthetic material. Expect to pay from $380 for a pair of the very best wool seatcovers. Soft wool underlays, which many claim perform magic during your sleeping hours, will cost about $195 to fit a queen-size mattress. Slippers and moccasins might creep into the $90 range, and these, along with wool-covered clothes hangers, sheepskin dusters, and bicycle seatcovers, make good souvenir-type presents to take back. Sheepskin coats or jackets will cover a wide gamut from about $380 and up.

Now, what about items made of **spun wool?** In the past 10 or 12 years, spinning and weaving has become a popular cottage industry and spare-time hobby for hundreds of women all over the country, so you will see all sorts of sweaters, hats, shawls, etc., for sale. Many use the term "natural colors," and that means undyed. So when you see a natural sweater ("jersey" or "jumper") with several white, black, and brown tones in it, you know those were the colors of the different sheep from whose backs the wool was spun.

The term "virgin wool" means yarn spun straight from the sheep, not recycled from other products. Products that have gone through the inspection process of the New Zealand Wool Board, a government agency, are allowed to receive the "wool mark." That's a trade symbol that looks rather like a ball of yarn, and it signifies not only that the product is made from virgin wool, but also that only a small percentage of other fibres may have been included, usually allowed for decoration only. The other brand that signifies quality is a distinctive fern.

If you're going to be traveling over much of the country, don't buy the first nice wool jersey you see. Unless you need it to wear right away, shop around. You could get one at a much better price after you are more sure of the kind of thing you want.

Many travelers return from New Zealand with items made from the mineral nephrite, generally called **greenstone** there. Nephrite, the hardest of all jades, should not be confused with the much rarer and more valuable *jadeite,* which is not found in New Zealand. All greenstone in the country comes from the South Island. The material was used by the Maori to make ornaments like *tikis,* as well as weapons, commonly the *mere* (hand club). The stone can be beautiful when well cut and perfectly polished, but beware that some advertising seems to exaggerate the worth of the finished product. (Do not buy greenstone as an investment.)

Over the years, the Maori have mostly deserted greenstone as a carving material (traditional methods are just too difficult), but several small factory operations in New Zealand have continued to work with it, albeit today with grinding wheels and other modern materials and often in much trendier designs than the ancient Maori dreamed of. Before you buy any greenstone, have a good look at some of the *objets* in the museums in order to be able to make an intelligent comparison with what is available in New Zealand today.

The traditional Maori art form that is as alive today as it was in pre-European times is **wood carving,** and Maori artisans are cutting and scraping over much of the North Island. The traditional woods are totara and kauri, trees that are seldom harvested, due to conservation laws. Consequently, much of the raw material comes from demolition sites. Again, visit the museums to see the old works first. Although the products are turned out in large quantities, relatively few are the kind of inauthentic schlock you may find in "native arts" in other countries. Maori carvings are copied from many, many traditional designs representing gods, spirits, ancestors, and the like. Any Maori carver who departed from these themes would probably soon find himself professionally ostracized by others in his tribe or profession. Nearly everything sold that is any good is accompanied by an explanation of the design.

Many, many other kinds of New Zealand handicrafts are sold, probably led by **ceramics and pottery.** In recent years, various New Zealand artists have achieved international recognition in the pottery field; you'll only see their works in the finest galleries. But many craft shops around the country display the works of enthusiastic and often talented part-time potters. Some of these craftsmen may have only a single retail outlet for their works.

Other handicrafts you'll find include batik, calligraphy, copperware, enameling, embroidery, glass products, puppets, silk screening, soft toys, stained glass, tapestry, and wrought iron.

WHERE THE STORES ARE

In the past we have recommended that Americans and Canadians skip the "duty-free" shops, where the "bargains" were largely limited to electronic products that cost less than New Zealanders normally shell out for these items but not less than we would pay at discount stores in North America. But the removal of a sales tax from many electronic items and the emergence of more competition among duty-free shops has meant greater and more interesting variety in these shops. Since early in 1990, two duty-free stores have opened for inbound passengers. You will find them just to the right of the entrance to the baggage claim area. So far their range is limited to liquor, beer, perfumes, and a small selection of confectionery, but they do beat lugging gifts halfway around the world. Inbound duty-free shops are a great invention.

The shopping scene at the lower end of Queen Street is anchored by the **Downtown Shopping Center,** on Elizabeth Square. Although it may look like a single department store, it is really a collection of about 70 shops on two floors, catering to both local and tourist traffic. In the last year it has undergone a major refurbishment. As well as a huge food hall, there are also fresh produce and retail stores. Another new shopping pavilion in central Auckland behind the Centra Hotel is the **Atrium on Elliott** in Elliott Street. Many clothing stores can be found here, as well as Dymocks bookshop, a favorite Australian store proving popular with New Zealanders.

In High Street, parallel to Queen Street, leading New Zealand designers such as Karen Walker, Zambesi, and World—all of whom are recent hits in London's international fashion show—have shops. Their creative apparel is accompanied by interesting cafés, galleries, and gift shops.

In the souvenir line, **United Crafts** (Tel. 379-0059) is at 101 Karangahape Road, as well as a newer branch on the Viaduct by the harbor. The selection of Maori carvings was good when we were there, but you might want to wait on any such work until you see what's available at what prices in Rotorua. Other reputable sheepskin outlets include **Exclusively New Zealand** (Tel. 309-5642) at 34 Queen Street East. A new one to open on Quay Street near the waterfront is **Hartings Authentic New Zealand Gifts** (Tel. 366-4739), which has a colorful range of sheepskins, leather, knitwear, and several innovative gifts. These are reliable outfits. (Unlike some Turkish *souk,* any New Zealand sheepskin shop can be relied upon to ship your goods as ordered.)

The last time we were in Auckland we bought several things at **Breen's Sheepskins** (Tel. 373-2788), at 6 Customs Street West, and saved a significant amount over prices in some of the fancier addresses around the country. Take a price list with you; Breen's ships to lots of folks who order more by mail or phone after they return home. Yet another woolly outfit in the Downtown Airline Terminal on the harbor front is **Woollywool Sheepskins Downtown** (Tel. 303-3779).

As a heritage from the days when fleets of cruise ships tied up in the area, and perpetuated by the several hotels and the airline bus terminal nearby, many shops catering to tourists are on the lower end of Queen Street, as well as on nearby lanes like Customs Street.

Absolutely loaded with gimcracks, knickknacks, and jiggumbobbery are stores like (catch these catchy titles!) **Aotea New Zealand Souvenirs,** on lower Albert Street, (Tel. 379-5022) open seven days and happy to post overseas. There are a dozen more to poke around in, some with a few decent items tucked in between tons of *paua* (abalone) shell and Hong Kong-ish junque. Any may be worth poring over on a rainy Sunday, since some of them are actually open daily.

Don't forget to wander through some of the little arcades (covered alleyways of shops) that open off of **Lower Queen Street.** Among them are (from the waterfront up) the *Queens Arcade,* near Customs Street, where you will find **Bast,** a shop specialising in lambswool coats and jackets; the *CML Mall,* which links Queen Street with Wyndham Street; the *Canterbury Arcade,* 170 Queen Street, in the "hub" of the city; and particularly the *Strand Arcade,* running from Queen Street to Elliott Street, a reproduction of Edwardian (not Victorian) architectural style. Also fun is *Vulcan Lane,* now a pedestrian mall leading off Queen Street. A recent and elegant addition to the tax-free shopping places in Auckland is **DFS Galleria,** in the Customhouse, on the corner of Customs and Albert Streets. The Customhouse is one of the city's historic buildings that has found new purpose in the share of a department store housing world-famous brands, souvenirs, and luxury items to tempt travellers.

More fun for us is rubbing shoulders with bargain-seeking locals at the **Victoria Park Markets,** which we referred to in section 6. This place is a sort of Kiwi casbah that has been carved out of a former garbage-incinerating plant and power station on Victoria Street opposite Victoria Park, just a little out of the central city area. It's open Monday to Saturday from 9 A.M. to 7 P.M., and on Sundays from 10 A.M. until 7 P.M. The weekends are more fun because there's live entertainment then. Almost anything you can think of might be sold there, from T-shirts to homemade jam. (It is also the home of Rick's Café Américain.) **From N to Z** (Tel. 377-2447), a souvenir shop near the eastern entrance, has some beautiful and quality souvenirs. They will post your purchases home for you, and those that take advantage of this will not be charged GST on their purchases. Look for the 125-foot-tall chimney that towers over the market. And here's a bit of Auckland trivia: When the destructor (incinerator) was completed in 1905, the mayor of the town ascended the chimney on a bosun's chair to ceremoniously lay the last brick.

Check out the shops on the first two floors of the BNZ Tower on Queen Street and the ground floor of the South Pac building on the corner of Queen and Customs Streets. These walk-through malls are worth inspecting. **Walker & Hall** sells quality antique and modern jewelry and a variety of interesting glassware. You can buy duty-free there, too. The born-again Ferry Building overlooking Auckland harbor contains an interesting collection of shops open seven days a week. New Zealand's flair for fashion design is evident in some of these shops. At 30 Queen Street, **BONZ in New Zealand** (Tel. 373-2248) sells a wonderful array of bright sweaters and cardigans with New Zealand motifs such as kiwi- or sheep-shaped buttons.

Don't forget the Polynesian precincts along **Karangahape Road,** off upper Queen Street; there the stores are allowed late-night hours on Thursday instead of Friday. The nearer "K" Road gets to the Sheraton Hotel, the more neutral its flavor becomes.

Auckland is surprisingly short on department stores, but one enduringly good one is **Smith & Caughey** (Tel. 377-4770) at 253-261 Queen Street. It rates as one of Auckland's oldest and most-respected stores. A budget department store is **DEKA,** at 48 Queen Street and 238 Queen Street. This New Zealand store is similar to the American Woolworth chain and in fact was called Woolworths (or Woollies) before the DEKA name change.

Elsewhere in the central city, we enjoyed looking at the silver and gold jewelry at **Fingers** (Tel. 373-3974) at 2 Kitchener Street. Products there are made by a cooperative of six artists. There are also periodic exhibitions of local jewelers' works. In Lorne Street (not dissimilar to High Street with its interesting array of fashion boutiques, small galleries, and cafés), look at **Compendium** for eye-catching works of art. If opals take your fancy you will find these sparklers at the **Opal and Jade Vault** (Tel. 379-3739). There are two shops on Queen Street. Remember, too, that there are very good crafts and other objects for sale at **The Museum Shop** (Tel. 377-3932), in the Auckland War Memorial Museum. It's open until 5 P.M. *daily.* Try to make your visit coincide with the first-rate Maori cultural show at the Museum. The times change, so it's best to check them out with the Auckland Visitors Centre. Take a stroll through the **Domain** that surrounds the museum. It's a verdant city oasis.

Antiques? Someone must be opening an antique store somewhere in New Zealand every day of the week, and you'll find them in almost any neighborhood. On the way to Auckland Airport at Mangere, notice the dozens of antique salons in the 400 and 500 block of Manukau Road (Route 12) in the Epsom district. Another group of antique stores has laid claim to Great South Road as it runs to the intersection with Market Road. If you're motoring farther out, on Highway 1, there are four or five nice antique shops in Cambridge en route to Rotorua. Ponsonby, Parnell, and Remuera Roads have also attracted antique dealers. **Portobello** (Tel. 525-2546), one of the longest-established dealers in Parnell, has moved to the suburb of Ellerslie.

PARNELL SHOPPING

Our favorite browsing is in the section of Auckland called Parnell, which is to say Parnell Road in the 200s and 300s. It's about a mile and a half east of the city center. (From the City Bus Terminal behind the post office, take any bus going to Meadowbank, St. Johns, or Glen Innes.) Parnell, once an exclusive residential suburb, fell into disrepair from about 1930 until the early 1960s. Then Les Harvey, a millionaire in a turtleneck sweater, got the idea of preserving and re-creating a piece of Victorian and colonial architecture that would attract shops and restaurants.

He went to work with wooden "lace," cobblestones, wrought iron, and the like, and today the shopping center called *Parnell Village* (from about 317 to 333 Parnell Road) is the happy result. The Village is expanding, and other businesses in the area jumped on the Harvey wagon, began redecorating, and have now formed an association that is making this delicate, tasteful area one of the joys of Auckland.

Here are some of the places we have enjoyed, beginning at the bus stop at the top of Parnell Road and continuing down the street for a three- or four-block serendipity. (Some of these may have moved by the date of your visit, or you may come up with a find we missed. If so, please tell us about it.)

There are numerous places for cups of tea or coffee along the way. You travel down past the BP station, now, and into the white gingerbread Parnell Village complex itself. We noted **Rosemarie Muller,** who makes top-quality knit garments, and also Elephant House with its range of New Zealand products from wood, leather, and greenstone, and all kinds of creative knickknacks. Close by is **Alpaca Heaven,** and it seems the gentle-eyed alpaca is giving the ubiquitous New Zealand sheep some woolly competition with fine-looking garments to keep us warm in winter. At 285 Parnell Road is Hoglund Art Glass Gallery, where items in bold colours and designs, hand blown by the artists in the South Island city of Nelson, are for sale.

Past the post office, **Aunt Agatha's Table Things** lays out modern settings, glassware, etc., at 285 Parnell Road. Across the street, at No. 272, we came close to buying one of the nice prints at the **International Art Center.** The ones we could afford were cut out of old books, hand-colored, then nicely matted until they looked like something much rarer and dearer. They also have lots of high-class New Zealand art at prices to match. You will be drawn to the window of the interior décor and antique shop adjacent.

Several fashion designers have their shops in Parnell. There's a little shopping cluster called the "Habitat Courtyard." Check out some interesting crafts in the co-op called **Elephant House** at No. 237. You'll probably find **Parnell Books,** now at No. 213, across from the 1861 Catholic Church. **The Gourmet Cookshop,** at the top end of Parnell Road on Birdwood Crescent, is full of interesting stuff, some of which you would sooner put in your living room than the kitchen.

Other than Parnell, Auckland's best suburban shopping centers are Remuera, Takapuna, St. Lukes, and Newmarket. The latter has burgeoned in the last few years to give Parnell a run for its money. Speaking of gifts to take home or leave with hospitable Kiwis, **Living and Giving** on Broadway (Newmarket) continues to maintaining its reputation for a fun place to shop. Across the street is **Saks,** a men's and women's fashion store stocking imports, some of which out-bound shoppers can purchase at duty-free prices. **Action Down Under** is the place to go for the latest in stylish sportswear.

Don't overlook **Devonport,** Auckland's gracious old waterside suburb in which the residents are content to live forever (and wouldn't we all be?). *St. Luke's* shopping center has a wealth of shops under one roof and is the only mall in New Zealand to have a two-year waiting list of retailers keen to get space. Among the many smaller shops selling everything from fashion to hardware are the **Farmers** department store, a branch of the **K-Mart** chain of Australian department stores, and a supermarket.

For bargain hunters, try **Dress Smart factory Outlet Store,** at 151 Arthur Street in the suburb of Onehunga. It has at least 40 shops offering decent savings on popular national and international fashions, footwear, and sportwear labels, as well as discounts off music and books. And if you arrive at Auckland Airport ready to fly home and still not shopped out, there are plenty of tax-free temptations.

BOOKSHOPS

Auckland has several interesting bookshops offering large collections of volumes produced by and about New Zealanders. We have two favorite nationwide chains. One is **London Bookshops** (Tel. 373-5355), the Auckland branch of which is in the Downtown shopping center. Incidentally, we have seen copies of our Mavericks on their shelves. The other, equally dependable chain is **Whitcoulls Ltd.** (Tel. 377-8329). This branch has been massively and expensively refurbished and now has three floors and a coffee bar. What used to be The Book Corner, mentioned in previous editions of this book, has now been absorbed by the new, larger store. Whitcoulls is now the place to buy government publications. In Elliott Street is the large **Dymocks Bookshop,** where you can easily lose track of time. **Pathfinders** (Tel. 379-0147) on Lorne Street has a particularly good art books section. In Newmarket, try **Techbooks** (Tel. 524-0132) for technical books on almost any subject. Used books can be purchased at **David Thomas' Bookshop,** (Tel. 378-0441) at 28 Lincoln Street in Ponsonby. Used and rare books are sold at **Dunsheath Rare Books** (Tel. 379-0379) at 6 High Street. **Unity Books** on High Street is another enthralling shop.

11. Night Life and Entertainment

Most of New Zealand's bright lights shine from Auckland. Here is a solid group of theaters, concert halls, and some pubs and clubs dedicated to night owls who want to fly as late as 3 A.M. As you might suspect, the scene changes quickly, so the following should be used only as a general guide. (Check the Entertainment section of the *New Zealand Herald* or the *Auckland Tourist Times* for more up-to-date listings.) For some reason—critics would say to gain votes in forthcoming national elections—the government, dominated by the National Party, has voted to lower the legal drinking age to 18 years.

NIGHTCLUBS

Many will serve up meals along with the acts, but all are known more for vitality than for victuals. **Stanley's Nightclub and Cocktail Bar** (Tel. 390-201) on Queen Street has some of the best live music in town and is the place to go to mix with the nocturnal crowd. The **Power Station** (Tel. 377-3488) in Mt. Eden is a local legend with the younger crowd and gets very noisy. On the other hand, **Club Havana** (Tel. 302-3354) on Beresford Street attracts South American music fans ranging from age 20 to at least 60. A Chilean immigrant band called Cantuta often plays live music there and has everyone on the dance floor.

The Las Vegas Theater Restaurant (Tel. 379-0938) is an upmarket strip club on "K" Road. Another such club is the **Firehouse Review Bar** on Fort Street. It is at Fort Street and Upper "K" Road, which are the "red light" districts. The nightclub scene in Auckland is active but volatile. Check that the options are still there before you go.

ROCK GROUPS

The young, hip crowd, of course, follows the internationally known rock bands of Britain, the U.S., and Australia. Also, they have their own groups grown at home quite successfully. You will find the pubs to be places where the music rocks along. The **Birdcage** in Ponsonby and **Windsor Castle** on Parnell Road are two of many in town where the beat goes on at least a couple, if not several, nights of the week.

Planet Hollywood, the rock-along restaurant chain that liked the way Hard Rock Café established a franchise around the globe and has tried to do one better, has an Auckland venue overlooking Aotea Square. You can't miss the 21st-century exterior, although the music inside is not the live variety.

PUBS AND BEER

Before looking into the pubs, any quaffer should have some idea about New Zealand beer. To us Yanks, anyway, it's more flavorsome than virtually any suds available from Maine to Hawaii. (Australians tend to think Godzone beer is either too sweet or too watery, but then the Diggers are notoriously chauvinistic about their beers—admittedly also delicious.) The clear, copper color of many N.Z. beers is said to be a result of the amount of caramel used in it.

In the past, there was a plethora of local beers in New Zealand, but all those independent brews have now evaporated. Today, there are several "brands," but they are all made by two large companies. Both own hotels or pubs, and have special arrangements with those they don't own. Dominion Breweries supplies DB and other blends to one group of hotels and bars. New Zealand (Lion) Breweries delivers Lion Beer and their other brands to their own hotels and other outlets. It is unusual to find an establishment that serves beer from both competing corporations.

Dominion's main line is *DB;* it also puts out *Waitemata* in the Auckland area. Then there's *DB Green Label, DB Double Brown,* and *DB Export,* which is supposed to be their premium beer. This very strong brew is only sold in small bottles. The draft (draught) beer is just called *DB Draught.* It's delicious. *Kuhtze* is a pleasant beer the ladies seem to go for. Dominion also owns Leopard Breweries, which produces *Leopard* beer, and the Waikato Breweries, which produces *Whitbread, Bass,* and some other dark English types. There's a strong ale called *Tui,* the approximation of Guinness Stout. It also churns out *Tennent's* under license from the Scottish brewery of that name. Tennent's strong ale packs the biggest wallop of any beer in New Zealand. DB's latest success story is *Kiwi Lager,* a lighter beer that's doing a steady export trade as well.

The Lion people pump two kinds of draught beer that is also sold in bottles—*Lion Red* and *Lion Brown;* the latter is positively my own first love in New Zealand, especially when it's on tap. There is also a *Lion Pilsner,* a *Lion Super, Lion Export, Lion Bavarian,* and their famous export beer, *Steinlager.* (I maintain that the Steinlager we buy in the U.S. doesn't taste nearly as good as that made for New Zealand consumption, and wonder if it might have something to do with altering the process so the brew conforms to American liquor laws. We would welcome any definitive information on this subject.) For the past few years now, "light" (low-alcohol) beers have been gaining popularity in New Zealand because of stricter drinking-and-driving laws. Both DB and Lion have introduced these less-lethal brews. (This forward-looking effort by New Zealand—and Australia—has unfortunately not been taken up in the U.S., whose own light beers are popular because they are low in calories, not in alcohol.)

A "boutique" beer is McCashins, brewed in Nelson and prized throughout New Zealand. The beer is naturally brewed according to the Bavarian Purity Laws of the 1700s and comes in small amber bottles with a rip-cap lid. It has no added sugar, is high in taste, and has a third fewer calories. The brew comes in Mac's Gold (lager), real ale, and the popular Black Mac, a deep, dark brew that looks like stout. The brewery also produces cider, ginger ale (root beer), and Snakebite. In the South Island, also try Speights from Dunedin.

When pouring beer, Kiwis carefully let it flow along a slanted glass so as to prevent even the slightest head from appearing. It's almost a national complex, and men have been known to forbid their wives to conduct so delicate and important an operation.

In pubs, it is common to belly up to the bar and order a "handle" of whatever kind of draft beer you want. That's a glass mug, or stein, and it holds 12 ounces (or 330 "mils") of beer. A larger container is a "pot," which used to hold 20 ounces, although these are probably metric pots now, perhaps up to 590 milliliters or so. If you ask for a "glass" of beer, the barman may ask you what size glass you mean. If you want a pitcher of beer, you ask for a "jug."

The prices of beer and alcohol in a "public bar" are set by law, and that's where you go if you want to drink most economically—probably for about half what you pay in the U.S. for the same poison. However, lounge bars are nicer places, especially when taking the ladies, and they are allowed to charge more for drinks. (Sometimes jeans are not acceptable dress in lounge bars, by the way.) Hotels, which the law says must have a public bar somewhere on the premises, naturally prefer that you drink in their lounge bars. We recall one flash hotel somewhere (I think it was in

Christchurch) that provided no internal connection from the hotel itself to the public bar!

By the way, for hard-liquor drinkers, a shot is called a "nip" in New Zealand, and it amounts to just about half as much booze as you're probably accustomed to. Some hotel lounge bars catering to international travelers automatically serve double-nip drinks, and charge accordingly.

There was a time when New Zealand celebrated an institution called the "six o'clock swill," which was when men had to consume all their beer in pubs before six, giving them exactly one hour after work to swallow as much as, or maybe more than, humanly possible. (This is sometimes referred to as "bolt drinking.") During those days, the beer came out of hoses in New Zealand bars, allowing a free-swinging barman to fill up hundreds of glasses almost at the same time.

Today the swill is, thankfully, a thing of the past, and the hoses seem to be all gone, too. The pubs with the tile walls (called "engine rooms") that could be conveniently hosed down with water after 6 P.M. have also disappeared, in favor of more commodious bars. The beer still comes to the establishment in tanker trucks, though, just the way gasoline is delivered in other countries. The tanks under the floor hold about 440 gallons each, and there are usually two in an installation. New Zealand still enjoys (that's the right word) a reputation as one of the highest per-capita beer-drinking nations in the world.

The live music pubs, including the many Irish bars, particularly jump on weekends. As well as the aforementioned **Windsor Castle Tavern,** at 144 Parnell Road, and **Bird Cage,** next to Victoria Market, you could try the **Empire Tavern,** at the corner of Victoria and Nelson, which is popular particularly for its garden bar. In Parnell, **Iguacu,** 269 Parnell Road near "Parnell Village," draws the crowds. Not far away, the **Nag's Head,** which we also mentioned earlier, is open at 117 St. Georges Bay Road. And on the North Shore, the **Birkenhead Trust Inn,** on Mokoia Road, serves up delicious harbor views along with sustenance and suds.

THEATER AND DRAMA

The dramatic arts are active in Auckland and all over New Zealand, with works by local and foreign playwrights. (Among the best-known authors of plays is Roger Hall.)

The **Kenneth Maidment Theatre** (Tel. 379-3685) is in the Maidment Arts Centre, at the corner of Alfred and Prince Streets on the Auckland University campus. In the same building is the **Maidment Little Theatre,** where we saw two excellent N.Z. performances. At both Maidments you'll probably find plays relevant to New Zealand. The **Howick Little Theatre** is a suburban-based group in Pakuranga but well worth the 20-minute drive to see one of their performances. The **Aotea Centre** regularly attracts top-draw performances and is home base to concerts by the resident and commendable Auckland Philharmonia. Bookings for Aotea performances can be telephoned through BASS (the local telephone booking agency) at 307-5000.

Sky City, referred to earlier in this chapter, has a good theatre and is the venue for quality drama productions. The same can be said for the **Bruce Mason Theatre** (named after one of New Zealand's talented playwrights), on the North Shore in Takapuna.

MOTION PICTURES

The movie business is alive and well in New Zealand, with a growing number of feature films turn being produced in Aotearoa, either by New Zealanders or foreign production houses taking advantage of superlative scenery and a softer dollar. In Auckland, most of the cinemas are on Queen Street. Also making its presence felt is the newly opened **IMAX Auckland Theatre** (Tel. 303-3345), which presents gripping films on the giant screen. IMAX is part of a new entertainment centre called The Edge and is flanked by Aotea Square and **The Civic Theatre.** The latter is the grand old cinema of Auckland that thankfully escaped the demolition gang and has been imaginatively restored. The doors had not quite reopened as the *Maverick Guide* went to print. The Civic will be well worth visiting.

An interesting cinematic offering is the North Shore's **Bridgeway** (Tel. 418-3308) at 122 Queen Street, Northcote. It screens prime film festival movies from the best of the international circuit. You will also find freshly perked coffee there. **The Berkeley** in Mission Bay is another "independent" that shows hand-picked movies for supportive locals. Newmarket is well catered for with **The Rialto,** specialising in art film and film festival movies, and Village 8 on Broadway, a complex of several cinemas under one roof. These are very accessible to Auckland accommodation houses. Contrary to the old days when New Zealanders had to wait months before "new" releases found their long way to the far reaches of the Pacific, movies often now open in Auckland, particularly within days of their general American release. Who knows, you might get to see the latest big picture on vacation before your friends back home!

CLASSICAL ENTERTAINMENT

You'll sometimes be able to catch performances by the **New Zealand Ballet** at the Aotea Centre or when it is on tour around the country, as well as concerts by the **New Zealand Symphony Orchestra.** Auckland's venerable **Town Hall** has recently undergone an expensive face-lift, and the city's highly regarded Philharmonia Orchestra performs most of its concerts there.

TELEVISION AND RADIO

The two main competing television networks in New Zealand are TVNZ (Television New Zealand) and TV 3. The first is government owned, but all its channels carry commercials. They transmit in much clearer colour than the American system. You'll find lots of American and British programs on both networks, plus considerable original programming. The TNZ channels do not compete head-to-head; that is, they avoid broadcasting the same kind of program at the same time. Nearly all programs are national ones. The privately-owned TV-3 is fighting a strong battle to build market share. Cable television is flourishing in New Zealand, too. It goes under the name of SKY TV.

Radio is more complicated and as keenly competitive. There are about two dozen non-commercial stations, divided into the "YC" stations, broadcasting classical music, etc., and the "YA" stations ("The National Program") of more general interest (and with almost no rock music). Sometimes the YA and the YC stations broadcast the same news programs simultaneously. (1YC and 1YA are Auckland stations.)

There are about an equal number of privately owned radio stations. Some have brand names, like the popular Newstalk ZB. Taupo's station is appropriately called "Radio Lakeland." Some of the community stations take news feeds from Radio New Zealand's news team or from Independent Radio News (IRN). In Auckland, 1XA was formerly a pirate station, and it's still called Radio Hauraki, a heritage from the days when it would broadcast from a ship in the Hauraki Gulf. FM stations are also well established.

12. The Auckland Address List

First, a few notes about telephones.

• All calls to the emergency number 111 (and a few other service numbers) from a pay telephone are free. Local calls from electronic telephones cost 50¢. Card phones use cards, which cost from $5. Toll calls can be made with coins or card.

• The telephones are partly numbered backwards compared to the rest of the world. The dial *turns* the same way, and the *zero* is in the same place. But then the numbers progress from 1—where the 9 is in other countries—through 9, instead of from 9 to 1. (Got that? Well, you may have to see it to believe it.) Luckily, push-button phones are now widely in use.

• To make long-distance ("toll" or "trunk") calls, you can go to the post office, where they'll have the necessary change, etc. (Of course you may also make these calls from your hotel or a private home.)

• Most hotel telephones are equipped for direct-distance dialing, called STD (subscriber trunk dialing). STD numbers for several N.Z. cities are listed in the front pages of the telephone directory.

• Toll calls are *less* expensive on Saturdays than Sundays. Toll calls in New Zealand have been reduced by the competitively run Telecom by at least half. Calls are even cheaper after 6 P.M. There is also a 50 percent savings for some cities now, if you place your call between 11 P.M. and 6 A.M.

• To look up a name in the telephone directory, it will help if you know the middle initial and the address. Many New Zealand telephone listings are by two initials and a last name only. You just might find a dozen blokes named J. J. Smith in a Kiwi phone book!

Airlines—See section 2.

Ambulance—St. John's Ambulance Association (Tel. 579-9099).

American Consulate—Corner Shortland and O'Connell Streets (Tel. 303-2724).

Australian Consulate—Union House, 38 Quay Street (Tel. 303-2429).

Automobile Association—Automobile House, 33 Wyndham Street (Tel. 377-4660).

Bank—The Bank of New Zealand, 80 Queen Street (Tel. 375-1300).

Barber—Top Half Salon, 8 Durham Street East (Tel. 379-7421).

Beauty salon—Cut Above, 20 Lorne Street (Tel. 309-0689).

British Consulate—151 Queen Street (Tel. 303-2973).

Bus information—Auckland Regional Authority (Tel. 366-6400).

Camping equipment rental—Pack 'N' Pedal (Tel. 522-2161).

Canadian Consulate—(Tel. 309-8516).

City Council offices—Civic Administration Building, Greys Avenue (Tel. 379-2020).

Dental emergency—122 Remuera Road (Tel. 520-6609).

Dry cleaners—New Zealand Dry Cleaners, Downtown Shopping Centre (Tel. 303-3736).

Emergencies of all types—Telephone 111.

Fire—Telephone 111.

Florist—Interflora (Tel. 0800-80-88-80).

Hospital—Auckland Hospital, Park Road (Tel. 379-7440).

Library—Auckland Public Library, Lorne Street (Tel. 377-0209).

Police station—Telephone 111 for all emergencies. Central Police Station, Vincent Street (Tel. 379-4240).

Post office—157 Queen Street (Tel. 302-1059).

Rest rooms—Underneath the Visitor Centre, Aotea Square.

Theater tickets—BASS (Tel. 307-5000).

Tourist information—Auckland Visitor's Centre, Aotea Square, Queen Street (Tel. 366-6889).

Train information—Tranz Rail. Railway Station, Beach Road (Tel. 0800-802-802).

Youth Hostel Association—(Tel. 309-2802).

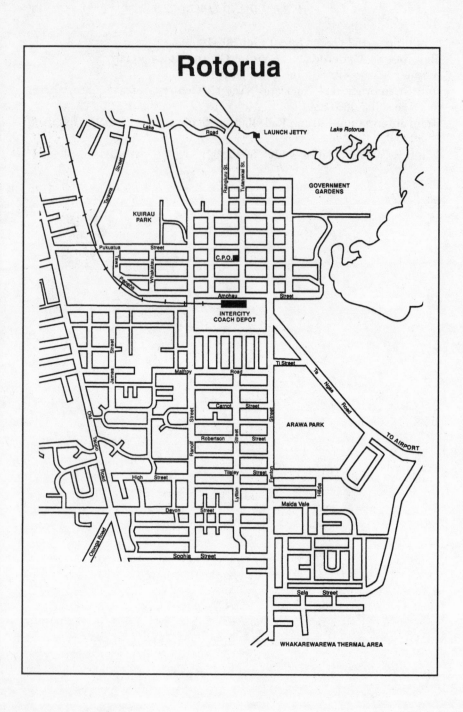

Rotorua

LAUNCH JETTY

Lake Rotorua

Lake Road

GOVERNMENT GARDENS

Rangiuru St.

Tutanekai St.

Tarawa Street

KUIRAU PARK

Pukuatua Street

Whakaue

Tawa

Capulha

Street

Amohau Street

C.P.O.

INTERCITY COACH DEPOT

James Street

Te Ngae Road

Malfroy Road

Ti Street

TO AIRPORT

Ranolf Street

Carnot Street

ARAWA PARK

Robertson Street

Fenton Street

Tilsley Street

Hilda

High Street

Lytton Street

Maida Vale

Devon Street

Teodore Road

Otonga Road

Sophia Street

Sala Street

WHAKAREWAREWA THERMAL AREA

6

Rotorua and the Central North Island

1. The General Picture

If the wind is right, you can smell **Rotorua** before you see it, even from an airplane. "Rotten eggs!" is the first reaction, but then you realize that it must be the sulfur in the air.

Rotorua is the unofficial headquarters of New Zealand's thermal area, where the very earth takes on a startling life of its own. It's a region of steam, hot water, and bubbling mud holes, often dangerous off the beaten paths. Things seem to seethe and boil, and to burble and spout all over the place.

For more than 500 years Rotorua has also been the seat of the powerful **Arawa** tribe—Maori who trace their ancestry back to the great canoe of the same name that arrived in New Zealand in about the fourteenth century. These people, more than many others, have successfully kept their culture alive in songs, dances, and traditional arts like weaving and woodcarving.

Combine the Maori and geysers, pour in some beautiful lakes, then stir with some of the biggest and healthiest trout in the world, add some springs and health spas, sprinkle over all of this a lovely little city of about

50,000, and you have the recipe for New Zealand's biggest and most successful tourist center.

Strangely, the odor that assaults your nostrils as you check in to your hotel seems to waft away after only a few hours. The residents of Rotorua have learned how to use this naturally hot water to their advantage. Many cook with it, heat their houses with it, and certainly bathe in it. Industries also use this ready source of free energy from under the ground.

On the other hand, there can be no indiscriminate digging in Rotorua; nature just won't allow it. The houses have no basements, and even graves have been built in special vaults that sit above the ground. To take spade to earth merely invites the surface to cave in and perhaps to keep falling away.

The citizens say that all this boiling and fuming is nonetheless beneficial to human health, and the Maori woman who guides you on a tour—and who has swum all her life in warm mineral waters—may point to her own even-toned, wrinkle-free skin as convincing proof. Thousands of Pakeha annually bring their aches and pains to Rotorua to "take the waters," and have been doing so since the early years of this century. You may recognize the 1909 **Bath House,** formerly the Government Bath House, next to the bowling green as one of the most photographed buildings in the country. It is now a museum (newly renovated) housing Rotorua's art and history and the home of the popular BHC (Bath House Café).

Rotorua is certainly not the only hot spot in the North Island. In fact, it is only one notch on a long belt of underground activity that runs generally north and south for about 175 miles, bisecting the island. Near Rotorua is **Mount Tarawera,** which blew up in 1886 in New Zealand's most massive volcanic eruption. South of town, there are thermal areas even more dramatic than those within the city.

At **Wairakei,** near the city of Taupo, the government has harnessed the steam in a set of geothermal power stations that have energy-conscious nations like the U.S. sitting up to take notice. The vapor carried by the spaghetti of pipes is used to generate nearly 200 million watts of electricity, and the area has the potential for even more power production.

Lake Taupo itself (whose waters can be bitterly cold for swimmers) is one deep, gigantic crater from an ancient volcano. Today the Taupo-Rotorua region seems to be the center of the trout fisherman's world, with rainbow and brown varieties weighing three to four pounds being caught in its lakes and rivers daily.

The geologically active area continues much further to the south, crowned by three volcanoes that form the bulk of **Tongariro National Park.** At least one of these high-altitude craters is often smoking and fuming with potential activity.

To the right of the north-south volcanic zone on the map lies the rich farming country of the east coast, particularly around **Gisborne, Napier, and Hastings.** Far to the west, one of the world's most perfectly formed snow cones, **Mount Egmont/Taranaki,** rivals Japan's Fujiyama as a study in symmetrical beauty. The mountain is the backdrop of the fertile region of **Taranaki,** the Maori name for the sacred mountain.

There is much more to the North Island than Auckland, Rotorua, and Wellington. If you're traveling between these cities by train, bus, or car, you'll experience some of the most pleasing green and rolling—and sometimes rugged and mountainous—countryside that the earth has to offer.

2. Long-Distance Transportation

Rotorua Airport terminal received a $600,000 facelift in 1992, and jet services now land and take off from the runway, just five miles out from town. It's kept relatively short because it abuts an ancient Maori burial ground. It's plenty of pavement to do the job, though, for the planes that land at the little aerodrome beside the lake.

The neat two-story red-brick terminal building features an enclosed observation lounge and a mural depicting Maori legends. When flights are due in or out, the single shop opens to sell tea, cakes, newspapers, souvenirs, etc. If you want a rental car at the airport, check at one of the airline counters. You can also phone **Rotorua Taxis** (Tel. 348-1111) or **FasTaxis** (Tel. 348-2444) for a cab from the airport; the fare into town will be about $16. You can also catch the city minibus **Air Port Super Shuttle** (Tel. 349-3444), which stops at most city hotels.

Airlines. Two airlines are represented in Rotorua. **Air New Zealand National/ Link** (Tel. 0800-737-000) and **Ansett New Zealand** (Tel. 0800-267-388).

Train and Bus Travel. Intercity (Tel. 348-0366) sends their buses to the rest of the North Island from the railroad station (Intercity Travel Centre) on Amohau Street. (It's a busy place; besides the long-distance buses, Intercity also handles local buses and guided tours; see later.) The **Geyserland Express** rail service operates between Auckland and Rotorua. The journey rolls through the green **Waikato** pastures before carving through the **Mamaku Ranges** and arriving in Rotorua. Buffet and bar facilities are available on board, and out of the window there's a feast of fine scenery. From the Auckland end you hop aboard at 8:04 A.M. and arrive four hours later. Tickets range from $32 per person to $64 each way. Intercity Rail's toll-free number is 0800-802-802.

Rental Cars. On our last trip, we easily found the offices of the Big Three. **Avis** (Tel. 345-6055) is parked on Fenton Street (and open Sundays, by the way). **Hertz** (Tel. 348-4081) you'll find at 77 Amohau Street, and **Budget** (Tel. 348-8127) has moved into town at 215 Fenton Street. You can also try **Link Low Cost Rentals** (Tel. 349-1629); **National Car Rentals** (Tel. 348-4518); **NZ Car Rentals** (Tel. 345-3918; **Rent-a-dent** (Tel. 349-3993); or **Thrifty** (Tel. 346-3050).

3. Local Transportation

There's not a lot of choice in this city. **City Line** runs the local buses, and there are about two dozen routes. You pay by the section; each section is about a mile. Most trips will cost about 80¢ to $1, unless you're going out in the country. Be prepared to wait at least half an hour for any bus. Phone 348-1035 to ask how to get from here to there, or just wander over to the City Line Travel Centre at the big bus/train station on Amohau Street. Generally speaking, bus travel just isn't very practical for visitors, and the service doesn't run very late into the night. You can get a cab by calling **Rotorua Taxis** (Tel. 348-1111), but they seem expensive. You can also contact **FasTaxis** (Tel. 348-2444). If anyone has their act together it is Mike and Doug Tamaki of **Tamaki Tours** (Tel. 346-2823; e-mail tamaki@wave.co.nz). These gentlemen will show you a time you won't forget. At the Tamaki Maori Village you journey back in time in a night of truly authentic, traditional culture and entertainment. Cost is $55 adult and $25 child and includes transport to and from your hotel or motel.

Otherwise try **Carey's Tours** (Tel. 347-1197; e-mail careys@careys.co.nz; Web site www.gisnz.co/careys.html) around the major city attractions as well as 4WD tours and hot bush-stream swims. Tours run from 8 A.M. to 6 P.M. Price is on application, as costs vary depending on the itinerary you want. Another option is **The Thermal Connection** (Tel. 377-6067), taking tours of Rotorua's thermal attraction. Price is also on application and tours run on demand. If the truth be known, if there's one city where you would be better off with your own car—or else on a guided tour—it's Rotorua.

Note: "Price on application," or "POA," means that there are many price brackets. The price that applies to the buyer depends on what the buyer wants, at what time or season. For example, a tour may normally depart at 10 A.M. every day, but the operator may be prepared to run that tour, or a similar one, at a different time to suit the client's needs. Therefore, the group needs to apply to the operator to do just that, and the operator will charge out the cost, depending on how much extra time he must hire his staff for, the weather conditions, a change of park fees, and other variables. So, when the price of something is described as "POA," it means that until you apply for the particular service or product and let the provider know exactly what you want, he cannot give you a set price.

4. Hotels and Motels of Rotorua

Show up in Rotorua without a reservation during Easter vacation, and your only choice may be whether to sleep in your car or in your suitcase. It can also be tough from late December through January; the long Christmas season finds Rotorua's population ballooning by an extra 30,000 holiday-makers, most of them from other parts of New Zealand. Although there are more than 200 centers of accommodation, they can be booked solid. And things are almost as bad during the August holidays.

At some other times of the year, many motels are virtually empty, and you can occasionally come up with excellent off-season rates—especially if you have the flexibility of a car so you don't have to stay in the middle of everything (unless you want to). Oddly enough, the better rates are offered at the top *hotels* during the summer "high" season when the *motels* are full.

We've inspected several places in Rotorua, but beyond a few obvious leaders, our choices of which to see were fairly arbitrary. You may well come up with some excellent motel bargains we didn't discover, and we would like to hear about them for future reference. Also, if you do show up on the scene with no bookings, better check in with **Tourism Rotorua** (Tel. 348-5179) to see what they can come up with. Sometimes they have temporary low prices available for some accommodations. (Tell them we said to ask if they have any sort of "special" running.)

EXPENSIVE ROTORUA ACCOMMODATIONS

Although Rotorua has never been a popular tourist destination with either New Zealanders or overseas visitors, the city has recently really come into its own in the tourism stakes. This has included the opening of several new hotels, some part of international chains.

As in any town, you can generally rely on a large hotel to give good service, although it is often the smaller establishments that provide the local flavour. An old favourite, although it's not situated quite as conveniently, is the **Sheraton Rotorua** (Tel. 349-5200; e-mail reservations_rotorua@sheraton.com; Web site www.sheraton.com/rotorua) at Fenton and Sala Streets, almost directly across from the **Arikikapakapa Golf Course.** It is a distinctively designed building under old-style multiple mansard roofs, with wrought-iron balconies, a garden with thermal pool and individual thermal pools for romantic bathing à deux, and a view of the famous thermal area of **Whakarewarewa.**

The Sheraton also has a *hangi* (Maori earth oven) feast and concert that is worth attending. Cost is $50 adult/$25 children. Concert only is $25/$14.

Steve Fawcett of Londonderry, New Hampshire, found himself there unexpectedly and although it wasn't quite what he wanted he was somewhat mollified by the great breakfast delivered to his room.

Within walking distance of the lake, Government Gardens, etc., is the aforementioned **Millennium Hotel** (Tel. 347-1234; Web site www.mill-cop.com), recently refurbished and upgraded from its previous life as the popular Quality Resort Lake Rotorua. Happily remembered and recommended, there is nothing to suggest that in its new life this established property will not continue to deliver the goods.

Facilities include the Nikau Restaurant with open kitchen and wood-fired oven, poolside brasserie, bar and swimming pool, sauna, and spa pool. Most rooms look out over Lake Rotorua. This hotel too, has a Maori *hangi* and concert. Cost is $45 adult and $22.50 child or $16 for the concert only.

The **Quality Hotel** (Tel. 348-0199) spreads out with a clean, modern, rectangular, and woody look behind a statue of a fierce-looking Maori spear carrier at Fenton and Maida Vale. It features a high-ceilinged, skylit lobby in pleasant timber tones; lots of greenery around every corner; many well-done Maori decorations; L-shaped swimming pool outdoors (thermally heated, of course, like nearly all pools in Rotorua); spas and saunas available; guest lounge with copper fireplace, waterfall, and bar; piano entertainment nightly; and air-conditioned restaurant. Not too expensive, and pretty good for the money. A *hangi* and concert here costs $42, or $15.50 for the concert only.

Rydges Rotorua is another new international hotel. On the edge of the racecourse, with views across the city, a thermally heated rooftop swimming pool, and plunge pools, the large rooms cost from just $95 per person per night twin share. Telephone free 0800-367-793.

Like the Sheraton, **Centra Rotorua** is adjacent to the Whakarewarewa thermal reserve as well as an 18-hole golf course. This property also has a heated swimming pool—welcome on frosty Rotorua winter days. Telephone free 0800-801-111. Ask about their *hangi* and concert.

The **Lake Plaza Rotorua Hotel** (Tel. 0800-801-440) offers many rooms with balconies overlooking the nearby lake, which, we believe, are the best rooms. One large hot pool and private mineral baths are available. The hotel is in a convenient location with another *hangi* programme offering the feast and concert for $43 and the concert only for $20. Half price for children.

How about $650 per couple per night, *including* breakfast and dinner (with wine)? Michael Seekings of Old Greenwich, Connecticut, wrote us to recommend the **Muriaroha New Zealand** (Tel. 346-1220), a luxurious guest estate that has just such an arrangement. The family-run lodge also features thermal pools and a freshwater heated pool. The garden suite costs $800 per couple, and the price includes all meals and beverages. Muriaroha is at 411 Old Taupo Road, about three miles from the center of things. Sorry, we missed it ourselves last trip.

Also worth a mention in this category are **Solitaire Lodge** (Tel. 0508-552-552 or 362-7823) and **Moose Lodge** (Tel. 362-7823), two exclusive resorts perched above lakes. Solitaire Lodge is above **Lake Tarawera** (see the map) on a spectacular site. It caters to people with a love for trout fishing and the great outdoors. Rates are $480 single and $680 double. The Solitaire Suite is also available. These rates include all meals and open bar. The hosts also include hot-air ballooning on their menu of activities. Moose Lodge is a former private holiday retreat. It has a gym as well as tennis courts and a sauna, and the golf, fishing, and hunting are close by. There at 12 suites at Moose Lodge with prices on application. Meals are included.

Another lodge to add to this handsome collection is **Okawa Bay Lake Resort** (Tel. 362-4599) at Rotoiti and also on the edge of the lake. A courtesy car is also on tap. A new hotel is the **Baden Lodge Motel** (Tel. 349-0634 or 0800-337-033), which offers luxury two-level suites with private spas. The Lodge is on Fenton Street and costs $150 to $180.

MEDIUM-PRICE ROTORUA ROOMS

Here are a few examples at the mid-range level. But remember, too, that Rotorua has motels scattered all over—and out of—town. You may come up with a gem by yourself, or throw yourself on the mercy of the Tourism Rotorua.

With a car, you can easily drive over to the colonial-style **Union Victoria Motor Lodge** (Tel. 348-7192 or 0508-765-765) at its easy-to-remember address at the corner of Union and Victoria Streets, and see what they offer in their charming two-story spread. Each unit is a full motel apartment with kitchen facilities, separate bedroom, and lots of luxury amenities like color tellies, etc., all in nicely decorated, wood-paneled surroundings. If you don't want to make your own breakfast, they'll deliver one to your room in the morning. Mineral and swimming pools on the premises. Doubles cost $70. (Don't confuse this with the *Victoria* in the next category.) Still a winner for the price.

We once spent several days in the dramatically sited **Regal Geyserland** (Tel. 348-2039, Web site www.vacation.co.nz/regal), next to Whakawerawera.

Many guests hardly look at the hotel itself, enjoying instead the glorious panorama directly out back—**Pohutu Geyser,** the boiling mud pools, and the general supernatural effect of a world in noisy, beautiful motion. This hotel was bought by the century-old Druids Friendly Society of New Zealand, which has spent a lot of money upgrading and increasing the size of the establishment, operating it both for society members and the general public. Currently doubles are running around $75-157, which almost pushes it up out of the category. Somehow on our last trip we missed getting back to see just exactly what the Druids did, but we understand the changes have been all to the good. We hear there's a good Maori concert most nights. Meanwhile, you can still thrill from dusk to dawn to the bloop-bleep of the mud and the whoosh of nature's own hot-water fountains. If you go, tell 'em we sent you—and then let us know how you got along.

The **Wylie Court Motor Lodge** (Tel. 347-7979 or 0800-100-879) has been a finalist in the NZ Tourism Awards three years in a row and has twice been the recipient of Flag Hotels of New Zealand's Excellence Awards. Each unit has a private hot plunge pool. Great for relaxing in after a day at the nearby golf course. **The Heritage** (Tel. 0800-999-393) has won a best mid-range accommodation NZ Tourism Award and offers a heated swimming pool and spa pools, is close to golf courses, tenpin bowling, the racecourse, and Whakarewarewa. Tariffs are between $124-185.

Last trip we took a quick peek at the **Sport of Kings Motel** (Tel. 348-2135 or 0800-508-246), where each of the 16 units has its own hot pool and there are private family pools available as well. With its peaceful location on Peace Street, just off Fenton, it seems to include most luxury facilities at a non-luxury price of $110 for two. An ideal parking place for motoring vacationers.

The Sport 'N' Spa Resort (Tel. 345-6799) is another good choice. It offers suites from $85 and leisure activities include bushwalking, kayaking, horseback riding and, of course, hot pools.

A new establishment that is already gaining a reputation for comfort is **Ann's Volcanic Rotorua Motel and Serviced Apartments** (Tel. 0800-768-683). Although close to the city centre, the property prides itself on being quiet. Cost is from $79 for a double studio.

Other good possibilities in the same price range include the refurbished 1899 **Prince's Gate** (Tel. 348-1179) at 1 Arawa Street; the **Ambassador Thermal Motel** (Tel. 347-9581) at No. 1 Hinemaru Street, down by the lakefront; and the **Midway Motel** (Tel. 347-7799) at 293 Fenton Street, where each two-story unit also has its own mineral pool. Ken and Sylvia Bardsley wrote to us from Oregon about the **Collingwood Gables** (Tel. 347-7795) at 325 Fenton Street, which they described as clean and well priced at $89 to $99 double.

ROTORUA ON A LOW BUDGET

Without meaning to confuse anyone, the best low-price motel rooms we found were at the little **Victoria Motel** (Tel. 348-4039) at 10 Victoria Street, which has no connection with the previously named Union Victoria, not far away. Strangely, each of this place's nine rooms has its very own thermal mineral pool, which you plunge into by jumping out the window of the bathroom. (We kid you not!) There are no cooking facilities, but there are things like a refrigerator, TV, tea- and coffee-maker, etc., and they'll even deliver a breakfast to your door on order. For other provisions a new shopping complex has recently opened across the road. Rates are from $65-80 for a studio unit. The property is part of Budget Motels, an Australasian chain that has recently begun operating in the United States. Previously we have told our readers about the hotel's little cat named Maverick, after this guide. The original Maverick departed with the previous owners, who retired. The new owners quickly followed tradition and adopted Maverick II. Unfortunately this Maverick, true to his name, took an independent stance in regards to who knew best in regards to road safety. Sadly he was wrong. This leaves Jimmy, a gorgeous, friendly Irish Setter. It was suggested that his name be changed to Jimmy Maverick, but no one has yet worked up the courage to suggest to the hound that he be renamed after a cat!

Fellow Mavericks have written us favorably about the **Tresco Bed & Breakfast** (Tel. 348-9611), just behind the aforementioned Victoria at 3 Toko Street. Since it's so small (just seven rooms), we almost fear a stampede, but the homey atmosphere around the hot pool sounds just great. At the moment, rates are just $70 double *including* breakfast, and they might even pick you up from the airport or bus station.

Another good choice in this range is the **Utuhina Hot Springs Fishing Lodge** (Tel. 0800-887-612). This fully equipped cottage sleeps from two to eight guests and sits right next to a trout-fishing stream. Better still, the property offers home-cooked meals, and a *hangi* too if you wish. Cost is from $80-105 for two people.

The **Cedar Wood Lakeside Holiday Resort** (Tel. 345-7773) stands on two acres on the shores of Lake Rotorua. Motel units are fully equipped and cost from $85-125. Amenities include a heated swimming pool, and indoor and outdoor spas. Continental or cooked breakfasts are available.

The **Coachman Motor Inn** (Tel. 0800-921-292) also has fully equipped kitchens as well as private in-room spas. Cost is from $79-89.

Other North Island cities? We haven't been able to make exhaustive comparisons of accommodations, but we'll mention some safe bets in our sightseeing sections covering these areas.

5. Rotorua Restaurants

Pick up a *Rotorua Visitor's Guide* from the Tourism Rotorua office at 67 Fenton Street. And while you're there, tuck a *Taste New Zealand Food Guide* under your arm. Both are free, and the latter is a helpful pointer in the right directions.

Rotorua has changed dramatically in the past few years. There is a lively new café society and many new restaurants to choose from. Take a good look around for yourself, as we can only list a few here.

Perhaps the finest restaurant in Rotorua, both for ambiance and quality of fare, is the **Landmark** (Tel. 349-2921). It occupies a historic old Edwardian home at 1 Meade Street, at the top end of Fenton Street, near Whaka and a short stroll from the Rotorua International or the Sheraton. Several rooms have been converted into dining rooms, but all offer the same French menu. Most "mains" are listed for around $24 to $28. The restaurant has recently acquired a new chef, who has introduced some very appetizing dishes. A charming location for an excellent, though not inexpensive, meal. (Reservations are required.)

The **Rendezvous** could be the place for appetizing lamb (Tel. 348-9273). It's on Himemoa Street and sports a Lamb Cuisine Award. It is also the place to try venison.

For vegetarians and seafood lovers, **Finally Found It** (Tel. 349-0984) is at 1284 Eruera Street. The **Copper Criollo** (Tel. 348-1333) offers Creole and contemporary Maori cooking at 1151 Arawa Street. (Warning: be *really* hungry before you go here, as the portions are not anywhere near as small as the prices. This restaurant offers an excellent value for big eaters.) **Zanellis Italian Cuisine** (Tel. 348-4908) is a popular and lively restaurant at 1234A Amohia Street.

Across the road from the cinema complex is **Sirrocco** (Tel. 347-3388) in a nicely refurbished house at 86 Eruera Street, so you can combine a night at the movies with a pleasant meal. Otherwise you can go back to your motel with a takeaway soup, pork, fish, lamb, or vegetable meal from **Fenwicks Bar and Café** (Tel. 347-0777).

The **Hoo Wah Chinese Restaurant** (Tel. 348-5271) has received a favorable judgment from Honolulu attorney Jeff Portnoy, who called the Chinese food there as good as any he's had in Hawaii. It's often crowded, noisy, and a little pricey. But it's worth every penny, Jeff said. Saturdays there's live music. It's changed premises since we last updated this guide and is now at 1266 Eruera Street.

More modest dining in town would include New Zealand's answer to the Howard Johnson chain, **Cobb & Co.** (Tel. 348-2089), offering nonstop meals in the Grand Establishment Hotel at the corner of Hinemoa and Fenton Streets. The original Freeman Cobb, who established stagecoach service in Australia and New Zealand, was an American, by the way, and the menu seems vaguely Americanized too, with milkshakes (watch it—these are watery by U.S. standards!) and hamburgers (strange but passable). Break into that hot bread, though, and step into the bar to bring back a great draft Lion Brown. Remember how to pronounce it by rhyming— "You'll get a glow, at Cobb and Co.!"

Pub dining is also fun at the **Lake Rotorua Tavern** (Tel. 348-5585), which has been overlooking the Maori village of Ohinemutu from Lake Road for more than a century. Some booths serve up a delicious view of the lake. Three in our party ate there for a modest total plus the beers, which we collected and paid for separately. (Entertainer Sir Howard Morrison was at a nearby table, too.) Another well-liked licensed chuck wagon is **Herb's Place** (Tel. 348-3985), formerly the Bar B.Q., at the lake end of Tutanekai Street.

An unusual high-level restaurant is the **Skyline** (Tel. 347-0027), a hilltop aerie that can be reached only by a gondola lift near Rainbow and Fairy Springs. We enjoyed the view from 700 feet, a salad, and a beer there one lunchtime recently. We haven't tried it at dinner, but the price of $22 includes the ride on the gondola, and that seems like a good combination. For more great views, you could try the **Aorangi Peak Restaurant** (Tel. 347-0046). There's smoked salmon on the menu and juicy scallops from the Bay of Plenty. Aorangi Peak is one of the more expensive restaurants in the city, but Mr. And Mrs. Stan Sayers, formerly of the U.S. and now living in Tokoroa near Rotorua, recommend it highly. The vote is that it's worth the extra dollars.

For substantial meals at really down-to-earth prices, try the **Prince's Gate Hotel** (Tel. 348-1179) on Arawa Street, opposite the Government Gardens. The five-course table d'hôte is usually very good for an all-inclusive price of perhaps around $15.

For fast food, there is a crispy wing of **Kentucky Fried Chicken** sizzling away at 20 Amohau Street and at Fairy Springs Road, a **Pizza Hut** on the corner of Lake Road and Tutanekai Street, and three McDonald's around the city.

The Kingsgate Hotel and the Sheraton's **Pavilion Coffee Shop** (Tel. 348-7139) also rate a mention in the N.Z.T.B. *Taste New Zealand* booklet. Remember—the booklet is free, and you can pick one up from **Tourism Rotorua.**

6. Sightseeing in Rotorua and the Central North Island

First of all, pick up the excellent sightseeing map "Rotorua—Gateway to Geyserland" for one dollar from **Tourism Rotorua** (Tel. 348-5179), open daily until 5:30 P.M. at 67 Fenton Street, opposite the central post office. The efficient staff stands ready to answer any question you may have about the island's biggest tourist center. Then ask them for a **Rotorua Fun Pass.** This provides discounted admissions in many of Rotorua's attractions. The Fun Pass came into being in 1992, and will no doubt continue if both vendors and visitors are happy with it.

Rotorua's principal tourist attraction is actually a combination of at least four different sites on the Maori-owned property in the thermal area called **Whakawerawera,** or just "Whaka" for short. (Pick up the brochure with the area map inside.) First, right next to Taupo Road is the **Maori Arts and Crafts Institute** (Tel. 348-9047). Weekdays, you can watch apprentice carvers, all men, learning the ancient art. Sometimes the women are at work weaving cloaks or making flax skirts and baskets.

The entrance to the reserve is through the nearby **Rotowhio Model Pa,** a 1901 reconstruction of the type of pre-Pakeha fortified village that once stood on the site. (Notice the carving above the gate depicting the lovers Tutanekai and Hinemoa. You'll learn their story on Mokoia Island.) Pick up one of the red-suited Maori guides near the gate; it's not nearly as much fun to go through it all on your own hook. (You can wander around later by yourself, if you want, and even return to see the institute if you had to skip it to be sure to catch the tour.)

After she explains the working of the *pa,* the guide will continue with you into the **Whakawerawera Thermal Region.** If you're lucky, the principal geyser, named **Pohutu Geyser,** will be spouting off (they call it "playing" in N.Z.), sometimes to a height of 100 feet or more. But even if it isn't, the smaller geysers, steam holes, boiling mud, and hot-water streams, all concentrated in a relatively small area, will make it all worthwhile. (*Warning: In this and all other thermal areas, keep to the marked paths!* If steam obscures your vision for a moment, stand pat until a gust of wind has blown it away.) At the end of the tour, you will come across the **Rahui Maori Village** (population about 50), and your guide may demonstrate how food is cooked in the boiling thermal waters and explain other aspects of how Maori life has adapted to the unusual environment. We were fascinated by the village's above-ground cemetery, where steam sometimes even emerges from the graves!

In downtown Rotorua, don't forget to stroll over to the **Government Gardens,** 100 acres of grass, roses, and white-garbed bowls players, capped by that wonderful old "pseudor-Tudor" building once known as the Government Bath House. As we've mentioned, it's often featured in stories and pictures of New Zealand. The building no longer offers baths. There's a well-organized Art and History Museum inside, however, which may be visited for a small charge, and a little art gallery, too. Newly restored, the Bath House now also offers the popular Bath House Café, or BHC as it is known to locals. Nearby is the privately owned **Polynesian Pools,** a thermal pool operation.

Alongside the lake, close to town, is a second Maori village called **Ohinemutu,** which also seems to blow off a considerable amount of steam on the premises. Don't miss the excellently carved **Tamatekapua Meeting House** (featuring nighttime concerts), and especially the **Church of St. Faith,** which is also carved. Inside the church there is a window that has a glass etching of a Maori Christ. When viewed from the proper angle, the figure appears to be walking on the real waters of Lake Rotorua in the distance (No photographs allowed, but postcards are sold inside). Each of the intricate carved panels in the church is from a different Arawa sub-tribe. Anglican services in the church are conducted in English and Maori.

About six miles out Highway 5 is Rotorua's famed **Agrodome** (Tel. 347-4350), where you see, hear, and learn about New Zealand's 19 principal types of sheep. If it sounds dull, it isn't. A legacy from the Osaka World's Fair of 1970, the shearing and shepherding demonstrations are dramatic and fun. The star of the show is Paul Bowen, who has taken over for his father Ivan, for many years New Zealand's champion shearer. Paul continues the show, together with his trained rams and sheep dogs. The whole thing finishes off with your going up on stage to hug a big, fuzzy ram with large horns while someone else in your party takes your picture. There are three shows each day, at 9:15, 11, and 2:30. Recheck those times, get there early (before all the buses), get a seat down front (to avoid the echoes), and don't miss it!

Now, besides all the hot water you can get into around Rotorua, there are several cold and delicious freshwater springs. Some of these have been developed into inviting private parks, demonstrating various types of native forests (bush) and serving as feeding areas for large rainbow and brown trout common to the region. If you have a car, you might combine a visit to a spring with a drive around the circumference of Lake Rotorua.

The biggest, most popular, closest, and perhaps best of the type are the **Rainbow and Fairy Springs** (Tel. 347-9301), now combined into a single destination just out of town on Route 5 North (the Auckland highway). For an admission of $9.70 you can stroll along a cool collection of trout streams and pools, New Zealand ferns, and other restful vistas anytime from 8 to 5. There's an underwater window, so you can get a fish-eye view of some of the most he-man trout you'll ever see; a special kiwi house, where day is turned into night so you can see these strange birds scampering around searching for grubs; other animals looking for a handout; various waterfalls; and different-colored waters caused by certain minerals. The entrance fee also includes admission to **Rainbow Farm,** a new development with shows not unlike the Agrodome variety. They go three times a day at 10:30 A.M., 1 P.M., and 2:30 P.M. The differences between these and Agrodome shows are enough to make them both worthwhile. The shop at the Springs sells leading New Zealand clothing, such as the world-famous Swanndri, the 100 percent woolen shirts that defy inclement weather. Rotorua's strong Maori culture is presented in fine, handcrafted carvings from native timbers. Creams, lotions, and soaps made from kiwifruit and the oil extracted from sheep wool are also doing steady trade.

Farther along the road, there is the smaller, much less crowded **Taniwha Springs,** named after a mythical Maori monster. There was no *taniwha* there or at the equally beautiful **Paradise Valley Springs** (Tel. 348-9667) when we were there, but we thought the presence of a couple of caged lions at the latter was the ultimate in irrelevancy.

Almost exactly opposite the town at the far end of the lake is **Hamurana Springs,** a park built around the island's largest spring, a trout-filled basin spewing out one million gallons of fresh water per hour. Here you can rent a rowboat, if you want, or just wander about, catching sight of a large variety of waterfowl and other birds, including the tui and the morepork. There's also a redwood glade. These trees grow six times faster in Rotorua than in their native California, by the way, but the wood is almost useless commercially, since, due to the speed of its growth, it doesn't have the same density as slow-growing, stronger wood.

Deserting the spring scene now, if you are on that highway circumnavigation of Lake Rotorua, take the side road when the sign comes into view directing you to Tikitere, now better known as **Hell's Gate Volcanic Park** (Tel. 345-3151). This is one of a couple of thermal areas where we were held more in awe of the violent activity than at Whaka. And we are in good company, for it was to this area that another maverick, George Bernard Shaw, was taken when he visited New Zealand in 1934. Asked later what he thought of Rotorua, the great British playwright, essayist, and devoted egoist paid the place a compliment almost in spite of himself:

"I thought it an uncommonly pleasant place, although it smells of brimstone like Hades," he began. "But I have no intention of writing an advertisement for every place I visit. Tikitere Hell's Gate, I think, is the most damnable spot I have ever visited, and I would willingly have paid 10 pounds not to see it."

It would cost the great wit around $12 to see Tikitere today, and we'll venture to say that he would again find it well worthwhile. (Several readers have also told us they preferred it to Whaka.)

About nine miles southeast of town, a charming country road first skirts the **Blue Lake** and then the **Green Lake** (and they really are these colors, because of subterranean mineral activity), and ends in the place now called the **Buried Village** (Tel. 362-8287). This was the site of Te Wairoa, a small settlement that served until 1886 as a staging area for tourists who wanted to visit the world-famous silica formations known as the Pink and White Terraces. Accompanied by Maori guides, they would take a canoe over Lake Tarawera and then Lake Rotomahana.

But on the night of June 10, 1886, nearby **Mount Tarawera,** a supposedly extinct volcano, suddenly erupted, killing more than 150 and burying Te Wairoa and two other villages. The Pink and White Terraces were destroyed, and the little town remained under the ashes until comparatively recently, when it began to be excavated. There isn't a whole lot left, but it's still appealing. Pay a few dollars at the tearoom to go through the area. (And don't miss the *tohunga*'s hut and the story posted nearby.)

About 16 miles south of town along Route 5 and then the Waimangu Road is the **Waimangu Volcanic Valley** (Tel. 366-6137). This area is also a result of the Tarawera eruption. At one time it boasted the world's largest geyser—a monstrous black thing that rose to a height of 1,500 feet. (Take a look at the photograph in the tearoom; it's unbelievable!) Today the valley consists of boiling pools and hot-water rivers, including the 10-acre Waimangu Cauldron, the world's largest boiling lake. Even if you think you're about thermaled out by now, you'll see effects here you didn't see at Whaka or Hell's Gate. *One caution:* There are a lot of ups and downs on the pathway, so you should be fit enough to tackle this, and should also allow enough extra time for some moderate climbing. We were glad we went beyond the main area to see the Warbrick Terrace formation. Probably the best and least strenuous way to see the valley is on the Waimangu round trip, the first tour listed in section 7. It's been almost the most popular Rotorua trip since it was first organized in 1904!

We'd skip **Leisure World,** a fun festival for locals, perhaps, but not terribly inspiring for international travelers. On the other hand, we did enjoy taking the **Skyline Skyride** (Tel. 347-0027). These are gondolas that go over the gorse and the goats near Rainbow and Fairy Springs for $8 round-trip. Next time we're going to screw up our courage and try the luge run on the

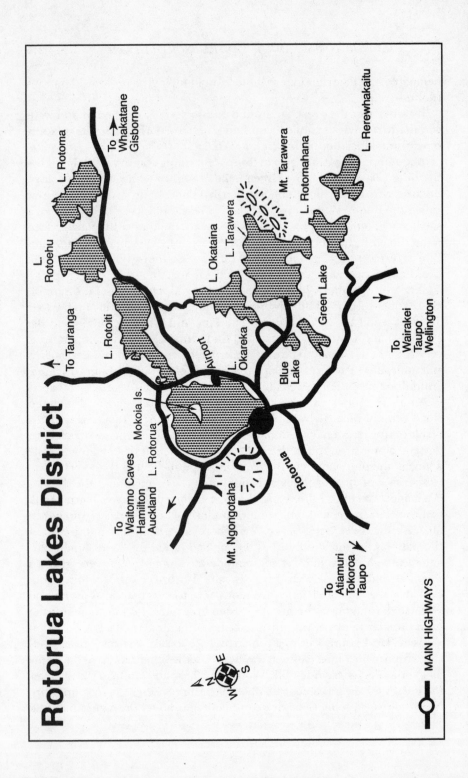

Rotorua Lakes District

L. Rotoma

To → Whakatane Gisborne

L. Rotoehu

To Tauranga

L. Rotoiti

L. Okataina

L. Tarawera

Mt. Tarawera

L. Rotomahana

L. Rerewhakaitu

Airport

L. Okareka

Green Lake

Blue Lake

To Wairakei Taupo Wellington

Mokoia Is.

Waitomo Caves
Hamilton
Auckland
To

L. Rotorua

Mt. Ngongotaha

Rotorua

To
Atiamuri
Tokoroa
Taupo

N
W E
S

⊸○⊸ MAIN HIGHWAYS

cement course that begins near the restaurant up there, especially since we hear the run has been extended to double its old capacity. One ride costs $6. These are sort of individually controlled, gravity-run sleds, in case you've missed them elsewhere in the world. More unusual rides were on the drawing boards when we visited this high-level property recently.

ELSEWHERE IN THE NORTH ISLAND

Digressing from the Rotorua area in order to round out this section, we'll proceed first to the **Waitomo Caves** (Tel. 0800-CAVING [228-464]), a single, small tourist attraction that almost rivals Rotorua itself in popularity. (From Auckland, you can do both in a round trip of two days.) There are caves and there are caves, but what makes these different is the unusual **Glow Worm Grotto,** where thousands of tiny, shining insects seem to create a star-spangled night sky inside the cave. The guides will explain it all while you sit craning your neck in a boat. You can also go Black Water Tubing there, floating through the darkness in an inner tube. Seeing the caves this way is described variously from awesome to romantic. Backpackers will find accommodations at the **Caves Motor Inn** (Tel. 873-8109) for $13 per person. At the same place there are beds with a few extra frills for around $55 single and $65 double. Driving time from Rotorua to the caves is about two hours, and it's three from Auckland. Recheck the closing time at the tourist office, then allow enough time to get there and back if you're not staying overnight. Admission is around $16.50.

One of the most challenging adventures to recently emerge from New Zealand's bounty of outdoor excursions is the **Lost World Adventure** (Tel. 878-7788) at Waitomo. Expert guides take the adventurous sort 300 feet down into an intriguing underworld of caves. The descent constitutes the highest guided abseil in the world. Down below in a mysterious world of ferns, fossils, and glow worms, an underground river journey is the next fascinating stage of the Lost World experience. You need one and a half days; the first day is taken up with abseil training (around $65). A softer option for those who prefer not to abseil is available. But people who have done the free-hanging abseil talk as if their lives began on that day. A third option is blackwater rafting, which means through underground streams instead of out in the open.

If the sound of all this builds an appetite, **Roseland's Restaurant** (Tel. 878-7611) on Fullerton Road at the caves could assuage it.

A short detour in a northwest direction will lead you to **Brooklands** (Tel. 825-4756), a handsome country estate on an large sheep, cattle, and deer farm. A swimming pool, tennis courts, a croquet lawn, and a billiard room await guests. And you'll be impressed with the cuisine. Down the road at

Waingaro Springs you can sink into hot mineral bubbles and kiss cares good-bye.

Up north and over to the east, the well-loved **Coromandel Peninsula** separates the Hauraki Gulf and the Firth of Thames from the Bay of Plenty. It hasn't seen much action of any kind since the gold rush, and this makes the isolated, rugged, and forested area a popular summer vacation site for New Zealanders. The surfing center of **Whangamata** has an excellent beach fronting an attractive community. In fact, the whole picturesque coast is dotted with camping sites and small motels. For a bit of luxury in the bush, try **Puka Park Lodge** (Tel. 864-8088) at **Pauanui.** Set in 25 acres of native greenery, its secluded, tasteful accommodations are adjacent to a fine restaurant. A sauna, pool, and golf and tennis courts are close by. So is a fine beach. Puka Park Lodge is the creation of Reiner Hoehn, a retired Lufthansa pilot who went on a careful search for a choice slice of the world to build his lodge. The Coromandel fit like a glove, and it is not difficult to see why Reiner put the foundations down in Pauanui. The lodge works with a variety of local tour operators, one of the local favorites being Doug Johannsan, christened Kiwi Dundee (after the Australian crocodile-hunting version). Two years ago Doug received a medal from Her Majesty Queen Elizabeth II, no less. The medal was for services to tourism. Doug has a keen interest in nature tourism and a knack for entertaining his tour parties and making them feel they would like to return. Called **Kiwi Dundee Adventures** (Tel. 865-8809), the company offers a wide range of programs including bush walking, visiting gold mines, caving, and much more.

At the other end of the accommodations ladder from Puka Park Lodge is the **Coromandel Backpackers Lodge,** with rates of $15 per person. And in the nearby coastal town of Whitianga, Rosaline Harper and Steven Catsiff wrote to us about **Cosy Cat Cottage,** which they recommend as a good place to stay. The name sounds inviting.

We introduced you to a natural history tour company called **Bush and Beach** in the previous chapter in the section on Auckland tours. The same company now operates interesting five-day tours to the Coromandel that include half of that time sailing the grand old Kauri schooner *Te Aroha. Te Aroha* was launched back in 1909 and has been refitted to give her guests a comfortable and memorable trip. After sailing and exploring the islands of the Hauraki Gulf, it's all ashore for adventures in the Coromandel. Contact Karin Platzer, P.O. Box 40-047, Auckland, if you are interested in this one. This special excursion is currently limited to one a year.

In **Thames** is the **Brian Boru Hotel** (Tel. 868-6523) where Agatha Christie-style "murder solving" weekends are the fashion (from $355).

Otherwise rates range from $66 to $125 single and double. There are eight larger units, too. Thames is well worth a meander through the streets, which contain several charming old buildings.

Another popular holiday playground with interesting topography is centered around **Tauranga** and **Mount Maunganui,** on the Bay of Plenty. The incredibly crenellated coastline hereabouts can't seem to make up its mind whether to become land or water, and you'd better pick up a map to know where you are. Try the 45-minute walk around the mount on a nice day for some great views. There are several nice hostelries in both communities. Glenna and Lloyd Hoffman of Hawaii liked the **Ritz-Carlton Motel** (Tel. 544-0779 or 0800-276-652) in Tauranga, where the rates are currently $79 double. **The Bay City Motel** (Tel. 578-0588 or 0800-997-788) has a good reputation and charges around $82 a double.

Farther east, if you're going to the hamlet of **Opotiki,** you may want to stop in to see the bloodstained pulpit at the Church of St. Stephen the Martyr. The minister was murdered by Maori religious fanatics in 1865 (the story is long and gory). Paul Bryan runs **Eastland Charter and Tour Co.** (Tel. 07-315-6146) and tailor-makes his East Coast tours for his clients. He offers an hourly rate, but the daily rate split between a small group is the better option, given the extent of the scenery. Paul offers overnight and day trips and travel is in his comfortable, 10-seater minicoach. The pearls in his string of scenic excursions would make a long necklace and, among them, the bush-lined Motu river and enchanting Lake Waikaremoana would add to their lustre.

About 30 miles offshore in the Bay of Plenty, you'll make out **White Island** from almost any point on the bayside. It's a constantly active volcano, and it's nearly always puffing out at least a little smoke.

Opotiki to **Gisborne** via the East Cape is a journey of about 209 miles. If you are driving yourself (and this is great campervan territory) it would be a mistake to take the shorter route because of the splendid beauty of the East Cape ride. This rather remote part of New Zealand is one of its most memorable from a scenic point of view. The stretch from Opotiki up to Hicks Bay is particularly fine. Giant *pohutukawa* trees cling to steep cliffs that drop to the ocean below. Periodically the rugged cliffs give way to coves circled with creamy sand. The East Cape remains sparsely populated and is predominantly the home of Maori communities whose families have lived there for generations. A first stop could be the **Te Kaha Motel** (Tel. 325-2830) about 50 miles from Opotiki. It enjoys a marvelous view of the ocean. The Te Kaha pub is typical of the smattering of watering holes along the coast. Within, the atmosphere is informal and decidedly friendly. On the East Cape, you can still see a horse tethered to the verandah of an old colonial pub, patiently waiting for his master to wet his throat. On the Gisborne side of the Cape there are accommodations at the **Tolaga Bay Motel** (Tel. 862-6888), where the rates are $60 double. The **Te Puia Hot Springs Hotel** (Tel. 864-6755) has rooms from $65 double and looks like a pleasant place to stay. There are several other good places to stay along the way, but the East Cape is the kind of place campervan holidays are made for. The places to pull up and soak in the scenery are numerous and not easily forgotten.

On the east coast of the North Island, the city of **Gisborne** is home base for the rich farming district very much misnamed Poverty Bay; it is supposed to be the first city in the world to be struck by the morning sun. It was also the first place at which Captain Cook set foot in New Zealand—a monument there marks the spot. And it just might be the only place in the world where railway tracks cross the airport runway. This area of New Zealand is rich in Maori carvings and history, having been a center in the 1880s for a warlike character called Te Kooti. Many of the earliest European buildings in the area were destroyed, but the Presbyterian Church at Matawhero survived and is worth a visit for those interested in the country's early settlement.

Tourism Eastland (Tel. 06-868-6139; e-mail info@eastland.tourism.co.nz) is the place to call for more information on the area, or you could write to the office at 209 Grey Street, Gisborne.

The **Urewera National Park** is also in this region and is a wild and wonderful slice of the country. The **Teal Motor Lodge** (Tel. 868-4019 or 0800-838-325) has rates at $85 double and **Sandown Park** (Tel. 867-9299) charges the same for its double rooms. These are two of a score of good motels.

For a good meal try **Pete's On The Beach** (Tel. 867-5861) an award-winning seafood restaurant on Midway Beach. Another good place to eat is the **Fettucine Brothers** (Tel. 868-5700) on Peel Street. We happen to like Gisborne a lot.

Backpackers and budget travelers (young and old) should try the **Gisborne YHA Hostel** (Tel. 867-3269) at 32 Harris Street, at $15 a night. It's basic comfort here, matched by a warm welcome.

South of Rotorua, more thermal areas beckon. We decided to skip **Waiotapu,** whose principal geyser (Lady Knox) is triggered faithfully at 10:15 A.M. daily by the pouring in of a bunch of soap flakes! Some other features, however, are more authentic.

We also missed **Orakei Korako** (Tel. 378-3131) and probably shouldn't have. We simply had overdosed on steam and sulfur by the time we passed that one about 30 miles south of Rotorua. But veteran American reporter John Anderson, a longtime associate, wrote us of his impressions:

"Located on the Waikato River, just above Lake Ohakuri, it reminded me of Yellowstone's Mammoth Hot Springs. A rich variety of siliceous and sulfureous colors and shapes flowed through hot springs, geysers, immense terraces, craters, ponds, and mud pools. An hour-long walk through the area is climaxed by a visit to the awesome Ruatapu (Aladdin's Cave), an ancient sacred Maori swimming hole." Access to Orakei Korako is by jetboat only. Readers continue to urge us to catch it next time around, and so we will.

Farther down Route 1, the thermal area at **Wairakei** also has its fans. It's more famous, however, as the location of the Wairakei Geothermal Power Station, where the escaping steam drives turbines connected to 13 electrical generators on the banks of the Waikato River. You can stay at the **Wairakei Resort Hotel** (Tel. 374-8021) and take in a game of golf at the Wairakei International Golf Course where you battle bunkers, the rough, *and* drifts of steam!

Still on the thermal path is **Craters of the Moon,** an intriguing stop off the main road from Wairakei to Taupo. The road is a little rough, but the drive off the beaten track is worth it. Entry is free. Just keep to the signed paths and you won't stray off the track.

Just five miles south of Wairakei, the resort city of **Taupo,** on the giant lake of the same name, rivals Rotorua as the center of the best trout fishing in New Zealand. There are lots of lake-related activities available, especially in the summer. For a complete rundown, see the **Taupo Visitor Centre** (Tel. 07-378-9000). They can tell you all the things you would like to know (how to get to Orakei Korako, for instance).

For overnights, you might try **Tui Oaks Motor Inn** (Tel. 378-8305), which is located slap on the lakefront. It also has a great view of Mt. Ruapehu and his volcanic neighbors. Tui Oaks has nicely appointed studio units and suites with private spas and prices ranging from $75 single to $100 double.

The **Mountain View Hotel** (Tel. 0800-800-128) is quiet but close to the town center and all amenities. Rates are normally from $59 for a studio, but double-check, as they can fluctuate according to season and need.

Brand-spanking new on the lake's edge is the **Caboose Taupo** (Tel. 377-2077; Web site www.taupo.caboose.co.nz). With wonderful views across the lake and to the mountains, the Caboose is a first for New Zealand. It is based on an African concept, and as such you'll find fine examples of African art and artifacts throughout the property. The log cabin-style building has spacious lounges overlooking the lake, the Serengeti Restaurant with an excellent menu, and a heated pool and spa. It is also totally accessible for the less mobile. Rates are from $89 for a compartment (double bed with en suite) and from $119 for a Train Suite. Budget travellers can doss down in the bunk room from $20 per person.

Some top-drawer pampering goes on at the internationally renowned **Huka Lodge** (Tel. 07-378-5791) back toward the Wairakei end of Taupo. In the summer season it pays to book well in advance, because the Huka Lodge combination of marvelous riverside site and top-notch hospitality makes it a hot favorite. It's a trout jump or two from **Huka Falls,** which thunders downriver. Lake Taupo is a mecca for fishermen around the world, and Huka Lodge is an enhancement to any sport. Nearby is **Huka Village,** a re-creation of an early village. Rates at the lodge are very up-market and include haute cuisine.

The Taupo region is geared towards entertaining people with a love of the outdoors. Cruises of the lake depart from the Waikato River mouth, in the center of Taupo.

From Lake Taupo, you can make out the peaks of three volcanoes on the southern horizon. They are **Mounts Tongariro, Ngauruhoe,** and **Ruapehu,** all classified as active, and at least one of them may very well be smoking at any given time. The three make up the bulk of **Tongariro National Park,** about 1.5 hours' drive south of Taupo. Park headquarters and the place to check on all the nature talks and bush walks is the hamlet of **Whakapapa,** on the slopes of Mount Ruapehu.

There is also the famed **Chateau Tongariro** (Tel. 892-3809), a well-preserved THC hotel (summer and winter rates vary from about $136 in winter to $118 in summer). The Chateau dates from the commodious 1920s. Also close by are the **Mount Ruapehu Ski Fields** (more in section 9). More modest accommodations can be found at the **Skotel Alpine Resort** (Tel. 892-3719 or 0800-756-835) from $82, near the Chateau, but unless you're a skier forget about staying anywhere in the park in August or September. Out of the park, if your route takes you through the army training town of **Waiouru,** stop in to see the **Queen Elizabeth II Army Memorial Museum** (open daily).

That bulge on the west coast of the North Island is caused by **Mount Egmont,** the hub of a national park of the same name. (Egmont has been officially renamed **Mount Taranaki,** although it will probably continue to be known by the previous name for some time.) The snowcapped peak seems almost perfectly formed, and it is often compared with Japan's Mount Fujiyama. It can be seen from almost everywhere in the Taranaki district. **New Plymouth** is the unofficial capital of Taranaki, but **Dawson Falls** is the staging area for hikes up the mountain slopes. Egmont is a nature-lover's delight. A botanist friend of ours, Meyric Williams, told us that of the 1,571 flowering plants in New Zealand, a total of 1,143 are found nowhere else in the world, and from others we learned that a considerable number of these are unique to **Mount Egmont National Park.** A good spot to get cultural in the area is the **Govett Brewster Art Gallery,** which is on Queen Street and has a stylish collection of contemporary and overseas art. The **Brougham Heights** (Tel. 757-9954) offers 22 suites with one or two bedrooms from $75 for two persons.

On the coast in South Taranaki, at the end of Route 4 from **Tongariro National Park,** is the port of **Wanganui.** If you go this way, stop to see the museum. We also enjoyed picnicking in one of its flowerful parks and later taking the 60-year-old elevator right up through the middle of the town hill, then climbing another lookout tower for a high-level view of the city, river, and ocean. See the **Tourism Wanganui** office (Tel. 345-3286). It's manned by helpful staff who know the best directions to send visitors in. One of the suggestions they are likely to make is to boat up the Wanganui River, at least as far as the poignant **Bridge to Nowhere.** Built by returned servicemen from the First World War who were given land, the bridge is a lonely memorial to their brave attempts to turn the thick forest into farms.

Try the **Acacia Park** on Anzac Parade for accommodations. The motel overlooks the **Whanganui River** and is on two acres of parkland. A historic homestead is also on the site. Tariff is from $65 for 2 persons.

On the east coast, a straight shot for 90 miles down Highway 5 from Taupo, are the twin cities of **Napier** and **Hastings,** both of which were nearly destroyed by a massive earthquake and accompanying conflagration on February 3, 1931. Among other things, the disaster raised the area by eight feet, creating many acres of new land along the shoreline. In Napier, many of the new buildings followed the art deco lines that were in vogue at the time, with the result that the attractive seaside town has the distinction of being a fine example of that style of architecture. The city has organized walks to see some of the best examples, and readers from Des Moines, Iowa, said theirs was "a real treat." Call the **Hawkes Bay Tourism Council** (Tel. 834-1918) for details. They will also tell you about vineyard and country tours in Hawkes Bay, which is as famous for its good wines as its rich pastureland. Hastings features **Fantasyland** (Tel. 876-9853) a wonder-filled place for the youngsters. **Splash Planet** (Tel. 876-9856; Web site www. Splashplanet.co.nz) is New Zealand's first fully themed water park for swimming in the summer and for a hot dip or ice skating in the winter. For a leisure activity or a totally relaxing visit, **Casa Lavanda** (Tel. 874-9300) is easy on the eye, the mind, and the pocket (well almost). Entry is free to this lavender farm, but there is a quality arts and crafts gallery on site, as well as the opportunity to stock up on the lavender body product range. A favorite sight on Napier's **Marine Parade** is the statue of **Pania,** the loveliest, most curvaceous maiden you ever saw in bronze. (Like the account of Hinemoa and Tutanekai in Rotorua, it represents an appealing Maori love story.) Nearby **Marineland** (Tel. 834-4027) produces some excellent dolphin shows. The **Visitor Information Centre** (Tel. 834-1191) on Marine Parade books accommodations as well as helping with visitor information.

Napier is our pick of the places to base the body for a general exploration of Hawkes Bay. Quality accommodations can be had for reasonable rates at the **Edgewater Motor Lodge** (Tel. 835-1148), on the corner of Marine Parade and Edwards Street, which has rates from $89 double, or at the **Harbour View Motor Lodge** (Tel. 835-8077), with rates from $110. The **Masonic Hotel** (Tel. 835-8689), on Tennyson Street, is also a good choice. And for backpacker accommodations, there's the **YHA Hostel** (Tel. 835-7039) at 277 Marine Parade, with rates of $12 per person.

For something wonderfully different, try staying at **The Master's Lodge** (Tel. 834-1947, Web site www.masterslodge.co.nz), high on Bluff Hill above Napier city, or **Black Barn** (Tel. 877-7985) in the heart of the Lombardi vineyard, looking over the vines to the mountains and the ocean. Private and self-contained, the interior features enormous beams, soaring ceilings, and a large riverstone fireplace. Otherwise there's **The County Hotel** (Tel. 835-7800) with its award-winning Anatoles restaurant and 11 luxurious and distinctive double rooms and a regal two-bedroom suite.

Mabel's Restaurant (Tel. 835-5655) is a good place to eat, especially as it is open from 6:30 A.M. until 9:30 P.M. You can find Mabel at 204 Hastings Street. For a lovely dining experience, try the **Ancient Oaks** (Tel. 876-3798), which offers outdoor dining under the very ancient oaks for which the place is named. This fine restaurant is just down the road in Hastings.

Shed 2 On The Quay (Tel. 835-2202) is a new restaurant on West Quay in Napier, with large picture windows overlooking the sea, and is rapidly gaining popularity. The menu offers a wide choice of both wines and food.

And there is McDonald's and KFC in both cities if you really must.

While you're on the East Coast, visit the gannet colony at **Cape Kidnappers.** For this try **Gannet Beach Adventures** (Tel. 875-0898, Web site www.napieronline.co.nz/attractions/gannetadventures). You can also try a wine tour. **Hawkes Bay in a Glass** (Tel. 836-7427, Web site www.qualityhb.co.nz) will take up to six people in air-conditioned luxury around the vineyards. The host is Noel Hunt, and he will also help you with accommodations, dining reservations, sightseeing, and just about anything else you need.

Hawkes Bay is otherwise know as the Fruit Bowl of New Zealand, so while you're there perhaps you should check out **Pernel Fruitworld**

(Tel. 878-3383). There are guided orchard tours with something for all seasons, but for lots of fruit go between late November and May, and for lots of blossoms be there during September and October. There is also a licensed café.

If you have access, surf the Internet all the way to www.hawkesbay-tourism.co.nz.

We can never think of Napier, however, without remembering the vignette of the earthquake told by N.Z. writer Jim Henderson: "The gravedigger, stripped to his tiny shorts that hot February, bent double trimming the bottom of the grave he'd just dug, leaping out to avoid burial in The Big One. A woman passerby seeing this sudden seminudity and convinced the graves were giving up the dead, justifiably fainting; and upon revival, in a town of ruin and fire, was possibly the only one to rejoice—it was *not*, after all, the Day of Judgement. . . ."

On State Highway 5 on the way to Napier is the **Riverland Outback Retreat** (Tel. 834-9756, Fax 834-9724), on 1,700 acres. Activities include whitewater rafting, horseback riding, bushwalking, and fishing. Accommodation in well-appointed cabins costs $55.

7. Guided Tours and Cruises

The **Tourism Rotorua Centre** (Tel. 348-5179) on Fenton Street is where most tours leave from, although some operators will pick you up from your hotel. However, Rotorua is very walkable, with nothing too far away. Check with your hotel or the Travel Office to find out exact times and fares. Not all of these are run daily, and departure times are subject to change. Prices vary, but generally speaking half-day trips run from about $27. (*Nota bene:* If you're taking more than one tour, let Tourism Rotorua help you plan, or you could find yourself retracing your steps.) The exact tours seem to change year by year, but here are samples of some that continue to be offered:

Waimangu-Tarawera: All-day bus and boat trip to Waimangu, the Buried Village, Lakes Tarawera and Rotomahana, etc. (Wear sensible shoes; you'll do some tramping in the valley.) This trip is probably the best way to get a handle on the dramatic events of 1886; **Waimangu Valley and Lake Rotomahana:** A morning or afternoon trip to the thermal valley and a short boat ride to the steaming cliffs; **Rotorua City Tour:** Morning or afternoon tour to several points including Ohinemuto, Government Gardens, Kuirau Park, Whakawerawera, and Rainbow Springs; **Rainbow Springs, Agrodome, Whakawerawera Special Tour:** All-day trip to the best-known sights and sites of Rotorua; **Agrodome and Hell's Gate:** Visit to the afternoon performance at the Agrodome, followed by the famous thermal area at Tikitere; **Buried Village and Hell's Gate:** Three-hour afternoon trip to the excavations at Te Wairoa plus the Tikitere thermal area; and **Buried Village and Lake Tarawera:** Another afternoon combination that also includes a short boat ride.

The Mount Tarawera Adventure Tour (Tel. 348-9929, Web site www.gisnz/rotorua/rotoopen) is an unusual and dramatic trip by four-wheel-drive vehicles right up to the crater that exploded in 1886. The half-day trip departs at 8:30 A.M. and 1:30 P.M. and costs $65. Try also **Mountain Magic Cultural Tours** (Tel. 348-6399), which also include Whakarewarewa and interactive participation in Maori arts and crafts. Cost is $70 for a half day and $140 for a full day.

Award-winning **Tamaki Tours** (Tel. 346-2823) will also ensure you have a good time, especially in regards to Maori Culture. Brothers Mike and Doug Tamaki will pick you up and deliver you back to your hotel accommodations. In between they will take you to the Tamaki Maori Village, where you will journey back in time through Te Tawa Ngahere Pa in a night of authentic traditional culture and entertainment. Cost is $55.

BOAT TRIPS

Lakeland Queen Cruises (Tel. 348-6634, Web site www.webline.co.nz/sub/lakelandqueen.html), a paddle steamer restaurant, takes patrons on breakfast ($24), morning tea ($16), luncheon ($26), afternoon tea ($16), and dinner ($42.50) cruises across Lake Rotorua. Or you can take the cruise only ($16), although they'll slip you a few snacks on the way with that one too.

Tarawera Launch Cruises (Tel. 362-8595) has fishing charter trips as well as daily scenic cruises of a couple of hours at a cost of around $22. **Lake Rotomahana Boat Cruises** (Tel. 366-6137) takes you on a cruise on Lake Rotomahana Crater Lake, which was formed by the 1886 Mt. Tarawera eruption, and then on a tour of Waimangu Volcanic Valley. Cost is $32.50.

AIR TOURS

Volcanic Air Safaris (Tel. 348-9984). We very much enjoyed the experience of taking off and landing right on the lake next to the downtown area. Float Plane offers eight different flights, from a 10-minute "Town and Around" to excursions more than an hour long. The one that goes way out to White Island, the active volcano in the Bay of Plenty, takes about 80 minutes. We took Flight 2, *Mount Tarawera-The Sleeping Giant,* which allowed us to look right down the mouth of the crater and to see other effects of the 1886 eruption. Cost is on application, as it depends on the type of aircraft being used.

Volcanic Wunderflites (Tel. 345-6077) has built its own small landing strip smack-dab on the edge of the crater of Mount Tarawera, 3,500 feet up! The company offers several flight programs, from around $100, and will include a landing on the crater with any of them for an extra charge. From the crater airstrip you can walk over in five minutes to take a look into the jaws of the volcano, a view similar to the one you get on the four-wheel-drive tour described earlier. Cost also varies depending on flight.

New Zealand Helicopters (Tel. 348-1223; Web site www.new-zealand-heli.nzl.com) is based at Whakarewarewa and offers fights to Mt. Tararewa and White Island and can combine the flights with jet boating, white-water rafting, and 4WD expeditions.

Marine Helicopters (Tel. 357-2512) also combines Mt. Tararewa with White Island and jet boating. Also check out **Lakeland Helicopters** (Tel. 366-5267) and **Heli-Kiwi** (Tel. 0800-435-454). As with the other air tour companies, cost depends on the tour and the type of aircraft.

If you're feeling really, really reckless, try **Tandem Skydiving** (Tel. 345-7520) and fork out $195 for the privilege of jumping out of a perfectly serviceable aircraft!

8. Water Sports

Two water sports are outstanding in the Rotorua and Lake Taupo areas—trout fishing and bathing (and that's not really swimming).

Anglers' Heaven. Even if you're not sure which end of a rod to put a hook on, this may be the place to learn. There are plenty of fish, so all you need is a good guide who knows all about the best places and will take care of all equipment and license worries.

Trout have been a dramatic and delicious feature of New Zealand life since the late 1800s. Brown trout eggs were brought from Britain in 1869, and rainbow eggs were shipped in from the Russian River in California and hatched in 1877. Both species have thrived more in New Zealand than in their native rivers and lakes. (In fact, their eggs are now shipped *back* to their homelands to purify the stock!)

Basically, you fish for brown trout in the rivers and rainbow trout in the lakes; either will average about two pounds. A few brown trout are caught in the lakes, too, and when they are they average about three pounds. Many of both varieties are even larger, of course—sometimes double those weights. If you go out on a guide's boat, you'll see two nails driven 16 inches apart on the side. Any fish that doesn't measure up to that from tip to tail must be thrown back to grow up a little.

Fishing guides (from around $72 per hour for a minimum of three hours) will provide any equipment you need, including tackle, wading boots, etc. If you haven't been given any personal recommendation for a guide, better stop in at the **Taupo Visitors Bureau,** where the experts based in Taupo can be tracked down. Otherwise try **Te Moana Charters Taupo** (Tel. 378-4839) or **Kinloch Fishing Charters** (Tel. 886-5116). Some of the best fly fishing you will find anywhere is on the **Tongariro River,** south of Taupo.

Of the 11 fishable lakes in the Rotorua District, Lakes Rotorua and Okareka are open year-round. The others are open from 1 October to 30 June. A license is required and can be arranged through your guide. Professional fishing guides include Kevin Coutts (Tel. 347-7479), Jim Flynn (Tel. 348-7120), Bill Loper (Tel. 345-6294), Dennis Ward (Tel. 347-4974), Terry Kelso (Tel. 347-9137), or Terry Walker (Tel. 347-1025), all of whom will be delighted to hear from you. Otherwise try **Still Water Fishing & Lake Adventures** (Tel. 345-4044).

Incidentally, if you want to dine on some delicious New Zealand trout, remember that you or someone you know is going to have to catch it first. Trout may not be sold commercially, so no dining room has it on the menu. However there are plenty of chefs who will happily cook your fish at a nominal charge. Your guide will know the best kitchens to apply to, so be sure to invite him for dinner!

Thermal Bathing. Rotorua's hot mineral pool scene has been a popular attraction for the past hundred years, ever since a rheumatic priest from Tauranga sat inside a spring for about a week and pronounced himself cured of his affliction. Today many hotels have their own hot pools, and guests enjoy lolling about in them, some claiming the waters do indeed have powers to banish whatever ails you. Nearly everyone says they feel better for the experience.

One of the best places to give this a whirl is the commercial establishment called the **Polynesian Spa** (Tel. 348-1328; Web site www.polynesianspa.co.nz), open daily from 6:30 A.M. to 11 P.M. on Hinemoa Street. Two kinds of mineral water are available—most of it the lightly alkaline, highly siliceous water from the Rachel Spring, which is supposed to have a soft, soothing effect on the skin. For $9 you can soothe your troubles away.

The water is controlled at an almost constant 100 degrees. If you want, you can step over to the special pit that still holds the water of the Priest's Spring (this one is slightly acidic—yup, diluted sulfuric acid!) to see what brought on the improvement for the good father. No control is exercised over this pool or three others near it. Temperatures may rise and fall, and mineral content will vary according to the whims of nature far under the ground.

For just $9.50 you can rent a private pool for half an hour, suitable for couples or families. No togs are necessary here. Just lock the door and soak in the six-foot-diameter pool clad in your birthday suit. You get the same Rachel water as in the two large pools, but you control your own temperature by manipulating the hot and cold valves.

You should take a few precautions along with your dip. The water is usually blood heat, and that portion of you that is underwater—everything but your head—has no way of perspiring. A total of 20 minutes is enough. Spending too much time in a thermal pool can alter your body temperature to dangerous levels, especially among those who are sensitive to hot and cold. Hot pools can raise your blood pressure and cause you to faint, possibly leading to you sliding under the water and drowning. (If you feel at all woozy, get out!) Do not put your head underwater. Don't do any genuine swimming, since you shouldn't exert yourself while soaking. And absolutely do not step in the pool after drinking any alcohol, an activity that raises the blood pressure and, in effect, lowers its boiling point.

Now, if just sitting around in hot water is not enough for you, you can take the best that Polynesian Pools has to offer—a combination of the aix massage (pronounced "aches," I think; it's a body rubdown with oil followed by jets of hot water and a vigorous hand massage), followed by a few minutes in a sauna, and capped off with (you guessed it) a cold "plunge pool." It will cost you $45 to do that to yourself, a process that takes about an hour, counting breathers in between steps. The cost also includes shampoo/conditioner, hair dryers, Japanese- and European-style showers, towels, and four pools of different temperature.

Conventional Swimming. Swimming along the lake front, especially near the city, is not really practical, with the amount of boating traffic and large flocks of swans and ducks. Further around the shore you'll find nice little beaches, but it can be cold. Otherwise trot along to the Aquatic Centre (Tel. 348-8833), which is adjacent to Kuirau Park. There are three pools—one 50 metres, one 25 metres, and a children's pool. The centre is open from 6 A.M to 9 P.M. and costs $2.70 for swimmers and 50¢ for spectators.

Whitewater Rafting and Jet Boating. If you're not going to Queenstown on the South Island, you can get a taste for these exciting sports with at least a couple of outfits operating out of Rotorua. **River Rats Rotorua** (Tel. 347-6049) offers "wildwater" rafting on the nearby Kaituna and Rangitaiki Rivers from $69 per person. **Raftabout** (Tel. 345-4652; Web site www.rotorua.nz.com/raftabout), **Kaituna Cascades** (Tel. 357-5032) and the **Great Kiwi White Water Co.** (Tel. 348-2144) also have programmes on these rivers. The **Whitewater Excitement Co.** (Tel. 345-7182) has a wide range of options with combinations that include 4WD adventures, jet boating, helicopters, thermal parks, geysers, and hot swims. Some trips are overnight. Cost is from $65 to $350 per person. **Wet and Wild Rafting** (Tel. 348-3191,

Web site www.wave.co.nz/pages.wetnwild/) also has a great degree of choice, offering from half-day up to four-day expeditions. Cost is from $65 to $396.

For some of the most exciting rafting on the North Island, **Rafting Fantastic** (Tel. 348-0233) has trips on the Wairoa River near Tauranga. You need to be fit and game for this one.

For windsurfing, parasailing, and other watersports, contact **Radical Water Sports** (Tel. 349-2828), which operates on all lakes around Rotorua. Wayne and Lee Gardner will look after you there. Cost is around $45.

The Taupo/Turangi area also has a number of excellent boat tours and river-raft opportunities. Call the Taupo Visitors Centre (Tel. 378-9000) for details.

9. Other Sports

Everywhere in this evergreen land you seem to find golf courses. Lee Tyler, the "Traveling Golfer" whose popular column runs in the *Los Angeles Times* and elsewhere, tells us that four of the top golf courses in the nation are in the Rotorua-Taupo area. The most sensational is the **Wairakei International Golf Club** (Taupo Tel. 374-8152), adjacent to the Wairakei Hotel. It's not really a private club at all, and tourists are more than welcome. Others, closer to Rotorua, include the **Arikikapakapa Golf Course** (Rotorua Golf Club) (Tel. 348-4051), which is across the road from Whaka and where you might lose your ball in a hot mud pool. This popular course has natural hazards and lakes. A round will cost about $50, or you can swing a short 9 holes for just $7. The **Springfield Golf Club** (Tel. 348-2748), at the western end of Devon Street, is an 18-hole, par-71 course of 6396 yards, and a round here will cost $40. For just a quick game, **Short Golf** (Tel. 348-3531) offers 9 holes varying from 45 metres to 85 metres, made up of par threes and fours. The first round costs $7 and the second round $3. There is a reduction for senior citizens.

Several games are available in the Government Gardens at nominal fees. There's a 9-hole golf course, tennis courts, croquet, and bowls (not the American kind). However, if it's tenpin bowling you want, you'll find it on Ward Street at **Geyserland Tenpin** (Tel. 347-8555). There are 16 fully automatic lanes, and to bowl on them will cost $7 and $1 for a pair of shoes.

If it's escaping on horseback you have a hankering for, try **Paradise Valley Horse Rides** (Tel. 348-8195; Web site www.webline.co.nz/leisure-time). Rides are from 30 minutes to two hours, and prices depend on how many of you want to go. **The Farmhouse** (Tel. 332-3771) and **Foxwood Park** (Tel. 345-7003) also offer horseback riding and guided treks, as well as farmstay accommodation. Cost at the former are from $15 for 30 minutes to $50 for two hours, and at the latter from $30 for 30 minutes to $150 for a full day including lunch.

If its hunting you're after, speak to your hosts at the Tourism Rotorua Centre (Tel. 348-5179), where will find out all you need to know. Time was when there were lots of horned beasts roaming the countryside almost asking to be picked off. There was even a bounty on them. Today the picture has changed, and professional hunters have reduced the wild herds considerably. However there are boar and wild deer if you know where to look.

SKIING

There is no snow in the steaming regions around Rotorua, and Taupo looks out to ski fields but has no snow of its own, so if skiing is your thing you'll have to be on a mountain; in the North Island some of the best schussing facilities in New Zealand are probably 7,000 feet up on the side of *Mount Ruapehu* in the **Tongariro National Park.**

The best-known runs are on the **Whakapapa Slopes** (also called the Chateau Ski Field) in the treeless heights four miles above the famed **Chateau Tongariro** (Tel. 892-3809), and a clutch of motels. Facilities include two double- and two single-chair lifts, four Poma lifts, and three T-bars—more total lifts than any other ski field in New Zealand—not counting several rope tows on the beginners' slope. A ski school, equipment rental, and the ski patrol are all there. Skiing is a lot cheaper in New Zealand than in the U.S., although after three consecutive years of bad snow and a grumbling, spitting volcano that coughed and spluttered all over the snow in a fit of pique, prices have gone up a wee bit in an effort to recoup losses and cleanse the equipment of ash.

Also at Ruapehu, the newer **Turoa Ski Fields** are a separate operation on the southwestern slopes, boasting two triple-chair lifts, two beginners' tows, a ski patrol, and group and private ski instruction. There are no ski rentals on the slopes, but all equipment is available by the day from shops in nearby **Ohakune.**

Like Mt. Hutt on the South Island, Ruapehu fields have a long season (from late June sometimes into November). In the spring (early October), the snow has been softened considerably by the sun. But in early morning and late afternoon, patrons clad in T-shirts and sometimes bathing suits put on suntan lotion and happily ski on "corn snow," an excellent surface for accomplished skiers.

Mt. Ruapehu is not as pretty without its mantle of snow, but if you're passing by outside of winter the Chateau is still a lovely place to stay. It is elegant and grand with an open fireplace, fine dining, and a large picture window that looks up the mountain. Cost is from $118. There are many treks you can do on the mountain, from just a couple of hours to a whole day. Check with **Ruapehu District Marketing** (Tel. 385-8364) for details.

10. Shopping in Rotorua

You may not find your best craft bargains on Tutanekai Street, or on any other street in downtown Rotorua. More likely they will be at the shops around the edges of the Whakawerawera Thermal Reserve or elsewhere. Establishments catering to visitors are often open seven days a week in Rotorua, by the way.

Be sure to see what carving, weaving, and flax products are available at the **Maori Arts and Crafts Institute** (Tel. 348-9047) on Hemo Road, right at the entrance to the Model Pa and Whaka. This is the main carving school, of course, and many of the totara wood products of its masters and students are for sale in the showroom. The same goes for woven and other types of items made by the women.

Excellent Maori carvings are also available in the group of shops that has sprung up on Tryon Street, near the exit to the reserve and the THC Rotorua International Hotel. Among that cluster, be sure to price and compare the *objets* offered in the **Eric Scholes Gallery** (Tel. 348-2219). You may note a distinct dearth of "airport art" there. Instead, you'll find hand-made reproductions of museum pieces, plus other new, different, and authentic Maori carvings. Some of the sweaters and wool products sold there we've seen for quite a bit more elsewhere.

Down in the town center, well-equipped souvenir emporia include **Tutanekai Souvenirs** (Tel. 348-7461) at 287 Tutanekai Street. You'll find wool and sheepskin products downtown at **Luxury Lambskin Products** (Tel. 348-1030). But we wouldn't buy any sheepskin until we had a chance to compare with the prices out at the **Agrodome** outside of town at Riverdale Park, where the sheep shows are given twice daily. They just might be your best bargains for fuzzy ruggies.

Lakeside Arts and Crafts (Tel. 349-2626) on Memorial Drive is well worth a look, and you will get a good idea of prices for future purchases. **The Jade Factory and Gift Centre** (Tel. 349-3968) has some quite lovely things that you will covet. You'll find this treasure trove at 1288 Fenton Street.

The **Tarawera Art Gallery and Handcraft Centre** (Tel. 362-8776) is on Spencer Road, although you'll be wondering how you will transport some of the larger pieces. If you're in town during the weekend, stroll down to the lake by the Soundshell and check out the craft market there. Don't expect great things, as a lot of stalls stock very folksy crafts, but don't dismiss it out of hand either. There can be some finds if you look, especially in native wood and pottery.

Bookstore? Probably the best-stocked bookstore in town is **McLeod's** (Tel. 348-5388) at 282 Tutanekai Street. Tell Mr. Trevor Thorp what you want, say "hello" for us, and ask him if he has a full complement of *Maverick Guides* on the shelf yet.

Food store? If you're setting up housekeeping for a few days, or just picnicking on the road, you can probably get just about anything you want to munch on at **Woolworth's Super Market.** If you didn't know that Woolworth's operates supermarkets, neither did we. But this one's right there at the lake end of good ole Tutanekai Street. Happy cart-pushing! The **Cambridge Country Store,** en route from Rotorua to Auckland, has won national tourism awards for presentation and insistence on quality. Owner Jan Seabrook seeks out New Zealand-made arts and crafts, leather and woolen goods, and wines and foodstuffs that exemplify the country's best retail qualities. You won't have to look too hard for the cerise building that looks like a church. Stop here also for lunch or refreshments.

11. Night Life and Entertainment

In Rotorua, this category means mainly one thing—the traditional Maori *hangi.* Like its Hawaiian equivalent, the *luau,* the word *hangi* has changed its meaning over the years. Strictly speaking, a *hangi* is a cooking pit in the ground. It's something nature provided for the Maori of Rotorua without their having to do much more than punch a hole in a thermally active region.

Later, *hangi* came to mean a feast of typical Maori food (wild pork, kumaras, etc.), especially when combined with a "Maori concert"—a costumed exhibition of traditional dancing and singing. The Maori concert may be unlike any other entertainment you've ever witnessed. Songs are presented, of course, often in beautiful, close harmony. But the dances and rhythm make the show—from the graceful flax poi ball dance, performed by high-born Maori women, to the fierce *haka,* traditionally a dance of defiance executed by warriors preparing to march into battle. This is the one that involves sticking out the tongue and rolling the eyeballs in ways designed to frighten and humble even the fiercest of one's enemies!

There are several other acts, including rhythmic and melodic games played by the performers on stage. The entertainment is capped by the singing of "Po Atarau," the Maori song of farewell that became popular in the U.S. some years ago under the title "Now Is the Hour."

Good concert venues are the **New Zealand Maori Arts and Crafts Institute** (Tel. 348-9047), which costs from $15.50, and *Magic of the Maori*

(Tel. 349-3949) from $16.50. This programme is based on the famous Te Papaiouru Marae at Ohinemutu. You can stay overnight too, if you choose. Price on application. And then, of course, there's Mike and Doug Tamaki's village at Tumunui (Tel. 346-2823) that we mentioned earlier.

The Ace of Clubs (Tel. 346-2204) is Rotorua's most popular nightclub, and if you feel like calling in, it is at 10 Ti Street. Another possibility is the **Towers Nightclub** (Tel. 346-2097) at 12 Eruera Street. For conventional drinking and dancing, there isn't a whole lot to choose from. Many finish off the evening with a few drinks in the hotel bar. Live music may be on tap at the **Lake Rotorua Tavern** on Lake Road, or the bar at the **Hotel Rotorua.**

Three television channels are available in Rotorua, with the same programming as everywhere else in the country. There's also cable Sky television, and some of the hotels are hooked up to it. Rotorua has its own radio station, 1ZC, "Radio Geyserland," which proudly broadcasts flight information, travelers' weather, and other news catering to the visitor in this tourist-oriented community. It's at 909 on the AM dial.

12. The Rotorua Address List

Ambulance—Dial 111 for all emergencies.

Bank—Bank of New Zealand, Corner of Hinemoa and Tutanekai Streets (Tel. 348-7069).

Dentist and doctor on duty—Tel. 348-1000 (weekends and holidays only).

Dry cleaners and laundry—Valet Automatic Laundrette and Dry Cleaners, corner of Amohia and Amohau Streets (Tel. 348-2986).

Fire—Dial 111 for all emergencies.

Health food shop—The Health Shop (Tel. 348-4883).

Hospital—Rotorua Hospital, Pukeroa Street (Tel. 348-1199).

Urgent pharmacist—Lake Care Pharmacy, corner of Arawa and Tutanekai Streets (Tel. 348-4385).

Police—Dial 111 for all emergencies.

Post office—GPO at 117 Hinemoa Street (Tel. 347-7851).

Taxi—Telephone 348-1111 or 348-2444.

Tourist information—Tourism Rotorua Centre, Fenton Street (Tel. 348-5179); Rotorua Activity Centre, corner of Fenton and Eruera Streets (Tel. 348-1048).

7

Wellington and Vicinity

1. The General Picture

Almost invariably, Americans compare the hills and harbor ambiance of New Zealand's capital city to those of San Francisco. The heights surrounding a large, circular bay have been molded into an enormous amphitheater offering excellent views of the ships and towers below to all residents lucky enough to find permanent positions on the steep slopes.

Charming, century-old buildings jam tightly against newer, more substantial constructions, apparently leaning on the younger walls for support. Like San Francisco, the city is prone to earth tremors, and Wellingtonians have been talking about—and preparing for—"the big one" for several years now.

There are even cable cars in **Wellington**—sort of. Exactly two red cars are winched alternately up a straight, steep slope and back several times a day on a single track. With this, then, the comparisons between the two cities begin to fall apart, and Wellington is seen to have its own personality—and its own standards of beauty—that need not be viewed as reflections of any other city.

There is no fog, for instance—or smog, smoke, or pollution of any kind—in the restless air that circulates through this political metropolis. New Zealanders have been calling the city "Windy Wellington" almost since its founding. The wind, which does indeed sometimes whistle between buildings at more than 80 mph, also has the effect of scouring the city clear of all but the purest, cleanest air. But the fact that it can also drive rain horizontally through the streets has prompted Wellington businessmen to forgo umbrellas in favor of raincoats and special plastic overpants to keep their trousers dry.

Wellington likes to trace its historical roots deep into the time of **Kupe,** the first Maori explorer of Aotearoa, who is said to have made a landing there in about A.D. 950. Captain Cook came across the entrance to Wellington Harbor (later named Port Nicholson) in 1773. The first colonials who arrived in the land in 1840 chose the site to build on, naming it in honor of General Arthur Wellesley, the first Duke of Wellington, who had helped them on their way to New Zealand. The city was not designated as the capital until 1865, after population had increased in the south and it was thought that Wellington would be more in the center of things than Auckland.

Because of its difficult, steep site and the fault line under the surface, Wellington is considered something of an engineering masterpiece. Its modern buildings are built to an expensive high standard of earthquake-proof construction. Older structures cling to the hillsides in the apparent hope that their tenacity will not be severely tested. It seems unfortunate that some of the city's fine old buildings are being razed after being judged unsafe. (A few are being braced from the inside, but not nearly as many are saved as sentimentalists would like.)

One of the newest buildings is **The Museum of New Zealand Te Papa Tongarewa,** which opened in late 1998. The building is the culmination of 140 years of cultural influence and events and burgeoning national pride. There was much political fighting over the establishment, which cost $317 million, and despite over 600,000 New Zealanders visiting in its first year, it still has its detractors. These criticisms are leveled mainly at the amount of public money that went into its construction. Museums are usually sponsored by their immediate local government, and often struggle for funding. Te Papa seemed, to those outside of the capital, to be funded from a bottomless purse. Te Papa (Our Place) is also criticized as a theme park because of the nature of some of its exhibits (such as a recent tribute to *Star Trek*) and because it has many, many exhibits stored away in comparison to what is displayed. If you compare the Auckland War Memorial Museum and Te Papa (which you must, as both are more than worth a visit), you will see for yourself where the great differences lie. Drift, in particular, through the exhibit Signs of a Nation, an interactive presentation of the **Treaty of Waitangi,** a document that is a great point of contention for many New Zealanders.

The Museum of New Zealand Te Papa Tongarewa is open year-round, from 10 A.M. to 6 P.M., except on Thursdays when the doors remain open until 9 p.m. Entry to the museum and most exhibitions is free.

Wellington might have had even more of a crowding problem if it were not for a massive earthquake in 1855. Casualties were low in the infant community, and the resulting seven-foot upheaval added considerable land to the coastline. Most of the commercial area is now built on this "reclaimed" land—as are the superhighways that lead out of the city to its principal suburbs in the **Hutt Valley.**

The valley not only holds many of Wellington's suburban communities, but is also the most highly industrialized area in New Zealand. Despite this, the entire southern peninsula of the North Island—which ends at Wellington—also contains thousands of acres of mountainous forests. This area includes the rugged **Rimutakas** and the long **Tararua Range,** which effectively separate the population in the elongated Wairarapa Plain from the second great suburban center stretched along the **Kapiti Coast** on the western edge of the peninsula.

Wellington, of course, is a government city, filled with the political trappings of any world capital. It is also a gateway, although not principally an aerial one (even if it does have a compact airport within five miles of the city center). It is much more important as a surface-shipping site for goods destined overseas or to the South Island. It is to this port that you travel to catch the large, green-and-white ferries that roll and heave over the often confused waters of Cook Strait between the two islands.

It's popular in New Zealand to put Wellington down, but that's of little concern to those fortunate enough to live on the precipitous terraces above the city. The homeowners who make like mountain goats every time they leave and enter their castles in the air take special pride in the city's motto—*Suprema a Situ.* It means, more or less, that they consider it the best place to be. We would agree—when the wind doesn't blow too hard and the earth doesn't shake too much, that is.

2. Long-Distance Transportation

Wellington's international airport is a continual source of embarrassment, considering that it serves the national capital. Its runway stretches across a narrow isthmus from Evans Bay to Lyall Bay, a distance of 6,000 feet, which is far too short for most jumbo jets. Consequently, nearly all flights in and out of the capital city are in smaller planes. Not even the international flights from Australia can come in on the big 747s. The largest craft seen at Wellington Airport now are Boeing 767s, twin-engine widebodies designed for short takeoffs and landings.

International flights (to Sydney, Melbourne, and Brisbane only) are served by **Qantas Airways** (Tel. 0800-808-767) and **Air New Zealand** (Tel. 382-2000). Domestic flights are all taken in and out by the 737s and an occasional 767 of the domestic services of **Air New Zealand National** and the smaller aircraft operated to provincial towns by **Air New Zealand Link**. **Air New Zealand Travel Centre** (0800-737-767) and **Ansett New Zealand** (Tel. 0800-ANSETT [0800-267 388]) also operate domestic services on main trunk and provincial routes.

The Domestic Terminal buildings have all the standard facilities, including a restaurant and cafeteria; Hertz, Budget, and Avis counters; bookstore; souvenir and art shop; and an amusement arcade. Buses to the city (with several stops, ending at the railroad station) are run every 20 minutes from right outside the terminal door for around $9. The taxi will cost three times as much. There's also a **Super Shuttle** (Tel. 387-8787), which operates door-to-door for $12. Otherwise try **Corporate Cabs** (Tel. 499-4649).

A long, covered walkway leads to the two-story International Terminal, which features a spiral staircase to the open observation deck. A bank opens there when flights are due in or out. To go into town, you can either take a taxi or catch the Vickers coach.

Interisland Ferries. The big Interisland ferries of **Tranz Rail** (Tel. 0800-802-802) take three hours to cross between the North and South Islands. On Sunday and Monday departure times are 6:30 A.M., 9:30 A.M., 2:30 P.M., and 6:30 P.M. On the remaining days they depart at 1:30 A.M., 6:30 A.M., 9:30 A.M., 2:30 P.M., and 5:30 P.M. Cost depends on when you sail and will cost at worst $46 one way and at best $23 one way. During the summer months The Lynx fast ferry also plies Cook Strait. This schedule usually starts in the second week of December and goes through the end of February. Departures are at 8 A.M., 1:30 P.M., and 6:30 P.M. Rates also depend on when you choose to sail, and at worst will cost $59 per person one way. The journey takes one hour and forty-five minutes. Both vessels also carry vehicles.

During the summer you can also take a **Top Cat ferry** (Tel. 0800-486-7228). Prices are released closer to the summer season.

Also check when booking to see what the current Travelpass could be. Depending on your schedule, some of these deals will afford you considerable savings.

If you're not driving to or from the ferry terminal, a bus runs from Platform 9 at the railroad station, leaving about 35 minutes before each ferry departure. (But it's a long walk from the front of the station.) Bus fare is free. The distance to the terminal is not great from most parts of Wellington, and many travelers say they were happy enough to take a cab between their hotel and the boat.

At the terminal you check your luggage in the same way you would at the airport.

The two ships—the *Aratere* and *Arahura*—are large vessels, and they look more like ocean liners than ferryboats. All have several lounges, including a television lounge, a bar lounge, and a children's play lounge. There is also a restaurant and a ship's store selling assorted candy bars and magazines. You'll find sitting and strolling space out on the decks, too, and if the weather is good the whole thing can be a beautiful 34-mile experience beginning at Port Nicholson and culminating in the scenic trip through the islands and along the peninsulas of Marlborough Sounds to the small port of Picton—or the reverse, of course, if you're coming up from the South Island.

Take something warm to wear, even in summer, because Cook Strait is known for sh-sh-shivvery temperatures any time of year. If you're prone to seasickness, take some Dramamine—or take the plane. Things often get choppy in the strait, even on a bright, clear day.

The ferries also operate a day trip for Wellington residents or anyone who is not going further on the South Island. Under the plan you catch the 10 A.M. ferry out, have a look around Picton and Marlborough Sounds throughout the day, and return on one of the evening sailings. The round-trip, same-day fare is currently around $57. Check out the *Saver Fare* deals, which shave about 20 percent off normal fares. They could suit your plans.

For any trip, be sure you book your ferry in advance. During peak periods, you just might not make it on board if you don't. Any travel agency or a branch of Intercity will take care of it for you. Bon voyage!

Trains. To or from Auckland or Napier by rail, you'll see the inside of the large **Tranz Rail** (Tel. 0800-802-802) on Bunny Street, just a hop off Waterloo Quay. Watch out, because your train might not come in on the exact platform predicted by the ticket seller.

The long-distance trains are Tranz Rail's Tranz Scenic services. The *Overlander* departs Wellington at 8:45 A.M. and arrives in **Auckland** at 7:35 P.M. Cost is between $69 and $138 depending on time of travel and type of ticket. The *Northerner* is the nighttime service between the two cities, and it departs Wellington at 7: 50 P.M. and arrives in **Auckland** at 7 A.M. Cost is between $61 and $122.

The Bay Express runs between Wellington and **Hastings** and **Napier,**

departing Wellington at 8 A.M. and arriving in Hastings at 1:05 P.M. and
Napier at 1:22 P.M. The return journey departs Hastings at 2:05 P.M., Napier
at 2:29 P.M., and arrives back in Wellington at 7:36 P.M. Cost is between $36
and $71.

Intercity Coaches. Into or out of Wellington, bus services up the west
coast and center of the island are run by **Intercity Coach** (Tel. 472-5111 for
bus and train information), now in the railway station. Buses arrive in town
at Platform 9 at the station.

East Coast Intercity services are operated by **Newmans Coachlines** (Tel.
499-3261). On the way into town, they will drop off passengers at the ferry
terminal and the railroad station. Prices depend on where you want to go
and when, of course.

Rental Cars. There are three U-drives with modest counters outside the
ferry terminal. One is **Hertz** (Tel. 384-3809), although their main address
is at 166 Taranaki Street, which you normally reach with that phone number. They also have a counter at the airport (Tel. 388-7070) and at the ferry
terminal (Tel. 384-3809). **Avis** (Tel. 801-8108) is mainly at 25 Dixon Street.
You reach their ferry terminal branch on Tel. 801-8108 and their airport
station on Tel. 802-1088.

Budget (Tel. 802-5428) has its garage at 81 Ghuznee Street, near the station. Reach them at the ferry terminal, Tel. 473-7588, and the airport, Tel.
755-7985.

You will also find cars in Wellington at **National** (Tel. 801-8483) at the
Plaza International Hotel, or **Thrifty** (Tel. 499-5691), in Miramar. Other reputable firms are **Pegasus** (Tel. 384-4883); **New Zealand Rent A Car** (Tel. 384-
2745); and **A1 Rentals** (Tel. 386-2888), who boast they have no hidden costs.

3. Local Transportation

The city bus system (electric and diesel vehicles) mainly operates south
of the city (toward Cook Strait). Residents commuting north would normally use a train—what they call a "unit" in Wellington. Buses are operated
by the Wellington City Transport, and you can pick up three separate
timetables (with small maps) for the Eastern, Western, and Southern
routes free from newsstands. The Western Route map seemed to cover
most of the areas we needed, and it hooks up conveniently to the Southern
Route map. Buses (Tel. Ridewell 801-7000 for information) work on a section fare system, with most starting from the main railroad station and
some from Courtenay Place. Check out the popular and useful *Daytripper*
fare, which saves money on the handful of bus trips you might want to
make in a day.

There are four commuter train lines to the city suburbs. The **Johnsonville** line runs about six miles northwest of the center. The local service up the main trunk line goes as far as **Paraparaumu** (mispronounced by virtually everyone, incidentally, as "pare-ah-per-*am*"). The other two go up the Hutt Valley, the first on a dead-end line to Lower Hutt and Melling, and the other through the hills to Upper Hutt. (Some of these units are inoperative on Sunday.)

Taxis. There are plenty of cabs available outside of the busiest hours. Pick them off the taxi rank or else telephone, as is usual in New Zealand. Most destinations in the central city will run four or five dollars. **Wellington Combined Taxis** (Tel. 384-4444) is one of the oldest established companies in Wellington and, despite recent deregulation of the Wellington taxi business, still seems to offer the best deal.

4. Hotels and Motels in Wellington

As a government and "home office" town, Wellington generally has more, better, and sometimes less expensive accommodations available on the weekends than it does from Monday through Thursday. If you're having trouble getting anything in the city, drop by the Visitor Information Centre (Tel. 801-4000). They may be able to set you up with something in the suburbs—perhaps in **Johnsonville,** about five miles north of the city, or even along the Gold Coast, the stretch of vacation coastline on Highway 1 from **Paekakariki** to **Waikanae.**

EXPENSIVE HOTELS

The overall commander of Wellington's fleet of top hotels is the **Parkroyal** (Tel. 472-2722 or 0800-80-11-11), on the corner of Grey and Featherston Streets. It is a proud member of the Parkroyal chain, with all the mod cons. Rates are $350 twin or double, moving on up sharply for the luxury of a suite. Special rates are offered on weekends. Two restaurants join the cocktail bars, and there's a health center inside and a helipad out.

The **Plaza International** (Tel. 473-3900 or 0800-655-555; Web site www.plazainternational.co.nz) also rates as another top Wellington hotel, and rises up from Wakefield Street at number 148.Tariff is on application, and special weekend rates are also available here. The Plaza Business Club operates on the eighth floor and includes complimentary breakfast, coffee and tea, and pre-dinner drinks. Rates are a little higher for this floor. You can ride the external glass elevator to Burbury's Restaurant, where dining is kept company by fine views out over the harbor. The property is close to Te Papa.

The 260-room **James Cook Centra Hotel** (Tel. 499-9500 or 0800-80-11-11) on The Terrace, high above the business district, has an architecturally inspiring entrance to a high-ceilinged lobby with appropriate Captain Cook trappings; an autograph board bearing the signatures of Bette Davis, Robert Morley, Raymond Burr, and other notable guests; lifts *down* to the city as well as up to the bedrooms; covered parking; well-maintained bedchambers, and excellent views over city and harbor. The real James Cook never had it so good. Like the Parkroyal, this is a South Pacific Hotel Group property.

The old Quality Hotel Plimmer Towers on Boulcott Street is now the **Copthorne Plimmer Towers** (Tel. 473-3750) and consists of one- or two-bedroom suites. Prices are also on application. After winding up in the hotel's business center, guests can wind down in the sauna and in-house gym.

It is also no longer the Terrace Regency at 345 The Terrace but the **Novotel Wellington** (Tel. 385-9829 or 0800-288-880). This property is perhaps more convenient, if you have a car. Tightly hugging the edge of a steep hill at 345 The Terrace, this establishment may be perfect for the physical-fitness buff—not only because of the uphill trudge from town, but also because of the facilities offered when you get back home. There is a cocktail lounge, Terrace Restaurant with a view over the city, large recreation/gymnasium area featuring exercise machines and a 40-foot heated, indoor swimming pool, and 108 newly refurbished and operable windows. Speak to them about their special leisure rates as well as weekend specials. The hotel makes a strong bid for the busy businessman, but it should also serve vacationers—especially if they want to do a few midwinter laps in the pool.

The **Airport Hotel** (Tel. 387-2189), also known locally as simply "The Lodge," may be better, but it's much further out on Kemp Street, on a bus line near the airport. It features a comfortable, spacious lobby; lovely, quiet setting with garden and lagoon; large, sunny outdoor swimming pool (unusual—and often unused—in Wellington); attractive and reportedly good Buccaneer Room restaurant; plenty of parking; and 122 colorful, tasteful rooms at rates from $96-157 for two. We have excellent reader reports on this hotel. If it were right in town, it would rival the James Cook in its overall attractions.

CityLife Wellington (Tel. 478-8588 or 0800-36-88-88; Web site wwwl.dynasty.co.nz) is a new all-suite hotel with generously sized, fully equipped and serviced apartments. Price is on application.

Just a little out of midtown, at 40-44 Oriental Parade, is the **Bay Plaza** (Tel. 385-7799 or 0800-857-799), with a small, neat lobby; friendly people in charge on our visit; award-winning Bohdan's Restaurant; a good guest laundry; no pool; and parking available. Its total of 78 bedrooms are often filled with business types during the week. Amenities include TV and standard equipment; no fridges; and some views from the upper floors. Light sleepers might like to know that the hotel sits very near the major metropolitan fire station, and the resulting cacophony during middle-of-the-night emergencies in the district just might spring you out of bed as quickly as it does the neighboring brigade. Thankfully, however, most nights in Wellington are peaceful. The hotel itself is very nice—and well protected, too!

The Hotel Raffaele (Tel. 384-33450 or 0800-739-333) is a romantic waterfront property also on Oriental Bay. All rooms have private balconies opening to harbour views, as does the gourmet restaurant. Cost is from $139 during the week and from $105 on the weekends.

The Shepherd's Arms Hotel (Tel. 472-1320) in Tinakori Road claims to be New Zealand's oldest hotel, established in 1870. Close to the Botanical Gardens and Lambton Quay, the boutique-style accommodations offer fourposter beds in some rooms, spa baths, and double showers. More accommodations are adjacent in the form of a fully self-contained luxury colonial cottage. Cost is from $85 per night in the regular rooms and $235 for the cottage.

The West Plaza at 110 Wakefield Street (Tel. 473-1440 or 0800-731-444), not to be confused with the Plaza International Hotel on the same street, is a comfortable hotel in the higher-priced range. Rates for singles and doubles are the same, around $145. Suites of course, cost more.

MEDIUM-PRICE ACCOMMODATIONS

The oddly named Museum Hotel de Wheels (Tel. 385-2809; Web site www.museum-hotel.co.nz) is adjacent to Wellington's popular night spots, business district, and convention centre. It has a licensed restaurant and bar and offers dinner and breakfast. Tariff is $84-135, and weekend rates are also available.

Although selling itself on its proximity to the airport, the 747 Motel (Tel. 387-3184 or 0800-747-668) nevertheless claims not to suffer from aircraft noise. Some of its units have fully equipped kitchens. Cost is between $90-100.

Five minutes' walk from the city, 15 minutes from the airport, and 10 minutes from the ferry, the Harbour City Motor Inn (Tel. 384-9809 or 0800-33-24-68) is centrally located. The hotel has facilities for the disabled and costs from $95-160 for two. There are also special weekend rates. The Willis Lodge (Tel. 384-5955) looks cosy at 318 Willis Street. Tariffs are from $79 single/double/twin.

Central to the city is the **Apollo Lodge** (Tel. 385-1849; Web site www.apollo-lodge.co.nz) on Majoribanks Street and the closest motel to Te Papa. There are also kitchen units here, and the tariff is around $95 double.

The **Marksman Motor Inn** (Tel. 385-2499; Web site www.yellowpages.co.nz/for/marksman/dp108.html) calls itself a rare and unique find for the astute traveller. So all you astute travellers out there, check it out and report back! The property is at 42 Sussex Street and consists of studios and one- or two-bedroom suites. Cost is between $90 and 137.

That wraps it up for the main recommendations. One reader has written to recommend the **Abel Tasman Hotel** (Tel. 385-1304). It has a convenient address at the corner of Willis and Dixon Streets. Doubles currently run around $95, suites from $145. The restaurant has the unusual name of *Razzamatazz*. The **Bucket Tree Motor Lodge** (Tel. 232-4898 or 0800-80-48-98) in the Wellington suburb of **Tawa** has a hard-to-miss name and a hard-to-pass-by restaurant. The food there is good, according to our reports. Tariffs range from $95.

ROOMS AT A BUDGET

Alas, the Railton Hotel has passed away since last we were in town, but **Trekkers Hotel** (Tel. 385-2153) on Cuba Street, with tariffs from $18 for backpackers, seems like a good substitute. There are also self-contained units from around $99, and these have one bedroom. Near Flanagan's on Kent Terrace is an appealing addition to the Wellington accommodations scene called **Halswell Lodge** (Tel. 385-0196). This hostelry has been converted from a delightful old colonial house. Double rooms cost around $120. Halswell Lodge is close to the city at Courtenay Place.

Several new guesthouses and small "private hotels" have been opening in the past couple of years. One good example is the **Terrace Lodge Guest House** (Tel. 382-9506), at 291 The Terrace. Rates are around $70. **Tinakori Lodge** (Tel. 473-3478), at 182 Tinakori Road, is a conveniently located, characterful, 100-year-old house and has such niceties as an included breakfast buffet and a complimentary morning *and* evening paper. We were pleased to receive a report from Walter Almon that he liked this one. Doubles go for $95 (includes GST). The hosts here are Mel and John Ainsworth.

One we've heard about is the **Rosemere Hostel** (Tel. 384-3041), which charges $13 per person. You can also go upscale at the Rosemere and pay around $35 for B & B. It's at 6 McDonald Crescent. Then there's the **Ambassador Travel Lodge** (Tel. 384-5696) at 287 The Terrace, which charges backpacker travelers $15 per person. Make a note, too, of **Waterloo Backpackers,** opposite the Railway station at 1 Bunny Street.

The official NZYHA **Wellington Youth Hostel** (Tel. 80-728-0271) is at the corner of Cambridge and Kent Terraces, and the cost is $18 a night.

Backpackers are well looked after in Wellington. **Ivanhoe Inn** (Tel. 384-2264), at 52 Ellis Street up on Mt. Victoria, has rates of $17 per person per night in dorm-style rooms. For privacy you pay $46.

5. Beef Wellington and Other Dining

Unless you've got a friend who's a backbencher, frontbencher, minister, or mucky-muck, you won't get into the city's most famous restaurant. That's the legendary **Bellamy's,** and it's reserved exclusively for members of Parliament and their special guests. Supposedly it's one of the best bargains in the country, but we can't confirm or deny it.

The Icon Restaurant, on the second floor of Te Papa, looks out over the city and harbour and boasts New Zealand's only Michelin star chef. Adam Newell's signature dish, crayfish cappuccino, has received rave reviews. Icon has been booked out since it opened, so reservations are a must.

Il Casino (Tel. 385-7496) is a renowned Wellington restaurant serving award-winning northern Italian food. It offers a piano bar, garden restaurant, and pizzeria with a wood-burning oven for delicious pizzas. The Bartelli Room is reserved for fine dining. You won't regret trying this establishment. Then there's **Angkor** (Tel. 384-9423), a good Cambodian restaurant around the corner at 41 Dixon Street. Choose carefully from an extensive menu. (Try the steam boat prepared at the table.)

Dixon Street to the east becomes Courtenay Place, where there are several delicious establishments. **The Exchange** (Tel. 384-1006) offers great New Zealand cuisine and specializes in beef. It is at 20 Blair Street and is open for lunch and dinner. While you're in Blair Street, have a look around, for it's the heart of café society. Nearby Dixon Street is another good eating area.

In Courtney Place itself, the **Coyote Street Bar & Restaurant** (Tel. 385-6665) is open seven days till late and does a weekend brunch that is well patronised.

The White House Restaurant (Tel. 385-8555) at 27 Willis Street has a new extensive wine list with a cellar book available. Here they use only organic vegetables, free-range eggs, and pure filtered water.

Logan-Brown (Tel. 801-5114) on the corner of Cuba and Vivian Streets promises an extra ordinary bankers' lunch menu. Three light and elegant courses as well as bread and coffee can be had for $29.50, and they guarantee to have you in and out in 60 minutes if you're pushed for time.

You can't visit New Zealand without trying at least three things—fat New Zealand mussels unlike any other seafood of the same name found anywhere else in the world; a hangi; and the Great New Zealand Sunday Roast. If you're not likely to be anywhere for some home cooking, try to be at **Whitby's Restaurant** (Tel. 499-9500, ext. 8600) at the James Cook Centra Wellington Hotel. Here you can indulge in roast meats, crispy crackling, golden roast potatoes, vegetables, and lashings of gravy. Then you can have a double helping of dessert. It may not be kind to your waistline, but it will do your gluttonous soul a world of good. Cost is $25 and reservations are a good idea for this popular menu.

Jane Henney and Bob Graham were most impressed by **The Grain of Salt** (Tel. 384-8642) in Oriental Bay at 232 Oriental Parade. They recommend the Walnut Dacquibise if it's on the menu when you get there. The **Skyline Restaurant** (Tel. 475-8727), at the top of the cable-car run in Kelburn, provides decent victuals at moderate prices for lunch or dinner, along with a delicious view. It's worth the drive to Marine Parade on Day's Bay.

There are several good Italian *cucinas*. One is called the **Las Casa Pasta House** (Tel. 385-9657) and it's not expensive. **Red Tomatoes Pizzeria/Café** (Tel. 475-7123) allows you to dine in, takeaway, or have your meal delivered to your accommodation. They offer a gourmet selection of pizzas cooked in a manuka (native New Zealand wood)-fired pizza oven, which will give it a distinctly New Zealand taste, as well as pastas and salads.

Otherwise try **Sfuzzi Bar and Bistro** (Tel. 477-4900) for Tuscan-style cuisine.

Another spicy choice is **Slows Malaysian Bar & Grill** (Tel. 801-7771), promising spicy food and a large menu. Somewhat similar is the **Armadillo** (Tel. 384-1444), a "Texan" restaurant at 129 Willis Street. We haven't moseyed in, so we don't know if Armadillo is merely the name or the main dish. Then there's **Arizona** (Tel. 495-7867) with a Tex-Mex style and plenty of atmosphere on the corner of Grey and Featherston Streets.

A cheap place to eat is the Wellington Polytechnic Training Restaurant. Don't be put off thinking you'll just be a guinea pig for baby chefs. **Finlay's** (Tel. 801-2794, ext. 8776) is becoming a popular place to eat, especially with a three-course lunch costing around $12 and a four-course dinner around $18. The menu also features quick and light meals for those in a hurry. The only downside (if you could call it that!) is the sometimes anxious faces that surround you, as the students bustle around trying so hard to please. Or maybe that is just a cunning marketing ploy—no matter what is on your plate you could only praise such anxious little faces! Seriously though, we haven't heard yet of a bad meal there. Try it out and do your bit towards fostering the confidence and careers of tomorrow's chefs and waiters. Bookings are essential.

Scorpio's (Tel. 383-7563) claims to be New Zealand's only Welsh restaurant—"Miners are welcome and beware of the dragon in the kitchen." The **Axolotl Mexican Walking Fish Cafe** (Tel. 384-3834) is smoke-free, they say.

Also causing some ethnic stir is an Indonesian dining room called **Satay Malaysia** (Tel. 385-7709), a fully licensed rice-and-peanut-sauce house. The **Boulcott Street Bistro** (Tel. 499-4199) is good for casual dining, and the **Bengal Tiger** (Tel. 385-1304) has a reputation for the best tandoori in town. You will find this one at 83 Willis Street in the city.

If you're looking for a Chinese restaurant, you might want to try the **Shanghai Café** (Tel. 384-4953); **Uncle Changs** (Tel. 801-9565), chef-owned and operated; or the **Gar Wah** (Tel. 384-6656). A good Japanese restaurant is **Fujiyama Teppanyaki** (Tel. 801-8699); Thai food is to be had at the **Chiang Rai** (Tel. 384-5455); and Mongolian at the **Genghis Khan** (Tel. 384-3592).

If you have a car, a good seafood spot is the **Shorebird** (Tel. 386-2017), at Greta Point on Evans Bay. Here might be the place to try N.Z. roughy, flounder, or John Dory. Prices (in the $18-to-24 range) all include clam chowder and the salad bar. The place also has its own fishing boat. We enjoyed it a lot. The family restaurant people are talking about is **Fisherman's Table** (Tel. 292-8125) at Paekakariki, a short drive from Wellington city. Superb city harbor views are to be had from **Tug Boat on the Bay** (Tel. 584-8884), and the Dockside practically sits in the water. **Greta Point Café and Bar** (Tel. 939-1030) a few bays on, also looks out over Wellington's spectacular harbor. Prices are lower here.

Just around the corner you'll see the familiar golden arches of **McDonald's.** A Big Mac and a milk shake taste pretty much the same here in Wellington, New Zealand as they do back Wellington, Kansas. The **Opera** (Tel. 382-8614) is an impressive retrieved building in the revamped Courtenay Place. There is a bar and restaurant here, and it is said to be a lively place. Wellington's waterside has also been revamped, and two very good restaurants there are **Shed 5** (Tel. 499-9069) and Dockside. The former is *the* place to be seen, and offers enormous meals and reasonable prices. Nearly next door, the **Dockside** (Tel. 499-9900) is gaining a following, with fresh seafood served in classic French style. **The Great New Zealand Farm Kitchen** (Tel. 566-1239) in Lower Hutt offers good home-baked fare, including casseroles (stews), soups, bread, salads, and desserts.

Look, we could just go on and on. Wellington's restaurant and café scene has surged ahead in the past few years with very few disasters. Pick up a copy of *Wellington's Wine & Food Guide* from the Visitor Information Centre (Tel. 801-4000).

The **Brix Café** (Tel. 385-1300) in Dixon Street is a relaxed bar with its own casino; the **Paris** (Tel. 472-4732) sings the blues; and there is jazz at lunchtime on Sundays at **The Ballroom** (Tel. 389-4828).

Some of these eating places are open for lunch, but for more modest dining, lunch or dinner, check into some of the old, established hotel/pubs in town.

6. Wellington Area Sightseeing

If you're going to take a guided tour of the city, check into it first to make sure you don't duplicate some of the sights you do on your own hook—unless you want to, of course. Many take the standard sightseeing buses and then, if the weather is clement, show up at the **Wellington Visitors Centre** (Tel. 801-4000) in Civic Square. Ask them for their booklet called *What's on in the Harbour Capital* and about walks and strolls in the parks or scenic drives around the city.

Firstly, take a good look around **The Museum of New Zealand Te Papa Tongarewa** (Our Place), which we talked about earlier in the chapter. As the most significant new building in recent New Zealand history, even eclipsing Auckland's Sky Tower in the controversy stakes, you really must go. Besides, it has a lovely shop with particularly nice examples of New Zealand art.

High-angle viewpoints are the thing in Wellington, and a popular way to reach one of them is to take the **Wellington Cable Car,** which you find by turning down narrow Cable Car Lane from Lambton Quay. For a token sum the car will lift you 400 feet in four minutes, right out of the business district, past Victoria University to the hilltop residential suburb of **Kelburn,** which offers one of the traditional vistas of the city and harbor below. (Sit on the left side going up for the best views.)

Until recently, the two cars were wonderfully old-fashioned, open-sided things that had successfully operated there for three-quarters of a century. Now they have been replaced by modern, larger, closed-in versions.

You can return on the cable car or the bus, but we prefer to walk through the **Botanical Gardens,** a meandering 62 acres of native and exotic plants that will lead you gradually downhill among the flowers. In the right season, see the Lady Norwood Rose Garden (best in November and February) and the Begonia House (which sometimes has other types of blooms in residence) along the route. Nearby is the **Richard Seddon Memorial,** a statue that may interest you if you've read about this remarkable prime minister in chapter 4.

From the lower boundary of the garden you can stroll to the **Parliament Buildings.** The most dramatic of the three structures is the unusually designed circular "Beehive," so called because of its shape. (Incidentally, the copper dome on top has been treated so that it will never turn green.) More formally, it is the Executive Wing of Parliament House, holding the offices of the prime minister and other dignitaries in the national government. It's not so interesting inside, though. The marble Parliament House, the central building, built in 1922, is currently closed for earthquake-resistant strengthening, so the wheels of government are creaking nearby in the Bower House. However, if the building is open when you are in Wellington, pay a visit. The House of Representatives is sitting when the flag is flying. There is a second, unused chamber inside, because New Zealand has had a unicameral legislature since 1951. Tours are given weekdays; you can watch from the visitors' gallery when the House is in session; phone 371-9457 for information. The third building in the group is the 1897 Gothic-style General Assembly Library.

Not far from Parliament is the new National Library building and the **Alexander Turnbull Library** (Tel. 474-3000), the leading research source for New Zealand and Pacific history. You'll find the original Treaty of Waitangi there, located in the National Archives in Mulgrave Street. You will also see some fine artworks by John Gully, who traveled the wilderness with Count Von Haast in the 1860s. Open Monday to Friday, 9 to 5, and until 12 on Saturday. The capital's new public library is a source of great pride. Go and visit it and admire the architecture and the peace and quiet.

My favorite building is down Bowen Street and across Lambton Quay. It has a plural name—**Government Buildings**—and to the casual eye it looks like any Italianate stone public building that might have been put up in 1876. But come a little closer; the entire 100,000-square-foot structure is built of wood, making it the second-largest wood structure in the world (after a temple in Japan). It was designed to survive an earthquake, of course, and so far it has lasted admirably. (Another wooden construction, in the style of the General Assembly Library, was never tested by an earthquake, but burned down instead in 1907!) If you are feeling like a half-hour walk, stroll along Lambton Quay and up Willis Street to 63 Boulcott Street. Here you will find **Antrim House** (Tel. 472-4341), home of the Historic Places Trust. This grand example of colonial architecture is staffed by helpful people and is open Monday to Friday.

Within walking distance of all these government edifices is the delightful 1866 wooden cathedral, **Old St. Paul's,** on Mulgrave Street. It's an excellent example of timbered Gothic construction, built all of New Zealand woods and now lovingly restored. The facade is not dramatic, but don't miss going inside. (Open 10 A.M. to 4:30 P.M.) On Jervois Quay, not far from Old St. Paul's Cathedral, is the Wellington Harbour

Board maritime museum, the Museum of Wellington City and Sea (Tel. 472-8904). It's open every day, and admission is free.

The inner-city "suburb" of **Thorndon** is one of the most pleasant to walk around. It was settled by immigrants in the nineteenth century, and just off Tinakori Road are two enchanting side streets called Ascot and Glenbervie, both of which contain some of the oldest "wedge" houses in the country. They were built tall and narrow to squeeze into a slim piece of land left over from a survey. The **Thistle Inn** on Mulgrave Street in Thorndon has the distinction of being New Zealand's oldest pub on its original site. At the other end of Tinakori Road at Number 24 is the restored house and birthplace of New Zealand's famous writer, **Katherine Mansfield.** The Botanic Gardens have an entrance off Tinakori Road also.

Besides the Kelburn Lookout, the other traditional bird's-eye view is provided by 558-foot **Mount Victoria,** on Alexandra Road, above Oriental Bay. On a clear day you can see almost all there is to the horizon in a 360-degree panorama. Near the lookout is the **Admiral Byrd Memorial,** honoring the great American explorer and aviator. It's shaped like an Antarctic tent. (Take Bus No. 20 to the end of the line.)

South of Mt. Victoria, about a mile as the magpie flies, is the **Wellington Zoo** (Tel. 389-8130), on Manchester Street. If you haven't yet seen a kiwi in a nocturnal house, this is a good place to do it (between 10 A.M. and 12 P.M.). The opossums you find victims of the automobile all over New Zealand roads you'll see here alive and well and happily scampering in the darkness, unblinded by any headlights. (This is one zoo that has licked the "elephant smell" problem, by the way; it has installed ozone-producing mercury-argon lamps that oxidize elephant odors!) Number 10 buses labeled "Newtown Park Zoo" will take you there. Or take a Number 3, get off at Constable Street, and walk a few minutes.

You can see Wellington from a whole new perspective on a cruise around the harbor. Try *Phantom of the Straits-NZL 3900* (Tel. 025-431-221) a 24-meter maxi-cruiser originally built for New Zealand's living legend of yachting, Sir Peter Blake. You can also contact **Sweet Georgia Cruising** (Tel. 384-3037) or **WestpacTrust Ferry** (Tel. 499-1282). You can get even closer to the harbour by hiring a kayak from **Fergs Rock 'n' Kayak** (Tel. 499-8898). If you're not keen to get that close to the wet stuff, you can hire in-line skates from Fergs instead, and skate around the waterfront.

You can also hire skates or cycles from **Wet & Wild Jet Safaris** (Tel. 235-9796) and skate the Petone waterfront while others take to the foreshore on Jet Skis.

You can wing your way across the capital with **Helipro** (Tel. 472-1550).

OUT OF TOWN

Before or after seeing Wellington, many Americans head for the **Kapiti Coast,** a holiday area that stretches from **Paekakariki** through **Paraparaumu** ("Para-pram") to **Waikanae.** At McKay's Crossing, near Paekakariki, are the **Memorial Gates to the U.S. Second Marine Division.** The division was stationed here in 1942 and 1943, before it left for the assault on Guadalcanal and other Pacific islands. (The episode was recalled in the 1957 U.S. film *Until They Sail,* with Paul Newman and Jean Simmons.) American Marine veterans revisit here from time to time, of course. Incidentally, records say that 1,400 New Zealand women married Yankee servicemen during World War II. Also in "Para-pram" is **Southward's Car Museum** (Tel. 04-297-1221), a mammoth motor display where the old cars are in virtually mint condition. The Nyco Chocolate factory is at Paraparaumu South, and a tour through there will either be a great delight or put you off chocolate completely. Nearby in Paekakariki are other tourist targets like the **Wellington Tramway Museum** (Tel. 292-8361) at Queen Elizabeth Park at Paekakariki, featuring the streetcars no longer in Wellington, and the **Engine Shed,** exhibiting retired steam locomotives. These three are all on State Highway One. On the same highway is **Lindale Tourist and Agriculture Centre** (Tel. 297-0916), open daily, where visitors are treated to sheep and cattle farming demonstrations and a short tour of Lindale's cheese factory. Their shop is stocked with farm produce. **Victoria Station Restaurant** (Tel. 297-0916), on State Highway One, serves meals in a building shaped like a railway carriage.

At nearby **Raumati Beach** is Trainscene (Tel. 298-2566), with one of New Zealand's largest model train layouts.

The beaches are excellent at all three towns, and some scenic flights over the Wellington peninsula from Paraparaumu Airport are popular. Paraparaumu is the jumping-off place for trips to **Kapiti Island,** once the redoubt of the "Maori Napoleon," Te Rauparaha. It's now a native bird sanctuary and somewhat difficult to visit without prior arrangements with the Department of Lands and Survey in Wellington.

However, if you ring Anthony Norris of **Tamarillo Sea Kayaking** (Tel. 025-244-1616), you can go with him to explore this conservation reserve. Anthony will tell you about the island's fascinating history as you paddle past endangered bird and marine wildlife.

There is also golf, horseback riding, fishing, and diving charters in the area.

Notable eateries in the area are **Alice's Beach Bistro** (Tel. 298-9404), which features fresh crab and smoked lamb; the **Great New Zealand Soup**

Kitchen (Tel. 298-8250), which is part of the Lindale complex—try the venison broth and crab bisque; and **Country Life** (Tel. 293-6353), which is licensed and fits well into the fine food category. While at Lindale indulge yourself at **Kapiti Cheeses** (Tel. 298-1352), home of gourmet cheeses and ice cream.

Going up the other side of the peninsula along Highway 2, you'll travel the windy **Rimutaka Range** (keep a tight hold on the wheel!). Tucked beneath the hill on the other side is the small town of Featherston, with an interesting museum housing the world's last remaining Fell locomotive. These brave engines hauled passengers and freight over a precipitous and windy way. You can walk the original track, but you will need energy to spare. The museum is open weekends only.

You may use this route to make a scenic round trip from Wellington by continuing through Masterton. (We stayed at the comfortable **Golden Shears Motel,** Tel. 377-0029.) Nearby Queen Elizabeth Park is nice for picnics. You could also try the **Masterton Motor Lodge** (Tel. 378-2585), winner of a Best Regional Accommodation Award. Costs are from $95-155.

Right next door is another hotel, once the Solway Park Travelodge, now the **Copthorne Resort Solway Park** (Tel. 377-5129 or 0800-47-65-92). Amenities include a 10-bay golf driving range, squash (racquet ball), billiards, pentanque (a European game like Lawn Bowls that uses a small wooden ball and six metal balls about the size of a baseball), bikes, tennis, a jogging track, and a heated swimming pool. Tariffs are from $95.

A couple of B&Bs in the nearby, historic town of **Greytown** look inviting. There's **Dinah and Max Edridge,** with their home set among lovely old trees (Tel. 06-305-9942). Our other pick is **Bright House** (Tel. 304-8047), owned by Paul and Karen Ratcliffe. The Ratcliffes own one of New Zealand's oldest inland homes. It dates from 1856. And slotting neatly into New Zealand's exclusive lodge style of accommodation is **Wharekauhau Lodge,** (Tel. 307-7581) owned by Bill and Anette Shaw. Their handsome house, surrounded by fine farmland and native bush, is close to Palliser Bay. The rates of around $350 per person include meals, and the lodge turns on the wealth of quality outdoor experiences we have come to expect from this distinctly New Zealand type of accommodation.

New Zealand's prolific sheep star at the **World Sheep Shearing Championships** every March in Masterton. And before leaving town you may enjoy *Laura's Wairarapa Tours* (Tel. 378-3534). Laura buses you around in a pleasantly personal way and turns on morning or afternoon tea, or lunch, depending on the time of day. Fifteen miles north on State Highway 2 is the **Mt. Bruce National Wildlife Centre,** which has a fine reputation for the conservation of endangered species. At Woodville, turn left to go through the awesome but notoriously unstable **Manawatu Gorge,** which cuts a mountain range in two. From the pleasant city of Palmerston North, return south to Wellington via routes 57 and 1. The whole trip takes about six hours—unless the Manawatu Gorge has washed out the highway again, of course!

If you don't turn left at **Woodville,** Route 2 continues to the east coast cities of Hastings and Napier, which we talked about in the previous chapter.

7. Guided Tours and Cruises

East West Ferries (Tel. 499-1273) service operates several times daily across the harbor. The half-hour trip starts from Queens Wharf in the city center and sails to Days Bay, an attractive stretch of water on the other side of the harbor. On some trips the ferry also stops at Soames Island, a wildlife conservation area.

Another good harbour tour is the *Dockside Jet Harbour Blaster* (Tel. 499-9900). The 12.6-metre jet boat seats up to 20 adults and thunders away for an invigorating trip out to Red Rocks and the Karori Lighthouse. Don't worry about getting wet; weatherproof clothing is provided, along with life-jackets.

Try also **Mountain Marine** (Tel. 586-0699), for a yachting experience or **Shed 5** (Tel. 499-9069) for a launch trip.

However, our personal choice would be **Hammond's Wellington Sightseeing Tours, Ltd.** (Tel. 472-0869), as long as the irrepressible owner, Wally Hammond, is conducting the tour himself. Besides his morning and afternoon city tours (leaving at 10 A.M. and 1:30 P.M.), which cover approximately the same places as the city government's, Wally offers several others by special arrangement. Wally's old bus costs a little more—$20 or so for the city tour this year—but he's worth it!

Walkers should speak to the people at the **Wellington Visitor Centre** (Tel. 801-4000). Tours to individual tastes can be arranged; some are just private strolls with like-minded locals.

Otherwise, the Wellington City Council's Parks and Recreations Department can set you off in interesting directions. Their eastern and southern walks will prove worthwhile, and you can pick up their brochures from the Information Centre. Being the coastal city that it is, and right at the southern tip of the North Island, Wellington's rugged coast offers an exhilarating coastal walk from Owhiro Bay to Sinclair Head, where you will see seal colonies in winter. The walk takes two to three hours and is about two and a half miles long. You can call the Parks and Recreation Department direct for information at 801-3600.

Town and Country Tours (Tel. 388-9124) of about two hours each cost $45 for up to four people and range as far afield as the **Wairarapa,** the Palliser seal colony, and the Kapiti Coast.

Intercity Scenic Tours (Tel. 385-9955) departs every day from the Information Centre at the Town Hall at 2 o'clock for a complete circuit of the city. The cost is $22, and there is also a hotel/motel pick-up service.

Aerial views are offered by **Flyaway Charters** (Tel. 386-1558), based at Wellington Airport. This company will fly you over to the wine region of Marlborough or up to the rich farming district of the Wairarapa in its four-seater planes.

The Wellington Civic Centre is an impressive cultural center. It consists of a civic square, often lively with events, a "hands-on" children's science museum, city art gallery, and the Michael Fowler Centre, which is one of the main concert venues in the city.

8. Water Sports

The single harbor and a relatively inhospitable Cook Strait tend to inhibit yachting activity in Wellington as compared to Auckland and other ports in New Zealand. You might not be surprised to learn, however, that Wellington is considered a paradise for windsurfers. Windsurfing may not be your passion but, just in case, **Wild Winds Extreme Sail 'n' Surf** (Tel. 384-1010) will show you how in Wellington's attractive Oriental Bay.

You can swim practically downtown in Wellington at **Oriental Bay,** and further out on Cook Strait at **Scorching Bay** and **Worser Bay.** You can even surf on the other side of the airport isthmus at **Lyall Bay** and further west at **Island Bay.** Nevertheless, serious beach-goers usually invest in a 30-mile ride up to the Gold Coast for the smooth, gentle sands of Paekakariki, Paraparaumu, and Waikanae. If the truth be known, most swimming goes on at indoor pools in Wellington. A popular one is the **Freyberg Pool and Fitness Centre** (Tel. 384-3107).

Hardy folks from the neighborhood find good fishing in Cook Strait. International visitors, however, had better skip it in favor of the many other areas covered in this book—which do not require cast-iron stomachs!

Even hardier folks could try diving in the incredibly deep Cook Strait and other parts of Wellington's coastline. Try **Island Bay Divers** (Tel. 383-6778) or **Divers World** (Tel. 385-8533).

9. Other Sports

Three excellent golf courses stand out among the 22 in Wellington and the vicinity. Right in the metropolitan area, only a seven-iron shot from the airport, is the **Miramar Golf Club** (Tel. 388-6344). It's open to visitors weekdays and sometimes on weekends. Then there's the **Wellington Golf Club** (Tel. 528-4590) at Heretaunga—and better known as Heretaunga—17 miles to the north. But the champion championship course is what the New Zealanders call Scottish links—a seaside course—at "Para-pram," or the **Paraparaumu Beach Golf Club** (Tel. 902-8200). Two of many golfers who extol the virtues of this course are Gary Player and New Zealand's own Bob Charles, who once shot a 62 there (par is 71). Wind, of course, is the principal hazard.

Tennis courts are for rent in several city parks; see the public relations office for exact locations. One we know about is in **Williams Park,** opposite the wharf at Days Bay on the other side of the harbor. There's also a putting green there. And there are tennis and netball courts for rent at **Haitaitai Park,** on the slopes of Mount Victoria.

Horse races are held regularly at **Trentham,** 19 miles from Wellington, and harness (trotting) racing is at **Hutt Park.** Greyhounds also race at Hutt Park. Rugby is played at **Athletic Park.** Soccer and cricket are played in winter and summer respectively at the **Basin Reserve.** It's just on the north side of Rugby Street (honest!). And, believe it or not, softball is a particularly popular pastime in the area. Wellington and Lower Hutt actually have separate leagues. Many games are played in **Haitaitai Park,** off Ruahine Street. Stop by the **Cricket Museum** (Tel. 384-5227) at the Basin Reserve, which has a host of interesting exhibits.

10. Shopping in Wellington

The main thoroughfares for buying and browsing are Lambton Quay (not a quay, but a street) and Lower Willis Street. (See the Willis Street Village at Flagstaff Lane.) The Cuba Street Mall is also popular and fun. Also, many stores are minded on Manners Street (which crosses Cuba).

Two local department stores are almost on top of each other on Lambton Quay—**Kircaldie and Stain's** (Tel. 472-5899), now generally called Kircaldie's or Kirk's; and **Farmers'** (Tel. 472-0010), the larger of the two (although Kirkcaldie's ranks as the top-quality one). Another **Farmers'** (Tel. 384-3969) is at 94-102 Cuba Mall.

Wellington is great for shopping in inclement weather, as it has many arcades, covered footpaths, and subterranean malls. Try **Capital on the Quay, Harbour City Shopping Centre,** and **The Cable Car Complex,** all on Lambton Quay and The Grand Arcade on Willis Street.

For poking around in small shops, Upper Cuba Street—beyond the mall—is interesting. There are lots of tiny places, generally with a colonial look about them, displaying antiques, bric-a-brac, etc. Their names, characters, and ownership seem to change from month to month.

Sheepskins, furs, suede, leather, and all kinds of dermal products are for sale at the **Sheepskin Warehouse** (Tel. 386-3376) on Evans Bay Drive, past the Shorebird restaurant to Greta Point on the inland side of the road. It has a warehouse look, but it may be the best bargain barn in the skin game.

The old James Smith department store from a bygone era is now the James Smiths Markets, which is worth a look for fun even if you don't buy anything. Earthsea Crafts and Gifts on the second floor of this complex has a wide selection, and Exotic Stuff on the ground floor will keep you entertained.

ArtWorks on Willeston Street and on Customhouse Quay offer "distinctly New Zealand gifts," including lovely pieces of jade. **Art For Art's Sake** is another good place to browse for a special New Zealand souvenir.

Fashion for 16 Plus apologises for not providing anything for those less than a size 16, but they are committed to the larger market. (Remember that a 16 in New Zealand is a 14 in the U.S.A.) They stock some beautifully designed clothes and are well worth a visit. Find them at 40 Johnston Street. For gentlemen who are either bigger than usual or smaller than usual, there is **Chicago for Men** at Cuba Mall. **The Mews** on Molesworth Street is where you'll find clothing from New Zealand designers, as well as at **Starfish** on Willis Street. The **Vibrant Handknits Lee Andersen Designer Gallery** is where you'll find unique New Zealand woolen garments.

Iko Iko is the place to go when you need that special gift for that unusual person.

Call to see Judith White at the **Potters Shop and Gallery** on Woodward Street. It's a cooperative of 16 top potters that steers clear of mass production. The items can be sent to your home address.

The Homestore, upstairs on Lambton Quay, has a wide selection of New Zealand preserves, sauces, marinades, and dressings, as well as special pottery, glassware, kitchen utensils, and other household items.

Get hold of a *Wellington's Shopping Guide* booklet for a good selection of worthy shops. If you are after antiques, pick up a copy of the *Great Time Guide.* You'll get both of them from the Visitor Information Centre (Tel. 801-4000).

Bookshops. There are a lot of Wellington readers, apparently, with a thirst for both new and used books. First there is **Whitcoulls,** the national chain that recently also took in the old London Bookshops, which has greatly increased its already extensive number of shops. New and old books are stacked together at **Quilters Bookshop** (Tel. 472-2767), with an entrance right on Plimmers Steps, off Lambton Quay. Scholars may want to ask for their catalogue of rare and out-of-print New Zealand and Pacific titles. **Roy Parson's Bookshop** (Tel. 472-4587) at 126 Lambton Quay has sold a quality range of books and records for a respectable number of decades. His shop is worth a good browse, especially the sections on art, photography, and New Zealand fiction and poetry. On a mezzanine floor above the books is a coffee shop where students, lawyers, and locals drop by for refreshments in intimate surroundings. The newest in town is the Australian franchise of **Dymocks,** which not only provides a great selection of books but also armchairs in which to sit and browse through them.

Galleries. Gallons of galleries are patronized by art-loving Wellingtonians, it seems. This is a scene we haven't been able to paint for ourselves, but our friends John and Virginia Port, who know their way around the brush-and-palette world of Wellington, have suggested several to see next time. Among them are the **McGregor Wright Gallery** (Tel. 472-1281) on Lambton Quay, probably the largest. There is also a branch at Paraparaumu (Tel. 299-4958). **Websters** (Tel. 570-6500) on Manners Street has antique maps and prints as well as other artworks, and the strangely named **The Art Walrus** (Tel. 382-8333) on Egmont Street is a definite place to browse. There are many more, however, and several are advertised in Wellington's weekly tourist paper, *Capital Times.* At this printing no fewer than 40 galleries can be visited in Wellington. The **Dowse Art Museum** (Tel. 570-6500) on Laing's Road in Lower Hutt is well known for its innovative approach to art education.

SUBURBAN SHOPPING

Actually almost urban is the attractive shopping area called **Tinakori Villas,** which you can walk to after taking the cable car to **Kelburn.** Instead of turning right through the Botanical Gardens, take a left and walk for a few minutes up Upland Road to about No. 87.

Located in Wellington's suburb of Lower Hutt is **Queensgate Shopping Centre,** consisting of about 48 specialty shops.

Out on the Kapiti Coast, 25 miles north on Highway 1, there is the **Coastland Shoppingtown** in Paraparaumu. This complex caters to day-trippers from Wellington, with dozens of little specialty stores with names like The House of Stamps or The House of Wines. Nearer the beach is another group of about 50 shops boasting such stores as The Bare Essentials and Huckleberry's Parlour.

In Waikanae, home of many retirees, there are a number of craft operations. Look for **Reikorangi Potteries Park and Café** (Tel. 293-5146), for a nice selection of ceramics. Open Tuesday through Saturday, it's actually about 5 kilometers out of Waikanae, toward Reikorangi.

11. Entertainment and Night Life

A few places are called "nightclubs," but they're more apt to be musical pubs and/or discos for the young set. Saturday and especially Friday nights, many popular pubs have 'em stacked up wall to wall.

Wellington's home of jazz and blues is at the top of the **Plaza Hotel** in Wakefield Street and is open every night. Phone bookings can be made at 477-3900. Wellington has live music or entertainment in at least 40 bars or clubs around the city. Check out the "gig guides" in the local papers. Trendy café/bars like **The Lido Café** (Tel. 499-6666) on the corner of Wakefield and Victoria and Expressoholic on Willis Street are convivial places for a pause. The **Diva Bar and Café** (Tel. 385-2987) on Dixon Street is a popular meeting spot for an after-work drink.

As much of a "theater district" as Wellington has is probably along Courtenay Place, an extension of Manners Street. One of the most popular houses is the **Downstage Theatre** (Tel. 801-6946), part of the Hannah Playhouse. Normally the Downstage serves dinner prior to the performance, but you can sometimes arrange to miss the meal and see the play at a correspondingly lower price. The **Wellington Repertory Theatre** (Tel. 385-4247) is at 304 Manners Street, and another professional company regularly performs at the **Circa Theatre** (Tel. 801-7992) on Taranaki Street, off Victoria. Bookings can be made by calling 385-0832.

Classical entertainment, such as the N.Z. Symphony Orchestra or the New Zealand Ballet or Opera companies, will be found at the **State Opera House** (Tel. 385-0832) on Manners Street or at the **Michael Fowler Centre** (Tel. 801-4242) at 111 Wakefield Street. During the summer, free concerts by the Sinfonia of Wellington or other groups may be staged in the outdoor **Sound Shell** at the Botanical Gardens.

The booklet *What's on in the Harbour Capital* lists current entertainment and sightseeing activities and is available from the City Information Centre. Two of the city's churches, Old St. Paul's and St. Andrews on The Terrace, give free musical concerts. Culture-conscious Wellington now boasts its own Festival of Arts, and you can catch top-rate international and local performers at the festival in the month of March.

Stay-at-homes can take their culture from three television channels, which are retransmitted from Wellington, and cable television.

Wellington also tunes in nine radio stations. The National Program is on 2YA (567 Kh—the YA stations are those that give the birdcalls just before the news). There are FM stations, including the rock fan's Windy FM. Student Radio is called "Radio Active," and the community radio is called "Access Radio." Concert FM is excellent. You will find it at 92.5 on the dial.

Be sure to check out the weather forecast on one of these before setting out for a day of sightseeing!

12. The Wellington Address List

Ambulance—111

American Embassy—29 Fitzherbert Terrace, Thorndon (Tel. 472-2068).

American Express—105 The Terrace (Tel. 499-7899).

Bank of New Zealand—1 Willis Street (Tel. 474-6000).

Canadian High Commission—ICI House, Molesworth Street (Tel. 473-9577).

Dentist—For dental emergencies phone 801-5551, or call ambulance number above for advice.

Fire—Dial 111 for all emergencies.

Pharmacy—Urgent Pharmacy (after hours), 17 Adelaide Road (Tel. 385-8810).

Police—Dial 111 for all emergencies.

Post office—Central P.O., Lambton Quay (Tel.0800-501-501).

Visitor Information Office—10 Wakefield Street (Tel. 801-4000).

Taxis—Telephone 388-8880.

Weather forecast recording—Meteorological department (Tel. 0900-99904).

8

Christchurch and the Upper South Island

1. The General Picture

Christchurch sounds like a religious sort of place. True, the town center is marked by an imposing, century-old Gothic cathedral, and the population of 312,600 is probably at least as devout as that of any city of its size. Loyal citizens speak well of Christchurch, to be sure, but when they write about it they almost invariably "deconsecrate" its name by abbreviating it to "Chch."

Actually, the pace and tone of the city are set more by the peaceful stream that meanders through its middle. **The Avon River,** with its grassy, willow-shaded banks and colonies of quacking ducks, seems to keep people in tune with nature. Office workers take noontime picnics along its banks and then lie back on the soft, green slope for a few minutes before returning to files and telephones. Schoolboys on bicycles pause to fish from its bridges. Lovers slip hand into hand while following its eccentric route.

Christchurch is described elsewhere in the country as "the most English city outside England" and as **"the Garden City of New Zealand,"** and there's truth to both statements. Architecturally, "Chch" is certainly English in its central areas, with dozens of Victorian and Edwardian buildings anchoring the urban landscape, spiked occasionally by the neo-Gothic towers associated with academia. The variety and concentration of trees and flowers can hardly be duplicated by any major city.

Only three blocks from the main square, a gigantic park awaits the pleasure of multitudes. The Avon makes a drastic loop there, too, thus enclosing the famous Botanic Gardens. But the flowers so often remembered from Christchurch are as much on private property as public. Not only do factories compete for the finest, brightest front lawns in the business world, but whole residential neighborhoods turn out with masses of spring blossoms in an effort to win their own annual awards.

With its vast Cathedral Square, forbidden to motor vehicles, Christchurch seems to put its people on display, too. On bright, clear days you see a large number of dignified elderly women, carrying umbrellas and wearing hats and sometimes gloves. Young mothers wheel their children this way and that across the wide-open space. The city's buses cooperate by providing special hooks on their fronts for Mum to place the pram on when it's time to go home.

Men in shirtsleeves and ties buy flowers or fruits from nearby carts. Groups of aimless adolescents, some playing hooky from school, dodge the cops. And another crowd gathers near the center of it all to listen to the tall, bearded man of about fifty who harangues them from the top of a stepladder: "People of Christchurch! I, the self-appointed Official Wizard of the City of Christchurch, say to you . . . !" He is indeed the "Official Wizard," a figure who demonstrates that the people of Chch have a tolerance, even a fondness, for diversity and eccentricity in their environment.

Christchurch is far from staid. It had the first casino in New Zealand, boasts international hotels, has hosted the Concorde more often than any other city, and is the jump-off place for Antarctica and its multinational contingent of scientists.

Unlike Auckland, Rotorua, Wellington, Queenstown, or Dunedin, Christchurch cannot point to a handsome bay or lake from its city center. The harbor is about ten miles east in **Lyttelton,** an attractive community that clings to the steep hills that separate it from the main metropolis. Christchurch was established just far enough inland to be conveniently tangent to the great Canterbury Plains, an immense, rich prairie between the city and the snowcapped Southern Alps, about 50 miles to the west.

Often perceived as one of the southernmost cities of the world, Christchurch is little more than one-third down the length of the South Island. But travelers who take the ferry from busy Wellington to the attractive little town of Picton still face a five-hour train or road trip to Christchurch by the most direct route, the largely deserted and lonely East Coast alongside the foothills of the Kaikoura Mountains.

It's also possible to take longer by traveling through the Marlborough Sounds area and the sunny coastal city of Nelson, then through tiny villages, twisting mountain roads, and the Lewis Pass to reach Christchurch. This route provides a pleasant hint and a gentle rehearsal for some of the really rugged and even more dramatic scenery waiting farther south.

2. Long-Distance Transportation

Christchurch International Airport, in the suburb of Russley, is the best in the country, both from the pilot's and the passenger's point of view. The modern terminal boasts a large number of comforts and conveniences as well as spacious, carpeted waiting areas. The whole building has been fashioned in a long, gentle curve; from the observation decks you not only overlook the active tarmac below, but can also see the Southern Alps on the distant horizon.

The city-owned facility is one of the busiest in the nation in number of takeoffs and landings, and it has been welcoming increasing numbers of international visitors flying in from Australia—and recently from the U.S. as well. The domestic and international wings are separated by a cafeteria, and facilities also include a licensed restaurant, cocktail bar, bank, post office, barber shop, beauty shop, gift shop, duty-free shop, nursery, first-aid room, hostess service, and the usual travel counters. Appropriately for the Garden City, there is usually a "flower barrow" stationed somewhere on the deep-purple carpet.

Christchurch International is also the New Zealand base for the United States Antarctic Operation Deep Freeze, which has been conducted since 1955. About 1,500 scientists and others fly the 2,382 miles between Chch and McMurdo Sound each year. There are 250 American sailors who live at the airport to help support this activity.

There are two major international airlines—**Air New Zealand** (Tel. 353-4899), which flies Christchurch, runs to and from Honolulu and Los Angeles, and **Qantas Airways** (Tel. 379-3100), the Australian overseas airline. Both fly wide-body jets between Chch and Sydney, Brisbane, and Melbourne. There's also a direct air link to and from Hobart, Tasmania, with Air New Zealand, which makes about two trips per week to Australia's Apple Isle. (There are more details in *Maverick Guide to Australia*.)

The domestic service of **Air New Zealand** (Tel. 379-7000) has nonstop Christchurch flights to and from Auckland (on a Boeing 767) and other nonstop flights on Boeing 737s to and from Dunedin, Hokitika, Invercargill, Napier, Nelson, and Wellington. Mount Cook Airlines has now been absorbed into the Air New Zealand Link Services, and the newest commuter aircraft belong to **Origin** (Tel. 0800-302-302), who fly their nifty little jets increasingly further. **Ansett New Zealand** (Tel. 371-1185 or 0800-267-388) makes nonstop runs to all the main trunk destinations.

Most of the rental car companies are found at the airport (see Rental Car section)

The seven-mile ride between the airport and Christchurch will cost about $24 by taxi or around $5 if you use the suburban bus service offered by the **Christchurch Transport** (Tel. 341-3134); buses leave from Worcester Street (pronounce it "*wooster*"), just off Cathedral Square. Allow about a half hour if you're busing to the airport. This is not a special airport express, but pauses at regular bus stops along the way. Bus timetable information can be obtained from Tel. 366-8853.

Trains. The railway station (Tel. 0800-802-802 for information) is on Moorhouse Avenue at the end of Manchester Street. Two main trains operate out of Christchurch, plus one interesting shorter route. The *Coastal Pacific* between Christchurch and Picton runs daily on a 5.5-hour, 220-mile trip. The service departs at 7:30 A.M. and gets into Picton at 12:50 P.M. Cost is between $31 and $73, depending on the time of travel.

The big train in the south, though, is the more comfortable *Southerner,* running between Christchurch, Dunedin, and Invercargill every day except Sunday. You'll find a hostess and a licensed buffet car (with about 20 bar stools), so you won't have to jump off to eat and drink. But if you want to have an alcoholic beverage at your seat, you'll have to sit in the smoking car. The train takes about 6 hours between Chch and Dunedin (230 miles for about 50), and another 3.5 hours for the additional 140 miles to Invercargill. The service departs Christchurch at 8:15 A.M. daily and arrives in Dunedin at 1:50 P.M. and Invercargill at 5:15 P.M. Cost is between $38 and $77.

The *Trans-Alpine Express* heads across to the West Coast daily at 9 A.M., getting into **Greymouth** at 1:25 P.M. Cost is between $41 and $68. A one-day excursion fare costs $109 return. This service is one of the great train journeys of New Zealand, and you enjoy some of the country's best scenery from large train windows. Like the Picton to Christchurch train, there's lunch, Devonshire teas, a liquor service, commentary from a train escort, and sheepskin-covered seats.

Buses. Four long-distance coach lines have Christchurch addresses, including the **Intercity Services** (Tel. 379-9020), whose depot is at the Christchurch railway station. Its principal route is between Christchurch and

Dunedin. **Gray Line** (Tel. 0800-800-904), at 40 Lichfield Street, operates a night bus to Dunedin, competing with the daytime Intercity run. You can book any of these buses or trains at the **Visitor Information Centre** (Tel. 379-9629) on the corner of Worcester Street and Oxford Trace. They are open seven days, and it's the place to go for visitor advice. The Centre is easy to find in the distinctive 125-year-old brick building on the banks of the Avon River. **Guthreys Pacific** (Tel. 366-8711) is a Christchurch-based company that operates tours throughout New Zealand. Tours that these coach-travel companies offer can be booked and paid for before leaving North America.

Rental Cars. Rental-car services include **Avis** (Tel. 0800-635-111), **Hertz** (Tel. 0800-654-321), **Budget** (Tel. 0800-652-227), **Letz** (Tel. 0800-358-973), **Thrifty** (Tel. 358-7533), **Avon-Percy** (Tel. 379-3822), and **Cross Country Rentals** (Tel. 348-8219). Not a bad selection for a city that is famous for its bicycles!

Christchurch is also the headquarters for several campervan outfits, one of which is called **Horizon Holidays** (Tel. 353-5600), at 530 Memorial Avenue. Their homes on wheels look attractive, but we have had no personal experience with them. Rates start at around $110 for a four-berth motor home, and go to $210 during the high season. Insurance and mileage is an extra cost.

3. Local Transportation

With its pancake-flat terrain, Christchurch is also known sometimes as the city of bicycles, and if you want to climb on a two-wheeler you can rent one from **City Cycle Hire** (Tel. 0800-343-848) at 96 Worcester Street. Cycles and motorbikes are certainly another efficient and popular way of getting about. Christchurch **Leisure Sports** (Tel. 365-7589) rents several kinds of motorized two-wheelers at rates that start at $55 a day. You can also try **New Zealand Motorcycle Rentals** (Tel. 377-0663).

Buses. An excellent service is run by **Christchurch Transport** (Tel. 341-3134), and nearly any CTB bus you want will leave from stations around the fringe of Cathedral Square. Look for the kiosk; you can ask questions or pick up maps and timetables there. As usual, fares are charged by sections. Off-peak (non-rush-hour) fares are about 50 percent off.

Taxis. You don't hail cabs. You either hop in at established "taxi ranks" or telephone for one (usually 50¢ extra). Two cab companies are **Blue Star** (Tel. 379-9799) and **Gold Band** (Tel. 379-5795), both of which offer 24-hour service.

Christchurch has just started running its old trams again. Spruced up and smart, they traverse the main shopping mall to and from the Bridge of

Remembrance. You don't have to be going anywhere in particular—just jump on and enjoy the ride.

4. Christchurch Hotels and Motels

EXPENSIVE HOTELS

The four top hotels in Christchurch, in our personal order of preference, are **The Parkroyal,** the **Kingsgate,** the **Quality Inn Chateau,** and **Noahs.** If you're paying top dollar, your travel agent should probably put you in one of those. A couple of others in this category are also described below.

The 300-room **Parkroyal** (Tel. 365-7799 or 0800-80-11-11) is next door to the Christchurch Town Hall, in a most convenient location. It's on the corner of Kilmore and Durham Streets, and rooms and suites are also available, some quite luxurious. Prices on application and ask about special weekend rates. The Victoria Street Café is a pleasant place from which to watch the world go by, and the Yamagen Japanese Restaurant is one we haven't tried yet but aim to next time 'round. For fine dining in the hotel, head for Canterbury Tales, which has a great reputation. There are three bars to sip cocktails in, and one has live music. There's also a courtesy limo to ferry guests from A to B. We feel this is the best of the best in Christchurch.

The famous Noahs Hotel now belongs to **Rydges** (Tel. 0800-654-994), and although overshadowed by the newer and more luxurious Parkroyal, this 208-room high-rise is an old favorite and its location right downtown and next to the river gives it bonus points. Its facade forms the slightly bent backdrop for many Christchurch scenes at the corner of Worcester Street and Oxford Terrace.

The **Millennium** (Tel. 365-1111) is another fairly new hotel, but it is built behind an old facade. Parts of Christchurch are protected as historic sites, and both the Millennium and the Heritage (see below) are bright new hotels hidden behind gracious old faces.

Although newish, the Millennium has already one awards for its Piko Piko Restaurant, and as it is right on Cathedral Square, it is a very convenient place to stay. The rooms are certainly large, and there is enough room in the generous bathrooms to hold a small cocktail party.

The Heritage (Tel. 377-9722 or 0800-36-88-88; Web site www.dynasty.co.nz) is also on the Square and offers self-contained suites of generous proportion. Prices for both are on application, and both also have weekend specials.

If you have a car, think about staying near the airport (seven miles from downtown) at the **Airport Plaza Christchurch Hotel** (Tel. 358-3139 or 0800-100-876) on Memorial Avenue at Orchard Street. Although it doesn't fit in with the top four mentioned above, it is included up front because of its proximity to the airport. Here's a spread-out layout that would never do in the city center, but is ideal here in big-sky country. There is a spacious lobby under an A-frame roof and hanging lamps; respected J.J.'s Restaurant to one side; Hunt Room Grill, open late for snacks; Maori entertainment some nights; and a pleasant garden with large outdoor pool for fine-weather swimming. The best downstairs doubles open right out onto the pool deck; the upstairs units with balconies overlook the splashing. There are excellent furnishings, most units are decorated in cool blues and greens, and there are good baths. The gardens have won an award and are lovely to stroll through. A high-flying *rara avis,* and recommended to those who don't mind roosting out at Russley. Prices on application.

Back in town—sort of—is the medieval-motif **Chateau on the Park** (Tel. 348-8999 or 0800-808-999) on the other side of Hagley Park at the corner of Deans Avenue and Kilmarnock Street. You may love or hate the looks of this Disneylandic version of a baronial mansion, but despite its Swinging Sir Lancelot architecture, the place is very comfortable: In 1999, 140 of its 190 rooms were refurbished. One walks across the cobblestone courtyard to a pleasant reception in a small lobby. There is a corridor along the moat leading to the Garden Court Brasserie, the deservedly popular Camelot Dining Room, and a bar called the Den of the Little Red Foxes. Amenities include golf, tennis, jogging, horseback riding, and cycling. The Chateau has had some tough crusades in the past, but now it's jousting with the best. We enjoyed our own stay, and it still looks like it could be your Canterbury Camelot. *Tally ho!*

The **Cotswold Hotel** (Tel. 355-3535 or 0800-65-35-35; Web site http://nz.com/travel/ScenicCircle/), away from the center at 88-90 Papanui Road, is an exercise in super-pseudo-Tudor. We can't fault the facilities, to be sure, and King Henry VII might have felt right at home.

But for double rates from $190, we'd rather bunk in the centre of town—and back in the twentieth century. (Some travellers may disagree; if you have a car, at least, you might check it out).

The **Chateau Blanc Suites** (Tel. 365-1600) is a luxury serviced apartment complex close to the city at 353 Montreal Street. If you feel like treating yourself, this is the right place to go. Each apartment has a kitchen, but if you dine in the Chateau Blanc dining room you are likely to be pleased with the food. It is also close to the Arts Centre. Special holiday and weekend rates apply.

Another hotel that should be now be in this category and has previously been in the medium listings is the **George Hotel** (Tel. 379 4569 or 0800 10-02-20; Web site www.thegeorge.com) a boutique hotel located across the road from Hagley Park offering views of the Avon River. The 54 luxurious rooms and suites have full facilities, some with a private balcony. It has the Pescator Restaurant, Roscoe's Bar and Brasserie, and has won awards for its cuisine. It also has a gift shop and Astroturf tennis courts. Prices on application.

MEDIUM-PRICE CHRISTCHURCH ROOMS

The Pavilions (Tel. 355-3633) is another new place to stay in Christchurch. More of a motor lodge than a hotel, Pavilions offers rooms from $142 to $200. For the latter price you can have one double bed, a queen, or two singles with lounge, kitchen, and spa bath. There's also a restaurant and bar. Pavilions is on Papanui Road, 5 minutes from the city and 20 minutes from the airport. This property is convenient to the casino.

The **Avon River Centra** (Tel. 379-1180 or 0800-80-11-11), 356 Oxford Terrace, was once the Christchurch City Travelodge and has improved immensely since changing hands. Overlooking the Avon River and five minutes from the city centre, it offers an indoor heated pool and gymnasium. Prices also on application.

The **Latimer Lodge** (Tel. 379-6760 or 0800-176-176), on Latimer Square, charges $89-137 for singles and doubles and slices 40 percent off the rate on either Fridays or Saturdays. It has both a bar and a restaurant.

If you're driving into Chch, there are two neighborhoods with several choices in motels. One is the Papanui Road area, before you get to Bealey Avenue. The **Adelphi Motel** (Tel. 355-6037) at No. 49 Papanui Road is one of several good ones out that way. The price is right, too; from $80 double.

The Camelot Court seems to be no more but Christchurch's English theme is carried through by the new **Buckingham Palace Motel** (Tel. 377-7059 or 0800-999-008; Web site www.buckinghampalace-motel.co.nz) three minutes from the city centre with a bus stop at the gate. Rates are between $85 and $120. Then there is the **Tudor Court** (Tel. 379-1465 or 0800-488-367), with rates between $79 and $145; and then the even more English-looking **Sherborne Motor Lodge** (Tel. 377-8050 or 0800-743-267) in the central city. Rates here are between $85 and $145.

There are also the Riccarton Road entries, for traffic from the south, including the **Riccarton Motel** (Tel. 348-7127) at No. 92, with 13 acres of park and with local buses to both the city and the airport stopping right at the gate ($88); or the **Christchurch Motel** (Tel. 348-9493 or 0800-252-258) at No. 252 ($75). If you don't need a restaurant, and do like the stove, these are a pretty good deal. Others just a little further from the city center range in price from between $60 to $80 for a double room. The **Airport Lodge** (Tel. 358-5119) has rates of $79 to $89 and, true to its name, is close to the airport at 105 Roydale Avenue. **Ferry Motel** (Tel. 389-1013 or 0800-184-900) is a bit further out of the city but still handy. It's comfortable and well priced at $68 to $85 double. **Hagley Park Motel** (Tel. 348-7683) is close to the Riccarton suburban shopping center in a quiet, tree-filled neighborhood. Rates are $76 to $100 double. It will be less noisy here than on Riccarton Road.

Carlton Mill Lodge (Tel. 366-1068 or 0508-800-170) is a centrally situated motel at 19 Bealey Avenue. Hagly Park is opposite, and the Botanical Gardens are a short walk away. It's not far on foot, either, to the Museum and Art Gallery of Canterbury. Architecturally designed studio units at Carlton Mill Lodge are modern and comfortable. The rates range from $85 to $140. Private spas are available.

The **Alcala Motor Lodge** (Tel. 365-8180 or 0800-22-44-41) is brand-new, with rates from $85 to $125. The **City Centre Motel** (Tel. 372-9294 or 0800-240-101) is also a new one, eight minutes' walk to Cathedral Square and asking between $85 and $135 a night.

Farmstays are popular choices for visitors to New Zealand, and a couple of South Island addresses to write to for further inquiries include **Homestays** (PO Box 309, Nelson), and **Friendly Kiwi Home and Farmstays** (195 Moana Ave., Nelson). These people can find you a farm in Canterbury or anywhere else in the South Island that takes the fancy. Also try **Rural Holidays New Zealand, Ltd.** They can find you a place from $80 with dinner and breakfast. Write to P.O. Box 2155, Christchurch, or phone 366-1919.

CHRISTCHURCH BUDGET ROOMS

As with the motels above, you may have to arrange for the following accommodations yourself, since their rates are too low to be interesting to travel agents outside the country.

American and Canadian budgeteers seem universal in their praise of the Victorian house converted into the 40-unit **Windsor Bed & Breakfast Hotel** (Tel. 366-1503) at 52 Armagh Street, within walking distance of the square, the park, and lots of other sites and sights. Register at the desk under the stairway. There's a lounge with a color TV for everyone to view together and free bottomless cups of tea and coffee. Nonsmokers are encouraged. Single rooms go for about $60 and doubles cost $90 for bed and breakfast this year. A bath and shower await you on each wing, and the water is *always* hot. We once enjoyed a brief incognito stay ourselves here, confirming everything good we've ever heard about the place. Tell enthusiastic Don Evans we sent you, and you may feel the Windsor is your castle in Christchurch.

Other good possibilities we haven't personally inspected at this price level include the following addresses, which are a little farther out from the center of things. First, **Eliza's Manor House** (Tel. 366-8584), a century-old house at 82 Bealey Avenue, with doubles or twins at around $100 with breakfast. ("What a find!" said one reader.) The **Strathern Motor Lodge** (Tel. 355-4411 or 0800-766-624) at 54 Papanui Road consists of 15 units, 6 with kitchens. There are two bedrooms and a lounge, and the tariff is $90 double. A fine old Canterbury house called **Highway Lodge** (Tel. 355-5418) is a lovely Tudor-style home and has single, double, or family accommodations available, and breakfast is served in the dining room. Singles cost $49 and doubles cost $65. Highway Lodge is a 20-minute walk into the city. Then there's what used to be Charlie Brown's but is now just **Charlie B's** (Tel. 379-8429 or 0800-224-222) at 268 Madras Street, with dormitory accommodations at $15 a night and room rates of $20. **The Holiday Lodge Motel** (Tel. 366-6584) on Colombo Street has accommodations from $65-75.

There's also budget-priced central city accommodation at the **Colombo Travelodge** (Tel. 366-3029) at 965 Colombo Street. Rates are $62 single and $69 double. The **Christchurch Visitor Information Centre** (Tel. 379-9629) is the place to appeal to if you've just flown in and are having trouble finding a nest for the night. They will also tell you if there is GST to be added to the room rate. The Christchurch accommodation rates we have quoted are mostly inclusive of GST. The Visitor Centre also has desks at both the domestic and international air terminals.

Youth hostels? There are two official NZYHA hostels, the **Rolleston House** (Tel. 366-6564) at 5 Worcester Street, and the **Cora Wilding Youth Hostel** (Tel. 389-9199) at 9 Evelyn Couzins Avenue. Rates are around $17 to $20 for qualified members. By the way, the national office of the Youth Hostel Association is in Christchurch, at the corner of Manchester and Gloucester Streets (Tel. 379-9535, Web site www.yha.org.nz). Here's the place to set up your membership, receive International Guest Cards, etc. Annual membership is $36.

More worthwhile accommodations in the B&B category will be found at **Turret House** (Tel. 653-900 or 0800-488-773) on Durham Street. You will find it at Number 435 in an characterful historic house with reasonable rates. *Cead Mile Failte,* they say—One hundred thousand welcomes!

Backpackers will find good pickings for just $13 per person a night. Try **Aorangi** (Tel. 348-3584) at 15 Riccarton Road, or Avon City Backpackers

(Tel. 389-8676) at 563 Worcester Avenue. Another good choice could be **Stonehurst Hotel** (Tel. 379-4620), which has dormitory accommodations as well as conventional hotel offerings. This lodge sits at 241 Gloucester Street.

Camping grounds and holiday parks are dotted around Christchurch, and all appear to be of similar standards. Try the **All Seasons Holiday Park** (Tel. 384-9490) at 5 Kidbrooke Street near Sumner Beach, just 5 kms from the city and on a bus route. Tourist flats are also available. The price for two is $57, but you have to bring your own linen. **Meadow Park Holiday Park** (Tel. 352-9176 or 0800-396-323) has won a N.Z. Tourism award and has cabins with carports, self-contained cabins, disabled facilities, caravan and tent sites, heated indoor pool, spa pool, and sauna. It's four kilometers from Christchurch's main Cathedral Square.

We have already referred to farmstays in Canterbury. The average nightly rate from about $90 per person for dinner, bed, and breakfast makes these well worth the while.

5. Restaurants and Dining

For some reason not easily determined, Christchurch is now blessed with an amazing number of dining rooms for its size. Reviewing them, however, is akin to reviewing a patch of mushrooms: They spring up quickly, and a number enjoy only brief popularity before they wither and die. If lamb is not on the menu, rich-flavored hogget should be sampled. And Christchurch's proximity to superlative salmon fishing waters means you'll find this tasty fish on several menus. We've tried to limit our selection here to those places we think will remain in good business health.

At the forefront of Christchurch's elegant BYO restaurants is **Dizzy Lizzies** (Tel. 389-6529) at 471 Ferry Road. She has taken over the former Portstone Restaurant and dressed herself in charming colonial attire. The blackboard menu changes almost daily and it's tempting to keep going back.

Vegetarians should try **Dux de Lux** (Tel. 366-6919), which specialises in seafood, vegetarian dishes, and pizza, and brews its own beer. Better still, the **Mainstreet Café and Bar** (Tel. 365-0421) offers vegetarian and vegan in a smoke-free atmosphere. It too, brews its own beer and is noted in the *New Zealand Micro Brewery & Good Beer Guide*.

Colonial Kiwi at Willowbank (Tel. 359-6226) at 60 Hussey Road, features a carvery where prime meats are on the menu. After dinner, step outside to view some wildlife, including Kiwis.

For carnivores, **Hay's Café** (Tel. 379-7501) at 93 Victoria Street is the place to go. This is Christchurch's specialist lamb restaurant, and it has a New Zealand Beef and Lamb Bureau Hallmark of Excellence award.

A collection of good fish restaurants resides in Christchurch. **Palazzo del Marinaio** (Tel. 365-4640) in the Shades Arcade is every bit as delicious as it sounds. You can feast on oysters and a variety of fishy favorites for under $30 (this covers three courses) at **Sarah's Brasserie** (Tel. 365-4699) in the **Quality Inn** on the corner of Durham and Kilmore Streets. Also excellent for ocean specialties is **Pescatore** (Tel. 379-4560), which is easy to find in the George Hotel. This particular restaurant has won many awards for its cuisine.

The **Landing Seafood Restaurant** (Tel. 379-9992) is upstairs on Cashel Street and has an extensive seafood menu.

One of the city's best restaurants for some time has been **Leinster House** (Tel. 355-8866) at 150 Leinster Road. The restaurant has been carved out of a fine old house with plenty of atmosphere and vast fireplaces to warm guests during the winter months. Seafood features on the menu here, but there are delicious dishes with game such as quail, hare, and pheasant. This is not the cheapest eatery in town, but many feel the prices are worth it.

For top hotel dining, the **Camelot Room** (Tel. 488-999) in the Chateau has a good reputation. We liked the food and found it generally more interesting, with its battle-axes and other trappings from days of yore. Sometimes there is dancing to a live orchestra in the castle, too. (Closed Sundays.)

Arthur's and Martha's (Tel. 355-9124) at Camelot court on Papanui Road has the full range of New Zealand dishes at reasonable prices. The service is tops, and their homemade chocolates will stick in the memory. (OK'd by Harold McKee of Kansas City.)

Grimsby's (Tel. 379-9040) is a licensed restaurant in an old school at Kilmore and Montreal Streets. One room is long and narrow, and the other is octagonal. It is popular for lunch and dinner. For Italian food try **Il Felice** (Tel. 366-7535), which promises unequaled cuisine and service. Dishes include fresh pasta, veal, seafood, and steak.

Christchurch has a colorful range of ethnic restaurants. There's Mexican fare at **South of the Border** (Tel. 379-7808) at 834 Colombo Street, and huge servings at reasonable prices at **Lonestar** (Tel. 365-7086) on Manchester Street. **Coyotes** (Tel. 366-6055) is also good at 126 Oxford Terrace. If you like Thai food (we do), try **Chiang Mai Thai Food** (Tel. 365-2400) at 376 Worcester Street, or **Kannigas** (Tel. 355-6228) at 18A Papanui Road.

You'll find Iberian and Mediterranean specialties at **Michael's** (Tel. 366-0822) at 178 High Street. Carry your own wine; a guitarist will provide the music. (Closed Sunday.) **Pedro's** (Tel. 379-7668) is, logically enough, limited to Spanish specialties. This BYO at 143 Worcester Street is also popular and good, but like many Chch restaurants is closed Sunday and Monday. **Santorinis Greek Ouzeri** (Tel. 379-6975) serves Greek food at the corner of Gloucester and Cambridge Streets.

A couple of excellent Chinese restaurants are around now. **Shangri-La** (Tel. 379-5720) is located at 321 Durham Street. Also good is the **Pagoda Court** (Tel. 366-3931), with a liquor license, at the corner of Colombo Street and City Mall. The **Jade Garden** (Tel. 379-5300) is at 109 Cambridge Terrace. You can also try the **Chung Wah II** (Tel. 379 3894).

There's an interesting vegetarian stop at **Gopals** (Tel. 366-7035), run by the Hare Krishna devotees. Prices range from $8 to $14. Gopals is on Worcester Street. **Sala Sala** (Tel. 366 6755) has classic Japanese food and an extensive menu. Despite its name, **Shanghai** (Tel. 379 7265) offers Malaysian cuisine and is popular with immigrants from there.

There are several candidates for casual pub dining. One of two we particularly enjoyed was the **Oxford On Avon** (Tel. 379-7148) on Colombo Street opposite the Town Hall. Get in line, place your order at the steam table, and pick it up later when they call out your number. Meanwhile, you can go into **Chloe's Bar** (on the same premises) and pick up a couple of delicious Kiwi beers. Choose a booth somewhere near the diamond-latticed windows, but not so far away you can't hear when your steak or chop is done. We recently enjoyed similar fare at lunchtime in the **Chancery Tavern** (Tel. 379-4317) in Chancery Lane, just off the square. (Braised sausages and onions, including salad and chips, cost around $15.50.) Entertainment is on tap in the evening.

Twiggers of Addington (Tel. 338-2572) is always reasonable but is best for atmosphere when the Addington horse races are on. The inexpensive **Wagon Wheel** in the Carlton Hotel (Tel. 355-6159), at the corner of Bealey Avenue and Papanui Road, is attempting to regain its reputation as a trencherman's palace.

There's also a branch of Lion Breweries' **Cobb & Co.** (Tel. 366-6035) at the Caledonian Hotel, 101 Caledonian Road. That's near the corner of Canon Street, north of Bealey Avenue. It's open seven days a week, 7:30 A.M. to 10 P.M. Cobb & Co. branches spring up all around New Zealand, but the Christchurch member of this family restaurant chain is especially good. Main courses cost between $18 and $28. There are also Cobb & Co. branches at the **Bush Inn** (Tel. 348-7175) at Riccarton and **Mackenzies Hotel** (Tel. 389-9014) at Linwood.

Midnight cravings can be catered to at **Matthews Restaurant** (Tel. 388-2472) in New Brighton. It's open every night until the wee small hours, and there are huge beefsteaks to keep you going. Matthew also serves what he calls "cute vegetarian dishes." You will find him at 186 Shaw Avenue.

Annie's Wine Bar (Tel. 365 0566) is an informal restaurant tucked away on the south quad of the Arts Centre. It has award-winning cuisine and over 70 local Canterbury and other New Zealand wines in its cellars.

The **Sign of the Takahe** (Tel. 332-4502) is a castle on the Cashmere Hills with pleasant views across Christchurch city. It is famous in Canterbury and probably further afield and offers traditional silver service. A baronial atmosphere prevails and New Zealand dishes, which include wild venison and pheasant, add to the flavor. The desserts are hard to beat. And **Strawberry Fare** (Tel. 365-4897) has the distinction of being a totally smoke-free restaurant and offers a choice of 24 desserts. Open most nights until midnight at 114 Peterborough Street.

For something different, how about the **Thomas Edmonds Restaurant** (Tel. 365-2888) in the band rotunda on the banks of the Avon River? It's a great place to sit outdoors on a fine day. They serve Devonshire teas as well as brasserie-style meals. This is both a BYO *and* a licensed restaurant, and the selection of Canterbury and New Zealand wines is good. The restaurant has a Taste New Zealand Award. Don't forget to visit **Death by Chocolate** (Tel. 365-7323) at 209 Cambridge Terrace for a totally indulgent hour or so swooning over 30 dessert choices.

There are also many vineyards around Canterbury that have attached restaurants. These include the **Akaroa Winery** (Tel. 304-8990), **Canterbury House Vineyards** (Tel. 314 6900), **Cider Garden Café & Wine** (Tel. 314-8030), the famous **French Farm** (Tel. 304-5784), and the **Rosebank Estate** (Tel. 323-7353) which has the added attraction of beautiful rose gardens.

The Christchurch Information Centre has an up-to-date restaurant guide for visitors. By the way, if you don't want to guzzle all the beer and wine available in Chch, you might like to try the local equivalent of Perrier mineral water instead. It's called Waimak, and it's bottled at 155 William Street at Kaiapoi, 12 miles north of Christchurch.

6. Sightseeing in and out of Christchurch

More than any specific sights in Christchurch, it's the general atmosphere of the place that captures most visitors. Many never set out to see anything specific at all, but come away satisfied after a serendipitous journey that leads them along the peaceful river, through the protective oak and elm trees, under Gothic arches, and into hallowed halls, virtually at random.

But for traditionalists who want to check things off the list, here are some of the musts or near-musts in this city. The first several of these can be easily walked to—in approximately this order; then they start getting more spaced out.

The center of town is dominated by **Christchurch Cathedral,** the result of a frustratingly long and difficult project of the past. Its cornerstone was laid in 1864, eight years after the Church of England colony was founded, but the Gothic-style building was not completed until 1904. Some years ago we climbed to the top of the 215-foot spire. It was all right, but we wouldn't do it again. You might enjoy the view more than the climb. The cost for this exercise is $1. More relaxing would be the Choral Evensong at 5:15 P.M. on Tuesdays and Wednesdays, and the boy choristers' performance on Fridays at 4:30 P.M.

The structure lends its name to **Cathedral Square,** which, now that traffic has been removed, provides a commodious stage from which to watch the world walk by. It's particularly interesting at noon on a bright, clear business day. Look then for the self-appointed "Official Wizard of Christchurch"—a man named Ian Brackenbury Channel—who, wearing any of a number of outlandish costumes, declaims to a willing crowd on any subject that comes into his head. The wizard usually goes into action at about 1 P.M.

A block east of the square is Christchurch's justly renowned **Avon River.** It is, for most of its length, not much more than a gentle stream winding between grassy banks while shaded by peaceful willow and oak trees. Children are allowed to fish for trout or eels between certain bridges. Since the town street pattern was laid out directly over the river, there are a dozen or so bridges, each one a different example of Victorian architecture.

At Cashel Street, the Avon was crossed by a bridge that two generations of soldiers marched over on their way from nearby King Edward Barracks to the railroad station and thence to war. To honor those who didn't return, the citizens of Christchurch have built the elegant **Bridge of Remembrance** there; it is now open only to foot traffic. Canoes and paddle boats are leisurely ways to view the Botanic Gardens and Hagley Park. Antigua Boat Sheds (Tel. 366-5885) rents canoes and paddle boats for $10, so you can meander down the Avon for a view from the water. Punting on the Avon is a great sport and a cruisy way to see the sights. Pick up a punt at the *Visitor Information Centre* from 10 A.M. to 6 P.M. daily, September to May; otherwise by arrangement. Twenty-minute rides cost $15 each. Thomas Edmonds does picnic lunches in willow hampers at a very reasonable extra cost. Call for information at 379-4834.

Farther downstream, on Durham Street, are the wood and stone **Provincial Government Buildings**—no longer used as such, since New Zealand officially abolished the provinces in 1876. They were built by Benjamin W. Mountfort, the architect responsible for many of the thirteenth-century-style Gothic structures all over the city. There's even a secret passage in there someplace. They are open weekdays, 9 to 4, plus free guided tours on Sunday afternoons, usually 2 P.M. to 4 P.M. (Tel. 365-3828).

Just back over the Armagh Street Bridge is **Victoria Square** (shaped more like a triangle). You'll find statues of Queen Vic and of Captain Cook, as well as the 1931-model Bowker Electric Fountain, which changes colors at night. Just over the Victoria Bridge is the **Floral Clock,** where the mums move and tell the correct time—at least within a begonia or two.

Nearby sits Christchurch's pride and joy, the modern yet stately **Town Hall,** the design of which somehow blends with all the ancient curlicues in other parts of the community. Opened in 1972, its two auditoriums are supposed to have just about the world's best acoustics. The building is generally photographed so that the river and the delightfully fuzzy Ferrier Fountain take up the foreground. (The spherical water display always reminds me of that kind of white dandelion that dissolves into hundreds of seeds when you blow on it.) Also in the structure is a restaurant that overlooks the Avon.

Figuratively speaking, at least, let's jump back to Worcester Street. In the block bounded by Worcester, Montreal, and Hereford Streets and Rolleston Avenue is the Gothic-spired former campus of Canterbury University. Recently it has been converted into the **Arts Centre of Christchurch** (Tel. 366-0989), an ambitious community project to keep the flavorsome old buildings in use as focal points for music, theater, painting, and other cultural pursuits. (The university has moved to a new and modern site at Ilam.) Most craft shops are open from 10 A.M. until 4 P.M. The restaurants are open every day from October through March and an arts, crafts, and antiques market is held every Saturday and Sunday from 9 A.M. until 4 P.M.

At the end of Worcester Street, and just across Rolleston Avenue, you'll find the **Canterbury Museum** (Tel. 366-5000). It houses the best stuffed-bird collection in the country, although we have been much more fascinated with the 1850 Christchurch street exhibit and, of course, the Hall of Antarctic Discovery. The latter includes remnants of the historic explorations of that polar continent, many of which were launched from Christchurch. (Open 9 A.M. to 4:30 P.M. daily—free admission) You'll be able to revive on light refreshments in the museum coffee bar. The **Brooke Gifford Gallery** (Tel. 366-5288) at 112 Manchester Street, has exhibitions of contemporary New Zealand painting and sculpture.

Just behind the museum is the **McDougall Art Gallery.** If you haven't seen any of the fine Maori portraits by Charles F. Goldie or Gottfried Lindauer, you should do that here (same hours as the Canterbury Museum). The buildings just to the north belong to **Christ's College,** an exclusive boys' high school where the students still wear formal English uniforms.

The school and the two museums border the city's **Botanic Gardens,** 60-some acres enclosed within a bend of the river. If you don't want to walk it, there's an electric vehicle popularly called the "toast rack" that offers guided tours for around a dollar during nice weather from about September through April. (The garden also features a small restaurant serving lunch or tea.)

The Botanic Gardens are surrounded by—or strictly speaking, are a part of—the 500-acre **Hagley Park,** which is otherwise devoted to venues for organized sports. Here are tennis courts, bowls fields, polo grounds, basketball courts, and so forth, all spread out over a massive greensward that is a monument to the foresight of the "pilgrims" who first settled Christchurch.

Off the northwest corner of the park you can find what was once a private estate along the Avon, **Mona Vale** (Tel. 348-9660). The mansion was built in 1905 in Elizabethan style, and the gardens include a collection of exotic trees. Now owned by the Christchurch and Riccarton city councils, it's often used for private as well as civic events. During the summer, it might be the site for the drama festival of the Canterbury Shakespeare Society. And forsooth, it's a wonderful place for a picnic. You can hire punts at Mona Vale from October through March (Tel. 348-9659).

If you're near Mona Vale during the warm-weather months—particularly January or February—find your way also to a short residential cul-de-sac called **Royds Street.** For several years, the neighbors along this block have been winning the annual street gardening competition hands-down. Turn into the road and you'll see why. It's spectacular, but surely some sort of exercise in floral obsession.

You'll need a car or some kind of transportation if you want to go farther west to see the present-day campus of **Canterbury University** at Ilam. (Today it's often miscalled Ilam University.) Frankly, we'd skip it except during October and November, when masses of orange, pink, red, white, and other colors of azaleas are abloom at the old farmhouse that was once the Ilam homestead. You'll have to ask your way to the University Staff Club to find it. Drive yourself there or take a Number 3 bus from Cathedral Square. Before we leave the center, a tip about the Cathedral tower: we've had a letter from a reader saying you can climb the stairs to the top for $1.50. The views must be worth several million.

A 100-acre piece of nostalgia for New Zealanders is represented by **Ferrymead,** the historical theme park at Heathcote, just southeast of the city line, reached via the Ferry Road (and then the Bridle Path Road). It's open daily from 10 A.M. until 4:30 P.M. There, volunteers have brought a once-important ghost town back to life and created yet another transportation and technology museum. If you haven't visited MOTAT in Auckland, Southward's near Wellington, or a couple of others around the country, you might drop in. Be sure to take a spin through the phonograph exhibit, too.

You may hear something about **Queen Elizabeth Park** (Tel. 359-7109), but generally speaking it represents more in thrills and spills for local funseekers than for international travelers. And **Orana Park** (Tel. 359-7109) is a 65-acre bird and animal park on McLeans Island, near the airport, featuring mostly African animals. Admission is $12, and the park is open from 10 A.M. to 5 P.M. There is also the Willowbank Wildlife Reserve (Tel. 359-6226), open from 10 A.M. to 10 P.M., which also costs $12 to enter.

Here are two more personal favorites within the boundaries of Chch, but not near anyplace else. One is the **Roman Catholic Cathedral,** unfortunately situated near the railroad line and the coal gas factory at Ferry Road and Barbados Street. The magnificent basilica was built in 1905 from Oamaru limestone and other fine local materials. In some ways, its appearance is more dramatic because of the contrast with its plain-Jane surroundings. When George Bernard Shaw visited Christchurch in 1934, he upset the Anglican city fathers by praising not the Church of England cathedral but "that other one down by the gasworks."

One of the most unusual cemeteries we have seen in a world of cemeteries is the **Oakland Gardens,** further out on Linwood Avenue at about Hargood Street. Here is one final resting place that does not wait for Resurrection Day. All those interred here are cremated, and each set of ashes is used to plant one single rose tree. Each is labeled, of course, with the name and dates of birth and death of the person from whose ashes it sprang, and today there are about 12,000 living rose trees on the property. Personally, I'm not sure I can imagine anything more heavenly than coming back to life again in a few weeks as a rose in the Garden City of New Zealand.

Since the seventies, Canterbury has been making a name for itself as a classic wine-producing area, and if you are fond of the grape, take the **Canterbury Wine Trail** (see Restaurants and Dining) Within striking distance of Christchurch, there are five highly recommended vineyards that sell award-winning wines. Some names to watch out for include Giesen, Larcomb, and St. Helena. Ask the Visitor Information Centre for directions, or hop on a tour.

DESTINATIONS OUTSIDE OF CHRISTCHURCH

The traditional day trip from Chch is the 50 miles or so to the Banks Peninsula. On the way out, skip the tunnel and drive on the Summit Road over the Port Hills. Keep your eyes open for the **Sign of the Takahe,** where you can stop for tea and cakes and soak up the view. Eventually, you'll get a takahe's-eye view of the port of **Lyttelton,** the flooded crater of a long-extinct volcano. Into Lyttelton sailed the "First Four Ships" with wide-eyed pilgrims in December 1850. After connecting with Highway 75, turn east. There's a pleasant pub with a magnificent panorama at Hill Top, where we couldn't resist investing several 10¢ pieces in one of those infernal gambling machines called Cascades. At the very end of Route 75 is the village of **Akaroa,** which, as we described in the restaurant section, began as a French settlement in 1840. There still is a little Gallic feeling about the town; some of the streets, at least, are called "rues." (The museum on Rue Lavaud is open 10:30 A.M. to 4:30 P.M. daily.) There is a full-day trip to Akaroa that includes a harbor cruise on the *Canterbury Cat* and public transport runs from the city every day.

If you head south, do call in to Wigram Air Base and the Air Force Museum, **Air Force World** (Tel. 343-9532) It is easy to find on the main road south, and features all kinds of intriguing exhibits. It's open from 10 A.M. to 5 P.M., and admission is $10. While you're heading in that direction, check out the International Antarctic Centre (Tel. 358-9896), which has gotten rave reviews. It has anything and everything you ever wanted to know about the snowy wastes. The site is open from 9 A.M. to 5 P.M. in winter, and from 9 A.M. to 8 P.M. in summer. The entry fee is $16.

If you happen to make your way to the obscure village of **Okains Bay,** don't miss their museum, if it's open. I'll never, ever forget the model of the rabbits' tea party—perhaps created long ago by a farmer for his little girl—made out of real stuffed rabbits dressed in dolls' clothing!

If you like the countryside here, there is a farmstay that has been bought to our attention. At Tai Tapu, there is the **Pear Drop Inn** (Tel. 329-6778) on a 20-acre orchard, probably one of the closest farmstays to Christchurch central. It is run by Brenda and John Crocker. Brenda is an art teacher and you can take a week-long live-in art course run by her for about $500 including full board, transfers, and tuition. Otherwise the cost is under $100 double for one night or more. We'd be interested to hear your views.

If, by some strange chance, you skipped the thermal areas in the North Island, you may want to make a short pilgrimage from Chch to the spa at **Hamner Springs,** about 80 miles up Route 7 on the way to Lewis Pass. As the Kiwis might say, it's "not a patch" on Rotorua, but the drive is certainly pleasant enough, through lovely countryside. There are three large, outdoor hot thermal pools. Call the **Hamner Connection,** a daily bus service, at 025-332-088.

By the time you read this guide, the **Hamner Springs Lodge** (Tel. 0800-80-50-85) will be open. It is promising top-of-the-range accommodation at rates yet to be published. If you visit, be sure to let us know how it is.

Not far from Hamner, just outside of Waiau, is the **Sherwood Country Lodge** (Tel. 315-6078), beautifully restored by John Clarke. This quiet retreat offers a heated outdoor pool (pool parties in mid-winter when the snow piles up around the pool's edge have been known), tennis court, gym and spa, and courtesy car for sightseeing. John is a chef of some renown, and his meals are little short of banquets. He'll take you salmon, freshwater or saltwater trout fishing, and cook up your catch for dinner. The Mt. Lyford ski area is just minutes away, as is golf. Prices are from $600 twin share per day.

In another direction from Christchurch, it's about 90 miles to **Arthur's Pass,** which is both a genuine mountain village and headquarters for the national park of the same name in that portion of the Southern Alps. (Look for a good walk to **Devil's Punchbowl Falls,** a 439-foot drop down a sheer cliff face.) In difficult weather, Highway 73 can be difficult, all right. You can also take the train into town (see section 2); the Chalet is a pretty fair guesthouse and restaurant there. Bed and breakfast costs $75 double. Both the road and the train also continue over the mountains to the West Coast town of **Greymouth**—160 miles from Chch. (The **Hotel Ashley** (Tel. 768-5135 or 0800-80-50-85) offers good food and lodging for $95 double. The **Willow Bank Pacifica Lodge** (Tel. 768-5339) sounds pleasant, with a room rate of $78 double.

About 30 miles north, New Zealanders like to visit the layered **Pancake Rocks** at Punakaiki. If you continue on up to **Westport,** you can take in the Coal Town Museum, but we would definitely skip Mitchell's Gulley Coal Mine. (The Barbary serves good tucker.) Some readers said they enjoyed visiting the lighthouse at Cape Foulwind. The **Ascot Motor Lodge** (Tel. 789-7832) is comfortable and has kitchens in each unit at a cost of $75 double. Try **Buller Bridge Motel** (Tel. 789-7519 or 0800-500-209) for a similar style of accommodations in a quiet setting and at about the same rates.

Ardwyn House (Tel. 768-6107) is a lovely circa 1929 art deco house in a quiet cul-de-sac. Bed and breakfast here is $70 for two. Be prepared to be loved to death by two resident elderly dogs. Just out of town at Dunollie is Kereru Lodge (Tel. 762-7077), with boutique accommodations on a bush-clad hill close to beaches, with "internationally praised cuisine." Price on application. E-mail them at kereru.lodge@xtra.co.nz.

Westport is small but friendly. **Marg's Travellers Rest** (Tel. 789-8627 or 0800-73 78-63) is one establishment we haven't tried, but it looks pleasant, with a scattering of outdoor furniture under a vine-draped pergola. Bed and breakfast is from $70 for two. There is separate hostel accommodation also, from $17.

Ten minutes off the main highway is **Punakaiki,** with a not unfriendly seal colony. The **Westport Information Centre** (Tel. 789-6658) offers plenty of holiday advice, and the **Greymouth Information Centre** can be contacted at Tel. 768-4300. Hokitika has its own information office, too (Tel. 755-8322). Oh, and Shelley Pogorelsky wrote us from California about the fascinating glow worm dell just three minutes from the center of town.

There's the **Shining Star Log Chalets** (Tel. 755-8921 or 0800-744-6464; Web site www.nzcentre.co.nz/hokitika/) opposite the dell, which asks $88 per night for two.

New Zealand's thickly forested west coast was settled largely by miners who dug for gold and coal. A potent mix of history and scenery on the west coast leaves its mark on visitors. So do the pubs, which are a legend in this part of the world. Try to fit one in and mingle with the unforgettable locals.

AREAS MUCH FARTHER AFIELD

Picton, the fishing and shipping community where the Wellington ferry lands, is also a resort town in its own right, as well as headquarters for cruises through Marlborough Sounds. (The Fifth Bank is a good restaurant.) If you're driving, the Queen Charlotte Drive from Picton to Havelock is slow but scenic. The best way to savor the magnificent Sounds is by boat, however. Picton Visitor Information can be reached at 573-7477.

In the heart of New Zealand's thriving wine-growing Marlborough region is **Blenheim,** which celebrates its fortunate position every February with an ambitious food and wine festival. It's a great time to be in Blenheim, and be sure to book ahead if you want to coincide with all the fun of this fair. Call the **Blenheim Information Centre** (Tel. 578-3399) for details of the festival and the region. The **Blenheim Country Lodge** (Tel. 578-5709 or 0800-655-079) sounds like a good place to stay in the city center. The rates here are $90 to $150. We can personally vouch for the **Chateau Marlborough** (Tel. 578-0064 or 0800-75-22-75) a family-run hotel in the center of Blenheim and one of the town's best. Rates are from $95 to $140 for two.

If the festival doesn't coincide with your visit, you should call into some of the vineyards, several of which have restaurants. Back in Blenheim, **Rocco's** (Tel. 578-6940) is a local favorite, serving Italian dishes and local seafood. Phone **Flying Kiwi Wilderness Expeditions** (Tel. 573-8126) to see what they have to offer in adventure and cycle tours as well as accommodations.

A trip out of Blenheim that we would very much like to do is to **Molesworth Station** (Tel. 575-7280) New Zealand's largest high-country property, stretching 445,000 acres all the way to **Hamner Springs.** The rub is that it's open to the public only for about six weeks each summer (late December through early February). The station runs 11,000 head of cattle

282   MAVERICK GUIDE TO NEW ZEALAND

and has been owned by the government since the late 1930s. Access to the
station is 80 miles southwest of Blenheim and about two hours' drive up
the Awatere Valley, off State Highway One. The long, winding road
through the property is in good shape, and the Department of Conservation
(DOC) has rangers on site to provide information. There is a road toll of
$10 a car and $5 a passenger, and camping sites are available on the way
through. It takes about five hours to drive through to the station's other
boundary near Hamner. The road rises to 3,500 feet and provides spectacular views. If you are taking a rental, make sure you get insurance for the
car! DOC's headquarters in Blenheim (Tel. 572-9140) will be able to
supply all the details on Molesworth.

Nelson, which might have grown into a large city but didn't, is still a favorite of many, especially beach- and sun-seekers. Nelson soaks in plenty of
sunshine, and artists in particular are attracted to its reliable climate. The
admiral after whom it is named is, of course, Horatio. The square, naturally, is Trafalgar (his last battle), and other plazas and streets are named
after other ships and conflicts.

Some of the delicious fruits, cheeses, meats, and fish of this region are
packaged so you can take them through Customs home. Craft Habitat is a collection of working studios open to the public seven days a week and worth a
visit. Otherwise there is a meandering art and wine trail through the region.
(Check the **Nelson Visitor Information Centre,** Tel. 548-2304.) There is even
a llama park with knitted garments at prices well below those paid in Europe
for similar-quality work. See the Queen's Gardens and the Suter Art Gallery,
with many John Gully works. There are probably nice accommodations at the
Leisure Lodge (Tel. 546-8502; Web site http://webnz.co.nz/leisurelodge),
the **Driftwood** (Tel. 548-2791), or **The Honest Lawyer** (Tel. 547-8850 or 0800-
92-11-92), a family-owned country pub just 10 minutes from Nelson city that
also offers accommodations and regional food, wines, and beers.

West of Nelson, some wanderers on wheels like to explore the peaceful
beaches and quiet shores via apple-rich Motueka to **Abel Tasman National
Park,** and then beyond to **Golden Bay** (Tasman's "Murderers Bay"). You'll
have to retrace your route, however, in order to plunge deeper into the
South Island. The Nelson Visitor Information Centre can be contacted at
548-2304. Nelson is also the home base for **New Zealand Home Hospitality**
(Tel. 548-2424), run by Dulcie and Allan Carson. Their farm- and homestays
stretch from Nelson to far beyond. At Golden Bay is **Northwest Lodge** (Tel.
524-8108), run by Philip and Angela England. The lodge has been built to
be ecologically friendly, and the couple are very much involved in conservation. Philip offers trout and sea fishing and eco-tours. Tariff is from $60 to
$115 double. The evening meal is about $30.

For trampers and lovers of the great outdoors, **Nelson Lakes National Park** is paradise. The tracks are suitable for all levels of fitness. Lake Rotoiti is the smaller of two lakes, and the larger magnet. Lake Rotoroa is less developed. **Lake Rotoroa Lodge** (Tel. 523-9121) on its shores is an upmarket retreat with rates of $225 double in the low season and $240 during the peak time. Nelson Lakes Transport (Tel. 521-1858) runs a twice-daily passenger service from Nelson during the summer and once a day in the winter. The **Nelson Visitor Information Office** (Tel. 548-2304) is a useful place for travelers. Outside of Nelson, at Richmond, visit the Hoglunds glass-blowing studio to see work sold in New Zealand's best galleries.

Major attractions to emerge in the south during the last couple of years are the **Kaikoura Whales.** Two-and-a-half hours' drive from Christchurch, the tiny little coastal town of Kaikoura has made a resounding impact with its schools of whales, seals, and dolphins. Whale-watching trips can be taken from Christchurch, or you can drive. **Whale Watch Kaikoura** (Tel. 319-5045 or 0800-655-121) will also take you out for $95. For something a little smaller, try **Dolphin Encounter** (Tel. 319-6777), which will set you back $85 if you wish to swim with the mammals or less if you go along as a spectator only. For something a wee bit smaller still, go on **Graeme's Sealion Adventure** (Tel. 319-6182). Watching these gorgeous creatures watching you will cost $40.

Almost directly west of Christchurch—although it seems much further south due to the northeast/southwest orientation of the island's axis and the winding, 233-mile route to get there—is **Mount Cook National Park,** also referred to in the Queenstown section of the guide. It is centered around the peak that is EnZed's highest at at least 12,345 feet. (It depends on how old your references are, as the country's mountains are supposed to be rising at the rate of about one inch per year.) Mount Cook was called Aorangi—the "cloud piercer"—by the Maori.

There are lots of walks in the park, on which you may see the famous Mount Cook lily and other alpine blossoms. But the most dramatic activities there are the flights from the little airport. Try **Air Safaris** (Tel. 0800-806-880). Cost is $210 per person. When conditions are right—i.e., "perfect," as they are about 50 percent of the time—they will land you smack-dab on the snow atop the Tasman or sometimes the Franz Josef Glacier as part of the standard flight-seeing tour. Twice we were to make that flight, and twice we've had to cancel our plans because the weather was far from perfect. Those who do make the landing label it a spectacular experience. (Skiers are also taken via the same planes to about the 8,000-foot level near the top of the glacier and picked up later at about the 2,500-foot level.) The scenic flights start at $185 for 40 minutes' flying over the spectacular Alps. A good place to stay at Mount Cook is **The Hermitage** (Tel. 435-1809), a rambling mountain retreat with fireplaces and large picture windows framing the alpine scenery. (The Panorama Room meals are nearly as delicious as the views, and make up for the somewhat plain rooms.) Rates begin at about $250 for two.

More modest but still decent arrangements are also available in chalets. Phone Mount Cook at 435-1809 for all accommodations, and don't go to the park without a reservation somewhere; it's a long drive out again. If you plan to fly in or out, be aware that sometimes the weather is too foggy for landings at Mount Cook. (South of the park, you could try the Ahuriri Hotel at Omarama.)

On one of our trips to the South Island, we chose to save Mount Cook for a northbound dessert later on the circuit. We drove instead from Christchurch to the south via the villages, rain forests, and glaciers on the other side of the Southern Alps, along the sparsely settled **West Coast.** It's a narrow strip of habitable real estate measuring more than 300 miles long by only about 30 miles wide.

After winding through Arthur's Pass, we paused long enough to look at the jade factory at **Westland Greenstone** (Tel. 755-8713) at **Hokitika.** The process was interesting, and the selection was excellent, but the retail prices seemed no better than at many other places. One of our readers liked the glassblowing factory at Hokitika and the fur factory 30 kms further south at **Ross.** Before leaving Hokitika for the Fox and Franz Josef Glaciers inland, make sure you've cash on hand. The glaciers turn on the scenery but not the banks. The **Fox Glacier** towers like a huge white tongue above the bush. Walk on the glacier, but take a guide with you. **Alpine Guides** (Tel. 03-751-0825) at Fox Glacier charges about $50 per walk. The Fox Glacier Hotel (Tel. 751-0839) is a cozy place to stay. Expect huge log fires, traditional cooking, central heating, and stunning scenery. Rates are from $105 double.

Inside the borders of **Westland World Heritage Park,** which achieved this global honor because of its superb and valuable wilderness, pull up for a morning, or preferably an overnight, at the village of Franz Josef. The best hotel is supposed to be the **Franz Josef Glacier Hotel** (Tel. 752-0729 or 0800-10-07-29; Web site http://nz.com/travel/ScenicCircle/), with doubles from $180 to $225, but if you can't get in or are counting pennies, there are a few good motels in the vicinity. (We liked the **Bushland Court Motel,** Tel. 752-0757, for $70 to $100 double, which efficiently mailed my forgotten trousers after we sent for them later.) Dinner in the Fern Room in the Franz Josef Hotel is usually fine.

The reason for stopping is to sign up for the morning excursion to the **Franz Josef Glacier,** conducted by a company called **Alpine Guides** (Tel. 751-08250). They'll give you the boots, and when sticks are being handed out be sure to take one of those, too. If you've got rain gear, better put that on, as well. Be warned that the hike is progressively more and more difficult, and almost inevitably a few in your party will decide to turn back before you get on the ice. When we were there, we had to negotiate our way around the crevasses, etc. after Peter McCormack, a former guide, chopped a few stairsteps in the glacier. Somehow, we made the entire round trip. We were pooped, wet, and a little frightened, but at the same time exhilarated by the experience. If you think you're in good shape, take a stab at it, but by no means push beyond the point of your own endurance! The rest of the gang will just have to pick you up on the way back.

One of the best ways to see this awesome glacier is by air. Try **Fox and Franz Helicopter Services** (Tel. 752-0764) who'll sweep you up there from $120 to $250. Otherwise go with **Air Safaris** (Tel. 0800-806-880), who'll take you on a Grand Traverse of Mt. Cook for $210.

Stop in at the Franz Josef Hotel or the **Franz Josef Visitor Centre** (Tel. 752-0796) for information and reservations.

In good weather, nearby **Lake Matheson** faithfully mirrors all the snow-capped mountains hereabout, and offers outstanding forest walks.

About 20 miles north of **Haast,** you will strike **Moeraki Wilderness Lodge** (Tel. 750-0881), which sits in an idyllic setting and is run by a prominent "Greenie," Dr. Gerry McSweeny. This former head of New Zealand's Royal Forest and Bird Protection Society has turned a mediocre motel into a rare treat. When we stayed there we were lucky enough to take a walk late at night with Gerry as our guide to see the glow worms light the banks on the sides of the road. Accommodation is in units and two larger, older-style cottages that sleep five. The dining room is intimate, and the home cooking is good.

Moeraki Wilderness Lodge is in the heart of **Southwest Heritage Park,** and Gerry has been a champion of the move to have the Southwest given World Heritage status. He is a man who has successfully married tourism with conservation.

Unless you're flying something or other, you'll cross the Southern Alps again at the most southerly and most rugged **Haast Pass,** in the forest, snow, boulder, and waterfall region that is also part of Mount Aspiring National Park. (Take these twists and turns cautiously in the winter, for the roads in the shadows of the tall peaks can get very icy.) The route will lead you to Wanaka and the lake country. Make a note of DOC's Headquarters' telephone number at Haast, 750-0809. A Haast telephone number—750-0728—rings into the **Westland Motor Inn,** where you can lay a weary head on a waterbed and sink into a spa bath for rates of from $110 to $140. The Inn has been a finalist in the NZ Tourism Awards for the last three years in a row.

7. Guided Tours and Cruises

A half dozen bus lines and a few chauffeured taxis will offer to take you around. The best-known trip is on the coach run by **Great Sights** (Tel. 358-9029). It leaves Cathedral Square at 10 A.M. most days on the two-hour *City and Suburban Tour,* for $35 per seat. The **Canterbury Transport** (Tel. 379-4600) also sends out a three-hour afternoon *Port, Hills and Harbour Tour,* leaving from the same square at 1:30 P.M. for an excursion as far as Lyttelton. It includes a half-hour boat trip around the harbor for an over-all price of $20. **Christchurch City Sightseeing Tours** (Tel. 366-9660) has a $22 half-day Chch tour. There is also an **Intercity** coach to **Hamner Springs** for $36, and don't forget that trip on the **Trans Alpine Express** to Greymouth.

Some interesting and slightly different tours include Akaroa Country Gardens, a fragrant and beautiful excursion through some of the most lovely gardens in New Zealand. Ring Lea Taylor (Tel. 304-7506) or Lee Dunster (Tel. 304-7660) to go on one of these.

Turf to Turf (Tel. 0800-279-479) takes you to remote areas of a coastal farm to visit seals and seabirds and study the flora and fauna. The trip includes a jet boat ride, 4WD safari, and sheepdog demonstration. Lunch is in a forest glade beside a stream. Contact Jeff and Linda.

Colmonell Wine Trails and Wagon Treks (Tel. 314-6827) is a day on a covered wagon pulled by gentle Clydesdale horses around the wineries of the Waipara Valley. Even those of you to whom covered wagons are hardly something new will enjoy this day out in the fresh air!

Open The Gate Tours (Tel. 315-6296 or 319-8667) will coordinate one-to three-day tours to gardens, farms, crafts, and artists on the Canterbury Plains. You can cover any or all of the above destinations, and each will give you a good prospective on rural New Zealand life. **The High Country Tour** (Tel. 318-6889) will appeal to those who come from the country or those city folks who have a hankering for the great outdoors. The one-day tour costs $65 and takes you to a High Country station (ranch) with dog trialling (sheepdogs) and gardens.

If you want to get up in the air, helicopter tours have recently been launched by **Garden City Helicopters** (Tel. 358-4360). At this writing, per-person prices run from around $65 to $210 per person, depending on whether you fly for five minutes over the city or whirl further afield and dine on crayfish and sip wine after a jet boat ride.

As far as cruises in Lyttelton are concerned, you can take the water trip included on the afternoon CTB bus tour separately with **Diamond Harbour Launch Services** for about $15 (Tel. 328-8368). One we know about goes to Ripapa Island for $12. For a scenic cruise of Akaroa, contact the **Black Cat Group** (formerly Akaroa Harbour Cruises) at 304-7641 for a Lyttelton Wildlife Cruise. Phone for exact details, or see the Visitor Information Office.

8. Water Sports

Of the beaches near Christchurch, probably the most scenic is **Taylor's Mistake**, even if it's a little difficult to get to. Supposedly it was named when the cove south of Sumner Head was thought to be the entrance to Lyttelton Harbor one foggy night by an unfortunate sea captain named Taylor. The hills, rocks, and trees make this, as well as the nearby ngaio tree-lined beach at **Sumner** (Bus No. 3), more interesting than the plainer beaches at **New Brighton** (Bus No. 5). All are safe and well patrolled, as well as exposed (sometimes unfortunately) to the prevailing and cool northeast winds.

You can rent a canoe and other small vessels for casual paddling on the Avon from the **Antigua Boat Sheds** (Tel. 366-5885), at the southern end of Rolleston Avenue, near the hospital. These antique sheds (open 9:30 A.M. to 5 P.M.) have been renting vessels out daily for the past century. If punting is too tame, try **Top Sport Kayaking** (Tel. 384-0410) for sea kayaking, whitewater, or multi-sport adventures.

Some of the world's best **freshwater fishing** is accessible from a Christchurch base. From November through April, the salmon fishing season is in full swim on rivers like the Waimakariri, the Rakaia, the Rangitata, and the Waitaki. You'll need a license, available for a reasonable cost from Visitor Information Centres. It allows you to fish for a month virtually anywhere in New Zealand.

Brown-trout fishing is also superb in wadable streams throughout the South Island. For either trout or salmon, sort out the many different tours and arrangements with the local Visitor Information offices or write to the NZTB in Los Angeles or Vancouver and ask them to send you a copy of *New Zealand Outdoor Holidays*, which they stock in their offices. It lists all the outdoor adventures to be enjoyed in New Zealand, who operates them, and for how much. **Mountain High Adventures** (Tel. 302-8733 or 302-9055) will take you fishing, and hunting too, if you want it.

Fishing and jet-boating tours are offered by a number of different companies. One that has been mentioned to us is **Outdoors the Canterbury Way** (Tel. 318-6574), which whisks out over the Waimakariri ("Waimak" to the locals). **Jetstream Tours** (Tel. 352-2961 or 025-321-104) also plies the Waimak from $55 per person, including pickup from and delivery back to your hotel.

Deep-sea fishing is not terribly practical from the Chch/Lyttelton area, although charter boats are available and recommended in Picton for some great fishing the length of Queen Charlotte Sound. However, you can enjoy a Dolphin Experience (Tel. 304-7866) from Akaroa for $65 per person.

9. Other Sports

In the spectator file, you'll find the big rugby matches (winter) and cricket matches (summer) out at **Lancaster Park** (Falsgrave Street, southeast of the center). Softball games are played in good old Hagley Park, just about across the river from the end of Chester Street.

Christchurch is the undisputed home of trotting races (the "trots") in New Zealand. Most of these are run at the **Addington Racecourse** (Bus No. 7), across the tracks southwest of Hagley Park. Going to the "gallops," on the other hand, you head out west to the **Riccarton Racecourse** (No. 8 bus). Both flat and steeplechase racing are run there.

Sports to take a hand in yourself include golf, of course; there are 11 courses within easy reach of the city. The best-known are the **Russley Golf Club** (Tel. 358-4612), 18 holes near the airport, and the **Christchurch Golf Club** (Tel. 385-2738) at Shirley, open to visitors on weekdays only. It's a colorful course with lots of pine trees and broom and gorse bushes. You can also golf at all-purpose Hagley Park. There are 12 holes, so you can play the first 6 again! (It *is* convenient, right in the center of the city, after all.) Call 379-8279 for more information.

Tennis fans will find plenty of courts. The unofficial headquarters for game, set, and match is **Wilding Park** (Tel. 389-7269), east of the city on Woodham Road. It boasts (and that's the right word) about *four dozen* courts—half grass, half hard surface.

Irie Tours (Tel. 318 7669) offers you a wealth of outdoor activity. They can take you caving, mountain biking, hiking, canyoning, rock climbing, and just about anything else your heart desires. Prices depend on the activity.

But the primary winter outdoor sport hereabouts is skiing—not in pancake-flat Christchurch, to be sure, but at mile-high **Mount Hutt,** near the town of **Methven** some 65 miles southwest of the city. The long season runs from late May or June into November, and sometimes slides clear into

December. Remember, this is high-altitude skiing, about 6,000 feet or so, and far above the tree line. (To phone the slopes, call 379-2720 in Christchurch.)

If you can take the rarefied air, the sky is usually sunny and clear at that height, above the clouds (if there are any). Lifts include one triple-chair lift, four double T-bars, two platter lifts, and three fixed-grip beginners' tows. You can rent skis, boots, poles, etc., if you need to.

Peninsula & Alpine 4x4 Tours (Tel. 384-3576; Web site www.penalp.co.nz) is just one of many companies that can arrange skiing and snowboarding excursions.

10. Shopping in Christchurch

The main center-city shopping is along **Colombo Street** and on the **Cashel Street Mall** (officially called the City Mall). These run at right angles, so the corner of Cashel and Colombo Streets is right in the center of all the buying and browsing. High Street has also been partly malled over and is part of the City Mall. And be sure to see Cashfield's Arcade. Other arcades with a wide variety of shops include the **Shades Shopping Precinct,** running between 110 Hereford Street and 99 Cashel Street, and **Canterbury Centre,** a smaller collection on the corner of High and Cashel Streets.

There are plenty of downtown stores not on these particular rights of way, however. Sometimes you'll hear of "Colombo Street North," an unofficial appellation for that portion of Colombo that is north of Cathedral Square. (In that area, too, be sure to note the Arabic-style upper stories of the stores along New Regent Street, off Gloucester.)

Normal shopping hours are 9 A.M. to 5:30 P.M. in the central city on weekdays. On Saturday morning most are open; during the summer they stay open all day Saturday and many shops are open on Sunday. All suburban shopping malls and some shops on the high streets are now open on Sundays. Late-night shopping is until 9 P.M. on Fridays. Suburban shopping centres have their late nights on Thursdays.

The big, exclusive department store in Chch is **Ballantyne's** (Tel. 379-7400), in City Mall, which traces its gilt-edge roots back to 1854. Ballantyne's also has a branch at the airport (Tel. 358-5121).

Other department stores include **Arthur Barnetts** (Tel. 379-9140) on Cashel Street, and **Farmers'** at 97-107 Gloucester Street (Tel. 379-8700), as well as in several suburban shopping malls.

For general souvenir sifting, we would first try **Lange's** (Tel. 379-1159), which you'll see next to the Visitor Information Centre. It's good for knickknacks and bric-a-brac. **Paua Jade Gems** is good, at 37 Cathedral Square. **Walker & Hall** (Tel. 349-0505) the quality jewelry shop, has a branch in the Triangle Centre at the corner of Cashel and Colombo Streets. You might find a nice gift here. **Jade and Opal** (Tel. 377-0956) at the Art's Centre, is another place to find New Zealand's semi-precious stone. **Aotea NZ Souvenirs** (Tel. 366-7814) is on the Square, and is another good gift shop. On the corner of Colombo and Gloucester is **D.F. Souvenirs** (Tel. 379-8670).

If you've been waiting to get to Christchurch to find those thick, wooly South Island sheepskins, you can feel your way through a dozen stores or so. There is some good stock at **Skin Pool Sheepskin Sales** (Tel. 366-4841). It's located not very conveniently at 76 Moorhouse Avenue, near the train station (take Bus No. 7). Other well-established establishments include **The Tannery** (Tel. 366-5406) and **Hartings in the Crystal Plaza** (Tel. 365-2534).

The **Artisan Fibre Centre** is in the Christchurch Arts Centre in the old university buildings on Worcester Street, and opens daily to sell its wooly and homespun contents. Thirty-five shops are in the centre and specialize in handmade and manufactured goods in leather, wool, glass, and pottery, Maori carvings, and weavings, among others. Some of the country's most talented artists combine with a local rug company to produce handsome floor coverings on display at **Dilana Rugs.**

Go to the Arts Centre market on Saturdays and Sundays for a wonderful collection of arts and crafts. This includes woodwork, pottery, jewellery, textiles, glass, confectionery etc., etc., etc! There are also live bands, food stalls, buskers, a restaurant, and a café.

Back in town, **Leather Image** (Tel. 365-3007) is a high-fashion leatherware shop that makes garments to measure at wholesale prices. **RUSA Leather** (Tel. 379-6578) is now at 174 St. Asaph Street. While on the subject of things warm and wooly, the Antarctic Centre sells Arctic-proof long johns. Other items here include toys, jewellery, works of art, and clothing. For handcrafted shoes, step back to 467 Colombo Street to **Last Footwear Company** (Tel. 366-1392). Once you've tried these on you'll know what quality footwear is all about, and you'll probably be ruined for mass-produced shoes for life.

Farther afield, a group of artists and craftsmen of several different types are represented at the **Artists Quarter Shop** (Tel. 379-4079), at 53 Tuam Street.

A little easier to get to are two shops near Town Hall. The **Thyme Cottage** (Tel. 366-3940), whose theme is both herbs and crafts, is at 809 Colombo Street. Also good for New Zealand souvenirs is **Langes NZ Gifts.** They have two locations—in the AMP Centre (Tel. 365-1031) and at the

Information Centre on the corner of Worcester Street and Oxford Trace (Tel. 379-1159).

We liked **Fusspots** (Tel. 379-1983) in the Shades Arcade, which sells innovative ceramics and pottery pieces. Some are quite unusual. Leading New Zealand artists have some of their wares on sale here.

Not Just Bears (Tel. 377 1311) is a delightful collection of dolls, bears, New Zealand souvenirs, and collectables at 137 Victoria Street. Besides the Canterbury shops that originated in Christchurch, **Rodd and Gunn, Action Down Under,** and **Rowlands** produce durable outdoor-oriented clothing that has flair. Visit Action Down Under for the latest in sports and outdoor clothing in moleskin, wool, and leather. They are at 772 Colombo Street, and the telephone is 366-5684. Victoria Villager has a collection of shops, galleries, and restaurants, and is worth a visit. We've also had a brief browse through the **Merivale Village Mall,** just up Papanui Road. It shows signs of becoming what Kiwis call a "trendy" shopping center. If you're up that way, poke into **The Village Pots** (Tel. 355-7130).

Two recently completed complexes worth a visit are the **Canterbury Centre** and the **Triangle Centre.** The Canterbury Centre is at the corner of Cashel and High Streets. It's a cluster of 20 specialty stores on a couple of floors. The Triangle Centre encompasses the Cashel and Colombo and High Street corners, and embraces about 60 shops.

Camping and hiking supplies? Christchurch has one very large store for outdoor gear: **McEwing's Mountain Sports Ltd.** (Tel. 366-6211) stores more packs, tents, sleeping bags, boots, lanterns, stoves, skis, etc. than you can shake an alpenstock at. It also rents out many supplies. You'll find them at 93 Cashel Mall.

Bookstores? There are several in Christchurch, an academic city, after all. London Bookshops, for whom we've always felt a particular affection, not only because of their large collection of Kiwiana, but also because their stock usually includes several strange foreign volumes—like ours—has been absorbed into the omnipresent **Whitcoulls** chain. We trust the stock will remain much the same. Cantabrians (those from the Canterbury Plains) are great readers, and you'll find lots of little privately run bookshops too. Try **Scorpio Bookshop** (Tel. 379 2882) for a wonderful selection of books with an emphasis on New Age texts, and also the **Arts Centre Bookshop** (Tel. 365 5277), which may be small, but has a powerful selection of books. It is also a good place to pick up New Zealand publications for all age groups.

At any pottery shop in New Zealand, you may see something called a "salt pig"—a fat jug with a big hole in its side. This appendectomied pig may run something between $15 and $25, and it's ideal for New Zealanders, who often prefer to spoon their salt instead of shake it. It keeps salt dry in a humid climate. Americans sometimes purchase the salt pig without knowing exactly what to make of it. We've seen them used as ashtrays and flower planters—or merely as "conversation pieces"—in American homes.

11. Night Life and Entertainment

As you might expect, after-dark carousing is traditionally limited in Christchurch—usually to a few pubs pouring out music to imbibe by—but things have been livening up a bit in the past couple of years. However, nightclubs can be fickle things, so check with the Visitor's Bureau for an updated list. Better still, talk to the bright young things behind the hotel reception desk—they're bound to have the lowdown!

Otherwise, try the **Chancery Tavern** (Tel. 379-4317) in Chancery Lane, which is a restaurant and pub. (The Chancery is known for having its own satellite receiving dish, regularly pulling in news and sports events from the U.S. and Australia and serving them up on a large screen in the bar. Here's where you might catch some American football live on the tube.) **Henry Africa's Restaurant and Bar** (Tel. 389-3619) at 325 Stanmore in Merivale has a resident pianist.

A popular cocktail lounge these days is modestly titled the **Elegant Cocktail Bar,** in the aforementioned Coachman Inn. (Not the wood-paneled bar by the restaurant, but the forties-style model with the comfy sofas one flight up.) You'll also find night-time music in the aforementioned **Dux De Lux** dining room and at the **Jazz Coffee Shop,** in the Arts Centre.

The Palladium Nite Club (Tel. 379-0572) on Chancery Lane will turn on plenty of bright lights for you. It is billed as the largest laser light show in Australasia, and you are sure to find some action, along with dining and dancing. Most of the pubs and larger hotels have live entertainment on weekends. Soothing late-night entertainment is found in the café bars, which have sprung up all over the city—as many as a dozen in the last 12 months. They tend to be small and cosy, sometimes with live music, and most have meals at realistic prices. The Cashel Mall is home to a few. Try **Bardelli's** (Tel. 353-0000) and Café Bleu (Tel. 377-2888). A third worth heading for is the popular Fresco's, now called **Blue Jean Cuisine** (Tel. 365-4130), at 205 Manchester Street.

Now, for theater, music, dance, etc.—the lively arts—Christchurch nearly challenges Auckland. The Christchurch Festival, held even-numbered years, features all those things and more. The city is especially keen on its annual Romance Festival. Other venues for entertainment include the following:

The **Town Hall** has two beautiful auditoriums that are often filled with fans of either modern or classical entertainment. There's the 2,600-seat main room, although even complicated ballets may also play in the smaller (1,000-seat) **James Hay Theatre.**

Events the Town Hall can't handle—concerts by American or English rock groups, for example—are staged outdoors in the sports arena at **Queen Elizabeth II Park,** on the road to New Brighton.

Other Chch theaters are the **Repertory Theatre** (Tel. 379-8866), at 146 Kilmore Street; the **Court Theatre** (Tel. 366-6992), with its own semiprofessional company, which sometimes welcomes out-of-town productions to its address at 20 Worcester Street, in the Arts Centre; the **Theatre Royal** (Tel. 366-6326), at 145 Gloucester Street, born in 1908 and now specializing in traveling British bedroom farces and the like; and the **Ngaio Marsh Theatre** (Tel. 364 3652), at the University of Canterbury Student Union on Ilam Road. The **Southern Ballet Theatre** (Tel. 379-7219) in the Arts Centre is also a talented company and you may be around to catch a performance.

Christchurch also has an aptitude for outdoor concerts—orchestras, bands, and pipe bands—in any of several parks. In good weather, outdoor theater is held, too, on a temporary stage and bleachers set up in the one-time estate at **Mona Vale.**

There are a number of cinemas in and around Cathedral Square. For slugabeds there are three television channels . . . and the international joys of CNN and Sky cable television. On Chch radio, you get the National Program at 3YA (675 Kh); the Concert Program at 3YC (963 Kh); community radio stations on 3ZM, "The New Sound of Christchurch" (1323 Kh); 3ZB, "You and Me Equals 3ZB" (1098 Kh); and the private stations, 3XA "Radio Avon" (1260 Kh); 3XG, a religious station called "Radio Rhema" (1503 Kh); and Radio UFM (983kh), an FM station. Chch also has a good morning newspaper, the Christchurch *Press*.

12. The Christchurch Address List

Automobile Association of N.Z.—210 Hereford Street (Tel. 379-1280).
Bank—Bank of New Zealand, Cathedral Square at Hereford Street (Tel. 353-2532).
Bus information—Tel. 0900-55-755 (24 hours).
Discount liquor—Liquorland, corner Fitzgerald Avenue and Hereford Street (Tel. 366-8461).
Fire department—Dial 111 for all emergencies.
Florist—Court Florist, Whitcoulls Arcade (Tel. 379-3255 a/h 366-2055)

Hospital—Christchurch Public Hospital, Oxford Terrace and Riccarton Avenue (Tel. 364-0640).

Laundry—Laundrette, 247 Armagh Street (Tel. 379-6622).

Library—Canterbury Public Library, Oxford Terrace and Gloucester Street (Tel. 379-6914).

Pharmacy (weekends and after hours)—Urgent Pharmacy, corner Bealey Avenue and Colombo Street (Tel. 366-4439).

Police station—(Dial 111 for all emergencies.) Hereford Street between Montreal Street and Cambridge Terrace (Tel. 379-3999).

Post office—General Post Office, Cathedral Square (Tel. 353-1899).

Visitor Information Office—Corner Worcester Street and Oxford Terrace (Tel. 379-9629).

U.S.A. Information Service—106 Gloucester Street (Tel. 366-1097).

U.S.A. Consular Agent—208 Colombo Street (Tel. 379-0040).

Youth Hostel Association—NZYHA National Office, 193 Cashel Street (Tel. 337-9970).

9

Queenstown, the Lakes, and Fiordland

1. The General Picture

We never met an American or Canadian who didn't love **Queenstown,** and most Australians are partial to it, too. Many Kiwis, however, aren't all that sure.

A village with a permanent population of about 7,000, Queenstown is nestled in a valley by the edge of a large, picture-perfect lake. Inhabitants in the nearby areas of **Arrowtown, Wakatipu,** and **Wanaka** bring the count up to about 15,000 persons. Mountains surround the scene, and during the colder months they are dusted or covered with snow.

In this spectacular alpine setting, in the midst of a grand display of nature, the little community hardly looks like a party town. Nevertheless, it is probably the most action-oriented hamlet for its size anywhere in New Zealand. In fact, it is the country's only true resort town.

Day or night, there is always something to do. This perpetual motion appeals to the battalions of the young and young in spirit who invade the valley for skiing in the winter and tramping in the summer. Many, of course,

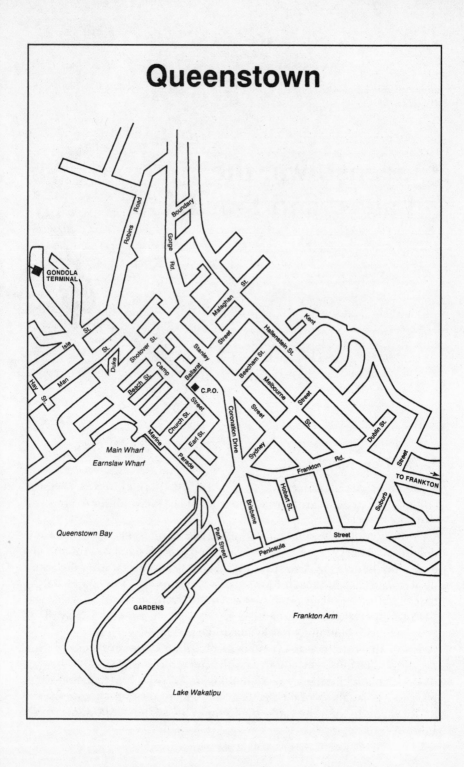

Queenstown

GONDOLA TERMINAL

Robins Road

Boundary

Gorge Rd.

Malaghan St.

Kent

Isle St.

Duke St.

Shotover St.

Stanley Street

Hallenstein St.

Beecham St.

Camp Street

Ballarat Street

Melbourne Street

Hay St.

Man

Beach St.

Church St.

C.P.O.

Earl St.

Coronation Drive

Sydney Street

St.

Dublin St.

Street

Main Wharf

Earnslaw Wharf

Marine Parade

Frankton Rd.

TO FRANKTON

Queenstown Bay

Park Street

Brisbane

Hobart St.

Peninsula

Suburb

Street

GARDENS

Frankton Arm

Lake Wakatipu

are from other countries, and their accents lend the town a cosmopolitan ambiance.

New Zealanders who prefer a quiet sort of vacation will forgo frenetic Q'town, perhaps in favor of a peaceful fishing holiday at nearby lakes **Wanaka, Te Anau,** or **Manapouri.** Some might even choose Kingston, a sleepier settlement sited on a calmer portion of the same lake whose middle Queenstown stirs up with music, motors, and merriment 12 months of the year.

Lake Wakatipu (the locals eliminate the final *u* and call it "waka-*tip*") is shaped rather like a sharp *s* or a backwards *z*. Scooped out by glaciers millions of years ago, it's a thousand feet deep in some places. A mysterious phenomenon causes it to vary several inches in depth every few minutes, giving some credence to a Maori legend of an ancient demon still breathing beneath the surface.

Seen from Queenstown, the lake is backgrounded by mountains that form a series of serrated peaks. This range was named by an early pioneer, whose laconic appellation—**"The Remarkables"**—inspires some amusement and several bad jokes today.

All the activity in Queenstown may be annoying to a few, but it is at least consistent with the roots of the community. In 1862, gold was discovered in the nearby Arrow River. The resulting rush there—as well as to the equally rich **Shotover River** and other lodes in the vicinity—soon brought a raucous vitality to the area that has not been equaled since.

Prospectors came from Australia, California, and China, and hundreds of bars lined the muddy streets. Nefarious characters like the American gentleman pirate "Bully" Hayes also poured into the town to cash in on the money that seemed to flow as swiftly as the Shotover, by this time known as "the Richest River in the World."

Some gold is still taken out of the neighborhood—in fact, about one million N.Z. dollars' worth a year—more than enough to keep the legends alive. But the richest experiences available to all on the Shotover today are the thrilling rides through its cliff-lined gorge, either by rubber raft or daredevil jet boat. Other nerve-wracking pastimes include the celebrated **bungee jumping,** borrowed from a remote Pacific community and refined by A.J. (Alan) Hackett, an Aucklander who had no doubts about the value of a resort town like Queenstown.

Tamer stunts in town include the dizzying ascent on the cable car to the peak almost 1,500 feet straight above the streets. Those who *really* want to take it easy can book passage on the 1912-model coal-fired steamer TSS *Earnslaw,* the Lady of the Lake, belching thick, black smoke over the water. It looks like a throwback to the Swiss steam yachts of Baedeker's day.

West of the lake country lies **Fiordland National Park.** At more than 3 million acres, it's the country's largest park by far, and one of the most sizable national parks in the world. Ancient glaciers like those that carved the inland lakes also gouged out the ocean fiords along the southwestern shoreline. Generally, the New Zealanders call them "sounds," and many are impossible to reach except by boat or the most rugged bushwalking.

The most famous fiord, and one considered a must for any visitor to the South Island, is the storied Milford Sound. In recent years, its high peaks and deep waters have come to symbolize the entire country for many travelers. There are three usual ways to get there—difficult, medium, and easy—and, at different times, we have enjoyed all three.

The easiest way is to fly over the rugged mountainscape from Queenstown. But you can also drive or bus there through the Homer Tunnel, in the shade of some of the most spectacular cliffs you'll see anywhere. Last, you can hike from Lake Te Anau over the 33-mile **Milford Track,** a three-day thrill for the physically fit. This remains the premier adventure in New Zealand for vacationers lucky enough to be able to arrange it. It's an experience to talk about for a lifetime.

2. Long-Distance Transportation

Queenstown's neat little airport, about five miles out, is actually closer to Frankton than Q'town. This compact little building has recently been extended to cope with increased traffic and now boasts money-changing facilities and several interesting new shops. The counters for Air New Zealand and Ansett New Zealand dominate the ground-floor room. The other desks are operated by Fiordland Travel, Milford Sound Scenic Flights, Waterwings Airways, and Air Fiordland. You'll find newspapers and such in the snack bar one flight up.

There's an airport bus between the airport and Queenstown to connect with the higher-density flights in and out. By taxi, the trip to town will cost about $13.

Rental Cars. Hertz (Tel. 442-4106 or 0800-654-321) and **Budget** (Tel. 442-9274) have counter space at the airport, as well as offices in town. You can also try **New Zealand Rent A Car** (Tel. 442-7465). Most of these companies have 4WD (four-wheel-drive) vehicles for excursions off the main highways. Mopeds are popular modes of transport in the summer.

Prestige Tourist Services Cars (Tel. 442-9803), on Shotover Street, operates limos. **Limousine Services** (Tel. 442-7377) is another option.

Airlines. Scheduled air services to Queenstown are run by **Ansett New**

Zealand (Tel. 442-4146 or 0800-800-146) and Air New Zealand (Tel. 441-1900). If you're coming to New Zealand via Australia during the ski season, check out Qantas flights between Sydney and Queenstown. The carrier runs a special ski flight with very competitive fares. Of course, if Queenstown is the end of your New Zealand sojourn, check out the fares departing Queenstown for Sydney. These can be remarkably cheap.

Air New Zealand Link services (which now incorporate Mt. Cook Airlines) provide short haul flights between Queenstown and other small centres such as Te Anau.

Except for air sightseeing tours, there are no flights scheduled *out* of Milford Sound. It's not that every plane goes into the water there (!), it's just that the weather is so unreliable that passengers might get stranded if they have made no other arrangements. You *might* get a standby seat out on the plane, but everyone prefers that you book the daily bus back instead. The flight between Queenstown and Christchurch soars over the Southern Alps via Mount Cook, and the bonus is a bogglingly good view.

Ansett operates scheduled air services into Queenstown using an all-jet fleet of Aerospace 146 aircraft. Their host airline, Waterwings, flies Queenstown-Te Anau, Queenstown-Milford when weather permits.

Other airlines are **Air Fiordland** (Tel. 442 3404), which will take you to Fiordland and Milford Sound for $75, and **Aspiring Air** (Tel. 443 7943), winging you to Mt. Aspiring, Mt. Cook, and Milford Sound for between $65 and $145.

Bus Routes. There are no trains into Q'town, but you can arrive via the coaches of **Intercity** (Tel. 442-8238), whose terminal is outside their offices on the corner of Shotover and Camp Streets. Intercity operates daily trips to Milford Sound that include morning tea at Te Anau en route and a two-hour boat cruise on the fiord. It's a full day, and the cost is $145. The daily departure for Franz Josef and into the glacier region is at 8:45 A.M. and costs $87. The bus to Christchurch via Mt. Cook leaves Queenstown at 8:45 A.M. and stops for 45 minutes at the foot of the great mountain for a refreshing break. The cost for this ride is also $85. Intercity also leaves every Monday through Friday for Invercargill (cost is $37), and there are several daily departures for Dunedin (via either Alexandra or Gore). The booking office for Intercity is open every day (Tel. 442-8238), and it is handy to know that Saver Seats are available on most services when you book and pay in advance. Check with the office on the duration of each journey, but reckon on about four and a half hours to Te Anau, five hours to Milford, and about four hours from Invercargill.

3. Local Transportation

Sorry, but Queenstown is just too miniscule for a municipal bus line. Taxis are reasonably plentiful from **Queenstown Taxis** (Tel. 442-7788), and most areas in town may be reached for about $10. Taxis can also be hired for day trips and sightseeing at an hourly rate.

You'll have to do a certain amount of huffing and puffing if you choose to trudge around the hilly streets. Unless you're staying right downtown, this might be one destination where you would be better off renting a car for at least part of your stay (see above).

In the section on bus tours from Queenstown (a little further on) we list a fun way or two to make excursions to such fascinating places out of town as the old mining village of Arrowtown other than in a rental car.

One interesting method of "local transportation," though, is the **Gondola Skyline and Cableway** (Tel. 441 0101), which you catch at the end of Brecon Street. It transports you seemingly straight up to the Skyline Restaurant at the top of 1,500-foot-high Bob's Peak. (Not to be confused with the chair lift at Coronet Peak—see section 9.) You don't have to buy anything to eat or drink up there, and we believe drinking in that delicious view is well worth the price for the dangling bubble-cars—about $12 for adults. The restaurant complex now includes the Kiwi Magic Showscan Theatre, which captures some of N.Z.'s best scenery on film.

4. Queenstown Hotels and Motels

We like all of these first four high-priced houses very much, and it's difficult to place them in order. Generally speaking, where facilities and basic comfort are very close to one another, we've tended to rank the hotels by preferred location and convenience. (As reports continue to come in from readers, evaluating service and other intangibles, things could always be different in the next edition.)

Queenstown recently completed a hotel/motel building boom, with existing houses expanding their capacity and new ones opening for business. Although the properties listed below probably will provide what you want, you can take a shortcut if you wish and contact **Queenstown Reservations** (Tel. 442-6340 or 0800-80-41-11; e-mail bookings@queenstownres.co.nz), who will do the walking for you, to steal a Telecom catchphrase. Ask them about their early booking bonuses.

EXPENSIVE ACCOMMODATIONS

Yes it's unoriginal, but we must give our top billing to the 139-room **Queenstown Parkroyal** (Tel. 442-7800 or 0800-80-11-11)—formerly the

Travelodge—scenically sited in two stair-stepped tiers on Beach Street, just across from the Earnslaw, the lake, the Remarkables, and all that glorious nature. There is an often busy, compact lobby; Bentley's Restaurant for dining and dancing, plus Steamer's Cocktail Bar; large swimming pool and sauna bath; well-appointed, balconied bedrooms; all units with TVs, tea- and coffee-makers, and fridges; good American-style bathrooms (lots of shelf space, mixer faucets, etc., which is unusual in EnZed); and the best rooms are in the front block or the seventh floor in the back block for views. In addition, third-floor units in the rear section have immediate access to the pool, a summertime plus. Rates on application.

Gardens Parkroyal (Tel. 442-7750 or 0800-80-11-11) offers a restaurant and bar, free laundry service, and skiers can hang their gear to dry in the ski room. The property is on the lakefront and has lovely rose gardens. Prices are on application.

Accor has moved into Queenstown in a big way with the **Novotel Queenstown** (Tel. 442-6600 or 0800-80-11-11), and the brand new **St. Moritz Suites** (Tel. 442-4990 or 0800-80-11-11). The former was the old Holiday Inn Queenstown, now revamped and refurbished. It offers a solar-heated pool, spa, tennis courts and gymnasium, two restaurants, and a bar. Price on application. The latter has suites and two-bedroom apartments, restaurant and bar, spa, and sauna. Special leisure rates are available.

Rydges (Tel. 442-7600 or 0800-7478-847; Web site http://nzcom.co.nz/Queenstown/Lakeland) has also moved in, taking over the former Lakeland Hotel. It is the town's largest hotel and its restaurant, Clancy's, is probably the most recognised and awarded dining facility in Queenstown. Prices are on application.

The Heritage Queenstown (Tel. 442-8611 or 0800-36-88-88; Web site www.dynasty.co.nz) is another new Queenstown hotel with attitude. The Dynasty Group, which is behind the Heritage collection, has already made a reputation for hotels of character. This one has one- and two-bedroom suites with open-plan dining room and lounge and fully equipped kitchen with the full complement of kitchen and dinnerware. Price on application.

Now, for those who want full kitchen facilities at this level of luxury, many are available in the design-award-winning **A-line Hotel** (Tel. 442-7700 or 0800-80-77-00; Web site http://nz.com/travel/ScenicCircle/). This collection of 80 sharp-roofed town houses is at 27 Stanley Street (be prepared for a short, sharp hike). Set in attractive surroundings, most of the rooms have superb lake views. There is a restaurant, convenient parking, and good laundry facilities. The rooms have TV, newspapers, refrigerators, and top-grade appurtenances. Rates are from $191-225.

Sorry, we haven't yet had a chance to see **Hulbert House** (Tel. 442-8767), a rambling, century-old house on a hill at 68 Ballarat Street, overlooking the bay. Two people with breakfast cost from $125 double, according to our information, a jump up from its former "bargain" category. Some readers have told us it was charming, but a steep walk back from town and not very warm in the winter. The owner is said to be colorful, though.

Highly recommended is **The Lodges** (Tel. 442-7552), at 8 Lake Esplanade, complete with kitchens. Rooms at The Lodges sleep five, and the tariff is $140 for two. **Alpine Village** (Tel. 0800-925-7463) and **Beachcove Apartments** (Tel. 441-8158) are two others in the luxury condo brigade that become value-for-money places to stay for small groups or families.

Nugget Point (Tel. 442-7630) is about four miles out of town on the road to Coronet Peak. It has the comfortable intimacy of other lodge-retreats in New Zealand and the advantages of a self-contained resort. There is a range of accommodations, but each unit or suite has its own cooking facilities if you want to do your own thing. A doubles apartment is $265, but you can also book into junior suites, which are two-bedroom units. The swept-up executive suites cost $3,450. There are squash courts, a spa and sauna, an indoor-outdoor swimming pool, and a good restaurant.

The **Millbrook Resort** (Tel. 441-7000 or 0800-800-604) continues to hold its own. Almost a village in its own right, it offers villas, villa suites, Village Inn rooms and cosy cottages, a café, and restaurants. It is placed around a championship golf course in an ideal setting. President Clinton took a break there. Cost is from $285 right up to "pretty pricey." Check with the hotel itself for rates, but expect to pay top dollar. Millbrook has already gained an international reputation.

MEDIUM-RATE ROOMS

If you're traveling by car, there's a pleasant stopover about halfway between Christchurch and Queenstown on Highway 8, just outside the township of Omarama. The **Briars Homestay B&B** (Tel. 438-9615) offers accommodations in rooms with separate facilities from $65 double. The house has views of the surrounding mountains and valleys, and the tiered garden falls away into the natural landscape. Give Marylou and Don Blue a ring.

For a comfort/convenience compromise, the best bet at this price level may be the **Ambassador Motel** (Tel. 442-8593), near the center of town on a hillside site at 2 Man Street. This motel features four floors of apartments, all with kitchen facilities; view over the village, the mountains, and a blue patch or two of the lake; tiny balconettes; color televisions; available continental breakfast; and rates of about $100 for two. Suites are also available. The Ambassador is no embassy, but it's clean and convenient. We like it for the prices posted, and the courtesy car to and from the bus depot.

Similar, but a little more inconveniently located, is the **Lakeside Motel** (Tel. 442-8976; Web site www.netprophet.co.nz/best/service/lakeside), at No. 18 Lake Esplanade. There are 13 living units behind an undistinguished facade; a small poplar park across the road; no central facilities, except a coin-operated laundry; all flats with full cooking equipment; long, shared balcony outside; fairly spacious rooms with wall-to-wall carpeting, some with wallpaper; all with TV; and better Remarkables panoramas on the top two or three floors, but ground-level units are more convenient for carrying in groceries, luggage, or ski stuff. Rates are between $95 and $104.

Try also the **St. James Apartments** (Tel. 442-5333 or 0800-243-254), which offers studio, one-, or two-bedroom apartments about one minute from the town centre. Rates start at $90.

Thomas's Hotel on the Waterfront (Tel. 442-4667) is "owned" by Thomas the cat, with the help of Jan Atkinson. All rooms are en suite and there is a communal kitchen/lounge as well as a waterfront café bar for outside dining. Rates are $55-84 double, and there are multi-share rooms for budget travelers from $16.

Caples Court (Tel. 442-7445 or 0800-282-275) is worth a look and costs from $89 to $110. So too is the Hotel Esplanade (Tel. 442-8611 or 0800-86-11-11), which is right on the lake with cosy heated rooms. Rates there are from $45.

Lomond Lodge (Web site http://nz.com/queenstown/LomondLodge; Tel. 442-8235 or 0800-45-66-66) at 33 Main Street, won praise from two of our California readers. Rates are around $98 for two. The **Hurley's of Queenstown** (Tel. 442 5999) has studios and two- and three-bedroom apartments from $80 to $120.

A little higher up the accommodation rate ladder, but with good facilities, is the **Gold Ridge International** (Tel. 442-6500 or 0800-65-61-11; Web site http://nz.com/travel/ScenicCircle/) at $144 single/double. **Turner Heights Townhouses** (Tel. 442-8383) also offers good value, with rates of $89-125 for two. Some units have their own spas, and there are those cracking good views of Queenstown. Queenstown House B&B no longer fits the budget criteria, with rates of $125.

LOW-BUDGET BARGAINS

In a town populated by and catering to so many young people, there have to be some bargains. The trouble is, of course, that the picture changes rapidly at this price level. Here are a few selections we liked the last time we scraped around for bottom-dollar bedrooms. You may well find some others, which we'd like to hear about.

The **Wakitipu View** (Tel. 442 7463; Web site http://nz.com/queenstown/wakatipu) is just three minutes' walk to the mall and has fully equipped kitchens with microwaves. There is also a washing machine and dryer in each unit. Tariff is $69-105 double. **Amity Lodge** (Tel. 442-7288 or 0800-55-60-11; Web site nz.com/queenstown/amity) has one-bedroom units that actually sleep up to five persons for $114 per unit.

Garden Court Motor Lodge (Tel. 442-9713 or 0800-247-336; Web site http://nz.com/queenstown/GardenCourt) has studios from $122; the **Colonial Village** (Tel. 442-7629 or 0800-22-66-52) has rooms from $50-100.

The next two are very close and very good for the all-in-the-family style they represent. The **Goldfields Motel & Breakfast Inn** (Tel. 442-7221) glitters the most for some. This modest old building at 41 Frankton Road, a five-minute walk from the center of town, has six clean bedrooms in the main house; four kitchen units to one side and four A-frame chalets on the other; breakfast and lounge room with community color TV and coffee-makers; all rooms with hot and cold washbasins and heated beds; and motel units and chalets with private loo, shower, and fridge. Rates are around $75 for two. Just down the road is the **Backpackers Downtown Lodge** (Tel. 442-6395) which charges $15 a person for dormitory sleeping, or $16 each for a twin room.

If you're really pinching pennies, the campsite at the **Queenstown Motor Camp** (Tel. 442-7252) has campervan sites among the pines and native trees that rent for $10 per person, or you can choose between motel or tourist flats that sleep up to six, have kitchens and, in the case of the motels, supply linen. You bring your own linen to the tourist flats, but they're just $50 for two per night. Motel units cost $68 for two. The tourist units cost $30 for two. There is a tourist lodge as well that costs $47 double and has tea and toast facilities. A camping ground is at **Frankton** (Tel. 442-2079) in a pleasant, lakeside setting, and we know of another at **Kawarau Falls,** right on the edge of the Kawarau River.

Campervan travelers are increasingly being catered to. In Queenstown you will find the **Kingston Stream Holiday Camp** nestled in mature trees at just $9 per person for a powered site. **Arthurs Point** has a full range of modern facilities as well as a shop and charges $8 per person for a powered site.

Pinewood Lodge is also cheap, with cabins from $18 per person double.

The **Bush Creek Health Retreat** (Tel. 442-7260) is located in three acres of garden that include a waterfall. All foods are organically grown, and the tariff is $40 per person.

The official **NZYHA Youth Hostel** (Tel. 442-8413) is at 80 Lake Esplanade; members pay $15 a bed. There's a blackboard menu in the restaurant, and a courtesy coach on hand. Despite all the nighttime activity around and about, they still enforce the curfew here. That aside, it's one of the newer and nicer youth hostels in the country. Others to note in the budget range are **Queenstown Lodge** (Tel. 442-7107), with rates of $23 a night and breakfast-making facilities, and **Mountain View Lodge** (Tel. 442-8246), which offers rates of $13 for a room with private facilities but sleeping four people. Sounds like a pretty good deal. The **Esplanade Hotel** (Tel. 442-8611) offers something similar; three in a room with private bathroom pay $17 per head.

The sheep stations around Queenstown are among some of the oldest in the country. You may want to book farmstay accommodations with your travel agent before leaving home. We can give you a toll-free number for the U.S. to find out more about farm holidays and self-catering cottage accommodation. It's 800-351-2323. Inside California the toll-free number is 800-351-2317. If you feel like some rural respite—either farmstays, staying in a private home in Queenstown, or just dining with one of the locals— try **Larch Hill Homestay** (Tel. 442-4811). This is one we think you will enjoy.

5. Dining in Queenstown

The cosmopolitan nature of Queenstown's residents and visitors has flavored its restaurants, too, and it's safe to say that the quality and diversity of the cuisine are greater than that of any other town its size in New Zealand.

The best all-around dining room in Queenstown for the past several years isn't in town at all, but about four miles' drive out, just past Arthur's Point. **Gantleys Wine Bar and Restaurant** (Tel. 442-8999), originally built in the 1860s as a hotel and trading post for the gold-rush era, has been restored as a gourmet restaurant. Inside it's thick, candlelit stone walls and fine cuisine, with specialties like rack of lamb and venison. There's also a good wine list, and we've dined here happily in the past. There are lunchtime barbecues in the garden during the summer months, and the establishment is closed Sundays. We don't know of anyone who ever had a bad meal here, and the fact that this paragraph has remained unchanged through several editions also proves enduring quality.

Treetops (Tel. 442-7238) is a seafood restaurant with a good wine list to keep its excellent menu company. It has smoke-free dining rooms and a courtesy coach to pluck you from your hotel and deliver you to your table at Sunshine Bay. Several of our readers have commented on the quality of Treetops, and we look forward to our next meal there. A more modest place in the Queenstown Bay Centre (an arcade running from 62 Shotover

Street to Beach Street) is the restaurant and coffee shop entitled the **Gourmet Express** (Tel. 442-9619). It chugs through the day offering three squares, of course, but we have it from Louie Leland, a longtime American expatriate from Dunedin, that this is one of the best places in Kiwiland for down-home Yankee breakfasts, including pancakes, French toast, etc. The hamburgers aren't bad, either.

There are several eating establishments in the Queenstown Mall, many of them not much more than carbohydrate-loading stations for skiers. One of the better ones, however, is **Chico's** (Tel. 442-8439). There is a cozy, fireside atmosphere that heats up with live entertainment most nights. **Beefeaters Steakhouse** (Tel. 442-9149) is popular. Call 442-9676. **Westy's** (Tel. 442-8635), in the Wakatipu Trading Post, is considered a BYO bargain. It has recently reopened after a total renovation, and we hear it's even better. Go for the food, not the somewhat diffident service. **O'Connell's Shopping Centre** (Tel. 442-7760), on the corner of Camp and Beach Streets, is a cheerful cluster of small restaurants with cosmopolitan menus.

No list of dining establishments would be complete without some mention of the **Skyline Restaurant** (Tel. 441-0101) at the top of the cable lift on Bob's Peak. The view is more delicious than the meal, although the nighttime vista suffers from too many lights at the restaurant. The lamb is a specialty here, and there's live entertainment.

Saguaro's Mexican Restaurant (Tel. 442-8240) has Mexican food at good prices. It's open every day. Locals strongly recommend **The Stonewall Café** (Tel. 444-6429) in the Mall. The specialties are char-grilled seafood and steaks at reasonable prices. Sounds good to us.

The Big Mac has arrived in Queenstown, and **McDonald's** occupies the front space in O'Connells. Not to be outdone, across the road on Camp Street, Colonel Sanders has opened a **Kentucky Fried** outlet. New restaurants in Queenstown have popped up like mushrooms in the past 12 months. It's worth putting on your Stetson and moseying down to the **Lone Star** (Tel. 442-9995) on Brecon Street. Be warned! The meals are BIG and the music is loud.

You'll find good food and plenty upon plenty of it at **The Cow Restaurant,** which is tethered on Cow Lane at the rear of the Bank of New Zealand. This is a very good-value restaurant. There are just a few tables, and you may be asked to share. Go early to avoid the lines. There's milk on tap. Otherwise, bring your own *vino tavola* (Tel. 442-8588).

The Japanese have discovered Queenstown, and the **Minami Jujisei Restaurant** (Tel. 442-9854) caters to them and everyone else with a taste for sushi and other Japanese flavors. You'll find the restaurant on the ground floor of the Queenstown Bay Hotel, formerly the Mountaineer. Chinese and Malay food fans can satisfy appetites at the **Dragon Place Restaurant** (Tel. 442-6293), and **Mandarin Restaurant** (Tel. 442-5222) restaurant. **Lai Sing** (Tel. 442-7131) is a popular Chinese restaurant on the top floor of O'Connell's Pavilion.

Giuseppe's Gourmet Pizza and Pasta Bar (Tel. 442-5444) is said to be good, and the **Boardwalk** (Tel. 442-5630) on the steamer wharf is a seafood restaurant and bar. **Berkel Gourmet Burgers** (Tel. 442-6950) are delicious, and the **Little India Bar and Tandoori** (Tel. 442-5335) also comes recommended.

6. Sightseeing in Lakeland and Fiordland

Because most of Queenstown's appeal traditionally falls into the area of "things to do" rather than "what to see," you'll find some of her most famous attractions straight ahead in section 7. Otherwise, Queenstown itself, with its backdrop of the lake and the Remarkables, is one lovely sight. We have wandered directionless over its lanes and streets, turning this way and that on pure whim, and enjoyed every step.

If you insist on a list, however, here it is. Queenstown's premier sight is the already described vista from **Bob's Peak,** and just about the only practical way to get there is the cable car. Just four minutes takes you to the top. (For the adventurous, there is a trail as well.)

Near the bottom of the cable-car station is the **Queenstown Motor Museum** (Tel. 442-8775), a collection of restored automobilia appealing to the car buff. It costs $5 to go through the gleaming establishment, open from 9 A.M. to 5:30 P.M. daily. (If you've already enjoyed Auckland's MOTAT or any of EnZed's many-fendered transport museums, maybe you could live without this one, at least in nice weather.)

Wander down to the wharves at **Queenstown Bay,** and have a look in the water for the tame trout that congregate there. These great, fat monsters know perfectly well that they're protected by law in the immediate area. They wait to be fed, secure in the knowledge that the bread you throw them wouldn't dare have a hook in it. Now open there is the new **Underwater World** (Tel. 442-8437), where for around $5 you can see some of the world's finest trout in their freshwater, natural environment. It's open year-round from 9 until 6, although during the long summer twilight it sometimes closes later.

Nearby is **Eichardt's Tavern,** still going strong, as it has been since the 1870s. Then it's only a few yards to the entrance of the spacious **Queenstown Tourist Gardens,** a green peninsula forming the demarcation between Queenstown Bay and the Frankton Arm of Lake Wakatipu. Fir trees, trim lawns, and rose gardens surround various sports venues, including even an ice-skating rink.

Kiwi and Birdlife Park (Tel. 442-8059), adjacent to the gondolas, has kiwis as well as the only black stilt on display in New Zealand. There are also lots of other rare, endangered, and common native birds in the park. The entrance fee is $5 and is well worth it.

THE ARROWTOWN TRIP

The most popular nearby road excursion, 13 miles from Queenstown, is to **Arrowtown,** the charming little hamlet that makes Q'town look like Auckland and Wellington by comparison. It began as a wild, gold-mining town when the precious metal was discovered in the Arrow River in 1862.

Heading out the Arrowtown Road, your first landmark is the **Arthurs Point Hotel,** a friendly country "local" that has been dispensing beer and good cheer for well over a century. You'll cross the **Edith Cavell Bridge** over the wild Shotover River, the site of many former gold workings. It is to this point you'll come for the Shotover jet boat rides (see section 7). Just opened below the bridge is **Cavells Restaurant,** which has a licensed bar as well as good food. Sit on the patio and watch the jet boats flash by. You will also see rafters arriving through the nearby Oxenbridge Tunnel. In the distance, you might catch sight of the skier's Elysian snow fields, **Coronet Peak** (5,413 feet). A connecting road will take you up there, if you want. In the spring and summer, when the Coronet skiers have gone home, you can ride the Cresta Run, a 600-yard stainless-steel toboggan ride, a thrilling ride for $6 a run. Avoid driving yourself along another side road into **Skippers Canyon,** a narrow and dangerous road for the inexperienced. There are tours to this area, though (see Section 7).

Close to Arrowtown is the aforementioned **Millbrook Resort,** on the right-hand side. It is New Zealand's first dedicated golf resort and is hailed as the N.Z. Tourism industry's flagship. The course has been designed by the notable Kiwi lefthander, Bob Charles—he's certainly well known on the PGA circuit. If you go there, please let us hear about it.

At **Arrowtown,** be sure to have a look at the tiny miners' cottages remaining under the tall, leafy sycamore trees at the end of the main street. It's a particularly colorful scene in the fall when the renowned *Arrowtown Autumn Festival* gets underway. The cottages are a favorite subject for painters and photographers at that time of year. Nearby is the small, well-organized **Lake District Museum** (entrance about $3). Another interesting excursion in the area is to the recently excavated Chinese camp at the far end of the town near the river.

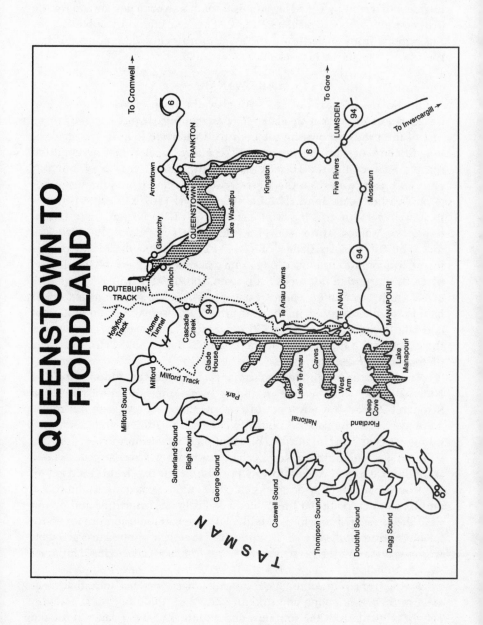

QUEENSTOWN TO
FIORDLAND

To Cromwell →
6
Arrowtown
FRANKTON
QUEENSTOWN
Glenorchy
Lake Wakatipu
Kingston
ROUTEBURN
TRACK
Kinloch
Hollyford Track
Homer Tunnel
Cascade Creek
94
Glade House
Milford Track
Milford
Milford Sound
Sutherland Sound
Bligh Sound
George Sound
Caswell Sound
Thompson Sound
Doubtful Sound
Dagg Sound
National
Park
Lake Te Anau
Caves
Te Anau Downs
TE ANAU
West Arm
Deep Cove
Fiordland
Lake Manapouri
MANAPOURI
94
Mossburn
Five Rivers
6
LUMSDEN
94
To Gore →
To Invercargill →

TASMAN

If you want, you can return to Q'town on a slightly different route, using Highway 6. It runs by **Lake Hayes,** a fisherman's favorite destination for the brown trout in uneasy residence there. The Red London Double Decker Bus departs from Queenstown to Arrowtown twice a day, and could be a fun way to take in the little town.

LAKE WANAKA

On the grassy shores of Lake Wanaka, the town of **Wanaka** is a slow-paced resort popular with many New Zealanders. It just happens to be one of the prettiest towns in the country, with more than its fair share of magnificent surrounding scenery. Like many travelers, we overnighted there after crossing the **Haast Pass** over the Southern Alps on our way east to Queenstown from the West Coast. Encircled by mountains, it has good weather year-round. The **Lakeview Motel** (Tel. 443-7029) is under new management and has wonderful views of Wanaka and the mountains. The **Wanaka Motor Inn** (Tel. 443-8216) costs from $125 for a studio. The **Te Wanaka Lodge** (Tel. 443-9224 or 0800-92-62-52; Web site http://nz.com.webnz.bbnz.wlodge.htm) has two lounges, an open fireplace, and a garden hot tub. Cost is from $110-125 for two.

Glendhu Bay Station Farm Cottages (Tel. 443-7055) are an excellent base for fishing, boating, hiking, and are set amidst magnificent mountain and lake scenery. Cost is from $50-70 per night for two persons. Towards the other end of the accommodations scale is the Wanaka YHA, with rates of about $15-18 a night.

Wanaka is also the headquarters for the nearby **Mount Aspiring National Park,** which features tramping over some wild countryside. You can climb Mount Roy, just out of town, via a moderately strenuous trail if you have a free afternoon. American writer John Anderson, at least, recommends that exercise for the "phenomenal" view from the top.

Wanaka is one of those New Zealand towns where you can feel isolated from the real world. We got up one morning in our hotel and could get no news on the radio. Only one weak station could be coaxed into the room, and that was carrying the Junior Request Program. Instead of finding out what the latest crisis was in the Middle East, we had to be content for about an hour with the "Story of Thumbelina." The radio waves are probably stronger now, but not too strong, we hope. Wanaka's charm has a lot to do with its isolation.

Driving from Wanaka to Queenstown, or vice versa, be aware that there are two roads—one long and smooth (Route 6), the other short and very rough, particularly at the southern end (Route 89). We've taken both and have decided that from here on we'd rather save our axles and our synapses than the 30 miles' difference. If you do insist on 89 (the Crown Range Road), however, be sure to have a look at **Cardrona,** the ghost town along the way. And don't go by the **Cardrona Pub** without a look-in. The facade has not changed in 100 years, and the rooms inside have heaps of personality. (But we're not kidding about the route; it's a toughie, and nearly always either dusty or muddy, too.) On the other road, keep your eyes open for **The Maze and Puzzle Centre** (Tel. 443-7489). You can lose yourself in here for a happy hour or more, finding your way around a two-story maze and then investigating the weird tilting room and the hologram display. When you finally find your way out, you may be ready for Devonshire tea, served on the premises. After the strawberry jam and cream-topped scones you may be ready to tackle the puzzle center, which owner Stuart Landsborough proclaims with pride is the largest in the world. Stuart doesn't charge any extra when you have a bash at the puzzles on open display.

Route 6, though longer, can be literally delicious, as it passes through the orchard country around **Cromwell.** Depending on the season, you may find lots of goodies for sale along the highway. An interesting new sightseeing possibility near Cromwell is the impressive **Clyde Dam.** Early in 1992 it began filling the future Lake Dunstan, and in 1993 boating, fishing, and other recreational pursuits started to make their way there. If *you* do, we would be interested to know how you found it all.

Wanaka has a surprising number of restaurants for a small town. One we tried and liked was **Ripples** (Tel. 443-7413) on the main street. We have also had good reports of **Relishes Cafe** (Tel. 443-9018) on Ardmore Street by the lake.

TE ANAU AND VICINITY

Part of this same lake country and Fiordland playground, the village of Te Anau, at the southern end of Lake Te Anau, seems to draw as many summertime visitors as Queenstown. It is generally regarded as the gateway to Fiordland. It takes about three hours to drive there via routes 6 and 94 from Q'town.

The town also houses the headquarters for **Fiordland National Park** (Tel. 249-7921), and it is to this building you should report if you're going to do the Milford Track as a "freedom walker." This hotel and the guided Milford Track walk are operated by the Helicopter Line and a Queenstown-based company called Trojan Holdings. Other good accommodations are at the Luxmore Resort Hotel and the Edgewater XL Motel. Rates for both are around $75 double. **The Village Inn** (Tel. 249-7911) is one of Te Anau's newest and best and offers a choice of kitchen or serviced units. Rates range from $115 to $179 double.

For good meal values, we like the Grubstake Restaurant. The Jintz at Te Anau Motor Park comes recommended. The Pizzeria, which has a genuine Italian chef, is a favorite of the locals, who swear by the pasta and pizzas. For $15 it's a good filler-upper.

A reader has recommended **Kepler's Restaurant** (Tel. 249-7909) as a good'un. It takes its name from the Kepler Track, one of the newer of Fiordland's famous tracks. It starts and finishes at Lake Te Anau. We'll give you more details on New Zealand's incomparable treks later in this chapter.

Guided excursions are run from Te Anau to the glow worm caves, to Lake Manapouri, and other places. You can book these and almost anything else from the Mount Cook Airlines office, near the Travelodge; it acts almost as an official tourist office for the community. **Fiordland Travel,** across the street, also has several good tours of its own (see section 7). A cruise on the lake gives the first hint of Fiordland's beauty.

THE TRIP TO MILFORD SOUND

New Zealand's most famous natural feature is generally reached by land from Te Anau, on a 75-mile road you'll never forget. You can bus or drive it round trip, or you can bus out of the sound after walking in via the Milford Track or flying in from Queenstown or Te Anau. (See the next section.) No matter how you go to Milford, though, take (a) insect repellent ("Dimp" is probably the best N.Z. brand) and (b) some kind of wet-weather gear. Milford Sound has more sand flies and rain than any other spot in the country.

By road, follow Highway 94 out of Te Anau along the lake, then through the Eglinton and Hollyford Valleys and via the tunnel to Cleddau Valley.

Just out of Te Anau, photographers often like to stop at the **Mirror Lakes,** which reflect the mountains in smooth, almost perfect symmetry. While driving along this part, you may see **Disappearing Mountain,** an optical illusion that makes the peak at the end of the road seem to grow smaller as you approach. Also, look for **The Chasm,** some unusual, near-vertical rapids about 300 yards off the road after the **Homer Tunnel.**

Milford Sound was described by no less an observer than Rudyard Kipling as "the eighth wonder of the world." It is a magnificent fiord that resulted when a canyon was carved by a prehistoric glacier, and the sea was admitted only after the ancient ice finally melted away.

The Milford Wanderer Overnight Cruise (Tel. 249-8090 or 0800-65-65-01; Web site http://fiordlandtravel.co.nz) is the ideal way to see the Milford Sound. The lovely old sailing scow takes its passengers on a scenic cruise with wildlife viewing and an onboard nature guide, kayaking, and walks ashore. She offers comfortable bunk accommodations, and a hearty evening meal and breakfast are included. Cost is $125. Day cruises are also available.

Milford Sound Lodge (Tel. 249 8071) has twin, triple, and bunk rooms at a reasonable price. There is a restaurant and bar and communal kitchen, lounge, and dining room. There are coach connections for there to the Routeburn, Greenstone, Holyford, and Kepler tracks, and to Te Anau and Queenstown. Cost is from $18-22.50 per person.

Although you can easily walk from the hotel to the spectacular, 500-foot **Bowen Falls,** most of Milford Sound—including lots of other waterfalls and hanging valleys—cannot be appreciated without taking one of the narrated boat tours. Fiordland Travel also runs the M.V. *Milford Haven,* which accommodates about 300 passengers. Lunch is served on board, and the delicious local crayfish is on the menu. The vessel leaves at 1 P.M., and the cost is $49. The same company also operates a combination of coach and cruise to Milford Sound, and a third option of flightseeing and cruising up the Sound. A high-speed jet boat, the *Milford Jet,* is also part of Fiordland Travel's fleet.

You can personally call in on Fiordland Travel at its Queenstown office on Steamer Wharf, or telephone at 442-7500. We took the two-hour Tourism Milford "Red Ride" cruise because it was included in our Milford Track excursion, but we've heard no discouraging words about the others. A big catamaran from Scotland is now doing the Red Boat run. It has obligingly changed its name from *Lady of the Loch* to *Lady of the Sound.*

If you've managed to experience Milford Sound without rain, put on that gear you brought anyway. Those boats are going to drive right up under **Stirling Falls,** and it's no fun unless you're standing on deck!

7. Guided Tours and Cruises

As we mentioned, the Queenstown area has so many group adventures that the very number and variety of choices make for a lot of potential confusion. They're run by several different companies, from big firms to small, individual operators. Rather than list these by companies, we group them here into the types of activities and break them down logically within those groups.

Visit the Queenstown Visitor Network Centre, on the corner of Shotover and Camp Streets (Tel. 442-4100), or the Destination Queenstown Web site, http://www.queenstown-nz.co.nz.

Following the Queenstown-based tours, we'll list the main ones leaving from Te Anau. (Keep in mind that during the busiest periods some special excursions and combinations of these may also be organized. During the winter, some of these activities may be canceled.)

VESSELS ON THE LAKE

• The most famous cruise on the waters of Wakatipu is, of course, aboard *T.S.S. Earnslaw,* a smoke-belching, Swiss-style, "twin-screw steamer" (which explains the "T.S.S."), built in 1912. A one-hour lunchtime cruise costs about $35. Then there's a three-hour afternoon cruise at $45 that calls at the **Walter Peak High Country Station,** on the other side of the lake. Here's the chance to see the famous New Zealand sheep dogs in action. You'll watch someone shear a sheep, and if you are brave you will jump on the back of one of the shaggy-faced Highland cattle for a trot round the yard. Walter Peak is famous for its pikelets and scones, piled with strawberry jam and served in the comfort of the Colonel's Homestead Restaurant. The original house was destroyed by fire, but it has been faithfully rebuilt with an authentic eye to detail.

There is a morning trip to Walter Peak that departs at 9:30 A.M., April through October, but it is by launch rather than steamer. Evening dining at the Colonel's is memorable and the cost, including the trip there and back via the *Earnslaw,* is $49. Bookings at Fiordland Travel on the Steamer Wharf can be made by calling 442-7500.

JET BOATS—AND HELICOPTERS

The Hamilton jet, a New Zealand invention, is a thrilling boat with an unusual design. It draws only three inches of water and works by means of a turbine system, sucking water in and throwing it out the rear with force enough to propel the boat through shallow water at speeds as high as 50 mph. The craft is highly maneuverable and can make sudden stops and starts—all features used to advantage in making the excursion as exciting as possible.

But look out, because there are so many competing jet boat operations now, set up in combination with buses, helicopters, etc., that it is just plain confusing. Competition in the jet boat biz is tough, so there will no doubt be some changes by the time of your Q'town adventure. Here is the situation as it exists at this writing, anyway. (Get the latest refinements over the counter at travel agencies in the town center.)

• The most thrilling ride—maybe a little *too* thrilling for the faint-hearted—is the original *Shotover Jet* (Tel. 442-2764). The 30-minute ride itself, with the skillful driver seeming to avoid outcroppings of rocks only at the last second, is along the often narrow upper gorge of the Shotover River, at about the point where it is crossed by the Edith Cavell Bridge. We loved it in 1979 and we loved it again in 1984, and—swallowing that lump in our throats—we might even go again. A safety point to remember is that the *Shotover Jet* has the exclusive permit to operate in its area, so there's no chance of screaming around a corner and running into another jet boat. Allow about an hour, counting a courtesy bus from Queenstown (or you can join it at the river). At this writing, the fare to frighten yourself silly is about $69. Treble the fun by booking into the Shotover Triple Challenge. For around $165 you shoot down the Shotover in the jet boat, soar overhead in the helicopter, and whack down the rapids in the raft.

• On the somewhat more peaceful Kawarau River is **The Kawarau Jet** (Tel. 442-6142). The vessel leaves from the Queenstown jetty so that it first covers a patch of Lake Wakatipu; then, like a crazed motorized salmon, seemingly shoots over the dam to finish off the experience on the scenic Kawarau River. The price for the one-hour trips floats at around $59 or so.

• There is also a variation that goes first to the Kawarau River and then finishes on the lower Shotover; it's called, naturally enough, the **Twin Rivers Jet** (Tel. 442-3257). Like some of the others, it starts on the lake and jumps the dam, but then it buzzes up and down the two rivers. The boat trip lasts about 90 minutes total, and the fare runs about $65.

• You can also combine jet boats and helicopters. We have mentioned the Shotover Triple Challenge above. **Glacier Southern Lakes Helicopters** (Tel. 377-8972 or 0800-80-16-16) can do you the whole package. Prices are on application depending on the combination. **Helijet** (Tel. 442-2239) is another option.

A trip with appeal is the **Dart River Safari** (Tel. 446-9992), a five- or six-hour adventure that drinks in the superb Dart River scenery at the head of Lake Wakatipu. It is not cheap, but is worth every dollar. There is also a combination "funyak" trip. Funyaks are inflatable canoes and you travel by bus from Queenstown to Glenorchy, take a jet boat ride, paddle a funyak, and have lunch. The trip costs $130. Most trips call into the Glenorchy pub for "afters," so don't count on an exact time for getting home.

WHITEWATER RIVER RAFT TRIPS

Queenstown is the self-proclaimed rafting capital of New Zealand. Several companies provide competing trips on both the Shotover and Kawarau Rivers, which have varying grades of whitewater rapids. (Rapids are graded from one, which is easy, to six, which is unraftable.)

The Kawarau River has grade three and four water, while the Shotover boasts five and six. The rapids go by such fascinating names as "the Mother," "Jaws," and the "Chinese Dog Leg." In most cases they have been named by rafting guides with humor to spare. And on the subject of guides, these young men and women are fully trained professionals who work to a strict code of guidelines and ethics. Rarely does anything go wrong. But with a sport of this nature, there is obviously some risk.

Dane's Shotover Rafts (Tel. 442-7318) is the oldest company operating, and their trips on the Shotover and Kawarau compete with **Kiwi Discover** (Tel. 442-7341). There doesn't appear to be much to choose between these companies—they offer similar products, similar prices, and are both well respected. In the end it will probably come down purely to your own convenience. Prices depend on what package you choose.

Extreme Green Rafting (Tel. 442-8517) includes helicopters, Shotover Jet, and bungee in its packages. Prices are from $79 to $320. Each offers a similar experience, and there is a mind-boggling mix of adventure trips that includes rafting. Any combination goes, and one of the most exciting is the Awesome Foursome, which has to be the thrill-seeker's ultimate dream. It starts with a leisurely coach trip to a helipad on the Coronet Peak ski-field road. From there the fun begins with a helicopter (locally known as a "chopper") roller coaster run over Skippers Canyon to Deep Creek on the Shotover River. A jet boat takes over, whipping through the narrow canyon to the famous Skippers bungee-jumping bridge. The 270-foot jump from the bridge to the river below connects you with a raft to beat the rapids down to the Oxenbridge Tunnel. The whole experience takes just over five hours.

Another rafting-type sport is river boarding, taking to the rapids on a boogie board (make sure you wear a helmet). You can try this mad and exhilarating sport with **Mad Dog River Boarding** (Tel. 442-3310); **Frogz Have More Fun** (Tel. 443-9130 or 0800-338-737 or 0800-338-738); or **Serious Fun River Surfing** (Tel. 442-5262). Prices are to either side of $100.

Book at any of the rafting company offices or booking offices in town. Make sure to check on the condition of the rivers. Things may not be as exciting when the water is very low, or may be *too* exciting when the rapids are running high and fast.

OTHER WATER TRIPS

There are lots of other things to do on the waters of the southern South Island. **Glacier Explorers** (Tel. 435-1077) takes inflatable boats to explore the huge dripping iceface of the Tasman Glacier. You can touch the icebergs and taste 500-year-old ice. Price on application. **Glacier Discoveries** (Tel. 435-1890) includes a hike exploring the inlets and bays of the Mueller Glacier Lake from $45.

To plunge down water-polished chutes, abseil down waterfalls, climb, swim, slide, and float through a spectacular green world of sculpted rock and sparkling, crashing cascades, you need to talk to **Deep Canyon Experience** (Tel. 443-7922). They will whisk you in and out by helicopter to and from the Matukituki Valley. Cost is from $145 and includes a gourmet lunch.

Vertigo Canyoning (Tel. 0800-8220999) offers a similar experience, although this particular company rates its programme as "challenging" and it is interesting to note that tours are accompanied by "swiftwater rescue qualified guides" (?!) **Funyaks** (Tel. 442-7374) we mentioned previously. You can check them out on www.funyaks.com and see for yourself their altogether more civilized and gentle programme. **Pioneer Rafting** (Tel. 443-1246) offers a combination of adventure and ecology and includes gold panning, photography, wildlife, and Manuka tea. Cost is from $85.

SOME BUS TOURS FROM QUEENSTOWN

Two land-based trips to see some rugged scenery and deserted mine workings are particularly exciting. **Skippers Canyon** is a three-hour, $55 excursion with Gray Line Tours (Tel. 442-4600), whose buses depart from their own terminal on Church Street. There are twice-daily departures, and you can try your gold-panning hand en route.

Try the **Milford Backroad Bus Adventure** (Tel. 442-7504) but be prepared to have the wits scared out of you as the bus crawls along some one-lane dirt roads cut into the sides of precipitous cliffs a thousand feet or more over the Shotover River. We tried a similar trek and we loved it, at least in retrospect. But once was enough! **The Milford Sound Barbecue Bus** (Tel. 442-0213) also sounds interesting. Let us know if you try it.

Full-day excursions to **Milford Sound** are offered by a half-dozen competing coach tours; they run around $155 round-trip from Queenstown. Most include a launch cruise on the sound itself. Check out **Milford Sound Daytime Cruises** (Tel. 249-7022); **Milford Sound Flightseeing** (fly-cruise-fly) at 442-2748; or **Milford Sound Red Boats** (Tel. 441-1197). Don't be confused if the same telephone numbers pop up under different options in Queenstown. A lot are run by the same company, under a different department.

Intercity is one such coach company, and their deal includes a gondola ride. Sounds like fun. There is only one trip from Queenstown to **Doubtful Sound;** a 12-hour excursion by Fiordland Travel with a price tag of $138. This includes two boat cruises (on Lake Manapouri and on the sound) and a visit to the electric generating station (probably a more popular trip for New Zealanders familiar with the story of the power project than for foreigners).

Buses also run daily from Queenstown to and from the Walking Tracks at the head of the lake. **Backpacker Express** (Tel. 442-9939) drops trampers at the start of the Routeburn for $22, at the Rees and Dart for $25, and at the Greenstone and Caples Tracks for $25. The services operate daily to and from the tracks during the walking season. A new tour with flavor is the **Queenstown Wine Trail** (Tel. 442-3799), which visits the world's southernmost vineyards. The four-hour trip calls by three vineyards named Taramea, Chard Farm, and Gibbston Valley. It also stops by the Kawarau bungee bridge en route.

"FLIGHTSEEING" FROM QUEENSTOWN

"Warbirds over Wanaka" is New Zealand's big airshow. If you're in New Zealand around April, check out the dates for the current display—usually over the Easter weekend. (Web site www.nzfpm.co.nz; e-mail wow@skyshow.co.nz.)

Breathtaking views of areas inaccessible by car or bus are offered by **Air Fiordland** (Tel. 442-3404) from around $75. Spectacular Fiordland and Milford Sound slide away under the wing tips in a far different way than how you see them off the deck of a boat. You can also take a day package combination that includes boating, coaching, jet boating, and flying (Phew!).

Combinations are also offered by **Glacier Southern Lakes Helicopters** (Tel. 377-8972 or 0800-80-16-16) for a price to be discussed with them first.

Aspiring Air (Tel. 443 7943) also does the scenic adventure thing, whisking you away across the Southern Alps with Mt. Aspiring and Mt. Cook reaching up and then across Milford Sound. Cost is between $65 and $415. So too does **Milford Sounds Scenic Flights** (Tel. 442 3065 or 0800-101-767). **Southern Lakes Helicopters** (Tel. 442-3016) and **Air Wakatipu** (Tel. 442-3048) could also be worth checking out for the flight-seeing adventures, as well as **Over the Top** (Tel. 442-3299) helicopter tours, which will also take you fishing.

Those daring young men do magnificent things in their flying machines at **Actionflite Aerobatics** (Tel. 442-2016) and **Biplane Adventures** (Tel. 443-1000 or 0800-47-59-74). Actionflite will flip you about on an aerobatic scenic flight, and if you know which way is up you'll see some magnificent flights. Cost is from $165, and this activity is rated from "moderate to extreme." If the "extreme" bit bothers you, talk to Wayne or King first. However, Biplane Adventures (from $170) describes their activity as "moderate to challenging," and if the "challenging" bit bothers you as much as the "extreme," maybe this sort of flightseeing is not your thing. Those who do take it up, however, won't regret it.

We can't finish this section without letting you know about parapenting, a sort of parachute hang-gliding. It's done from the top of hills around Queenstown in the company of a professional. We can't pass on personal experience yet. For information, contact **Queenstown Tandem Parapentes** (Tel. 025-324-663).

Speaking of parachuting, you can jump over the **Remarkables. Skydive Tandem** (Tel. 021-325-961) will be with you all the way, at prices from $245. **Skydive Wanaka** (Tel. 443-7207) also offers the big jump from $225.

SOME EXCURSIONS FROM TE ANAU

Like Queenstown, Te Anau offers tours on land, water, and in the air. The **Te Anau Visitor's Centre** (Tel. 249-7921), run by the Department of Conservation (DOC) on the lakefront, is a great starting point for information for visitors. While on the subject of DOC, this switched-on government department runs commendable summer trips into New Zealand's national parks. They cost next to nothing and rate among some of the best nature trips the country has to offer. Contact DOC in Auckland, Wellington, or in the various National Park headquarters.

There are two types of tours of the underground power station across Lake Manapouri, both offered by **Fiordland Travel** (Tel. 0800-65-65-01). The half-day **West Arm Manapouri** tour skims across the lake and then drives by bus into the station for about $57. The all-day tour, or the **Heart of Fiordland Triple Trip,** includes the West Arm power station visit, a bus trip over Wilmot Pass to Doubtful Sound, and a cruise on the sound itself. It is run by Fiordland Travel and costs around $130. Doubtful Sound has one of the finest rain forests in the world, and it's well worth making time on your itinerary to visit it.

Backroads Bus Adventures (Tel. 442-7504) which you've already come across in Queenstown, also has an office in Te Anau.

Adventure Charters Kayak and Cruise (Tel. 249-6626) also take you around Lake Manapouri. They'll guide you, or you can take off on your own. All gear is supplied. **Fiordland Wilderness Experience** (Tel. 249-7700) also offers sea and lake kayaking, with guided trips from one to six days. **Fiordland Ecology Holidays** (Tel. 249-6600) take a maximum of 12 people on their sailboat for three- to seven-day (longer by request) voyages around Fiordland. You can swim with sea lions and dolphins, snorkel, dive, visit historic sites, and hike. Price is $165 per person per day. Berths are also available on scientific research ships.

Waterwings Airways (Tel. 249-7405) offers three sightseeing flights: a 10-minute seaplane run to **Hidden Lakes,** which also hops over to South Fiord; a 35-minute flight to **Doubtful Sound** that covers nearly everything else in the area; and **Catch a Crayfish.** On the "Catch a Crayfish" tour ("crayfish" being "lobster" to Americans), you take a four-hour tour by a Waterwings float plane to Doubtful Sound to transfer to a licensed cray-fishing vessel. As you cruise to the fishing ground you pass at close hand seals, penguins, and, on most days, friendly dolphins. At the crayfish beds you catch your own crayfish with a cray pot and enjoy the fruits of your labours with champagne for lunch. You also get to take some crayfish with you. The tour departs twice a day, and costs $475 per person. You can still fly over Milford Sound on the **Milford Sound Overhead Flight,** taking in

Milford Sound, Tutoko Glaciers, Sutherland Falls, and the Milford Track. The tour lasts one hour and costs $187. Being float planes, these aircraft can land you in places inaccessible in any other way, so you can be sure you've seen a part of the world that very few other people have, and that's something to treasure. Cost is on application.

THE MILFORD TRACK

In every vacation destination, there is always one special achievement— the kind of thing that not quite everyone can do, but that provides the ultimate experience the area has to offer. In Hawaii, it's hiking through the crater at Mount Haleakala; in Australia, it's climbing Ayers Rock; and in New Zealand, it's walking the Milford Track.

"The Finest Walk in the World" is the traditional appellation, the echo of a breezy British headline of 100 years ago. However, it should not be considered merely a "walk" at all. It's a three-day, 33-mile, sometimes grueling hike from the northern tip of Lake Te Anau, through the Clinton Canyon, over the 3,400-foot McKinnon Pass, and down through the Arthur Valley to Milford Sound. Despite what you've been told, it is not "easy," and it should not be approached without a certain amount of research and advance preparation.

There are two ways to do the track. One is as a "freedom walker," but you have to book huts and boats and pay before you go. Book through the **Centra Te Anau** (Tel. 249-7411) or the **Te Anau Visitors Centre** (Tel. 249-8900). If you are in Queenstown you can book at the **Great Sights Track Information Centre** (Tel. 442-9708) on Shotover Street. For details and rules, write to P.O. Box 29, Te Anau, New Zealand.

We did the Milford Track the *other* (which is not to say *simple*) way, as members of the five-day group tours conducted over the same route by the Tourist Hotel Corporation. The walk is now in the hands of new owners, but follows the same format. Now known as the **Milford Track Guided Walk** (Tel. 441-1138 or 0800-659-255), the experience consists of groups of about 40 with at least three departures a week beginning about November. From early December the walks depart almost every day except Sunday. The last walks leave early April, and then the track hibernates through to spring.

The cost is around $2000 (just under half that for children), and includes packs and ponchos, transportation by bus and by boat across the lake to the point where the track begins, three nights at special hostels along the track, all meals, transportation by water again from Sandfly Point at the end of the track to Milford, a last night's stay in the Milford Hotel, and the long Red Ride cruise on Milford Sound the following morning. It does *not* include transportation from Milford back to Te Anau or other destinations, for which you'll have to book a bus. (It would be a good idea to do that at the same time you make your track reservations.)

After the half-day by bus from Te Anau and boat across Lake Te Anau to the hut at the beginning of the track, the hike itself takes three days. On the first real walking day (called "Day 2" in the package), the track goes for 10 miles, and all but the last mile or so is over relatively flat territory through woods and clearings, largely along the Clinton River. The second day is the toughest, but certainly the greatest; it's another 10 miles, but it includes the steep ascent and descent of McKinnon Pass. The third day features 13 miles of walking, but again over relatively level land in Arthur Valley. Day four is mostly downhill, before the final night is spent at Milford with the launch trip before returning to Te Anau.

Whether you are a freedom walker or a trekker, you may get closer to nature than you've ever been. The most attractive benefits of this experience include such rewards as learning the call of the bellbird; making your way through moss-green forests, waving grasslands, and interesting swamps; coming across dramatic waterfalls and clear, silent lakes; and even feeding the almost-tame keas (New Zealand parrots) at the top of the pass.

But the trek also includes exposure to the awesome aspects of the wild—facing the almost inevitable rain showers, helping each other ford swollen streams, and fighting against the high winds way up in the mountains. The Buerstatte family of Wisconsin related, "We hit the worst weather for this time of year on record . . . lifted by helicopter over the Pass . . . would do it again tomorrow if we could." They relate that there is a man from New York who does it every year, rain or shine.

In our own case, we began our second day in the dark of early morning and in the pouring rain, but there was no turning back. We were far behind schedule as we trudged the apparently endless zigzags above the tree line up to the pass. At the top, we tried to remember the words of others who have turned their gaze back to Clinton Canyon and ahead to Arthur Valley. One was the British author A. J. Harrop, who made the ascent in the early 1930s:

> "A superb panorama is seen from the top of the pass which lies between Mount Balloon on the east and Mount Hart on the west. The wild architecture of the mountains, rising in myriad shapes to the sky, capped by snow and scored by glaciers, has baffled the descriptive powers of a hundred writers, and we are content to gaze upon it, hoping to preserve in the mind's eye some at least of the details of this astonishing spectacle."

Don't be put off by the seemingly large groups. When you string 40 people out along several miles of trail, you'll find yourself as alone as you

MAVERICK GUIDE TO NEW ZEALAND

want to be, not a member of a stampeding herd. Most walkers gravitate to 3 or 4 people whose pace matches their own and find they are often exploring together with them. On other occasions, they still have the trail apparently to themselves.

Some of your party you will see only at the huts or hostels along the way, and there you will exchange tales of your day's experiences. On the final day, you will be exchanging addresses and promises to visit one another. The shared experience of walking the Milford Track is a guaranteed friend-maker, and some of these friendships may last a lifetime.

As soon as you know you're going to New Zealand, and if you want to take the trek, ask your travel agent to try for reservations (with alternate dates, if possible). Take what you can get, and schedule the rest of your trip around those dates. If you're not working through a travel agent, in the U.S. you might try for brochures and information through the N.Z. Tourism Board. In any case, do as much advance reading on the track as you possibly can, starting in the public library (look for the January 1978 *National Geographic* article). Most especially, read the excellent *New Zealand Milford Track Guide,* available from Air New Zealand, Qantas, or the N.Z. Tourism Board. This will tell you about good footwear, wool sweaters, and zillions of other things you'll want or need on the track, as well as answer scores of questions that potential track walkers have asked.

Try to find members of hiking clubs or other veterans of the track in your community to talk to. The **Department of Conservation** (Tel. 442-7933) in Queenstown has an excellent pamphlet on the Milford Track that is free of charge.

If you land in New Zealand *without* having made arrangements and you still want to walk the Milford Track, stop at the first tourist information office you can find, as soon as you arrive. Maybe there will be a cancellation around the date you want. Normally, departures are Monday, Wednesday, and Friday, but sometimes there will be additional departures on Tuesday, Thursday, or Saturday.

One more outfit to contact is **Bev's Tramping** (hiking to us) **Gear Hire** (Tel. 249 7389; e-mail bevshire@teanau.co.nz).

One last word about the Milford Track: Don't listen to anyone who says the track is a breeze or that "any normally active person" will have no trouble. That may be true for a lot of Kiwis. It was *not* true for at least one of us Yanks.

OTHER TRACKS IN FIORDLAND

Two other walking tracks nearby are almost as famous in New Zealand, and both may be taken independently or on conducted tours. The

Routeburn Track, a three- to five-day, 25-mile excursion, includes a 4,200-foot pass over the Humboldt Mountains linking the Dart and Hollyford Valleys. Conducted rates are about $950 (plus GST) for adults, and the track can be taken in either the northbound or southbound direction. For information contact the **Routeburn Guided Walk** (Tel. 442-8200), email routeburn@xtra.co.nz) There are three slightly different itineraries ranging from three to five days and you have the choice of flying or walking out at the end of the hike. Constance Roos of San Francisco says the crossing of the *Harris Saddle* is every bit as spectacular as the Milford Track's *Mackinnon Pass.*

The **Hollyford Track,** in the same vicinity, is also popular. Four- or five-day conducted walks are available from the **Hollyford Tourist & Travel Co. Ltd.,** P.O. Box 205, Wakatipu, New Zealand (Tel. 442-3760). There are two slightly different itineraries, depending on whether you choose to walk out or fly out at the end of the hike. All tours commence from Te Anau. Fly-out tours finish in Milford Sound, and walk-out tours finish at Te Anau.

Three other tracks are well worth the walking, and we list them here. They are **Greenstone Valley Track, Caples Track,** and **Rees/Dart Valley Track.** Freedom or guided walking is possible on most of them, with transport connections from the entrance and exit points. The **Destination Queenstown** (Tel. 442-7420; Web site http://www.queenstown-nz.co.nz) is a mine of useful information on these walks and everything else about visits to the area. They will give you comprehensive information on guided treks for each of the tracks above, and possibly others that we haven't discovered yet. Let us know if you walk your boots along one we should make tracks for.

There are Shell guides available that describe the Routeburn and Hollyford Tracks in detail. We would like very much to hear from readers who have walked the Milford Track, as well as either or both of the Routeburn and Hollyford Tracks. To date, we have not taken the latter two hikes. The N.Z. Tourism Board also recommends the Greenstone Walk, which links with the Routeburn Track. You can also speak to Richard Bryant at **Guided Walks NZ Ltd.** in Queenstown (Tel. 442-6722).

8. Water Sports

The world's principal water sport, swimming, is hardly practical in Queenstown, outside of the hotel pools. The deep, deep waters of Lake Wakatipu are quite cool most of the year. If it's a hot day, and you can't resist the sparkling waters of the lake, drive to Frankton before taking the plunge. The Frankton Arm, being shallower, is relatively warm. You can also try Lake Hayes, on the road to Arrowtown. The water is warm in the summer, and it's a peaceful picnic spot.

For fast, individual fun for the younger set, your jet boat hire is available from Fisherman's Pier by the marina at Frankton Road. No license is needed, by the way, just nerve. Windsurfing, Hobie-catting, and water-skiing on Lake Wakatipu are gaining some popularity. And we're not sure whether it comes under water sports or not, but parasailing—in a parachute pulled for about 10 minutes above the lake by a jet boat—is also available, although it is not a sport yet indulged in by us chickens. To take part in any of these things, just bring money and enough nerve, and let the Visitors Centre point you in the right direction.

Fishing in the neighborhood is excellent. After you have obtained your license, you can try for trout from October 1 to September 31 on Lake Wakatipu. River fishing is allowed from November 1 to May 31. Most visitors to New Zealand would be better off hiring a local guide. They were charging about $75 or so an hour, at last report, and they provide everything; equipment, transportation, and, best of all, the experience needed to know where to go and how to catch 'em. Better figure a minimum of about two hours for lake trolling or four hours for fly-fishing, since they have to take you right up to the head of the lake to one of the river mouths in the Glenorchy area. If you get a trout or one of those Quinnat freshwater salmon, you can bring it back to a hotel dining room, and they'll usually cook it for you. You can book fishing guides through any of the booking centers in town. The **Wakatipu Anglers Club** meets the first Tuesday of every month, and visitors are welcome. For information on where to join them, check with the Promotions Board or the booking centers. There is also excellent fishing on the rivers, but the season differs from the start of November or December until the end of May.

Fishing and Hunting Services (Tel. 443-9257; Web site http://www.flyfishhunt.co.nz) reckons they'll fnd the best stream, river, or lake for your fishing pleasure. Try also Michael Bedner at **Southern Cross Fly Fishing** (Tel. 249-7249) or Ken Cochrane at **Southern Trout Fly Fishing** (Tel. 442-9404).

9. Other Sports

There are three sets of golf links in the immediate vicinity of Queenstown. The main one is the **Queenstown Golf Club** (Tel. 442-9169), an 18-hole course in Kelvin Heights, just across the Frankton Arm from the Queenstown Tourist Gardens. Greens fees are about $20 per duffer. You can also rent clubs and a "trundler" to carry them with. Interestingly, it's

11 miles by road, but you can get a jet boat water taxi to take you across in just a few minutes (get their phone number before you disembark). When you've finished, pick up the phone, call the number, and the boat will be back to pick you up.

There's also the very flat, 9-hole **Frankton Golf Course** (Tel. 442-3584) near the airport, and the 18-hole **Arrowtown Golf Course.** No reservations are needed.

Tennis anyone? There are two courts available in the **Queenstown Tourist Gardens** at minimal cost. Rackets are for rent at **Queenstown Sports Ltd.** There are also squash courts adjacent to the Memorial Hall.

Yes, there is horseback riding available from Queenstown. Trail rides have been set up by **Moonlight Stables** (Tel. 442-1229) on half-day plans (about three hours) for around $65. Trails go up the Shotover Gorge to the old gold mining areas of Moonlight Valley. Trips are guided, and they say no experience is needed for that one. Another outfit that caters to riders who *have* been on horses before is the **Shotover Stables** (Tel. 442-7486). **NZ Backcountry Saddle Expeditions** (Tel. 443-8151) has a gorgeous bunch of Appaloosas.

A. J. Hackett's name may have made its way into your vocabulary by now. He perfected the thrill-seeker experience called **bungee jumping,** using the Eiffel Tower and the French Alps to get it right. Now hundreds are queuing to take the plunge off the historic Kawarau Bridge and the even higher Skippers Canyon Bridge. Walter Almon, who wrote us a good account of his travels in New Zealand, took the bungee plunge and sounds like he'd do it again. He is one of the more than 100,000 proud people who have jumped from the Kawarau Bridge, 143 feet above the river. Many thousands have so far bungied from Skippers. Walter has a certificate to prove he's done it, and he says you can have your daring feat recorded on film. For $30 can have the photographer on hand take the picture. An 80-year-old has done it and loved it, but even if it is not your thing, you should at least go along to watch the men and women who dive from the bridge, ankles firmly tied to the bungee rope so they can yo-yo ride through space. The telephone number to call is 442-7100. Cost is from $65. *Beware, however, if you have had eye surgery—some bungee jumpers have experienced displaced retinas.*

The latest sport to take off in Queenstown is *Rap Jumping*. The literal translation is to abseil forwards down a cliff face. It's not everyone's idea of fun, but it is another challenge for adventurers. It's $45 for this head-first thrill.

You can also try **Off Road Adventures** (Tel. 442-7858) for three-hour to three-day motor bike expeditions; **Cardrona Alpine Resort** (Tel. 443-7341) for mountain biking; or **The Adventure Centre** (Tel. 443-8174 or 0800-684-468) for everything else!

SKIING

Queenstown's principal winter sport is skiing, often on the 5,000-foot slopes of **Coronet Peak,** 11 miles out. Coronet Peak is like the Little Girl with the Curl. The slopes are treeless, avalanche-free, wide open, and sunny. But the same sun can be the area's downfall. Entire ski seasons have been ruined by too much sun. However, those problems are probably over with the installation of a multi-million-dollar snowmaking system. It debuted in 1991 and has proven its worth a thousand times over. Now skiing at Coronet is guaranteed, and skiers can book ahead with confidence that conditions, either manmade or natural, will be good. Snowmaking means a June opening, but the nicest conditions are usually from July through September. In good seasons they remain open into October for extended spring skiing. The August school holidays bring the crowds, when families from all over the country converge here.

One mile-long double-chair lift carries skiers from the restaurant area at the 3,800-foot level on up to the summit at around 5,413 feet. There's also a triple-chair lift serving a different area, a T-bar, and some poma lifts and rope tows on the beginners' slopes.

There's a ski school, and the ski patrol is on duty. You can rent just about anything you need to get on the slopes. All-day lift passes cost around $55 per adult. Rental equipment is $30, and a lesson costs about $30, too. The air temperature is seldom below freezing, and you'll find many skiers schussing happily along in light jackets or sweaters. Buses chug up and down from Queenstown frequently during the day, from major hotels and designated stops. You can drive up to the parking lot, but it's a practice that is discouraged by requiring chains on the tires.

Slopes and three chair lifts at Rastus Burn, a shady area 5,500 feet up in the Remarkables overlooking the village and about a half hour's drive from town, prolong the season considerably. A good base building has all kinds of facilities, including a *Penguin Club* for four-year-olds and up. There is an excellent creche (babysitting service) for little ones in downtown Queenstown. It works in with the ski hours, and you can call them at 442-9217.

The Remarkables is one of the few commercial ski areas to offer **cross-country and Nordic skiing,** although the Pisa Range to the north has a cross-country field. Once you have skied your heart out on these Queenstown slopes, the ski fields of Cardrona and Treble Cone just outside Wanaka are a feasible alternative for the day. The crème de la crème is **heliskiing.** New Zealand has pioneered this sport, the ultimate skiing experience. Two companies, **Southern Lakes Heliski** (Tel. 442-6222) and **Heli-Guides Heliski** (Tel. 442-7733 or 0800-123-HELISKI), run trips in the mountains around Queenstown and Wanaka. Skiers who have done it say it's unforgettable to ski untracked slopes and to be picked up at the bottom by "chopper." Expect to pay from $125 for a day out. That's about three powder ski runs plus lunch and refreshments.

10. Shopping in Queenstown

Let's face it. Q'town is not "downtown," and there are no department stores. Still, there are some attractive stores and a couple of unusual addresses for dedicated shophounds. Incidentally, you'll find souvenir and N.Z. product stores opening in Queenstown from 9 A.M. to 9 P.M. every day. Some boutiques and clothing stores close Sunday, but all shops in town are allowed by law to be open 24 hours. Only a few stay open 'round the clock.

Like all resort towns, there are those who come for a holiday and then decide to stay. One way to make a buck is to get into retail. This means some shops in Queenstown can come and go, but it also means that these kind of stores are bound to be interesting, perhaps a little off-beat, and nearly always staffed by interesting people.

Jim Robbi's **Artistry in Wood,** just a few kilometers out of town, reflects the true character of the area. Robbi and fellow artists are inspired by the magnificent scenery that surrounds Queenstown, and some of their work can be found at the Central Art Gallery. **The Mountaineer Shop** (Tel. 442-7460) sells leather coats, sheepskins, oilskins, and greenstone jewellery, and **O'Connells Shopping Pavilion** in Queenstown houses restaurants, bars, and shops under its attractive glass roof. You'll find it on the corner of Beach and Camp Streets. For some truly New Zealand gear, go to the **Canterbury Shop** for casual clothing and New Zealand rugby jerseys. **Action Down Under** is also here. It is the Queenstown brother of the Auckland and Christchurch shops of the same name, and you will find top-quality fashion sports clothing here.

Wander along the Queenstown Mall for most of your browsing for wool products, leather, suede, sheepskins, and all that are perennially the rage in Queenstown. If you've already been looking in the larger cities, you might be able to make some intelligent judgments on these materials here. For sheepskins and other enticing woolies, check out **Sheeps** (Tel. 442-7064), at 75 Beach Street. They post overseas. Lots of suede and leather products are available at **Settler's Mill** (Tel. 442-9248). Also, the **Craft Boutique** (Tel. 442-7054) displays some attractive wool and leather at 65 Beach Street (the Queenstown Bay Centre).

In the **Eureka Arcade,** in the center of Queenstown, is one of the city's best-equipped sporting-goods stores, **Bill Lacheny Sports** (Tel. 442-8438). Lacheny also rents out a lot of camping gear to those who don't want to be encumbered after they leave the wilderness. **Queenstown Sportsworld** (Tel. 442-8452), 17 Rees Street, is also considered a dependable outdoorsy address. For good secondhand sports gear, **Recycled Recreation,** at 27 Shotover, and **R and R Sport** (Tel. 442-7791), on the corner of Shotover and Reese, have excellent bargains. A good place to trade in anything you don't want to carry any further, Recycled Recreation also has shops in Christchurch and Dunedin.

Just opened at 4 Brecon Street is **Sheep Country,** which is the brainchild of Liz Smolenski. She is a spinner, weaver, and entrepreneur, and has combined her talents to open a "sound and light" show that spotlights sheep and wool. City dwellers will find her show both informative and professional. Liz sells woolen products on the premises as well as posting them overseas. Attractive woolen goods can also be found at **Aotea Souvenirs.** This shop stocks New Zealand mementos, and you will find it on Beach Street, opposite Earnslaw Wharf. On the sports clothing and equipment scene there's a heap of choice, which is not surprising in a town where there is an emphasis on the great outdoors. Try **Mountainworks** on Camp Street. They will equip you for adventure, and they also have guides willing to take you anywhere you may want to explore.

11. Entertainment and Night Life

There's plenty of action after dark, but the scene shifts season by season (sometimes week by week) and this is a little too quick a step for this guidebook. Most of the nighttime fun and frolic is geared to the younger set, and much of it will be booked into the established hotels.

There are several public bars that draw a happy, drinking crowd, and all provide some kind of music or entertainment on busy nights. The historic **Eichardt's Tavern,** at the waterfront end of the Queenstown Mall, has been there forever, which proves it must be a good thing. The Steamer Wharf has had a complete about face and is now full of bars and eateries. It is also the site of Queenstown's first casino (another is in the process of being built). Here you will find the restful and quietly elegant **Cigar Bar.** The **Bordeaux** wine bar, in the Mall, is also civilised.

For a taste of Ireland go to **Pog Mahones,** where you'll have a rollicking good time, the same kind of time you'll have at the bar in **Chico's** restaurant. About three miles out of town, there's another excellent pub, the **Arthur's Point Hotel** (Tel. 442-8352), enjoyed by locals and newcomers alike.

On the nightclub scene, try **The Edge,** which swings till very very late, in fact so late that it barely closes before it opens again! Another good choice is **The World.**

A favourite, if you can find it, is the **Bunker.** Small and cosy, with an open fire, it is Queenstown's worst-kept secret. You'll find it behind an unmarked wooden door on Cow Street. It might take some looking, but once you've found it you'll be glad you did.

Most restaurants feature live music some night of the week; check the local papers for the guest bands and vocalists.

Cultural activities are waxing, and a new commercial theatre is underway upstairs in The Mall. It should attract the talent. Movies are up-to-date and the movie house is the Memorial Hall. If the film is good you won't mind the seats.

You can now pick up all three national television channels in Queenstown and on ITV (Information Television and Video) screens in all the major accommodations houses, with freshly updated happenings in the area. The community also has two radio stations, "Resort Radio" (99 FM/1395 AM) and "Radio 92QFM." Radio New Zealand's National Program is transmitted to Queenstown. Three major daily papers (*Christchurch Press, Southland Times,* and *Otago Daily Times*) compete for readers in the region.

12. The Queenstown Address List

Automobile Association—A-Line Queenstown Motel, 13 Frankton Road (Tel. 442-7700); breakdown reports (Tel. 0800-500-222); road conditions (Tel. 0900-33-222).

Baby-sitting service—Queenstown Child Care, Brecon and Shotover Streets (Tel. 442-9217).

Bank—The Bank of New Zealand, Rees Street (Tel. 442-7325).

Bus information—Mount Cook Landlines (Tel. 442-4600).

Dry cleaners—High Peaks, Gorge Road (Tel. 442-8621).

Florist—Lakeview Nursery, Perkins Road (Tel. 442-3044).

Hospital or medical emergency—Queenstown Medical Centre, corner of Stanley and Shotover Streets (Tel. 442-7301).

Pharmacy—Wilkinson's, Queenstown Mall (Tel. 442-7313 a/h 442-9140).

Police—Queenstown Police Station, 11 Camp Street (Tel. 442-7900).

Post office—G.P.O., corner of Camp and Ballarat Streets (Tel. 442-7670).

Supermarket—The Mall (Tel. 442-7444).

Taxis—(Tel. 442-7888).

Visitor Information Centre—Queenstown Visitor Information (Tel. 442-4100).

10

Dunedin and
the Deep South

1. The General Picture

Dunedin is a relic of several periods of the past. Founded in 1848 by serious Presbyterian Scots, its religion and Highland cultural traits have survived in some measure to the present. Otago University, which opened its doors only two decades later, also continues to set a high intellectual tone for the town.

After gold was discovered in **Otago,** Dunedin captured—and for many years, held—a reputation as the largest, wealthiest city in New Zealand; at the same time, it became the financial and construction headquarters for the colony. Its richly ornate facades are evident everywhere today, a hundred years after they were conceived and built. Dunedin, said writer Errol Brathwaite, is "the most perfectly preserved Victorian city on earth."

Its citizens look back on a proud era of "firsts"—first in the country with gas lighting, first city with water mains, first to use hydroelectricity, first with steam trams and then with electric trams. For years its seven hills were traversed by cable cars that now survive only as museum pieces.

331

MAVERICK GUIDE TO NEW ZEALAND

Early in this century, with glittering memories of commercial wealth behind it, Dunedin became the country's leader in social welfare programs, setting the pace for the north to follow. Today it is an important port and manufacturing center.

Dunedin is the old Celtic name for Edinburgh, and although much of the city's high religious ambition was lost during the Gold Rush, its basic Scottish heritage has remained. The street names were taken straight from Edinburgh's, and there is a statue of the poet Robert Burns standing downtown. More modern manifestations include Dunedin's singularity as the sole city to distill whiskey in New Zealand, and as the home of a man you might meet, the last surviving kiltmaker in the country.

With a population of 116,000, Dunedin is the second-largest city on the South Island. It sits on Highway 1, which leads straight down the coast from Christchurch. That route also continues farther through dozens of agricultural towns, many with Scottish names, to the bustling little city of Invercargill (population 49,000) on the south coast of the South Island, considered by some to be the hub of the region. Actually, Invercargill is not quite on the shoreline. The distinction of the "southernmost point" goes to the nearby oyster-dredging center of Bluff, which is also the traditional jumping-off point for Stewart Island.

Stewart Island, should you get to know it well, could be the high point of a New Zealand trip, at least for outdoors people. Populated by fewer than 500 people, and boasting about 5 miles of paved road, it consists mainly of nothing more nor less than 700 square miles of rugged mountains, virgin forest, and scenic hiking trails.

2. Long-Distance Transportation

If you come in by air, you haven't landed at Dunedin at all, but at **Momona,** some 18 miles out, which is by far the greatest distance between touchdown and downtown of any New Zealand city. Unless you are part of a group of four or five, taxis into town are expensive. But other options are available. Look for **Ritchies Coach Lines** (Tel. 477-9238), a bus service that will take you into town in about 40 minutes for $12. There are two other companies that provide a similar $12 bus service, the **Dunedin Airport Shuttle** (Tel. 477-6611) and the **Airporter Express** (Tel. 476-2519). Otherwise try **Airport Shuttle City Taxis** (Tel. 479-6594).

Dunedin flights via the 737 jets of **Air New Zealand** (Tel. 479-6594) are nonstop to and from Christchurch (45 minutes), Wellington (70 minutes), and Invercargill (45 minutes). **Ansett New Zealand** (Tel. 477-0146 or 0800-800-146) also has direct flights from Dunedin to Invercargill, Christchurch, and Wellington.

Train Travel. There are three major train journeys to take in the South Island. The **Southerner** departs Christchurch daily at 8:15 A.M. and arrives in Dunedin at 1:59 P.M. and in Invercargill at 5:15 P.M. Fares are between $38 and $77, depending on what type of ticket you buy. The **Coastal Pacific** departs Christchurch daily at 7:30 A.M. and arrives at the top of the island at Picton at 12:50 P.M. Cost is between $31 and $73. Finally, the Trans Alpine takes passengers across to the rugged West Coast, departing from Christchurch daily at 9 A.M. and arriving in Greymouth at 1:25 P.M. Cost is between $41 and $81. This is a particularly scenic trip, and it is possible to make a round trip in a day for a $109 excursion fare. Contact **TranzRail** (Tel. 0800-802-802).

Bus Travel. Dunedin is served by **Intercity** (Tel. 477-8860) from several points north and south. From Christchurch, the Intercity bus will cost you $47. That's around 5 hours and 30 minutes on the road, whether you choose to travel via Gore or via Alexandra, by the way. (The Dunedin depot is on Cumberland Street, near the Early Settlers' Museum.)

Rental Cars. Look for **Hertz** (Tel. 477-7385) at the airport and at 59 Great King Street. **Avis** (Tel. 486-2780) is also parked at the airport, as well as at 25 Stafford Street. And **Budget** (Tel. 474-0428) has an airport counter as well as its headquarters at 101 Great King Street. Other firms that are probably offering competitively priced deals include **New Zealand Rent A Car** (Tel. 477-3895), and **Thrifty** (Tel. 477-7087). A company specializing in four-wheel-drive vehicles and vans is **Cross Country Rentals** (Tel. 477-9950) at 124 Andrew Street in Dunedin.

Except for rush hours, you'll find Dunedin driving a piece of cake, at least with a map in your lap. There are wide streets and an efficiently designed one-way system. You'll have to keep your wits in gear as you cruise over the hills, though.

3. Local Transportation

The public bus system is called **Citi Bus** (Tel. 477-2224). Buses run frequently Monday to Saturday, but don't count on frequent runs on Sundays. Most leave from the city square called the **Octagon** (where there is a DCT information office). Some go from the area they call the Exchange, where the stock exchange used to be some years ago, at the corner of Princes and High Streets. There's a "Shopper's Special" that offers cheaper fares between 10 and 3 weekdays.

Bus lines are named after features or streets at their farthest points. You would take the Gardens Service, for instance, to either the Botanical Gardens at the end of the line or to Otago University, which is on the way. Some bus lines change names and route numbers according to the direction they are going. Once the Opoho, Route 6 bus reaches Opoho, for example, then turns around and becomes the Shiel Hill, Route 5 bus, following the exact same route, but in reverse.

The service may be confusing to nonresidents, so if you're staying long in the city pick up a free book of timetables from the Civic Centre, Arthur Barnetts, or the Manor Place Office. Remember that Dunedin is very much an up-and-down city. You may want to take a bus to hilly areas that seem to be only a short distance away on the map, but turn out to be more suitable for goats than bipeds.

Taxis. You'll find cab ranks downtown, or you can order a taxi by phone. Three of the larger companies are **City Taxis** (Tel. 477-1771), **Call A Cab** (Tel. 477-7800), and **Dunedin Taxis** (Tel. 477-7777). The ride in from the airport to the city is about $48.

Dunedin also offers limousine transport. Call **Regency Stretch Limousine** (Tel.455-7221), and be prepared to pay $60 an hour for the service. During the weekend the hourly rate rises, and there's a further rise in price for the limo after 6 P.M.

4. Hotels and Motels of Dunedin

There are dozens of places to stay in Dunedin, and we have had some complaints about some accommodations in the city. We have excluded these establishments from the following recommended list, and, on the plus side of things, accommodations seem generally less expensive in Dunedin than in many other New Zealand tourist centers.

EXPENSIVE ACCOMMODATIONS IN DUNEDIN

At the top of our list is the **Abbey Lodge Inn** (Tel. 477-5380), and the choice is *not* merely alphabetical. You'll find it behind a cobbled courtyard at 900 Cumberland Street, not far from the Botanical Gardens. It has 38 international-class bedrooms, including suites and very comfortable motel units. Two white stucco buildings, including the original two-story *motel* plus a three-story *hotel* addition with individual balconies out back; an indoor heated swimming pool (the only place with a pool we found), in addition to a spa and sauna; Portraits Restaurant and Bar; several different kinds of bedrooms—some bargain basics, some luxurious and expensive; color tellies, fridges, and other conveniences in all rooms; fully equipped kitchen in the motel units; and lots of artificial wood paneling everywhere you look. Cost is from $80-270.

The **Albatross Inn** (Tel. 477-2727 or 0800-44-14-41) is in a beautiful Edwardian House (circa 1900) on a main street close to the city. It has just

8 comfortable rooms with private facilities, television, and phone, and some have cooking facilities. Breakfast is available. Cost is between $85 and $125 double.

Larnach Lodge (Tel. 476-1616; Web site www.larnachcastle.co.nz) is on the Otago Peninsular and part of Larnach Castle. There are 12 themed rooms with "spectacular views," dining is within the castle, and breakfast is in the historic stables. Cost is between $140-180. Ask about their out-of-season discounts.

The **Pacific Park Hotel** (Tel. 477-3374 or 0800-730-400) is about three quarters of a mile from the Octagon and overlooks Dunedin from a peaceful, leafy location above the city. You will find it at 22-24 Wallace Street. The property offers 48 hotel rooms and 8 one-, two- or three-bedroom units with kitchen facilities. The licensed restaurant has a great view; there are private tennis courts, miniature golf, and a trampoline; an outdoor picnic and barbecue area; and it is close to the Moana public swimming pool. Cost is $150 double.

If you are without a car and need a central location in Dunedin, perhaps the expanded **Southern Cross** (Tel. 477-0752), at 118 High Street, will fill the bill. Some years ago this place took over the century-old Grand Hotel, and part of the establishment has some museum-like interest. When we visited the address a while back, we were not impressed with the facilities, housekeeping, maintenance, or staff that we saw. Recently, however, the hotel has been considerably refurbished and enlarged, with new management. Rooms all have luxury amenities, including satellite television reception of American and Australian TV. There is a deli café that stays open around the clock from Thursday until Saturday and goes to bed at 12 P.M. the other days of the week. The Lobby Restaurant and Exchange Brasserie and bar are accompanied by Club 118, the hotel's own nightclub. The Southern Cross is the traditional hotel leader, and it's one of the most expensive places in town. Now part of Scenic Circle, it should be a safe bet. It certainly looks like a whole new establishment. Tariffs are between $191.25 and $309.40 for two persons.

Cargill's Motor Lodge (Tel. 477-7983), at 678 George Street, remains a favourite with regular visitors to Dunedin. It has a bar and dining rooms behind a street-front facade; floodlit cherry-tree garden in the rear, appealing in October and November when the blossoms check in; living units on two floors, some with skylight and all with amply proportioned rooms; TV, coffee, and tea, of course; fridges in the suites only; and 50 rooms. Rates are $112.50-195. Cargill's is a pleasant choice in the springtime.

Also on George Street, at number 590, is the **Allan Court Motel** (Tel. 477-7526), with its own expensively furnished kitchens, 18 units, and rates of $92-120 double.

The **Boutique Hotel** (Tel. 477-1155 or 0800-515-155) offers 42 individually decorated rooms, à la carte restaurant and JW's café and bar, and is close to public transport. The cost is $95 double.

MEDIUM- TO LOW-BUDGET ACCOMMODATIONS

On one trip to Dunedin, we stayed in the **Alcala Motel** (Tel. 477-9073 or 0800-503-883), which was pleasant for the price. It's in a convenient location at the corner of George and St. David Streets, has modern stucco with Spanish arches over three floors around a brick court, and a sauna and spa pool are available. There is a total of 23 flats with high ceilings and good furnishings; several units with interior balconies, all with good kitchens and baths; and rates about $78-84 for two this year. About the only complaints we had were that our mattress fought back at us, and we had to carry our bags up the long stairs, problems that might have been solved if we had drawn a different unit. Overall, however, we think it's a good choice, and when you get there someone will probably carry your bags.

A couple of other motels worth mentioning and still in the $65 to $75 range include the **Commodore** (Tel. 477-7766) at 932 Cumberland Street, and the **Carisbrook** (Tel. 455-2169) at 169 Main South Road, Caversham, with rates at around $68 double. Both come recommended. The **Cable Court Motel** (Tel. 477-3525), at 833 Cumberland Street and in walking distance of the city, is also on our "yes" list. Rates are from $65 double.

One reader has written of his happiness at the **Best Western** (Tel. 477-4270) at 842 George Street. Rooms there go for around $84 double.

The **858 George Street Motel** (Tel. 474-0047) is a new establishment and has luxury studio, kitchen, family, and executive units serviced daily. Facilities include in-room spa baths, in-house video, and cooked or continental breakfasts. It is within walking distance of almost everything. Try it out and let us know. Rates are from $85 per unit.

The Cumberland Motel (Tel. 477-1321) is well priced and located on Cumberland Street at 821. We think it offers good value, too, with rates of from $84 double. The **Garden Motel** (Tel. 477-8251) at 958 George Street is in the same category, and units include kitchens. Rates are from $60 to $90 double. There are off-season and long stay specials available.

Chy-an-dowr Homestay and Self Contained Cottage (Tel. 478-0806) is said to be a bit of a bargain. It is a luxury, self-contained cottage that will actually sleep up to four, and is two minutes to shopping. Tariff is $95 for two persons and includes full breakfast.

Motel Esplanade (Tel. 455-1987) is Dunedin's only beachfront motel. It overlooks St. Clair beach and has a hot saltwater pool. It is also close to the golf course and restaurant, café, and bar, seven minutes from the city, and

60 feet from the surf! Four one-bedroom apartments and two two-bedroom apartments are what you are looking at here, and the cost is between $99 and $115 for two persons.

We haven't seen the **YWCA** (Tel. 477-6781) at Stafford Gables at 77 Stafford Street. It's within walking distance of the Octagon. Couples are welcome. **Manor House** (Tel. 477-0484) is another backpacker favorite. It's an old colonial house in attractive surroundings at 28 Manor Place. The rates are $15 per person. **Chalet Backpackers** (Tel. 479-2075) is at 296 High Street and charges $17 per night. **Next Stop Dunedin** is one block from the Octagon and has facilities for the disabled. Rates are $15 and you can phone them at Tel. 477-0447.

At the **Tahuna Park Motor Camp** (Tel. 455-4690), you can rent some rustic cabins for $26 for two per night or pay $16 per person for tent sites. It's at 41 Victoria Road, next to the beach in the suburb of St. Kilda. The official hostel for YHA members is **Stafford Gables** (Tel. 474-1919) at 17 Stafford Street, within walking distance of the Octagon. The **Manor Motel** (477-6729), at 22 Manor Place, is in a handy location off Princes Street, and the rates are $55 per person or $60 to $70 for two.

5. Dining in Dunedin

The university influence seems to have given a cosmopolitan flavor to the city's cuisine, and new restaurants constantly seem to be opening up. And closing down, too, for that matter. We would especially like to know of your own culinary discoveries in Dunedin this year.

There have been great changes since this guide was last edited, which old friends will realise as they read on.

A Cow Called Berta (Tel. 477-2993) is at 199 Stuart Street—not an actual living cow, just her image. This has become a popular watering hole, and you might have to make reservations. **95 Filluel** (Tel. 477-7233) at (95 Filluel Street, an award-winning, intimate restaurant with fine cuisine to match the elegant décor, still remains. Readers talk about the quality of food and service, and the team at Number 95 continues to maintain a good name.

There's a great line in international cuisine too, with the **Ananda Indian Café and Takeaway** (Tel. 477-4499); **Bahnthai Restaurant** (Tel. 471-9500), **Asian Restaurant** (Tel. 477-6673); **Paasha Turkish Café (Tel. 477-7181); Khmer Satay Noodle House** (Tel. 477-1861); **Da Vincis Pizzeria** (Tel. 489-0008); **China Palace** (Tel. 455-0771); **Café Zambessi** (Tel. 477-1107), **Emiles Lebanese Cuisine** (Tel. 477-7210), and **Café Tokyo** (Tel. 477-7631).

Roganos Seafood Restaurant (Tel. 477-5748) is the place to go for seafood. You'll find this restaurant at 388 Princes Street. They turn on an early-bird special, a three-course dinner that could be the value treat in town. **The High Tide Restaurant** (Tel. 477-9784) is, understandably, on the sea shore and, despite its name, not so close to the surf to wet your feet, but just about. It has a good reputation for seafood and probably requires a reservation to get a seat. Two *Taste New Zealand* awards have been picked up by **Settler's Restaurant** (Tel. 477-6784), which serves traditional dishes. You will find it opposite the Town Hall.

Dunedin also offers several Eastern dining rooms, mainly Chinese. **The Canton** (New Canton) (Tel. 477-7169), goes from strength to strength, even having to enlarge its premises to cope with its popularity. Also fancy and very good is the **New Dynasty** (Tel. 477-6263), a BYO at 509 George Street. Recommended, too, is the **Nanking Palace** (Tel. 455-4218) at 198-200 King Edward Street in South Dunedin.

For noontime nibbles, nip into **Glenfallock** (Tel. 476-1006) in the Woodland Gardens for a very pleasant sojourn amongst the trees. Also with a garden theme is Croque-O-Dile in the Garden (Tel. 477-0026), which is in the municipal Botanic Gardens. Otherwise, there is **Potpourri Natural Foods,** an informal salad, sandwich, and soup emporium at 97 Stuart Street, near Cumberland. It may be the best for vegetarians.

One of the best addresses for pub dining is the **Captain Cook Tavern** (Tel. 474-1935), where midday meals are served 12 till 2 at the corner of Great King and Albany Streets. The **Fuel Café** (Tel. 477-2575) sounds just the place to stock up on some energy. **Ruby in The Dust** (Tel. 477-4690) is unknown to us, but the name sounds extremely enigmatic. Check it out and tell us what you think. Break it to us gently if it's awful—it sounds so romantic. On Moray Place, at number 368, is a favorite of the locals called **Parisettes**, with good dining at reasonable prices.

Taverns are something Dunedin is cheerfully dotted with. **Cobb & Co.** (Tel. 477-8036) serves family fare on the corner of Cumberland and Stuart Streets. **Thyme Out** (Tel. 474-0467), at 5 Stafford Street, has both good selections and prices, and the **Huntsmans** (Tel. 477-8000) serves great steaks.

If you're really homesick then try the **Arizona American Kitchen** (Tel. 477-1777). We haven't actually tried it, and we're not sure what the kiwi idea of an American kitchen might be, but we want one of you to give it a try. Let us know.

6. Sightseeing in Dunedin

Pay a call first to the **Dunedin Visitor Centre** (Tel. 474-3300) at 48 The Octagon. You may pick up some well-designed *Know the City* and *Know the Region* pamphlets, outlining some popular walks and drives in and around Dunedin. They can also launch you on the seven-mile Golden Arrow Drive, which hits several scenic and interesting points throughout the city. Before you begin a round of sightseeing on your own hook, you may want to find out exactly what is covered by the standard city tour, or to take it first (see section 7).

A visit to Dunedin traditionally begins in the center of the city in a grassy, eight-sided area they call the **Octagon** (it's not a square, after all). There you'll see the statue of Robert Burns, a poet with a permanently poised pen. Also across from the Octagon, those with an architectural bent will be interested in St. Paul's Cathedral and the Municipal Chambers. The Dunedin City Council has spent millions restoring these buildings, and the result is impressive.

A block away, on the southeast leg of equally eight-sided Moray Place, you'll come across the **First Church of Otago,** finished in 1873 and now considered one of the finest in the nation. First Church was built of that white Oamaru limestone used to face so many public buildings in New Zealand, especially in the South Island.

A premier tourist attraction since the day it was completed in 1906 is the **Dunedin Railway Station,** although its excesses today bring more smiles of amusement than of civic pride. The outside of the bluestone building is flamboyant enough, but it is the reverent railroad motif worked into the mosaic flooring, the intricate scrollwork around the ticket booths, and especially the colorful stained-glass windows (featuring steam engines instead of saints) that provide evidence of the exaltation with which the railroads were regarded at the turn of the century. (Be sure to climb the stairs for a turn around the internal balcony.)

A short walk away you come across the **Otago Settlers' Museum** (Tel. 477-5052). Designed to illustrate something of the life of the nineteenth-century residents of Dunedin and Otago, it has been much improved over the past few years. The nearby **Cadbury Factory** (Tel. 474 1126) on Castle Street gives free tours twice daily from Monday to Thursday and then rewards you with chocolates. Apparently they're wise to chocoholics who finish the tour then run around and rejoin the end of the queue! This is a popular tour and you would be smart to book for this one, according to Margo Vagliardo. Similarly, **Speights Brewery** (Tel. 477-9480) offers four-dollar, two-hour excursions at 10:30 A.M. Monday through Friday at 200 Rattray Street. A cool glass of ale awaits you at the end of the tour.

In the northern section of the city is the **Otago Museum** (Tel. 477-2372), an internationally respected institution with worldwide interests and exhibits. Several Maori weapons and other artifacts from the region are preserved there. (On Great King Street, between Albany and Union, the museum is open from 10 until 5 Monday to Friday and from 1 until 5 during the weekend.) Admission is free.

Near the museum is **Otago University** (Tel. 479-1100). The 120-year-old central complex of bluestone buildings is on the banks of the Leith Stream north of Union Street, and has now been augmented by many modern structures. Besides offering basic courses, the university is the nation's training center for such specialties as dentistry, theology, home economics, physical education, pharmacy, surveying, and mining, and one of two locations for the study of medicine. The students let their hair down during "Capping Week" each May. In Dunedin, traditions die harder than in many other parts of the country.

You'll find the **Dunedin Public Art Gallery** (Tel. 477-8770) a few blocks west in Logan Park. The New Zealand paintings there include a major collection of works by Frances Hodgkins, one of Dunedin's favorite daughters. Several English oils and watercolors are also on display, as well as some European old masters. (Open weekdays until 4:30 and Saturday and Sunday from 2 to 5 P.M.)

Northwest of Logan Park, the city's **Botanical Gardens** (Tel. 474-3309) are pleasant, if not usually as dramatic as the corresponding facility in Christchurch. It's best to visit from late July through January, when the azaleas, rhododendrons, and other flowers are blooming most beautifully.

The outstanding park is the **Town Belt,** a 500-acre green buffer zone stretched along the hills between the older part of the city and some of its suburbs. A good portion of the aforementioned Golden Arrow Drive winds through the Town Belt. The southern part of the park is planted with non-native trees, and it is most dramatic in the fall. The northern section is New Zealand bush, sometimes ablaze with yellow kowhai and red rata trees (the latter similar to the North Island's famous pohutukawa "Christmas" trees).

If you are visiting Dunedin in spring, your trip will happily coincide with rhododendrons blooming in glorious profusion all over the city. In the third week of October every year, the city celebrates Rhododendron Week and these flowers are at their vibrant best in the Botanical Gardens. Dunedin's Visitor Information Centre organizes tours for rhododendron fans from around New Zealand and the world.

If you visit Dunedin with time to see only one sight, make it **Olveston** (Tel. 477-3320). The home was built from 1904 to 1906 by David E. Theomin, an importer and world traveller. Architecturally, it has very little to do with Dunedin. It is a Jacobean-style house, designed by a well-known English residential architect, and filled with the treasures gathered in a lifetime of Theomin family travels. The 35-room mansion has been left furnished exactly as it was during the 1920s, when it was the most elegant home in the city. It was also equipped with such up-to-date devices as modern plumbing, central heating, and intercommunication systems long before these items became generally available. The dining-room table is set with the original place cards, exactly as it was for the 1907 founding dinner of the Plunket Society, New Zealand's model mother-and-baby-care system.

Phone for reservations first to make sure a guide is available. Tours are on tap about four times a day. Drive to the corner of Cobden Street and Royal Terrace. (Walking up the hill is quite a workout, but some do it. Or take a bus from the Octagon up Stuart Street to Queen's Drive, check the map, then walk generally downhill from there.) The hour tour costs $3 or so, and it's well worth it. Our only criticism is that the taking of photographs is forbidden, an unnecessary rule.

The Visitor's Centre (Tel. 474-3300) will tell you when **St. Paul's Cathedral Choir** of 24 boys and 16 men will be in voice. Visitors are welcome to sing along with this accomplished choir at services in the soaring cathedral.

OTAGO PENINSULA

The long, narrow Otago Harbor is formed between the mainland and the hilly Otago Peninsula, which stretches for about 15 miles. Its shoreline is so convoluted that there are even peninsulas on the peninsula. Good roads go out to many of its extremities, however, and a few also lead to some traditional tourist sights. (Before leaving, read the next four paragraphs, particularly the one about the albatross colony.)

Near the village of Macandrew Bay, **Glenfalloch Woodland Gardens** (Tel. 476-1006) is noted for its rhododendrons, azaleas, roses, and other flowers spreading over 25 acres. The Swiss-style chalet there is a great place to stop for lunch or tea. The gardens are particularly attractive in September and October, although we enjoyed them even in May. (Admission by donation.)

A little farther out is the second famous Dunedin residence, **Larnach Castle** (Tel. 476-1616), whose story reads like an Italian opera. Briefly, it was built in the 1870s by the Hon. W.J.M. Larnach, a successful banker and member of Parliament, for his first wife, a titled Frenchwoman. He spared no expense, importing workmen from Europe, etc., but his wife died shortly after the castle was completed; a second wife also died young. Altogether, three Larnach wives lived in the "castle," until the day wife number three ran off with Larnach's son by wife number one. Larnach, who was also suffering some financial reverses at the time, shot and killed himself—an act his son repeated some years later. The neo-Gothic castle remains, however, valiantly kept up by a husband-and-wife team, Mr. and Mrs. Barry Barker, who bought it for a song and now run it as a tourist attraction. During the last three years the Barkers have continued to add to the castle's antique furniture and to restore it to full splendor.

The castle's artistic construction is obviously superb, and Lanarch is without a doubt an interesting excursion. There's a wonderful view of the harbor and peninsula from the top of the parapet. Admission is about $10. You can also stay at Lanarch Castle Lodge or in the refurbished stable. Meals are available in the castle dining room.

Eco-tourism, a nineties buzzword, is taking a strong lead in New Zealand, and Dunedin certainly has a head start in the world of "green tourism." The city really started waking up to the potential inherent in its natural and historic assets in the early eighties and, as a result, now has much to offer. Albatross colonies, the rare yellow-eyed penguin, and schools of seals live on the Otago Peninsula and have become prime attractions for an international audience. Wildlife in its natural habitat can be viewed close at hand, a situation that is comparatively rare these days.

Way out near the tip of the peninsula is **Penguin Place** (Tel. 478-0286), where the **yellow-eyed penguins** (the rarest penguin in the world) come in from the ocean and go to bed in the late afternoons. The bird is found only on the Otago Peninsula and in the Catlins area in Southland, on Banks Peninsula near Christchurch, and in North Otago. The greenies have gone to bat for the survival of the unique little *hoi-hoi* (the Maori name for the yellow-eye penguin) and the New Zealand branch of the Worldwide Fund for Nature (WWF NZ) has purchased land to ensure its survival. Admission to Penguin Place is $9. Turn off the road where you see the Penguin Place sign and pick up the key. Late afternoon is a good time to go if you are staying overnight on the Peninsula, as the next morning you can catch these penguins on their early-morning march to the water. (A little further north, at Oamaru, you can visit the Blue Penguin Colony, home of the world's smallest penguin. **Oamaru Visitor Information Centre** Tel. 434-1656.)

At the **Royal Albatross Centre** (Tel. 478-0499) you can visit the world's only mainland albatross colony, as well as historic Fort Taiaroa, built in 1886. Cost is $8.50 and this excursion can be combined with a Southlight Wildlife tour for viewing the yellow-eyed penguins. Contact the Dunedin Visitor Centre for information.

Monarch Wildlife Cruises (Tel. 477-4276 or 0800-MONARCH) also take in both kinds of penguins, the albatross colony, seals, and wading birds. The little vessel, *Monarch,* cruises the harbor year-round and is a double NZ Tourism Award winner. Cost is from $23 to $150.

While in the area, visit the **Portobello Aquarium** (Tel. 479-5826). It's part of the Otago University's marine research station at the end of the Portobello Peninsula. It's open only from midday until 4:30 P.M. during the weekends. If you strike school holiday time, however, you will find it open every day. The marine life is displayed in "touch tanks." Some species, such as crabs and starfish, you can touch if you are feeling brave. There are also videos for boning up on the local natural history and the work of the research station.

After several years of negotiation, the Otago Peninsula Trust was given the green light to go ahead with the redevelopment of underground military fortifications. The star attraction is the century-old "Disappearing Gun," which was forged in 1886. The gun is the sole survivor of eight coastal defense guns mounted on Taiaroa Head during the so-called Russian Scare of the 1880-90s. During World War II the Taiaroa gun fired 100 pounds of explosives for a range of five miles. Combine an inspection of the gun and its surrounding Coastal Defence with a visit to the albatross colony. Bookings are essential, and tickets are obtained from the Visitor Centre.

The Peninsula's **Portobello Village Tourist Park** (Tel. 478-0359) is a good place for campervans and campers, and provides a handy base from which to explore. In the tiny town of Portobello, golf, tennis, salmon fishing, and boating are just some of the activities on hand.

INVERCARGILL AND BLUFF

A pleasant provincial town, Invercargill often suffers from invidious comparisons to some of the more dramatic cities of New Zealand. The town and its port, Bluff, are the two southernmost municipalities on the South Island and the traditional jumping-off places for Stewart Island and Fiordland.

The most luxurious place to stay, and Invercargill's pride and joy, is the **Ascot Park Hotel** (Tel. 217-6195), which is away from the center of town. Rooms are $145 double. **The Kelvin Hotel** (Tel. 218-2829) is popular downtown with rooms from $108, and the **Balmoral Lodge** (Tel. 217-6109 or 0800-BALMORAL) is also a good bet, and rates are from $90-100 double.

The **Birchwood Manor** (Tel. 218-8881) is a new property close to the airport, golf course, and central city. For those being self-reliant, there is a large supermarket opposite. Tariffs are between $82 and $112 double.

Invercargill's Queens Park is large and pleasant, and is also the location of the **Southland Museum and Art Gallery,** which we zipped around in about 15 minutes. It's near the park's Gala Street entrance. See the section of fossilized forest in front of the building, too. Some restaurant names to note are **Strathern Inn** (best licensed restaurant), **Aino's Steakhouse** (best BYO), and **Donavan's** (best wine list). **Anderson's Park** is another pleasant interlude just north of the city. Artwork displayed in an historic Georgian-style mansion and afternoon tea in a quiet bush setting are two restful things you can visit and partake of.

The village of **Bluff** is a fishing center, and the processing site for those wonderful Bluff oysters enjoyed all over the country during the season (April through about August).

The town is also known as the location of one of New Zealand's large industrial operations, the **Tiwai Aluminum Smelter.** It buys its massive amounts of electrical power from the hydroelectric operation at Manapouri. The raw material comes from Australia, and the operation is considered a way to "export" some of New Zealand's electrical potential by attracting outside industry and providing industrial jobs. You can see the smelter from **Bluff Hill** across the harbor, and there are even tours through the operation. Far below, oyster boats dredge the sea bed for plump, juicy oysters. Bluff oysters in season are delectable, but they are becoming a scarcer treat these days. The *Takaroa II* (Tel. 212-8170) operates out of Bluff Harbour, taking passengers fishing, diving, bird watching, and just cruising. There is accommodation on board, and a dive compressor. **Lynette Jackson** (Tel. 025-338-370) can take you on one of her scenic sights tours for two-hour, half-day, or full-day excursions all around Southland. Her garden tours are very popular. **Driver Guided Tours** (Tel. 235-2827) also offer possibilities, including Stewart Island.

The **Invercargill Visitor Centre** at Queens Park is a first port of call for local and regional visitor information (Tel. 218-9753).

Not far from Invercargill, in the far right-hand corner of the South Island, is the **Catlins** area. It is so remote that your cell phone won't work here! However, it is a beautiful and peaceful spot to visit.

Catlins Wildlife Trackers (Tel. 0800-CATLINS/228-547) can take you on an eco-tourism walk and nature experience. The company has won eco-tourism and activity and adventure tourism awards. Two or four full-day tours take in the forest, estuarine, and marine wildlife. Cost is $250 for two days and $500 for four days, including accommodations and meals.

Inland, at **Alexandra, Safari Excursions** (Tel. 448-7474) will take you on wildflower walks. The personally guided walks take in flowers, general scenery, and historic sites from the valley floor to the summits. They operate year-round, and tour costs range from $35 to $95.

STEWART ISLAND

You haven't really seen all of New Zealand, of course, until you hop over to its "third island." **Stewart Island** is a large area of wilderness populated by only about 500 people, and most of them are gathered in the small community of Oban at Halfmoon Bay. The rest of the island is as wild and rugged as it has always been, although laced with numerous hiking trails. There are huts for backpackers, maintained by the N.Z. Department of

Conservation. There's also **Stewart Island Lodge** (Tel. 219-1885), a cozy and comfortable small hotel that has rooms with top views across the bay at $210 single/twin/double including meals. Kitchens and living rooms are included with the bedrooms at the **Rakiura Motel** (Tel. 291-1096), and rooms are about $77 double. Although this is the southernmost area of the country, warm sea currents keep the island frost-free, even in the depths of winter. The **Shearwater Inn** has rooms from $55 double. There are about seven backpacker hostels, so you should be able to find at least one to suit.

If you drop in for a quick visit, chances are you'll fall into the one-hour guided tour conducted by Lloyd Wilcox, a man with a delightful sense of humor. A catamaran service runs between Bluff and Stewart Island, which has made the island much more accessible for day trippers. The *Foveaux Express,* named for **Foveaux Strait,** which separates the islands, is vastly superior to any of its predecessors. What was once something of a nightmare journey in rough conditions is now a breeze. It takes just one hour to ride the waves, and there are two trips there and back each day. It's a good deal at $45 an adult and half price for children. A swifter alternative is the 20-minute flight with **Southern Air** (Tel. 218-9129) from the Invercargill Airport. The regular round trip costs about $170, but the company still has a lower-priced special sightseeing flight, over and back in a couple of hours, in an arrangement that includes the Lloyd Wilcox tour and a bite of lunch. If you're on a tight schedule, it's well worth it. But re-check this first. **Stewart Island Travel** (Tel. 219-1269) will steer you in the right direction.

There are too many charter boats off the island to mention, and they include a glass-bottomed boat and cruisers. While you're thinking about it, you can go and have a round of golf at the **Ringa Ringa Heights** course. Sea kayaking sounds like fun on the Paterson Inlet, 100 square kilometers of bush-surrounded, sheltered waterways, mostly uninhabited. It has two islands and two Dept. of Conservation (DOC) huts. There are guided tours, independent trips, and overnight trips. Kayaks are $10 for three hours or from $30 per day, with the sixth and seventh days free. You can get a double kayak, too, if you need a bit of moral support (Tel. 219-1080).

NORTH OF DUNEDIN

A side trip up Highway 88 will eventually lead you to **Port Chalmers,** the original and still important deepwater port for Otago. The massive cranes and other equipment contrast strangely with the turn-of-the-century mansions and stone cottages in the area. Check the view from the flagstaff. It, by the way, was once the mainmast of a ship owned by the notorious American pirate Bully Hayes.

North on Highway 1, 36 miles from Dunedin, you'll run across the town
of **Palmerston.** We remember it best as the site of an excellent fish-'n'-chips
shop, the **Palmerston Fish Supply,** just a few steps off the highway near the
Shell station. (Delicious battered sausages and hot dogs on a stick, too!
And still famous after all these years!) A good place to eat these things, by
the way, is the picnic spot at **Trotters Gorge,** 7.5 miles to the northeast. For
non-picnickers, there's also an excellent restaurant (and good accommodations) at the **Mill House** at Waianakarua, a few miles further north. The
Mill House, a former flour mill more than a century old, offers accommodations with plenty of character in individual apartments for $76. A few
miles further north, at **Moeraki,** are uniquely formed boulders formed by
the erosion of sea cliffs. You can view them from **Boulders Restaurant.**

Another 37 miles from Palmerston is **Oamaru,** home of all that white
stone of the same name and of the little blue penguins we mentioned earlier. You'll see the stone widely used in many buildings there in the quarry's
own hometown. The Whitestone Trust has commenced a redevelopment
of the Harbour-Tyne Street precinct to preserve the fine nineteenth-
century buildings for posterity. After a wander down this lane, it's worth
having a look at the Parkside Limestone Quarry, which produces huge
slabs of cream-colored, quality limestone. Kaye and Keith Dennison run
the **Sunny Downs** farmstay (Tel. 431-1741) near Oamaru, on a 1,000-acre
merino sheep and cattle farm. You can go fishing or jet boating, help
about the working farm (one Japanese tourist found his field of work docking lambs' tails), or just observe. Golf, tennis, squash, and skiing are
nearby. Cost is from $45 per person for full board.

Fifty-three miles up the same pike is **Timaru,** a town in a fruit-growing
region and on a magnificent sandy beach called Caroline Bay. The Pioneer
Hall Museum there specializes in relics from the "moa-hunter" period of
New Zealand history, which predates the Maori. In nearby **Temuka,** try the
unusual Redwoods Restaurant.

7. Guided Tours in Dunedin

The several tour options available all leave from outside the Visitor
Centre. **Newton's Tours** (Tel. 477-5577) offers excursions around the city
center as well as to the various attractions on the peninsula, including a
call at Olveston, Larnach Castle, Glenfalloch Gardens, the Royal Albatross
colony, and a visit to the seals and penguins. The tours are reasonably
priced and good discounts are offered.

The **YHA** (Tel. 474-1919) also operates a guided tour that focuses on
the wildlife on the Otago Peninsula. Additionally, they take tours for a look

at the **Otakou Marae,** the site of a prominent pre-European settlement. And for a later stage in New Zealand history, there's a tour to a whaling station. All of these tours are subject to change according to the season, and prices vary according to the options you select. Contact the Visitor Centre for the current status. They will also book you into the tours.

Something different is the **Taieri Gorge Railway** (Tel. 477-4449), a set of old carriages restored to their former glory that now carries passengers on trips to the Taieri Gorge and other scenic areas. We received word of this train trip after our last visit to the area, so you're on your own. However, R. E. McBride of Highlands Ranch, Colorado, took the trip and can "unequivocally recommend it. The scenery was spectacular, the commentary is well done, the cars are very comfortable." Thanks for telling us.

The train runs year-round through spectacular scenery, viaducts, and tunnels dating from 1879, across ravines and hugging cliffs. There is a commentary, sightseeing stops, an onboard bar, and refreshments. The train departs Dunedin at 2:30 PM. You can also make a connection from Queenstown, where a coach will pick you up at noon and take you to the Dunedin station. Cost is $49 return from Dunedin and $99 return from Christchurch. From April to September the schedule is 12:30 P.M. from Dunedin and 10 A.M. from Queenstown.

The **Otago Harbour Fish 'N Cruise** is a lively trip that departs at 10 A.M. during the late spring and early fall, when the salmon are running. The thrill of the catch is fostered by the *Salmon Anglers Association,* which seeds the harbor each winter with 40,000 darting young salmon. Keen anglers can get into the action on fishing trips that depart at the good fishing hour of 7 in the morning.

The surf-rafting trips are more adventurous. You'll go out to sea in motorized rafts for a thrilling trip past memorable scenery. You may also see dolphins frolicking in the water. The Visitor Centre will help out with bookings. **Silver Peak Tours** offers jet boating, rafting, and four-wheel-drive safaris in the scenic **Taiere Gorge** (Tel. 472-8191).

8. Water Sports

In the height of summer you might enjoy the wide sand stretches on the south edge of town. **St. Clair Beach** and the adjoining **St. Kilda Beach** are considered the best. A few miles north of Dunedin, **Warrington Beach** is warmer.

Most Dunedin denizens seem to prefer to get in the swim at the **Moana Pool** (Tel. 471-9780), an enclosed Olympic-sized pool, learner's pool, diving pool, spa pool, weight room (getting puffed yet?), and two waterslides.

Prideful residents list the pool as a tourist attraction and a major point of interest in the city. It's in the Town Belt, just up steep Stuart Street from the Octagon. The water temperature is maintained at 80 degrees or so year-round. It's open until late most evenings. Meals are available at the pool café. The St. Clair Hot Pools are heated saltwater pools overlooking the sea.

Freshwater fishing is possible in several nearby rivers and lakes. Beautiful trout are pulled right out of the mouth of the Clutha and from the stocked waters at Tomahawk Lagoon. Some salmon fishing is popular north of Oamaru on the Waitaki River; trout are occasionally pulled out of the Water of Leith, the gentle stream on the campus at O.U.; and you'll find both trout and salmon at Lake Mahinerangi. The city's sporting goods stores will have lots of information on these activities.

Wild Earth Adventures (Tel. 025-721-931) will take you sea kayaking in all seasons. Prices are on application.

9. Other Sports

Several good golf courses are spread around Dunedin, including the famous **St. Clair Golf Course** (Tel. 487-7076) at the south end of town. Considered the most scenic on the South Island, it winds through pine groves and along the rugged shoreline. The 6,500-yard course is also the site of the Otago Charity Classic. Visitors are welcome any time except Tuesday mornings (Ladies' Day) and Saturdays. The **Otago Golf Club** (Tel. 467-2099), a 10-minute drive from the city, is the oldest in New Zealand, founded by golf-loving Scots in 1871. **Chisholm Park Golf Club** (Tel. 455-0715) qualifies as Dunedin's most scenic links, overlooking the Pacific Ocean.

You'll find some tennis courts in the public parks, and the **St. Clair Tennis Club,** on Victoria Road, also welcomes visitors. You can also check out the Logan Park Tennis Courts in Logan Park.

For spectator sports, the famous rugby (winter) and cricket (summer) ground in Dunedin is **Carisbrook,** just off Highway 1 on Burns Street. For the "trots," **Forbury Park** is known the world over by the racing set. You'll find it on Victoria Road, next to St. Clair Beach. The flat-racing track is **Wingatui,** over near Mosgiel.

Wild Earth Adventures will take you mountain biking and on other outdoor pursuits. Prices on application.

10. Shopping in Dunedin

A recent facelift to the city center has produced some more flavor in the form of an early colonial shopping center. Cobblestone pavements add to the atmosphere and sense of history.

George Street, from the Octagon to Knox Church, is the main shopping area of Dunedin. You'll find the big department stores like **Arthur Barnett's** and **Farmer's Trading Company** there at the beginning of Princes Street, on the south side of the Octagon. **Penrose's** is at George and St. Andrew Streets. There is also some shopping further on Princes, which is the continuation of George on the other side of the Octagon, although it tends to be more the venue of banks and businesses. Late-night shopping is on Fridays (except in South Dunedin and Port Chalmers, where stores stay open until 9 on Thursdays). Most shops are open on Saturdays, too. The **Golden Centre** (Tel. 477-8544) at 251 George Street, contains an array of shops under one convenient roof.

There are several souvenir shops in the main shopping area. Try **Hides, Leather, and Sheepskin Merchants** at 185 George Street, or **Glendermid** (Tel. 477-3655) at 192 Castle Street. **The Golden Leaf International, Ltd.** (Tel. 474-0063), posts overseas tax-free and is at 16 Manse Street.

Mackenzie Country, in the Civic Centre next to the Visitor Centre, specializes in original designer handknits. **The New Zealand Shop** (Tel. 477-3379) also has a range of quality fashion garments as well as gifts. The **Canterbury Shop** (Tel. 477-6039) is in the Civic Centre Plaza, and stocks a colorful selection of ethnic N.Z. gear. Canterbury exports around the world, and their distinctive gear also sells in the U.S. But you could do better to buy on home base from the chain of stores in the major N.Z. cities.

Rumours (Tel. 447 1113), at 21 Andrew Street, sells crafted pieces, and **Variety Handcrafts** (Tel. 474-1008) at 368 Moray Place, sells goods fashioned by the Otago Craft Cooperative. The **Otago Museum Shop and Crafts Council Gallery** sells a selection of crafts, books, cards, prints, and quality souvenirs.

Antique shops are good in the city, and so are their prices. The aforementioned Rumours on St. Andrew has both old and new goods. The **Orchid** on George Street sells great knickknacks and is a favorite of out-of-towners. Call into **Dimension Interiors** on King Street to view their top-of-the-range collectibles. They pack and post overseas.

The **Southern Cross Lobby Shop,** at 118 High Street, and the **Lobby Shop,** next to the Visitor Centre in the Octagon, are another couple of good-quality souvenir shops worth poking around in. One that specializes in imported as well as local handcrafted gifts, soft furnishings, and apparel is **Acquisitions** at 320 George Street.

Perhaps Dunedin's most interesting shop, and certainly unique in New Zealand, is **Helean Kiltmakers,** at 8 Hocken Street (Tel. 453-0233). Frank Helean is the last kiltmaker in the country, carrying on in the tradition of his father, grandfather, and great-grandfather. Some of his more than 70 different tartans are imported from Scotland, but most come from New

Zealand wool woven at a factory near Dunedin. Prices can vary, of course, but when we dropped by a lady's handmade kilt sold for less than a man's. And if Scotland is not on your itinerary this time 'round, the **Scottish Shop** (Tel. 477-9965) at 187 George Street will compensate with its range of Scottish goods.

New Zealand books are a specialty at **Otago Heritage Books** (Tel. 477-1500) on Moray Place. Dunedin has branches of **Whitcoulls,** the large, well-stocked chain, at 168 Princes Street and in the Golden Centre arcade. In July the **Great 24-Hour Book Sale** is held at the Regent Theatre, where, from Friday night until Saturday, thousands upon thousands of books change hands. Who knows what treasures you might find?

11. Night Life and Entertainment

Because of the student influence in Dunedin, there is a proliferation of pubs for drinking, dancing, and sometimes dining. A favorite watering hole for the students is the **Captain Cook Tavern** (Tel. 474-1935) at 354 Great King Street. The **Albert Arms Tavern** features tartan carpet, in deference to Dunedin's Scottish heritage. Bistro meals are served here daily. It is also one of the homes of the famous Dunedin Yummy Doorstep Toasted Sandwiches. We haven't tried one of these yet but we keep hearing about them. Another entertaining stopover could be **George's Tavern** (Tel. 474-1955), at 419 Princes Street. It swings on weekend nights. **The Outback Inn** (Tel. 477-4414) has a bar, brasserie, and nightclub. Other nightclubs include **Orbit 107** (Tel. 477-1824), **KC's Bar** (Tel. 474-1133), and **Shooters Bar.**

Dunedin is a city of bands, and most of the hotels have live entertainment on weekends. The Visitor Centre can tell you where the best play.

The local brand of beer is Speights, still brewed in Dunedin, although the company is now owned by Auckland-based Dominion Breweries. Above Speights is the **Clarendon Hotel** (Tel. 477-9095), at 28 Maclaggan Street. It's smack in the area known as the Devil's Half Acre during the Gold Rush of the last century. It's decked out to suit, and offers à la carte and buffets on Sunday. **Bentley's** (Tel. 477-0572) restaurant in the Alglen Motor Hotel serves a variety of dishes in a pleasant atmosphere. **Regines** (Tel. 755-5196) is the name of the nightclub at the Shoreline Motor Hotel, and the place gets going from Thursday through Saturday. But real night owls should probably head for later-opening nightclubs like **Club Nouveau** and **Foxys.** There's good jazz at the latter, as well as regular poetry readings.

For a town its size, Dunedin boasts considerable theatrical activity. We enjoyed a comedy-thriller by the professional company at the **Fortune**

Theatre (Tel. 477-8323), which occupies a former church at the corner of Stuart Street and Moray Place. The big traveling shows are more likely to go on the boards at the **Regent Theatre** (Tel. 477-6597) at 104 London Street. Other live productions are sometimes performed at the **Playhouse** (Tel. 477-6544) on Albany Street, and at the **Mayfair Theatre** (Tel. 455-4962), which is also the home of the Dunedin Opera Company, an amateur group with a long history. Most of the cinemas are centered around the Octagon and neighboring side streets.

Performances by the Dunedin Civic Orchestra and other classical productions are occasionally staged at the **Town Hall** (Tel. 474-3614) on the Octagon, or its Concert Chamber next door. Ask at the Dunedin Visitor Centre.

For stay-at-homes, well, the three national TV channels can be tuned in Dunedin. On the radio, you'll get the National Program at 4YA, Dunedin (810 Kh); the Concert Program at 4YC (900 Kh); community radio at 4ZB, "The Entertainer" (1044 Kh); and two private radio stations, 4XD, "Radio Alpha" (1035 Kh), and 4XO, "Radio Otago" (1206 Kh). For FM tune in to 91 Mh.

Dunedin's newspaper is the *Otago Daily Times*. Founded in 1861, it was the first daily newspaper in New Zealand.

12. The Dunedin Address List

Automobile Association (Otago) Inc.—450 Moray Place (Tel. 477-5945).
Airporter Express—(Tel. 476-2519), or Dunedin Airport Shuttle—(Tel. 477-6611).
Candy store—Edinburgh Confectionery, 314 George Street (Tel. 477-2757).
Discount liquor—Robbie Burns Shoppe, 374 George Street (Tel. 477-6355).
Emergencies of all types—Dial 111.
Emergency advice service—Dial 477-1111 at any hour.
Fire department—Dial 111 for all emergencies.
Hairdressers (for men and women)—Headquarters, The Octagon (Tel. 477-0472).
Hospital—(Tel. 474-0999).
Ambulance—Dial 111 for all emergencies.
Information of all types—Dunedin Visitor Centre, 48 The Octagon (Tel. 474-3300).
Library—Dunedin Public Library, 230 Moray Place and George Street (Tel. 474-3690).

Pharmacy—95 Hanover Street (Tel. 477-6344).

Police Station—Lower High Street, opposite the railroad station (Tel. 476-6011).

Post office—Central Post Office, Princes Street, opposite Wains Hotel (Tel. 477-0999).

Index

THE MAVERICK GUIDE TO HONG KONG, MACAU, AND SOUTH CHINA

By Len Rutledge

A land of contrasts—traditions and modern ambitions, Eastern and Western influences, skyscrapers and mountain monasteries—the Hong Kong, Macau, and South China area is one of the world's most fascinating regions and the new China's most dynamic area.

As with all Maverick Guides, the culture, people, and geography of this land as well as the main points of interest for visitors are described. You will find everything from Hong Kong Island's double-decker trams to the Happy Valley racecourse, from the ferry to Lantau Island to Macau's A-Ma Temple. Covering transportation, hotels, dining, sightseeing, events, shopping, and entertainment, Rutledge has created a pleasant-to-read guide designed to get you ready for a trip as well as act as a handy reference during your stay. An excellent aid for those traveling on business.

296 pp. 5½ x 8½ Photos Maps Index
ISBN: 1-56554-071-9

THE MAVERICK GUIDE TO
AUSTRALIA: 11th Edition

By Robert W. Bone
Edited by Kevin Voltz

For fifteen years one of the best guides to take down under, with current information on lodging, food, sightseeing, the language, getting on and off the continent, and more. Cities dazzle with shopping, dining, and the arts. Natural wonders such as the Great Barrier Reef abound.

416 pp. 5½ x 8½
Maps Index
ISBN: 1-56554-151-0

THE MAVERICK GUIDE
TO SCOTLAND

By June Skinner Sawyers

Alongside practical knowledge and advice are the intangible histories with which every stone of Scotland seems filled. This Maverick Guide enhances a journey through modern Scotland by revealing bits of its past, which is ripe with figures of poets and kings. It details the country's timeless features that have driven people to its shores— the ruined castles and highland cliffs—but highlights the timely attractions as well. Today, the thriving art and theater of Glasgow and Edinburgh and the recent renewal of interest in Celtic language, music, and culture are just as noteworthy.

Whether visitors are interested in golfing the famous courses of Saint Andrews, walking the battlefields of William Wallace at Stirling, or visiting Glamis castle, the haunting setting for Shakespeare's *Macbeth*, *The Maverick Guide to Scotland* is a useful tool for enhancing their travels.

608 pp. 5½ x 8½ 54 photos 19 maps Index
ISBN: 1-56554-227-4

THE MAVERICK GUIDE
TO BARCELONA

By Richard Schweid

This guide describes each facet of Barcelona's personality in detail, giving tips on hotels and lodging, restaurants and cafés, sightseeing, sports, shopping, and entertainment and nightlife in the thorough manner associated with the Maverick Guide Series. Since Barcelona is the capital of Catalunya, this region is covered as well.

Introductory chapters discuss the best ways to reach Barcelona, traveling within the city, banking and changing money, procuring health and emergency services, and other valuable information for the traveler.

There is much to see and do in Barcelona, from walking the scenic streets to resting on the beach to dancing all night in lively discos. The cuisine is an important part of the Barcelona experience: It is varied and tasty, and going out to eat is an event in itself. Artistic diversions abound. Whatever the visitor's interest, this book covers it.

This new addition to the Mavericks also offers eight maps, a glossary of words in Castilian and Catalan (Catalunya's two official languages), and a sample translated menu.

160 pp. 5½ x 8½ 8 maps Glossary Index
ISBN: 1-56554-191-X

THE MAVERICK GUIDE TO MOROCCO

By Susan Searight

With much more to experience than just Tangier and Casablanca, Morocco offers delicious local cuisine in Fès and Marrakech, bargain-filled kasbahs in the Dades Valley, and prehistoric sites at Volubilis. The High Atlas Mountains, Sahara Desert, and Berber villages present diverse terrains to explore and equally distinct peoples to encounter. Regardless of location, or budget, accommodations ranging from the luxurious to the spartan are profiled to fill every possible need.

This guide utilizes the familiar Maverick format to communicate everything a first-time traveler needs to know, including the customs, history, and culture of the country, as well as how to get along with the natives in the best possible fashion. Advice is given on everything from what type of vehicle to drive in certain areas, to what kinds of clothes to wear, and even what topics of conversation are considered taboo.

288 pp. 5⅜ x 8½ 41 maps Index
ISBN: 1-56554-348-3

THE MAVERICK GUIDE
TO HAWAII: 20th Edition

By Robert W. Bone

Edited by Carol Greenhouse

WINNER OF FIRST PLACE HONORS
HAWAII VISITORS BUREAU TRAVEL JOURNALISM AWARDS

"The best guide to Hawaii, and one of the best travel guides I've ever read, is *The Maverick Guide to Hawaii.*"

Chicago Sun-Times

"It's just about as good as you can get in one package; we've yet to find a better one."

Hawaii Magazine

"They give the necessary practical information, but are also strong on local history, geography, and lore."

New York Times

The lively and informative text includes background on each island's history, the people, the language, and the best ways to travel from island to island. In addition, for the traveler who values choice, the guide provides the most current information on everything from hotels and sightseeing to entertainment and recreation.

432 pp. 5½ x 8½ 9 Maps Appendix Index
ISBN: 1-56554-312-2

Please tell us about your trip to New Zealand.

(This page can be folded to make an envelope.)

CUT

CUT

FOLD

FOLD HERE. FASTEN LIP ON FRONT WITH CLEAR TAPE.

PLEASE FASTEN SIDES WITH CLEAR TAPE.

PLEASE FASTEN SIDES WITH CLEAR TAPE.

CUT

FOLD HERE

PLACE
FIRST-CLASS
POSTAGE
HERE

RE: Maverick New Zealand

THE MAVERICK GUIDES
Pelican Publishing Company
1000 Burmaster Street
P.O. Box 3110
Gretna, Louisiana 70054